WITHDRAWN
W9-CNQ-055

Encyclopedia of

Family Health

ENCYCLOPEDIA OF

FAMILY HEALTH

CONSULTANT
DAVID B. JACOBY, MD
JOHNS HOPKINS SCHOOL OF MEDICINE

VOLUME
6

HEMORRHAGE–INFECTIOUS MONONUCLEOSIS

DEKALB COUNTY PUBLIC LIBRARY

MARSHALL CAVENDISH
NEW YORK · LONDON · TORONTO · SYDNEY

Marshall Cavendish Corporation
99 White Plains Road
Tarrytown, New York 10591-9001
© Marshall Cavendish Corporation, 1998
© Marshall Cavendish Limited 1998, 1991, 1988, 1986, 1983, 1982, 1971

All rights reserved. No part of this book may be reproduced or utilized in any form or by any means electronic or mechanical, including photocopying, recording, or by an information storage system, without permission from the copyright holder.
Update by Brown Partworks
The material in this set was first published in the English language by Marshall Cavendish Limited of 119 Wardour Street, London W1V 3TD, England.

Printed and bound in Italy

Library of Congress Cataloging-in-Publication Data

Encyclopedia of family health
17v. cm.
Includes index
1. Medicine, Popular–Encyclopedias. 2. Health–Encyclopedias. I. Marshall Cavendish Corporation.
RC81.A2M336 1998 96–49537
610'. 3–dc21 CIP
ISBN 0-7614-0625-5 (set)
ISBN 0-7614-0631-X (v.6)

This encyclopedia is not intended for use as a substitute for advice, consultation, or treatment by a licensed medical practitioner. The reader is advised that no action of a medical nature should be taken without consultation with a licensed medical practitioner, including action that may seem to be indicated by the contents of this work, as individual circumstances vary and medical standards, knowledge, and practices change with time. The publishers, authors, and medical consultants disclaim all liability and cannot be held responsible for any problems that may arise from its use.

Introduction

We Americans live under a constant bombardment of information (and misinformation) about the latest supposed threats to our health. We are taught to believe that disease is the result of not taking care of ourselves. Death becomes optional. Preventive medicine becomes a moral crusade, illness the punishment for the foolish excesses of the American lifestyle. It is not the intent of the authors of this encyclopedia to contribute to this atmosphere. While it is undoubtedly true that Americans could improve their health by smoking less, exercising more, and controlling their weight, this is already widely understood.

As Mencken put it, "It is not the aim of medicine to make men virtuous. The physician should not preach salvation, he should offer absolution." The aims of this encyclopedia are to present a summary of human biology, anatomy, and physiology, to outline the more common diseases, and to discuss, in a general way, the diagnosis and treatment of these diseases. This is not a do-it-yourself book. It will not be possible to treat most conditions based on the information presented here. But it will be possible to understand most diseases and their treatments. Informed in this way, you will be able to discuss your condition and its treatment with your physician. It is also hoped that this will alleviate some of the fears associated with diseases, doctors, and hospitals.

The authors of this encyclopedia have also attempted to present, in an open-minded way, alternative therapies. There is undoubtedly value to some of these. However, when dealing with serious diseases, they should not be viewed as a substitute for conventional treatment. The reason that conventional treatment is accepted is that it has been systematically tested, and because scientific evidence backs it up. It would be a tragedy to miss the opportunity for effective treatment while pursuing an ineffective alternative therapy.

Finally, it should be remembered that the word *doctor* is originally from the Latin word for "teacher." Applied to medicine, this should remind us that the doctor's duty is not only to diagnose and treat disease, but to help the patient to understand. If this encyclopedia can aid in this process, its authors will be gratified.

David B. Jacoby, MD
Johns Hopkins School of Medicine

CONTENTS

Hemorrhage

Q My husband has recently noticed blood in his urine but is reluctant to go to the doctor. What can I say to him to make him understand that he should have this checked?

A Anyone who notices blood in the urine should see a doctor as soon as possible, even if he or she feels perfectly fine, simply because the blood may indicate the presence of a serious disease of the kidneys, bladder, or sex organs—particularly the prostate gland in men. If such problems receive prompt treatment as soon as they are noticed, they are almost always curable. Tell your husband this right away.

Q Is a cerebral hemorrhage another way of saying someone has had a stroke?

A A stroke can have several causes, but one of the most common is bleeding or hemorrhage from a burst blood vessel into the brain. As a result some of the brain cells are starved of blood and so cannot work properly; this is what causes the characteristic loss of movement in various parts of the body. It also explains why a cerebral hemorrhage can be fatal, because death follows the total failure of the brain.

Q Why do some parts of the body, such as the scalp and mouth, seem to bleed profusely when they are damaged, while other parts don't bleed nearly so much?

A The main reason is that the scalp, tongue, and lips have a very rich supply of blood vessels that tend not to constrict as much as those in other parts of the body. Also the skin of the scalp forms an attachment for muscles, unlike elsewhere in the body, and so tends to pull open when cut and takes longer to heal.

Any hemorrhage from the mouth area may continue for a long time because the saliva in the mouth and the movements of the tongue dislodge the clots that are forming to dam the broken blood vessels.

Hemorrhage—bleeding from any severed or damaged blood vessel—should always be treated immediately as an emergency. A knowledge of first aid will help to minimize its effects.

Bubbles/Jennie Woodcock

To stop a nosebleed, sit up, bend the head forward very slightly, and pinch the soft part of the nose for ten minutes.

A hemorrhage threatens life because it means that the body loses blood, the vital fluid that supplies the tissues with oxygen and food (see Blood). Whether the bleeding is external or internal, a hemorrhage is always a cause for concern.

Medically the term *hemorrhage* simply means bleeding from any severed or damaged blood vessel in the body. Whether it is caused by an accident, disease, or surgery, a hemorrhage is described as external if the blood from the vessels is lost to the outside of the body and internal if the blood is retained unseen within.

Types of hemorrhage

The blood lost in a hemorrhage may come from any of the arteries, veins, or capillaries in the body, and each type of bleeding has its own distinctive characteristics that are important to effective first aid and treatment.

If an artery has been severed, blood spurts and pumps out on its way from the heart to the body tissues, often with enormous force. (The blood is bright red because it is full or oxygen.) As the heart goes on pumping regardless of the damage that has been done, an enormous amount of blood can be lost in a very short time. Arterial hemorrhage is thus the most dangerous form of hemorrhage and should always be viewed as a medical emergency that requires immediate hospital treatment.

Veins are the vessels that carry blood low in oxygen from the body tissues back to the heart. For this reason the blood that issues from a vein hemorrhage is a dull, dark red. It seeps from a wound, rather than gushing as it does from an injured artery.

Blood lost from capillaries, the tiny vessels that link arteries and veins, is usually the familiar dark red color, but it is released very slowly so that it seems to ooze out of the body.

FIRST AID

Treating hemorrhage from special areas

Clotting of blood at the site of the wound is a protective reaction, but it cannot take place while the blood is flowing.

The tongue

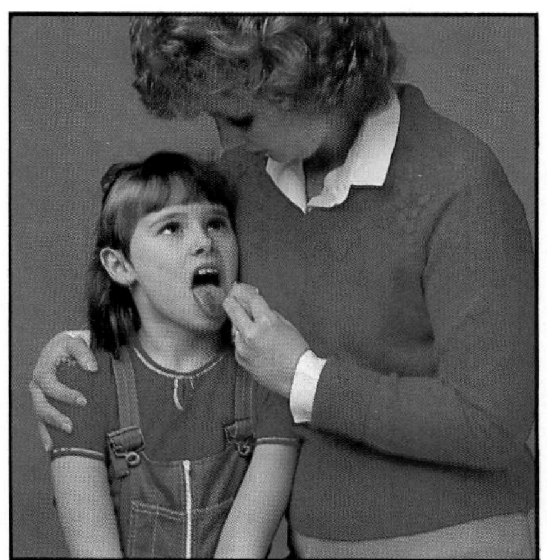

The tongue can often be bitten in an accident and may bleed profusely. Unless the patient is unconscious, sit him or her up and grasp the tongue over the part that is bleeding, using a clean dressing or a piece of material. If this is not possible (for example, if you are treating a struggling child) place ice on the tongue or give him or her an ice cube to suck; this will make the blood vessels contract.

The palm of the hand

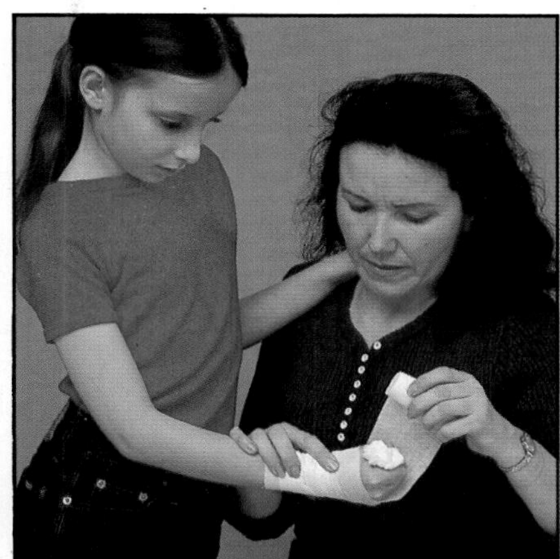

Roll a pad of some clean material into a sausage shape, and get the patient to grip it as tightly as possible for ten minutes. In treating a child it may be better to bind the fist in this clenched position. Give additional help by lifting the patient's arm if he or she is unable to do this. This will decrease blood flow to the hand. If the patient is unconscious, lie him or her on one side.

For a serious wound, always follow up first aid by getting medical help.

The thigh

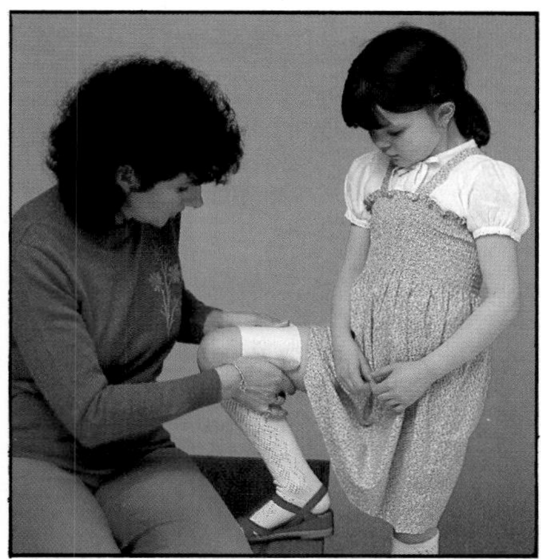

Raise the injured leg to reduce the blood flow through it. Press firmly on the wound, after first covering it with a pad of gauze or other clean material. Keep up the pressure for at least five minutes. If blood oozes through the dressing, do not remove it because this might disturb a clot that is forming: cover with a clean bandage. If the wound is serious, get medical help immediately: heavy blood loss can result in shock due to lowered blood pressure.

Causes

The most common cause of hemorrhaging is a direct injury to the blood vessels, but diseases of the vessels can also lead to bleeding. For example, fatty degeneration may weaken the muscle coat of an artery, causing it to become progressively thinner and weaker until it bursts like an overinflated balloon. High blood pressure, which often accompanies the fatty degeneration, puts even more strain on the damaged vessel (see Blood pressure). Fatty degeneration and hypertension are most common in the aorta and its major branches and can cause an aneurysm (a bulge in the blood vessel wall; see Heart disease). A ruptured aneurysm is an extreme medical emergency with a high fatality rate. Syphilis was once a common cause of aortic aneurysm but is now quite rare.

Blood vessels may also be involved in diseases that cause secondary hemorrhages. Infection may produce abscesses (see Abscess) that erode vessel walls. Ulcers (see Ulcers) in the stomach or intestine may eat into a vein or artery and cause a hemorrhage. Tumors (see Tumors) may also produce similar results anywhere in the body.

Congenital abnormalities may cause hemorrhaging. The most common, berry aneurysms, involve the vessels of the brain and may cause cerebral hemorrhages. Arteriovenous malformation (fusion of an artery and vein) can also cause bleeding anywhere in the body from either the arteries or the veins.

Berry aneurysms are due to congenital weakness in the vessel wall, and usually occur at the point of branching of arteries on the underside of the brain. They cause no symptoms and give no warning of their presence. They may burst and often do so in comparatively young people, in their late 30s or 40s. Because the vessel concerned lies under the middle, or arachnoid, layer of the brain coverings (the three meninges) the resulting bleeding is called a subarachnoid hemorrhage.

External hemorrhage

General rules

- Call the local emergency service immediately
- While waiting, place a clean gauze or material pad over the site of the bleeding
- Raise the bleeding body part
- Press firmly on the site of the bleeding for at least five minutes
- If an artery has been severed, press on artery at side nearest to the heart for 15 minutes at a time
- Do not remove a blood-soaked pad. Bandage it in place and put a clean dressing over the top

The body's protective reactions

Except when hemorrhaging is severe, the body is usually able to put a whole series of protective reactions into effect, first to dam the bleeding and then to repair the damaged vessel (see Blood). The damming reaction involves the clotting of blood around the site of the injury, but in some diseases, including hemophilia (see Hemophilia), certain types of jaundice (see Jaundice), and vitamin K deficiency (see Vitamin K), the clotting mechanism is impaired, making a hemorrhage much more serious than in a healthy person.

Scurvy is another important cause of spontaneous hemorrhaging. It is caused by a deficiency of vitamin C (ascorbic acid) and occurs only in people whose diets contain almost no vegetables and fruits. Scurvy still occurs occasionally even in our well-nourished Western societies, as a result of fad diets or severe poverty and general incapacity (see Scurvy).

Vitamin C is required for the normal production of the body's structural protein, collagen. People with scurvy do not form strong, healthy collagen so their blood vessels are weak and leak easily, causing hemorrhage into the gums and into the deep tissues of the body. This can lead to bruising and to the development of large accumulations of blood (hematomas) in the tissues. In such people blood levels of ascorbic acid are low and other vitamin deficiencies are usually present as well. The condition can be rapidly cured by taking 500 mg of ascorbic acid twice a day.

Blood clotting is a complex process involving a sequence, or cascade, of a dozen sequential biochemical processes, each of which must be completed before the next can occur. At least 13 different substances, known as clotting factors, are required. Some of the disorders that lead to the failure of blood clotting and hemorrhages are due to a genetic deficiency of these clotting factors. Lack of Factors 8 and 9, for example, cause two kinds of hemophilia.

Effects

The effects of hemorrhaging vary greatly according to the amount of blood lost, where the hemorrhage occurs, how fast blood is lost, the health of the person involved, and any other injuries received.

As a general rule very rapid blood loss is more serious than slow bleeding because it puts more stress on the heart, causes collapse of the general circulation, and gives the body no chance to make up the blood volume quickly enough. In a healthy adult or child the amount of blood that can be lost without the need for emergency treatment (and blood transfusion to make up the loss) depends on the amount of blood in the system but not on the site of the hemorrhage: the effects are the same whether the patient is found lying in a pool of blood or has lost the same amount of blood into the alimentary canal from an ulcer. The safe figure for blood loss is usually taken as 15 percent of the total blood in the system, but this total varies according to body weight. Each person has an average of 1 pt (475 ml) of blood for every 14 lb (6.3 kg) of body weight. This means that a child or a small woman is endangered by losing much less blood than a man of large build. For most adults the rough figure for the upper limit of safety is usually rounded up to 2 pt (950 ml) of blood loss.

Another common and important cause of considerable blood loss is the fracture of one of the larger bones, especially the thighbone (femur). Such a fracture is often associated with the internal release of a large volume of blood. This causes great swelling and discoloration. As much as 4.2 pt (2 l) of blood may be lost from the circulation into the soft tissues surrounding a fracture of the femur. The body is wholly deprived of the use of this blood and the effects of this loss are the same as they would be if the same volume were lost by external bleeding. This is why femoral fractures are commonly associated with severe shock.

Slow hemorrhaging that occurs over several days may not pose such an immediate threat to life as the sudden loss of a lot of blood but is still dangerous and can be deceptive. In this case fluid percolates back into the blood vessels from the tissues to make the blood up to the correct volume and keep the circulation going. However, the body's capacity for making new red blood cells to carry oxygen works much more slowly so that the potential result is fatal anemia. In anyone who is already anemic, a slight hemorrhage can quickly reduce the oxygen-

An internal hemorrhage that has led to shock

Danger signs indicating internal bleeding and shock:

- Skin, especially on the face, turns very pale, almost ashen
- Skin clammy and cold to the touch
- Pulse weak and racing
- Fast, gasping breathing
- Coughing up blood
- Patient anxious and very weak
- Patient may complain of thirst, cold and dizziness
- Patient may complain of feeling faint, with restlessness and confusion or of buzzing or ringing in the ears and may lapse into unconsciousness

What to do

- Call the local emergency service
- Never move the patient except to lie him or her down, and keep him or her calm
- Check for pulse and breathing
- Put a pillow or folded blanket under the head and several more pillows under the calves so that the feet are higher than the head and blood can flow to the brain easily
- Keep a person in shock as cold as possible, preferably on ice. This slows the metabolism and constricts the blood flow until help arrives

CAUTION: Do not try this without first consulting a doctor unless you are properly trained

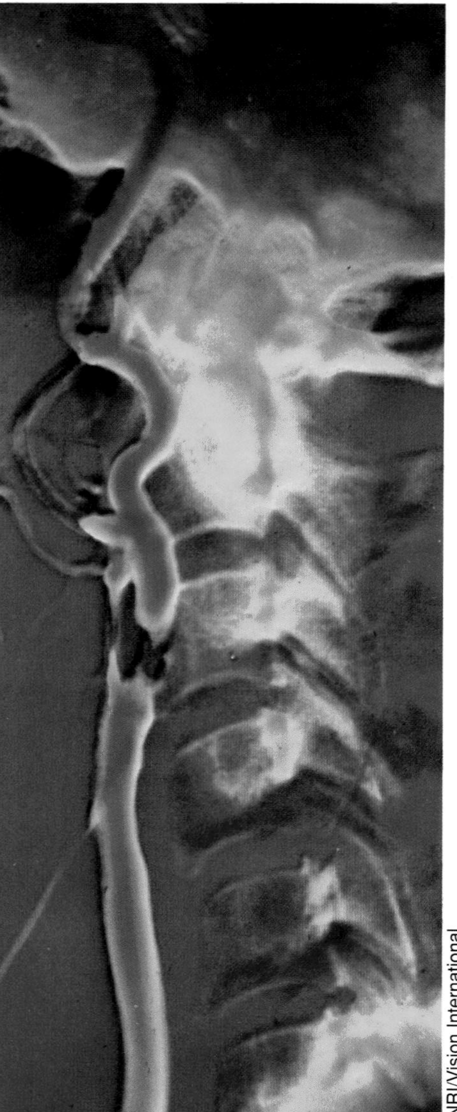

CNRI/Vision International

Arteries can be weakened by deposits of fatty material on their inner walls to such an extent that they can rupture.

transporting capacity of the blood to a dangerously low level (see Anemia).

Shock

The unfailing symptom of severe hemorrhaging is shock, a term used to describe the failure of the blood circulation. When a lot of blood is lost, the immediate result is a fall in blood pressure. The blood vessels then constrict (narrow) and so increase the resistance to flow, to keep the blood pressure up. Despite this, and despite extra work by the heart, the flow of blood to tissues may fall. Life is then threatened because vital tissues—particularly the brain—cannot get enough oxygen to survive, although the body does its best to divert blood to where it is needed most: the brain, lungs, and the heart itself.

Shock, which may be accompanied by raging thirst because the body has lost fluid, is typified by extremely pale skin, that feels cold and clammy to the touch; a weak, fast pulse; and panting or gasping for breath (often described as air hunger, because the person in shock tries to boost the oxygen in the blood by taking more air into the lungs).

Anyone who has lost more than the critical amount of blood is likely to go into shock and needs an immediate transfusion to save his or her life. This explains why someone suffering from hemorrhaging must be taken at once to the hospital, preferably by ambulance. At the hospital a transfusion of blood is given as soon as the patient's blood group has been determined (so that there is no risk of an adverse reaction to blood of an incompatible group; see Blood groups).

Fluid volume

One of the most dangerous features of shock is the reduction in the circulating volume of fluid in the blood vessels. This is called hypovolemia, and the first and most urgent requirement is the restoration of blood volume. This loss of volume may, in itself, be so serious as to cause death. For this reason a transfusion of fluid other than blood, perhaps of slightly salty water (saline), can be life-saving. Paramedics dealing with a person in surgical shock may therefore start an infusion of saline at the location of the accident. Blood transfusion will, of course, be started in the hospital as soon as blood grouping and crossmatching permit. Such blood may have to be given very rapidly to save the person's life. Severe shock is very dangerous.

Shock due to fluid loss from burns actually causes concentration of the blood because, in this case, the main loss may be of water rather than whole blood. In such a case there may be a greater immediate requirement for saline than for blood.

In a major hemorrhage the urgency to restore the blood volume may be acute. This is because the reduction in available blood to the organs and the selective shutdown of supply to certain less vital organs can quickly lead to such severe organ damage that survival becomes impossible for the patient. In many cases the organ damage passes the stage at which recovery is possible. Multiple organ failure is a common cause of death following severe hemorrhaging.

In the case of a hemorrhage that is not bad enough to result in shock, the body's natural systems are able to work unaided. The blood vessels are sealed off with clots, then gradually repair themselves over a period of weeks. At the same time the blood gradually recovers its full potential to carry oxygen through the addition of new blood cells that are formed in the bone marrow, a reaction that is automatically stimulated by the loss of any blood.

Hemorrhaging after surgery

Anyone who has to go into the hospital for surgery worries about the amount of blood that may be lost during surgery. However, the patient can be sure that the surgeons and nurses are all intensely aware of the dangers of hemorrhaging and will do their utmost to prevent the excess loss of blood. They will give transfusions if necessary to make up the loss.

The anticipated blood loss for most surgical procedures is a known quantity, and a suitable amount of compatible blood is made ready at the blood bank.

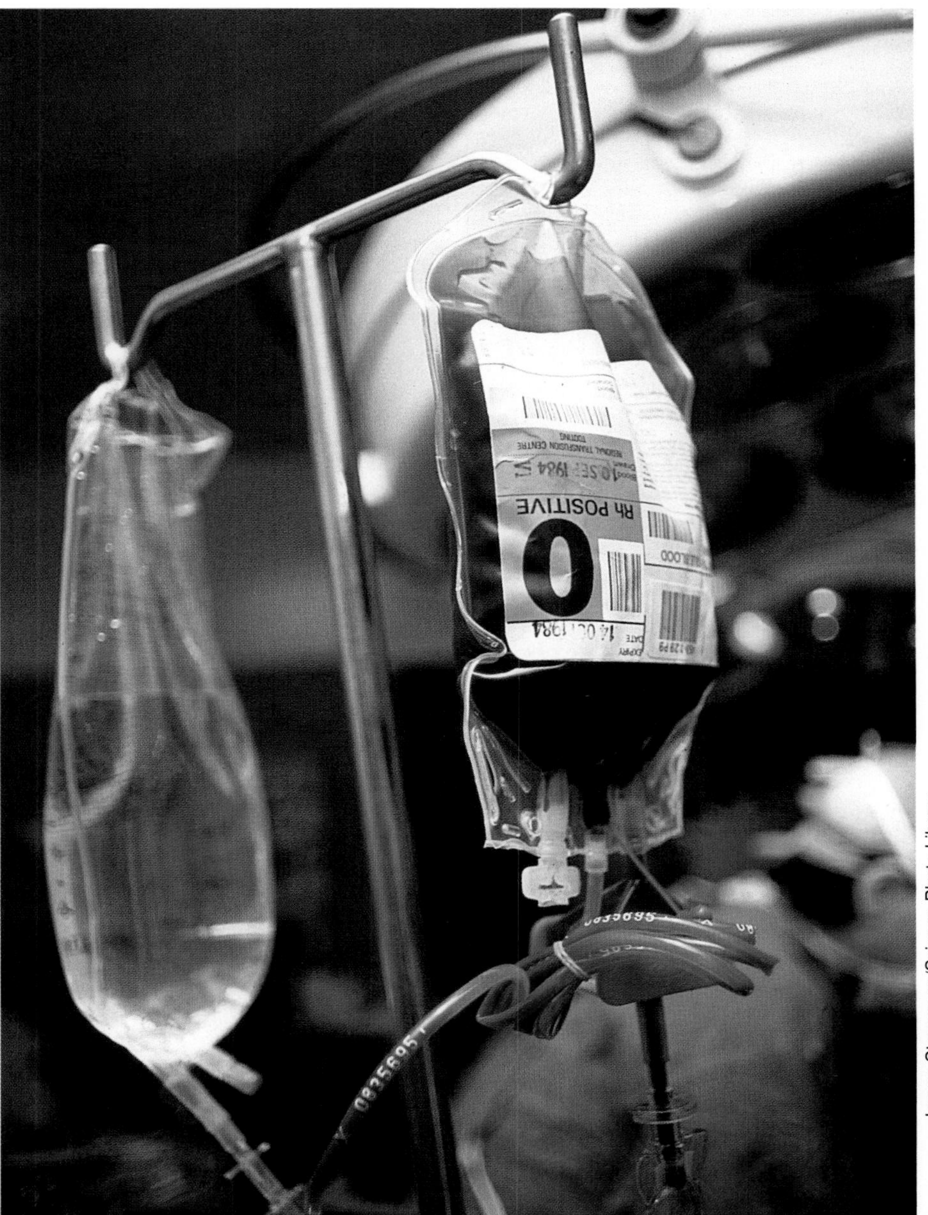

James Stevenson/Science Photo Library

During an operation a blood transfusion bag hangs on a nearby stand. The type of blood is carefully matched to the patient.

Hemorrhoids

Q Are people with high blood pressure likely to suffer from hemorrhoids?

A Internal hemorrhoids are very common in people of the Western hemisphere and so are bound to occur in those with high blood pressure. A person with high blood pressure may be more likely to bleed from hemorrhoids than a person with normal blood pressure, but they are not caused by this condition.

Q Do hemorrhoids and varicose veins go together?

A Hemorrhoids used to be thought of as a type of varicose vein in the anal canal. However, this has now been shown not to be the case. The two conditions do often coexist though, and both can be made worse by pregnancy. Both varicose veins and hemorrhoids are swellings of the veins. Both are caused by increased blood pressure. During pregnancy, the total volume of blood in the body doubles.

Q Is hard toilet paper bad for hemorrhoids?

A Hard toilet paper does not cause hemorrhoids, but it can cause injury to the skin, leading to minor abrasions with bleeding.

Q Is it true that you can get hemorrhoids from sitting on a hot radiator?

A Sitting on a hot surface does not cause hemorrhoids. However, it is possible that in a person who already has them, increased local heat could make hemorrhoids swell and therefore become more pronounced.

Q Can some types of food give you hemorrhoids?

A Some foods are good, and some bad, for hemorrhoids. Anything that tends to cause diarrhea is likely to aggravate them, and any food with a high roughage content, such as vegetables, fruits, and nuts, is likely to help prevent them.

While the condition commonly referred to as piles can sometimes cause extreme pain and much embarrassment to the patient, hemorrhoids are essentially minor medical problems that can be easily and often painlessly cured.

The word *piles* can refer to several different conditions of the anal canal, each with different symptoms. Most commonly the word refers to hemorrhoids, which are swellings of the veins in the rectum that usually cause irritation. However, it is often also used to denote anal fissures (tears), thrombosed (clotted) external hemorrhoids, and simple anal skin tags (flaps of extra skin).

Structure of the anal canal

The anal canal is a short tube, about 1.5 in (3.8 cm) long, that connects the rectum (the last part of the large intestine) to the outside. Its upper (innermost) half is lined with mucous membrane—the type of lining found throughout the gut. The lower half is lined with skin, and is very sensitive to painful stimuli, whereas the upper half is insensitive to pain.

The anal canal is surrounded by a ring of muscle called the anal sphincter, which is normally tightly contracted but can relax to allow a bowel motion (see Excretory system).

Conditions and their symptoms

Internal hemorrhoids are swellings of the veins in the upper part of the anal canal and gradually become larger over a period of years. They are probably caused by prolonged straining to pass small, hard feces, but they are made worse by pregnancy. Internal hemorrhoids are thought to be made of spongy tissue rich in small blood vessels. They generally occur in threes, and the first symptom is usually bright red bleeding. The bleeding is slight, occurs at the end of defecation, and does not usually cause any pain.

People with small internal hemorrhoids have minimal symptoms and often tolerate them well for years. If the hemorrhoids become larger, in addition to bleeding during defecation, they may come out of the anal canal and be visible as a lump. Occasionally these kinds of hemorrhoids can become painful, and the pain may last for several days. This is known as an attack of piles. Normally, however, these hemorrhoids are not painful, and when they are it is because they have become strangulated, or squeezed (see Strangulation), by a tight anal canal.

An anal fissure is a split in the skin of the anal canal in a longitudinal direction. This is probably caused by straining due to constipation. There is extreme pain during defecation, together with a small amount of blood, often only on the toilet paper. The pain may be so severe that the patient is afraid to defecate. Anal fissures can sometimes heal spontaneously; others may require a minor operation.

In thrombosed external piles a small blood vessel bursts just beneath the skin's surface at the edge of the anal canal. The patient feels severe pain during and after defecation. Some time later a painful lump appears that becomes red, sore, and inflamed. The condition is easy to treat.

Tags of extra skin around the anal canal are not strictly speaking an abnormality, but they do cause problems with hygiene. They are commonly diagnosed as piles and treated as such, even though the treatment is not usually necessary.

The condition known as anal fistula (see Fistula) is also occasionally diagnosed as piles. The main symptom is a discharge of fluid, often like pus, and there is seldom much pain or bleeding, or a lump. Anal fistula is usually the aftereffect of a tiny abscess (see Abscess) in the lining of the anal canal. There is an abnormal connection between the skin next to the anal canal and the inside of the canal. Secretions leak out through this channel, leading to soiling of underclothes.

Treatment

Treatment of true internal hemorrhoids takes several different forms. Initially the doctor will want to make sure that there is no other serious cause for the bleeding by examining the lower part of the rectum. If the hemorrhoids are small, there are a number of ways in which they can be treated.

The hemorrhoids can be injected with a substance that makes them shrivel up. This may sound painful, but if it is done properly it should not hurt at all, because the injection is put into the upper, insensitive part of the anal canal. Other methods of treatment are to use a special freezing instrument called a cryoprobe that shrinks the hemorrhoids, or to put tiny rubber bands around them that cut off their blood supply (see Freezing).

None of these treatments is painful, and they can all be done in the outpatient

Anatomy of the anal canal

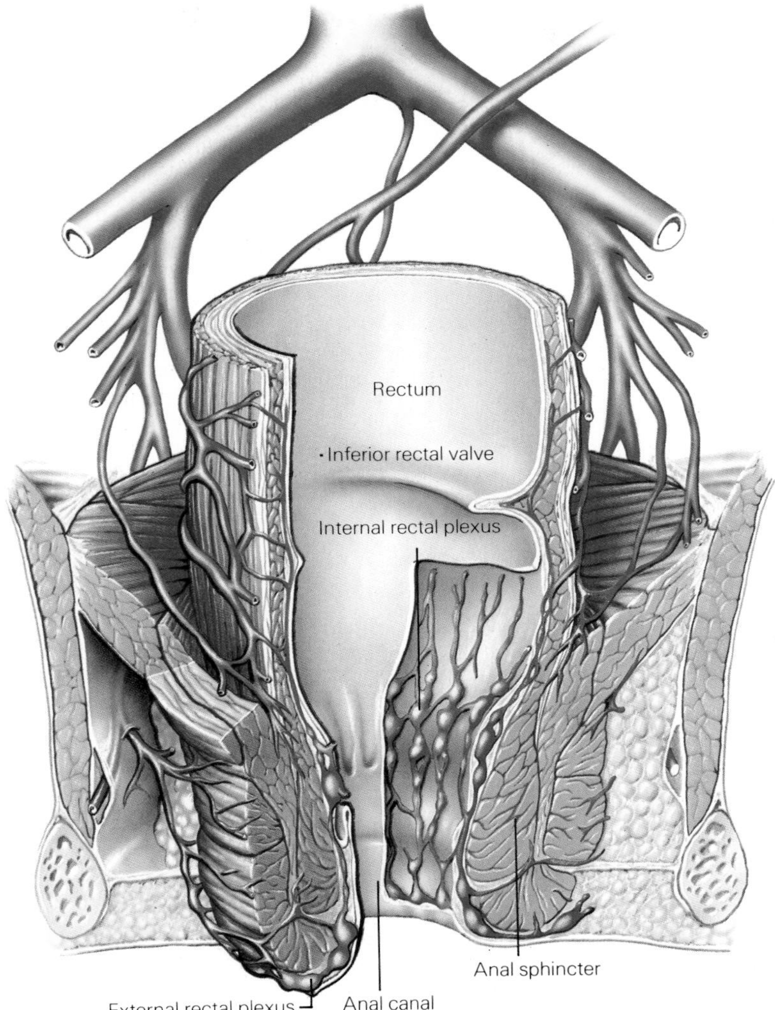

department of the hospital. A high-fiber diet (see Diet) is also recommended, because it is thought that a lack of fiber is one of the main causes of hemorrhoids.

The treatment of an anal fissure depends on whether it is a small, recent one, or a larger one of some months duration. In a mild form the use of some local anesthetic cream, together with the intake of increased amounts of dietary fiber, which makes defecation easier, may allow the fissure to heal. In more severe cases there may be so much pain that the doctor may give the patient a general anesthetic before attempting an examination. If a fissure is found, then a canal stretch is performed; the ring of muscle around the anal canal is stretched so that it is unable to contract strongly. This allows the patient to defecate more easily and the fissure to heal quickly. Most patients notice an immediate relief from pain.

Thrombosed external piles can easily be treated under a local anesthetic. After cutting through the skin, the blood clot is removed and there is instant pain relief.

Anal skin tags do not usually need any specific treatment. However, they can be removed easily during a small operation, sometimes under a local anesthetic.

Most cases of anal fistula can be treated by opening the abnormal channel and draining it. Sometimes a longer operation is necessary but this is a very rare occurrence nowadays.

Home remedies

If hemorrhoids prolapse (appear externally as lumps) then a warm bath with a handful of salt dissolved in it often helps.

When hemorrhoids become strangulated, a polythene bag full of crushed ice applied to the enlarged hemorrhoids may ease the pain.

Frank Kennard

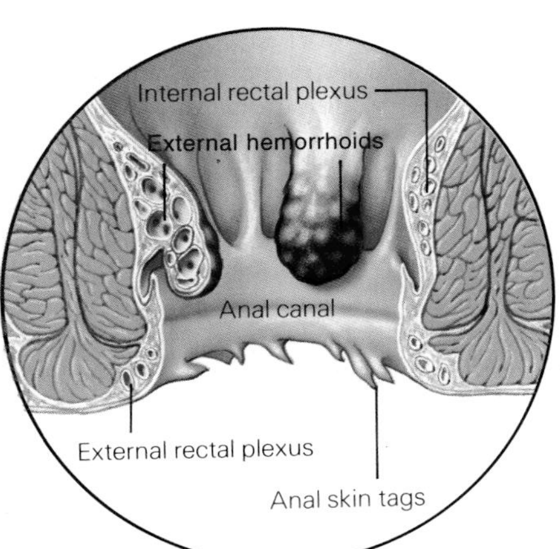

The diagram above illustrates how networks of veins (the plexuses) are concentrated in certain areas of the rectum. It is in these areas that piles may occur, either as external hemorrhoids (inset right) or internal hemorrhoids (inset left). Skin tags (inset left) are not true hemorrhoids but are often diagnosed and treated as such, although they seldom cause any serious problem.

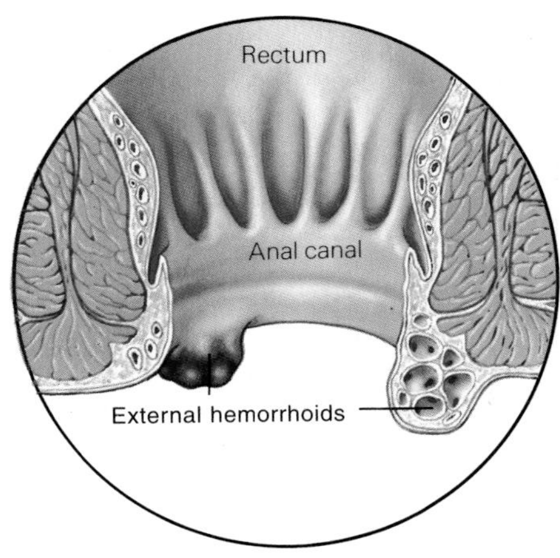

Hepatitis

Q My brother has just gone to sea. He now writes that he wants to be tattooed when he reaches the next port. Is there any risk involved?

A You are probably referring to the risk of contracting hepatitis, but this is purely a question of hygiene. Although there are many competent practicing tattooists around, it is still possible to be infected with a hepatitis virus through the use of unsterile needles, which could introduce the infection into the recipient's body.

Unfortunately there is no central regulatory body for tattooists, nor is there a code of professional practice that would act to protect the public as well as reputable tattooists. Although there are moves being made to get a professional body organized, at the moment people must simply use their common sense and not patronize tattooist's premises that look dirty and unhygienic.

Q I would like to go on the Pill but have had hepatitis. People tell me that this means that it will not be allowed. Is there a special reason for this?

A Medical opinions vary on this point, but most doctors would agree that if you have had chronic (infectious) hepatitis you should never use this means of contraception. The reason is that the Pill contains powerful chemicals that could cause further damage to your liver if they did not pass through it very quickly, and the result could be complete liver failure. You should use other methods of contraception rather than run this risk.

Q I am five months pregnant and have just been told that I have caught hepatitis. Does this mean that my baby will catch it from me?

A Unfortunately your baby may also develop hepatitis and may have the virus in its blood when it is born. However, both of you can be treated with an injection of gamma globulin, which is given shortly after the child is born to deal with the infection.

Hepatitis—inflammation of the liver—can be a serious illness, but fortunately many people recover completely. However, it is advisable to give up alcohol for at least six months after an attack as a preventive measure.

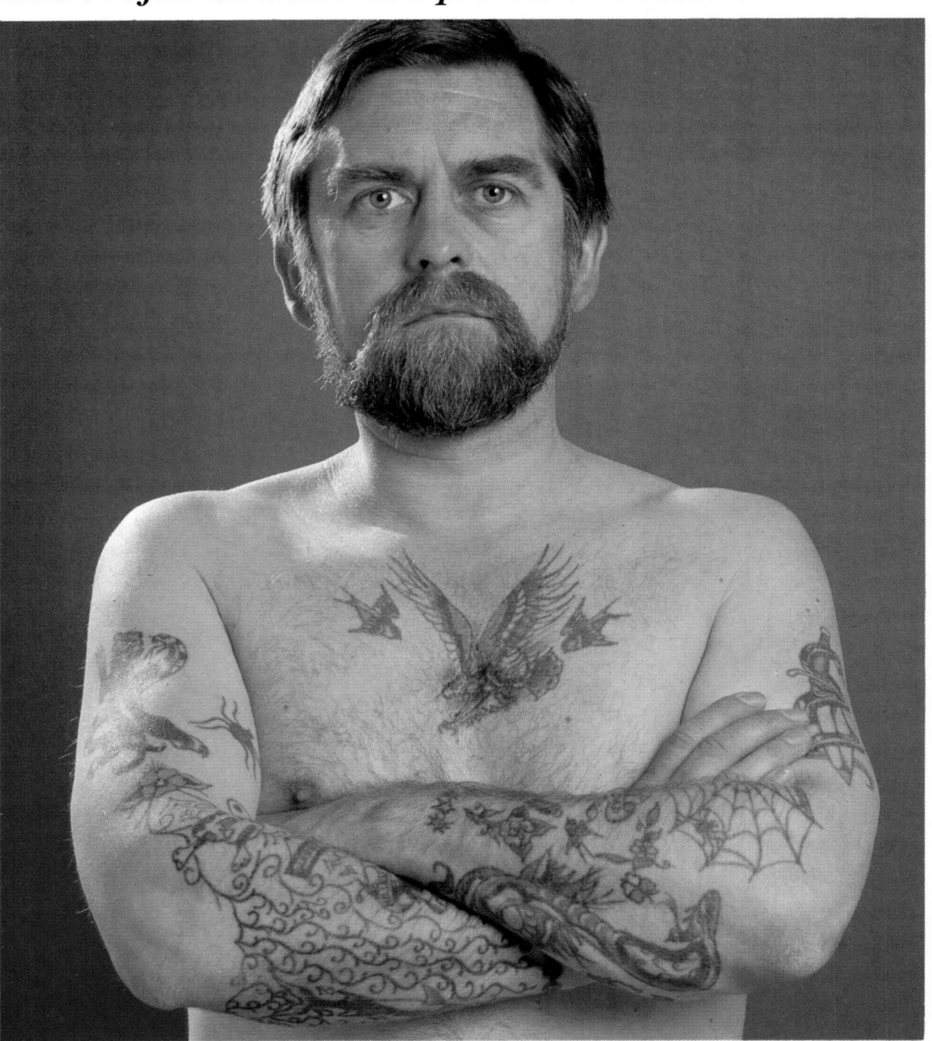

Tattooing must be done with sterile needles to avoid the risk of hepatitis infection.

Hepatitis is a highly infectious viral disease involving inflammation of the liver (see Liver and liver diseases). The virus is transmitted in blood, feces, or saliva. It is a disease that affects people of all ages but tends to occur more in the young and among those whose work involves handling contaminated material.

Causes

There are two viruses that are chiefly responsible, known as hepatitis A (formerly called infectious hepatitis) and hepatitis B (serum hepatitis). A third kind of virus that resembles hepatitis B in its method of transmission occurs in the absence of either the A or B virus. This is called hepatitis non-A, non-B (or hepatitis C).

Another agent (cause), called delta hepatitis, has also been discovered. This virus (hepatitis D) cannot cause disease on its own, but if it is acquired together with hepatitis B, or if it is superimposed on a hepatitis B carrier, it causes a virulent form of liver infection. Other less common viruses that can cause hepatitis are known as hepatitis E and F.

Hepatitis A is usually transmitted by food or water that have been contaminated, although this virus can also be transmitted in infected blood. The disease is only infectious in the incubation stage, and it is not transmitted by carriers.

Outbreaks happen from time to time in areas with overcrowded housing and poor sanitation.

Hepatitis B takes longer to incubate, sometimes several months. Although it may be transmitted in the same way as hepatitis A, the B virus is more often transmitted in infected blood, either from hypodermic needles or as a result of a transfusion of infected blood or plasma. The use of disposable needles and blood screening tests have made this virtually unknown in Western hospitals. However, about 40 percent of heroin addicts are carriers of the B virus, and transmission still occurs through the use of unsterile tattoo needles and razor blades.

This virus also has the ability to infect an unborn child by crossing the placenta and so getting into the fetal bloodstream.

A group of people especially at risk are members of hospital staff, particularly those whose work involves handling blood on a regular basis in operating rooms or renal dialysis units (where sick patients are treated on kidney machines).

Symptoms

The majority of infections with either the A or B virus are mild and may even pass unnoticed, although both viruses leave chemical evidence in the blood after an infection, and signs of this can be found in blood tests.

When the disease is severe enough to cause sufficient inflammation of the liver to block the drainage of bile, the sufferer becomes jaundiced. When this happens the skin and the whites of the eyes develop a yellowish tinge. This is caused by bile pigments made by the liver entering the circulation instead of being eliminated through the intestine.

Jaundice may occur fairly rapidly after an infection by hepatitis A but is usually slower if the illness is due to hepatitis B.

How hepatitis affects the liver

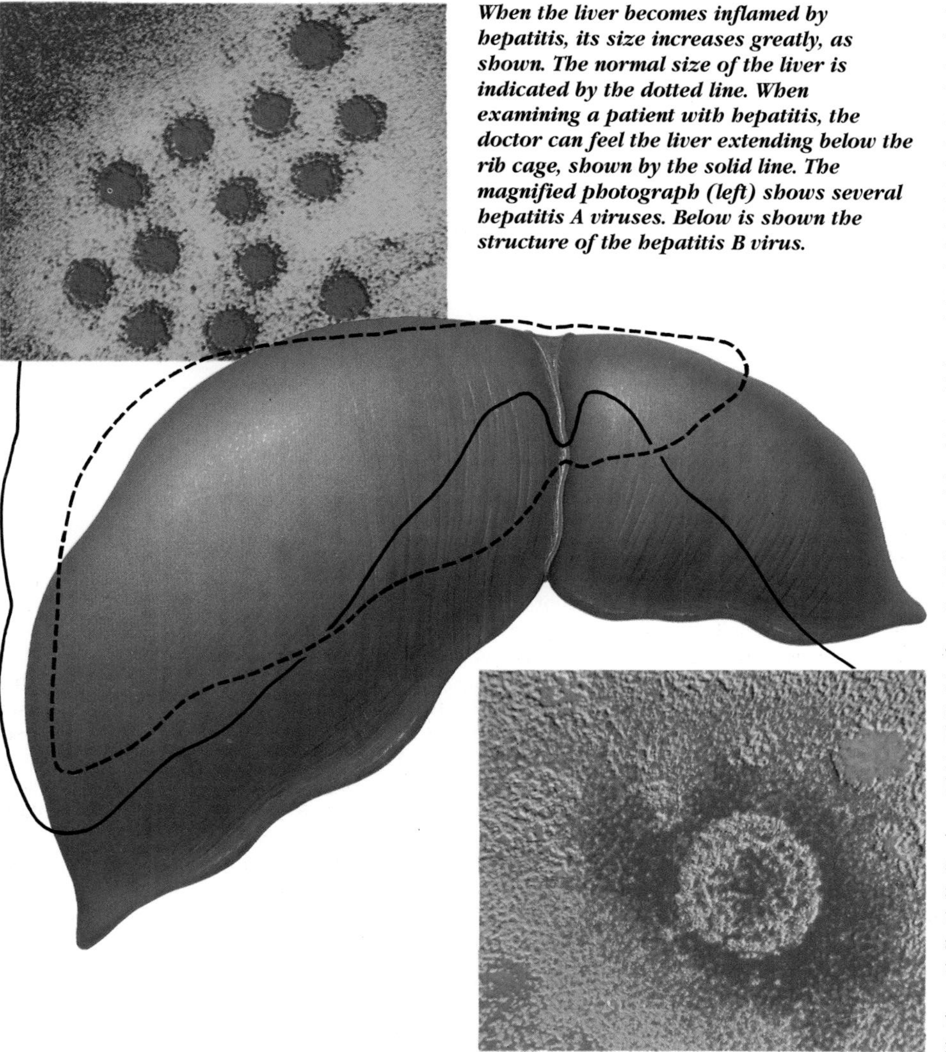

When the liver becomes inflamed by hepatitis, its size increases greatly, as shown. The normal size of the liver is indicated by the dotted line. When examining a patient with hepatitis, the doctor can feel the liver extending below the rib cage, shown by the solid line. The magnified photograph (left) shows several hepatitis A viruses. Below is shown the structure of the hepatitis B virus.

Mike Courteney

Very often the victim feels unwell for some time beforehand, rejecting food and losing any desire to smoke (if formerly a smoker). Pain is felt high in the abdomen on the right side. There may be arthritic-type pains in the joints, and also a rash. While the jaundice is most marked, the patient feels sick and frequently vomits. The jaundice does not usually last for more than two weeks and recovery takes place within six weeks or so.

Unfortunately in a few cases of hepatitis B or C, the virus is not eliminated and the patient becomes a carrier. In some of these patients, chronic inflammation of the liver develops, which progresses to cirrhosis. This does not occur in hepatitis A, since there is no carrier state.

Doctors can easily diagnose hepatitis if typical symptoms are present, which can then be confirmed by blood tests.

After having a hepatitis A infection, the antibodies made against it can be detected in the blood. Hepatitis B is more complex and therefore more difficult to detect. During infection a portion of the virus called surface antigen is found in the blood. When the patient has overcome the infection, antibodies to this virus antigen appear. If no antibody is made, it indicates that the patient is still carrying the virus. If the doctor suspects that a virus carrier is developing chronic liver disease, blood tests for chemicals leaking from damaged liver cells will be done. If the tests show any abnormality, then a liver biopsy is performed and a minute sample of tissue is examined under a microscope (see Biopsy).

Dangers

Until the recent increase in liver disease produced by alcoholism, viral hepatitis was without question the most common cause of cirrhosis of the liver, which can be fatal. Some sufferers from viral hepatitis do make a complete recovery, but others fail to eliminate the virus from the body. They then become chronic carriers and may infect others.

Treatment

It is not necessary to admit all hepatitis sufferers to the hospital—only those who become extremely unwell or who are at risk, for example, expectant mothers, diabetics, or the elderly.

Both while the liver is inflamed, and while it is recovering, its cells will be sensitive to all kinds of drugs, and it is advisable not to take any medicines at this time. It is particularly important to avoid alcohol, which has a poisonous effect on the liver.

Whether the patient is being treated in the hospital or at home, it is essential to reduce the chances of cross-infection by

Q My friend is a very heavy drinker. Is he in danger of getting hepatitis?

A People who drink heavily do suffer more from chronic hepatitis or from cirrhosis of the liver, which could result in death from liver damage. The message is clear; persuade him to cut down.

Q My baby son had jaundice soon after he was born. Does this increase the danger that he might develop hepatitis?

A No, this is not significant. Young babies sometimes develop jaundice through the destruction of red blood cells that are no longer needed. It is rarely due to inflammation of the liver, as in hepatitis, but hospitals watch out for symptoms of jaundice in newborn infants so that treatment can be given if necessary.

Q My mother has infectious hepatitis and is being treated at home. Must we take special precautions?

A During the infectious stage you should cook her food in separate pots and use different utensils; you should also take extra care with personal hygiene. However, your mother will stop being infectious soon after the jaundice begins to disappear.

Q I have read that you cannot be a blood donor if you have had hepatitis. Is this true?

A Yes. The organisms that cause this disease can go on living in your blood long after you have recovered. If this blood was given to someone else, they could contract the disease.

Q My teenage daughter has had glandular fever and has now developed jaundice. Isn't this rather odd?

A Not at all. It is not uncommon for people with glandular fever to develop jaundice due to hepatitis. This also happens in a number of other viral diseases, because numerous viruses are potential causes of inflammation of the liver.

Abstinence from alcohol is essential if you have had hepatitis. Orange juice can provide a healthy alternative.

using separate cooking and eating utensils for the patient and being careful about personal hygiene.

There has been a good deal of medical argument as to the importance of complete rest in bed. Some doctors feel that the later complications (cirrhosis or chronic hepatitis) can be avoided, provided that the patient rests as much as possible while jaundiced. There are no particular dietary restrictions but the patient should eat properly.

People who are exposed to infection by hepatitis or who intend to live cheaply on walking or camping vacations in areas such as southern Europe, India, or Africa can be protected against hepatitis A by an injection of gamma globulin. Vaccination against hepatitis B is also available but is only recommended for very high risk groups. Accidental exposure to hepatitis B can be treated with hyperimmune globulin, given within a week of exposure to the virus. Infants born to mothers with hepatitis can also be protected in the same way if they are injected within a week of birth.

Outlook

The majority of hepatitis attacks are mild, can be nursed at home, and are followed by complete recovery.

Hepatitis can recur, but it is rarely caused by the same type of virus. It is, however, possible for patients who are carriers to suffer a relapse.

If you have had hepatitis the best advice is never to drink alcohol again, but if this is too hard to bear, abstain from all alcoholic drinks for at least six months.

Herbalism

Q Can you make your own herbal remedies at home?

A Yes. Some plants can be used raw, either eaten or applied directly to the body. An onion, for example, is a strong antiseptic. It can also be cut in half and applied to the skin to relieve insect stings or to soften corns. Many herbs can be made into a medicinal tea by pouring hot water over them and leaving them to infuse for several minutes. Peppermint tea, for example, is an old remedy said to be useful in relieving the symptoms of a cold—headache, sore throat, and a runny nose.

Q Are herbal medicines safer than doctor's drugs?

A There is no real evidence that they are any safer; just because something is natural does not guarantee that it is safe. In fact, some very dangerous materials may be found in herbal remedies that are prepared under uncontrolled conditions. Although some herbal remedies do have a good safety record, the lack of official monitoring is a concern.

Q Do herbalists have to have any medical qualifications?

A There are a few doctors and pharmacists who know about, and use, herbal medicines. The majority of practicing herbalists have had training in herbal medicine but few have had orthodox medical training of either a specialist or a general nature. For this reason you should use caution when seeking a herbalist's advice. However, this may well change in the future.

Q What is the difference between the herbs you put into food and the herbs used for medicines?

A There is no difference at all. A herb is any plant used for culinary, medicinal, or cosmetic purposes, and many herbs are used in several ways. Sage, for example, is a popular flavoring for food; it is also used in gargles for a sore throat, and as a hair rinse to restore the color in graying hair.

Many people use herbal remedies for minor ailments, but herbs can also be used effectively to treat many diseases. Research into their medicinal value is increasing.

At the end of the 19th century almost all the medicines prescribed by doctors were based on plants. In Europe and the United States, where herbal medicine almost completely disappeared after the discovery of potent, effective synthetic drugs, there has been a revival of interest in medicinal plants. More and more people are turning to herbalists because they want medicines that are more natural than synthetic drugs.

A different approach

The one big difference between herbal medicines and conventional drugs is that the former are natural substances derived from plants, while the latter are mostly synthetic chemicals. Of course many well-known medicines—such as digitalis, the heart drug, and novacaine, the painkiller—do come from plants. But although modern drug manufacturers owe a lot to herbs, they have a very different approach from that of the herbalists. A herbalist prefers to use medicines that are made from the whole plant, while the drug manufacturer—if he or she cannot make a synthetic version of a plant medicine—tries to isolate the single chemical ingredient of a plant that seems to have the most medicinal value.

An onion, which is a strong antiseptic, can also be placed on the skin to relieve insect stings.

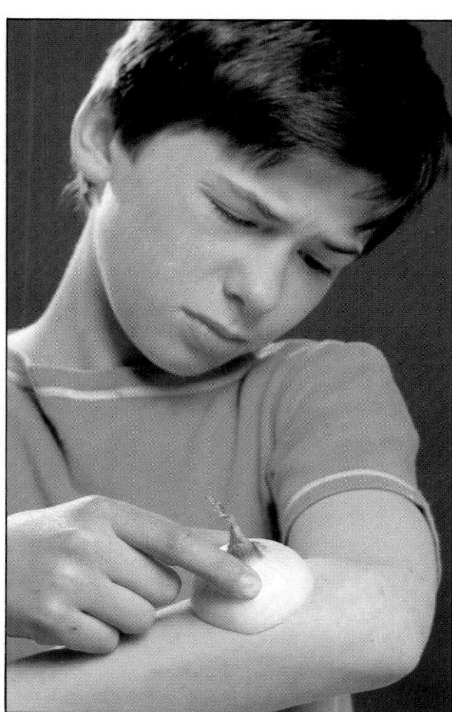

Herbalists disagree with this approach, claiming that whole-plant extracts are better for the body and cause fewer side effects because they contain a whole variety of substances that tone down the harsh effect of a single potent chemical. An example of this is the plant ephedra, which herbalists use to treat asthma. Ephedra contains a chemical, ephedrine, which has been used in conventional medicine to treat asthma, but which also raises the patient's blood pressure. The plant, on the other hand, contains other substances, such as norephedrine and pseudoephedrine, which modify the effect of ephedrine on the blood pressure while not interfering with its antiasthmatic properties too much. However, many doctors believe that using ephedra to treat asthma is unsafe, since the dosage is difficult to control. They prefer to use the isolated chemical.

As yet it is not known whether herbal medicines are more or less safe and effective than synthetic drugs, because few researchers have tried to compare them directly in action. We know about the hazards of some synthetic drugs, because they are widely prescribed and many doctors are on the watch for potential side effects; herbal medicine has not come under the same scrutiny.

Medicinal plants

It is undeniable that herbs can be used effectively to treat many diseases, even serious ones. Willow bark, for example, contains salicylic acid, which is chemically the same as aspirin (acetyl salicylic acid); tea made by infusing (soaking) willow bark in hot water is an effective treatment for rheumatic and arthritic pains—indeed, the same kind of complaints for which aspirin would be used.

There are several herbs that can reduce the amount of sugar in the blood and are therefore an effective treatment for diabetes. One often used by herbalists is goat's rue, *Galliga officinalis* (*officinalis* in the scientific name of plants means that they can be used as medicine). It is so effective at reducing blood sugar levels that patients should not take this herbal medicine with conventional diabetic drugs—they risk bringing their blood sugar level down so low that they

Garlic is an antiseptic, and in herbal medicine it is also used in the treatment of colds, influenza, asthma, and flatulence.

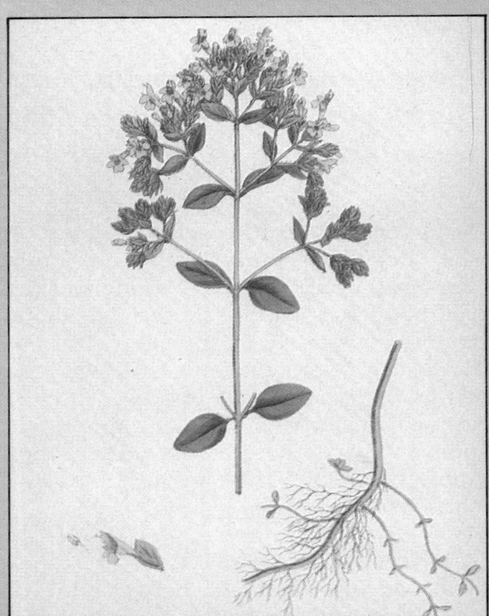

Marjoram, a remedy for diarrhea, can also be used to stimulate the digestion and as a diuretic (to encourage urine production).

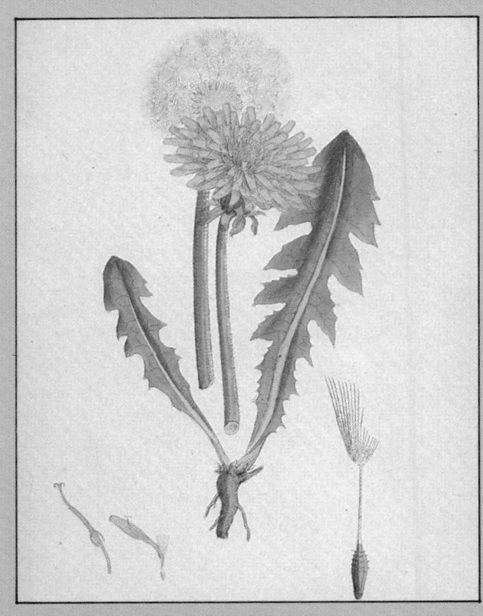

Dandelion tea, made from the leaves of the plant, has a tonic and cleansing effect, and is mildly laxative.

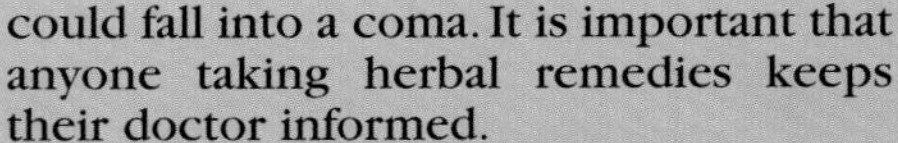

could fall into a coma. It is important that anyone taking herbal remedies keeps their doctor informed.

Garlic has a reputation for protecting from cancer, and research at the US National Cancer Institute suggests that garlic juice might be able to inhibit the growth of tumors in laboratory animals.

What do herbalists treat?

Most of the people who visit herbalists tend to have chronic complaints that have failed to respond to conventional medical treatment; arthritis, skin complaints such as acne, and cancer are all familiar to the herbalist, who in many cases can help such patients.

Most herbalists are reluctant to make claims that they are able to treat successfully specific conditions such as cancer, arthritis, venereal disease, glaucoma, cataracts, or diabetes. It is too easy for unscrupulous quacks to make such claims. Therefore, to protect patients, all

The nettle contains several vitamins, including C, K, and E. One of its properties is the ability to reduce blood sugar levels.

Peppermint tea is a long-established remedy for relieving indigestion and the discomfort of cold symptoms.

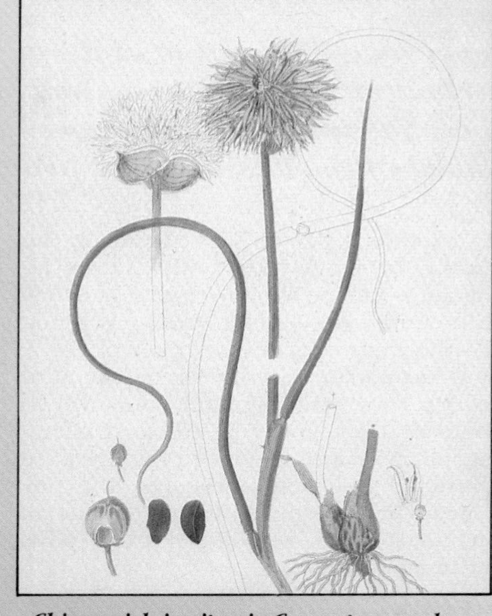

Chives, rich in vitamin C, carotene, and vitamin B_2, are also regarded as useful in reducing high blood pressure.

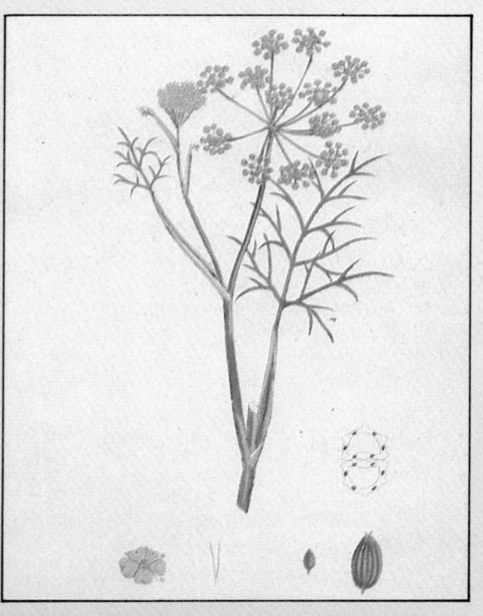

Dill water, which is made from the seeds of the plant, is used as a mild medicine for gas, especially in babies.

The Mansell Collection

Borage, another herb whose leaves can be made into a pleasant medicinal tea, has diuretic and mild laxative properties.

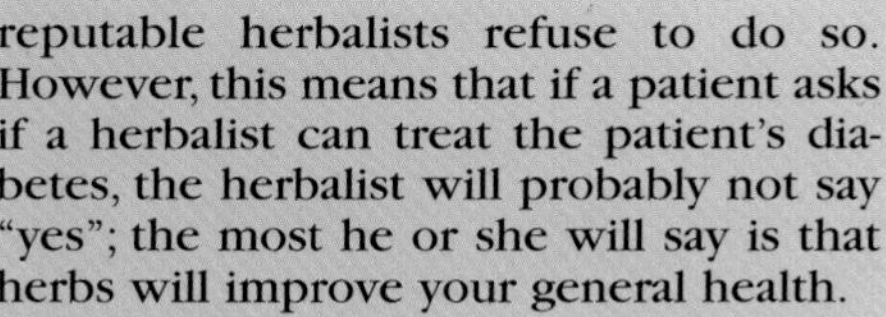

reputable herbalists refuse to do so. However, this means that if a patient asks if a herbalist can treat the patient's diabetes, the herbalist will probably not say "yes"; the most he or she will say is that herbs will improve your general health.

Herbal treatment

Most herbalists try to be holistic in their approach, treating the whole patient, not just the symptoms that are causing obvious distress (see Holistic medicine). So a patient with a skin complaint, for example, in addition to being given a herbal lotion or an ointment for the skin, might be given a liquid stomach medicine to aid digestion and a tonic to ease the nerves. They might also be given dietary advice.

Many plants

Of the 300,000 or more known species of plants, only about 10,000 have so far been investigated for their medicinal properties, and most herbalists make use of no more than two or three hundred of these. In Western countries research into herbal medicines is on the increase, and some years ago the World Health Organization set up a research institute to study plant remedies.

Heredity

Q My parents were both overweight, and I've turned out that way too. Why do heavy parents so often seem to have heavy children?

A Being overweight seems to be a problem that is both inherited and also caused by environment. Overweight parents tend to have heavy children, not simply because the children are overfed or encouraged to eat fattening foods, but also because they inherit certain physical and chemical tendencies.

Q I suffer from dyslexia, and I think my son may be developing the same problem. Is dyslexia inherited?

A Yes. Dyslexia is sometimes called word blindness and it causes severe problems with reading. It is a disability that can be inherited, so if a parent suffers from it, there is a risk that it will be passed on to the children. Given early and expert treatment (which is what you must get for your son), most children with dyslexia can learn to read. This demonstrates that many inherited problems can be overcome in a favorable environment, i.e., if they are treated properly.

Q My mother went through menopause early—at the age of 43. Will I be the same?

A It is likely. The length of the female reproductive life (the years when she may bear children) does tend to be inherited. It is not understood exactly how this happens, but it is thought that many different genes (inheritance factors) are involved, which regulate such mechanisms as egg release and hormone production.

Q My husband is a twin. Does this mean our children are likely to be twins?

A No. This tendency is only inherited through females. If there are no twins in your family tree, you are unlikely to have them. Also this only applies to nonidentical twins, when two eggs are fertilized.

Everyone knows that children resemble their parents, grandparents, brothers, and sisters to some extent, but just how far is it possible to predict the way they will turn out? Some of the answers are provided by the study of heredity.

Every time a person says "it runs in the family" or "she has her mother's eyes" he or she is talking about heredity. In scientific terminology this is known as genetics,the study of genes (see Genetics).

Genes can be described as biochemical codes. They are tiny, much too small to be seen even under an electron microscope. Research has shown that they are carried on the chromosomes (the tiny threadlike structures within all human cells that can be seen under a very powerful microscope).

Everyone has 46 chromosomes arranged in 23 pairs. One member of each pair comes from the father's sperm, the other from the mother's egg. Together these structures make up a complete chemical blueprint for a person's entire lifetime.

Simple forms of heredity

The pairing of chromosomes is most significant to the way heredity works, because each pair contains similar genes, and the most simple form of heredity can be traced to the operation of single pairs of genes. Genes acting in this way can occur in two different forms: one will be dominant, the other recessive. Dominant genes are distinguished by the tendency to display their character-

Children of racially mixed parents will reflect characteristics of both parents.

istics in the physical makeup of a person, even if they are only present in a single dose. A pair of similar recessive genes, with one gene inherited from each parent, must be present if they are to become obvious in an individual.

Geneticists have identified various dominant and recessive genes. For example, the gene for curly hair is dominant, so if a child inherits it from, say, the father, and also a gene for straight hair (which is recessive) from the mother, the curly hair gene will dominate and the child will have curly hair.

In practical terms this does not mean that you can predict whether your child will inherit your curly hair. The actual passing on of genes is a random occurrence, the curly-haired dominant trait having slightly better than even chances of being transferred. However, the principle does help us in a negative way, making it clear that we cannot count on a child having straight hair (if that is preferred) if one partner is curly-haired and the other is straight-haired.

Normality

A form of heredity, known as single-factor inheritance, or normality, is relatively simple and tells us some important and reassuring things about how our children will turn out in terms of their general health and makeup. This is because the majority of healthy characteristics are governed by dominant genes. So, as one might expect, most babies born to healthy mothers are themselves healthy.

Just a few hereditary diseases are inherited on dominant genes, but recessive genes can cause many more, including albinism (lack of pigment, or coloring; see Melanin) and some types of deafness.

Another important point to understand is that recessive genes, by nature, can be carried by a human all through life without the characteristics they convey actually showing up. Also, there is nothing to stop them from being passed on to the next generation and, if the circumstances are right, showing up there.

It is important to realize that this is putting the theory as simply as possble. There are complications even in single-factor inheritance.

Other types of heredity

There are several other ways in which genes can work. These vary in complexity. Perhaps one of the most interesting is the polygene system, which governs such characteristics as skin color, height, and probably intelligence.

Polygenes can be thought of as groups of genes working together. The rules of dominance apply to each gene in the group, and the effect of the genes is cumulative (they build up to produce an overall effect).

So although it is impossible to lay down a general rule, it is fair to say that tallness or shortness tends to run in families because the polygene for height contains more tall or short genes in some families than others. If a taller-than-average man has children by a shorter-than-average woman, the geneticist would expect them to be closer to the average height than either parent.

In a similar way the polygenes governing skin color produce a whole range of complexions among the races of the world, ranging from very dark to extremely pale.

Children born to parents of completely different skin colors—say, a pale Caucasian and a dark African—will tend to be intermediate between their parents, although because the darker skin genes are dominant over the pale skin genes, such a child would tend to be darker than the exact halfway shade. So there is no simple pattern of either dark or pale skin being inherited. There is also no truth to the myth that a child born with a different skin color from his or her parents is due to an ancestor of a different race somewhere back in the family tree.

Intelligence is the most argued-over aspect of the whole subject. The only certain fact is that intelligence is both inherited and affected by a child's environment, the atmosphere and conditions in which a child is raised and then lives during adult life.

The reason why certain talents, such as musical ability, tend to run in families to such an extent cannot be exactly explained. No one knows how much of it is inherited and how much occurs as a result of being brought up in an environment where music is part of family life. The same applies to acting ability, sports skills, literary ability, and other talents.

Environment may also act as the trigger for an inherited physical characteristic. Two people may, for example, be born

Physical features are passed on genetically from parent to child. It is obvious that actor Kirk Douglas and his sons are related.

Rex Features

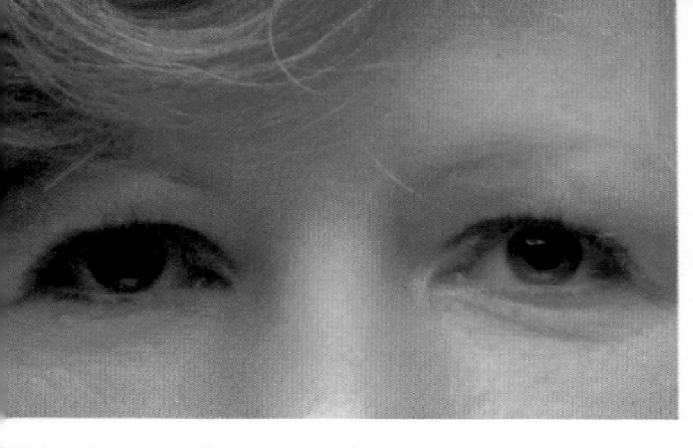

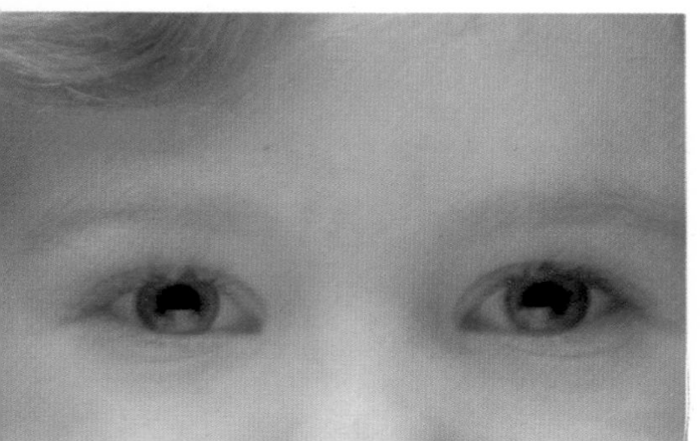

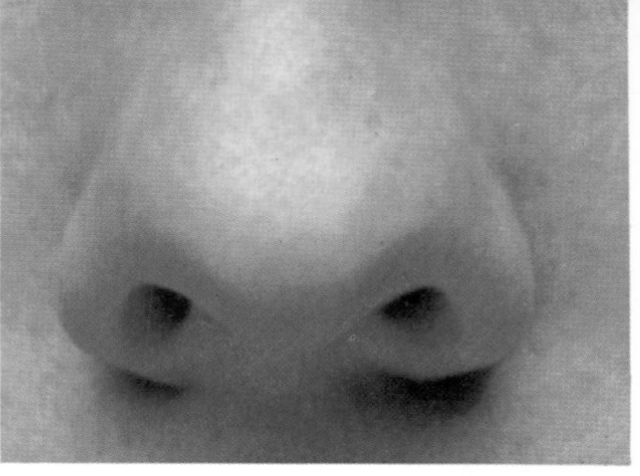

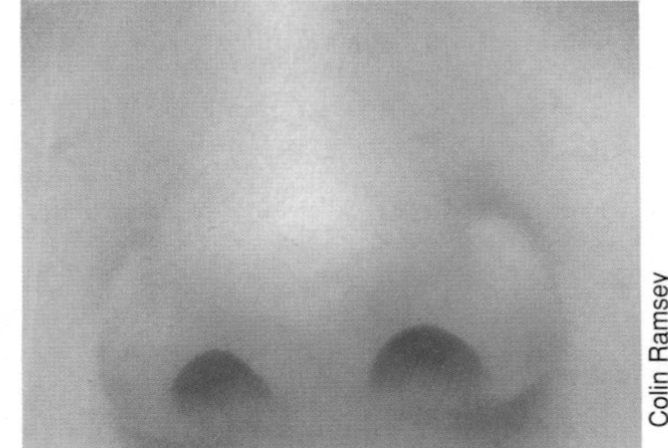

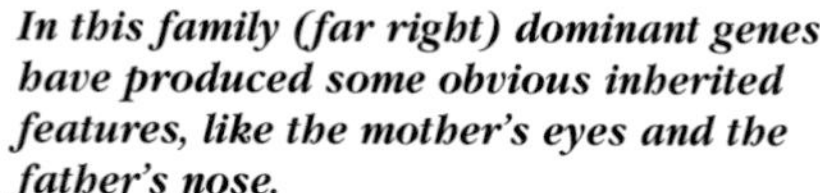

In this family (far right) dominant genes have produced some obvious inherited features, like the mother's eyes and the father's nose.

with a tendency to tan easily (which involves the ability to make the pigment melanin in the skin). However, if one of them stays indoors for most of the time, his or her skin is unlikely to tan, while the other, doing an outdoor job, will quickly develop a tan.

The question of heredity is further complicated because genes show their strength not only in terms of dominance over other genes, but by the degree to which they penetrate; geneticists call this penetrance.

Penetrance may be weak or strong. For example, the defect of the fingers known as camptodactyly is produced by a dominant gene and can thus show up by being inherited in the single-factor method. However, the degree to which a person suffers from it will vary from severe stiffness in several fingers (full penetrance) to stiffness in just one finger (partial penetrance).

Geneticists suspect that longevity (the ability to live a long time) is determined by genes, possibly by polygenes. On the other hand they also recognize that however long a person's genes have programmed him or her to live, their effect can be counteracted by maltreating the body in any of the usual ways, such as smoking, drinking, or overeating.

These various principles of heredity are only tiny corners of an extremely complex jigsaw. Most geneticists are concerned with trying to unravel the way diseases and abnormalities are inherited. Doctors now believe that almost all traits in the body are determined by the polygene theory.

Theories about eye color

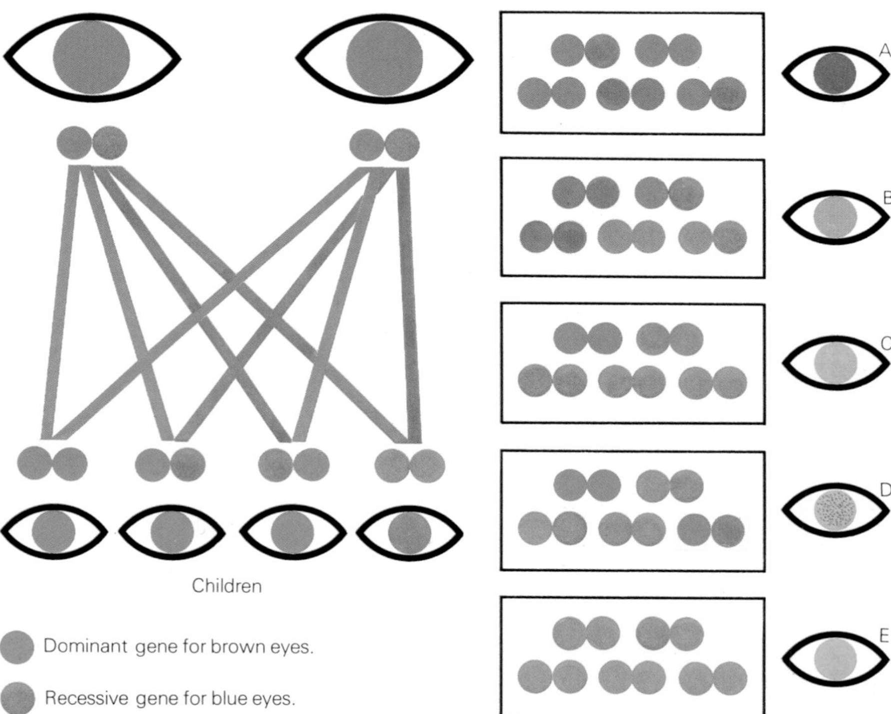

According to the single-factor theory of heredity (above left), children of brown-eyed parents will have pure brown or pure blue eyes. So how are color variations explained? The polygene theory (above right) suggests that several pairs of genes determine color. Parents with blue eyes will have children with blue eyes (E), but the eye color of children whose parents have other eye colors cannot be predicted because the greater number of genes and the ways in which they can interact (A, B, C, and D) produce a greater potential for color variation.

Hernia

Q Does a hernia hurt? My uncle's hernia looks awful but he says he is not in pain.

A Hernias do not usually hurt, except when they first occur, for example, during heavy lifting. Afterward they may be a bit uncomfortable but are usually not actually painful. If a hernia does become painful, it may be strangulating. This happens when the blood supply to it is cut off by pressure on the neck of the sac; medical advice should be sought.

Q Can a tendency toward hernias run in families?

A Yes, but there is no definite hereditary link. It may be that members of some families always tend to do the same types of jobs—e.g., those involving heavy labor—which are more likely to cause a hernia.

Q Is a big hernia more serious than a small one?

A No, and it may be the other way around. Some very small hernias, such as femoral hernias that occur in the lower part of the groin, may be so small as to be only detectable by touch, especially in an overweight person, but they commonly strangulate.

Q My mother has a big hernia in the wound left after her hysterectomy operation, but the doctors say that it does not need to be repaired. Is this right?

A Probably. Most of these incisional hernias have a very wide neck so there is very little likelihood of strangulation. In addition they can be difficult to repair satisfactorily. A surgical belt is likely to control them very well.

Q I have just had a hernia operation. When can I go back to work?

A This depends on what work you do. If you have a desk job, you could go back after about 10 days. If your work involves heavy lifting, you should stay away for at least six weeks and some surgeons would say three months.

Hernias are a common problem. Sometimes they cause no discomfort at all, but when they do require treatment, they can be cured with complete success.

A hernia occurs when an organ (usually the intestine) protrudes through the muscle or tissue that usually contains it. It can be external—so that it shows as a lump on the surface of the abdomen or in the groin—or internal, like a hiatal hernia, caused by a weakness in the diaphragm.

Types of hernia

The most common types of hernia occur in the groin and are called inguinal or femoral hernias, depending on the site of the weakness. They can also occur in the diaphragm (hiatal hernias); near the navel (umbilical hernias); in the upper part of the abdomen in the midline (ventral hernias); and through weakness in the posterior (back) wall of the abdomen, when they are usually not visible as lumps.

Hernias that develop at an operation site where the muscles have failed to heal strongly are called incisional hernias.

Common sites of hernias

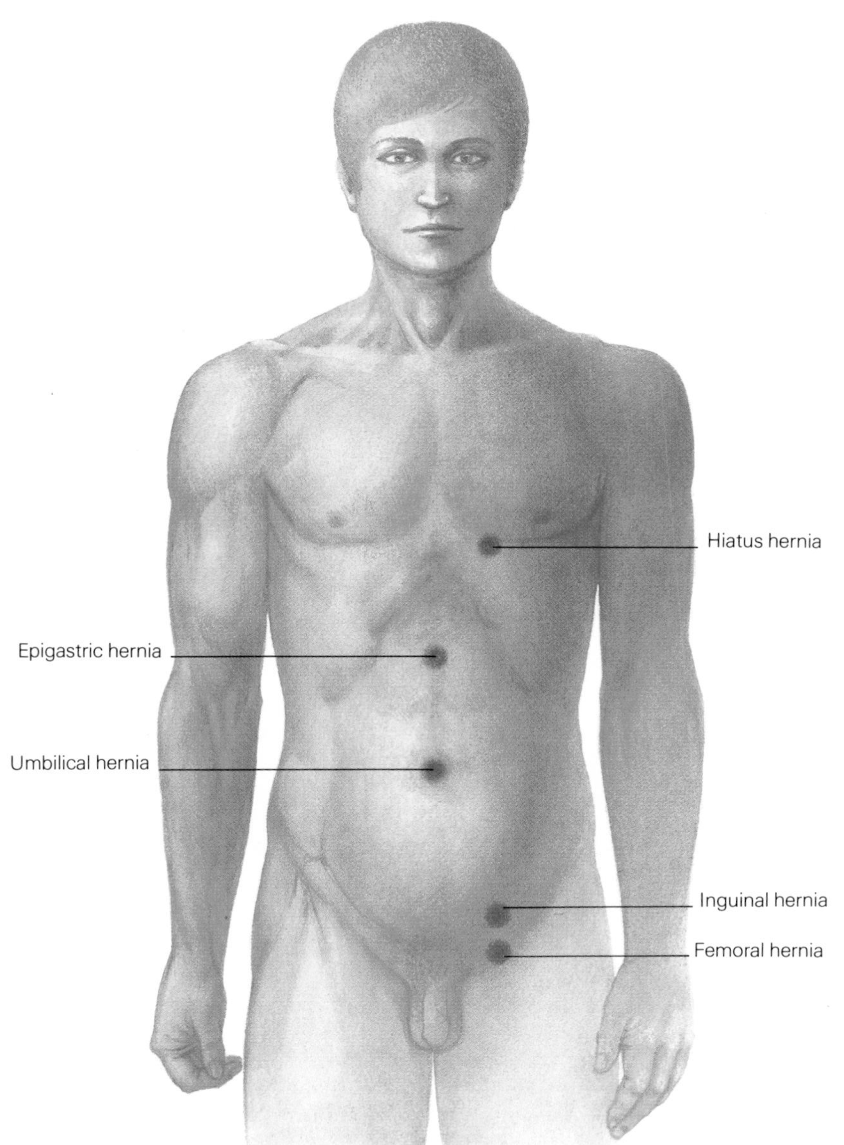

A hernia usually consists of a sac made of peritoneum (the thin membrane lining the abdominal cavity) that protrudes through a weakness in the muscular wall of the abdomen. If it is an external hernia, the sac will be covered with a layer of fat, over which will be the skin.

The sac contains either part of an intra-abdominal organ, usually a loop of small intestine, or of the omentum, the fatty membrane that covers the intestines. The omentum often fills the sac completely, preventing other structures from entering it, and this helps to prevent the complications that may result from the presence of a hernia.

Causes

Hernias are very common and various conditions may cause them. People may be born with a particular weakness in the muscle wall that makes them prone to develop a hernia. This may mean that they develop a hernia in infancy, or later in life due to heavy lifting, for example. Anything that weakens or strains the muscle wall until it breaks can cause a hernia. This includes coughing and straining to lift heavy objects.

A common type of hernia is the groin (inguinal) hernia, which occurs more often in men than women. In men a part of the intestine protrudes into the inguinal canal (the passage through which the testicle descends to the scrotum early in a boy's life). Women are more prone to develop a hiatal hernia (where the upper part of the stomach moves upward into the chest through a weakness in the diaphragm), and this is probably related to the increase in intra-abdominal pressure during pregnancy (see Pregnancy).

Symptoms

An inguinal hernia caused by heavy lifting will often occur suddenly; the patient may describe a feeling of something giving way, accompanied by some pain. This usually lasts only for a short time, and the patient then notices a lump in the groin. This lump is usually soft, bulges when he or she coughs, and goes away completely when he or she lies down.

If it gets very large it may extend down into the scrotum in a man, but hernias can get surprisingly large before they cause many symptoms. Of course if the patient's job involves a lot of heavy lifting, the hernia may become uncomfortable all the time and prevent him or her from working. Sometimes a hernia develops so slowly that the first thing the patient notices is a lump in the groin.

A hiatal hernia, because it bulges into the chest, is never seen or felt as a lump, but makes itself manifest by its effect on the junction between the esophagus and the stomach. Usually there is a valve at the lower end of the esophagus, just at the point where it joins the stomach (see Alimentary canal), which allows swallowed food to pass into the stomach but prevents it from going back up the esophagus. When a hiatal hernia is present, the effect of the valve is lost, and so food (and acid) can pass freely out of the stomach and up into the esophagus. Because the lining of the esophagus is not designed to withstand acid, it becomes damaged and inflamed (the condition is known as esophagitis; see Heartburn).

The symptoms of this type of hernia are burning pain behind the sternum (breastbone), which is made worse by bending down or lying flat. If the esophagus is severely damaged over a number of years, it may become narrowed and make swallowing difficult. Hiatal hernias are very common, especially after middle age. Many people may have a small one of which they are unaware, and which causes them no harm whatsoever.

Dangers

If strangulation occurs (see Strangulation) a hernia becomes extremely serious and potentially lethal. It happens when the punctured muscle wall surrounding the protruding herniated intestine tightens. The muscle squeezes the contents of the hernial sac, cutting off its

Types of hernia

Inguinal hernia (below), the commonest type, occurs more often in men than women. In men it is usually located at the point where the inguinal canal meets the peritoneum. The soft lump that develops in the groin (*inguinal *means "of the groin") bulges when the patient coughs and disappears completely when he lies down.

Muscular wall of abdomen

Peritoneum

Intestine

Fat

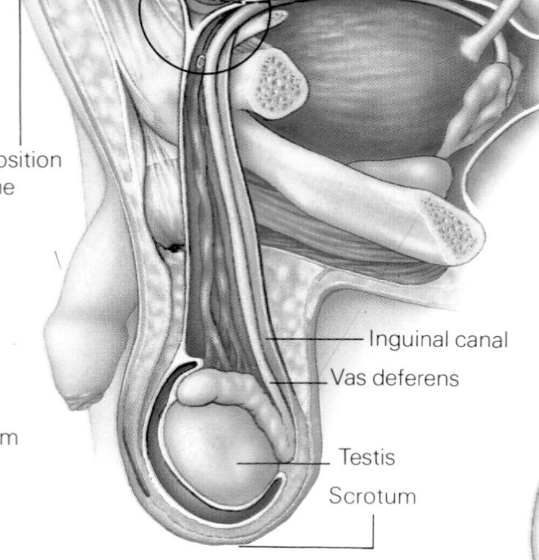

When the testes descend into the scrotum, they may drag on the peritoneum and weaken it so that it sags downward slightly into the groin. Later a hernia may develop at this weak point.

A strangulated hernia (below) is dangerous and could cause death. When the blood supply to the contents of the hernia is cut off, it swells and may eventually become gangrenous. If this happens, the gangrene may be followed by perforation and peritonitis.

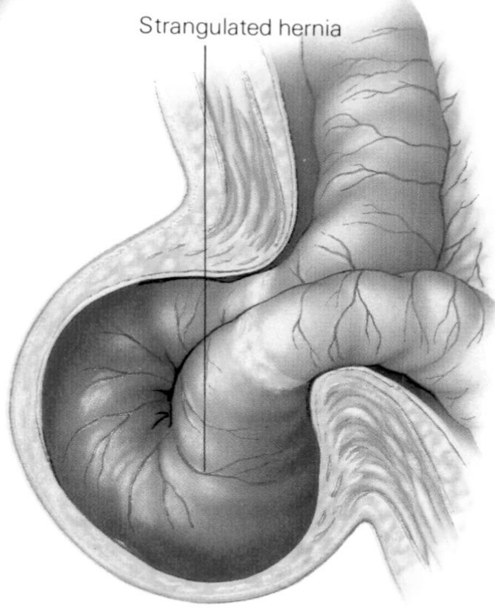

Frank Kennard

blood supply. First the veins are obstructed. This causes the contents to swell, putting further pressure on the arteries, and eventually this can lead to gangrene of the contents (see Gangrene). If the hernia contains intestine, gangrene of the latter may develop followed by perforation and peritonitis (see Peritoneum).

The hernia, which had previously been soft and perhaps only uncomfortable, becomes tense, tender, and irreducible (does not go away when the patient lies down). If the intestine is strangulated, the patient may develop symptoms of intestinal obstruction—vomiting, abdominal pain, distension, and constipation. If this happens an emergency operation is needed to free the strangulated intestine and repair the hernia. If it is left for more than a few hours, the intestine may become irreparably damaged, so that part of it will have to be removed and the two ends joined together again. Of course, if strangulation occurs in one of the rare internal hernias, there will be no lump to feel and the patient will become ill because of an intestinal obstruction.

The commonest hernia to strangulate is a femoral hernia, followed by inguinal and umbilical hernias. Hiatal hernias can strangulate, but because the abdomen is large they rarely do.

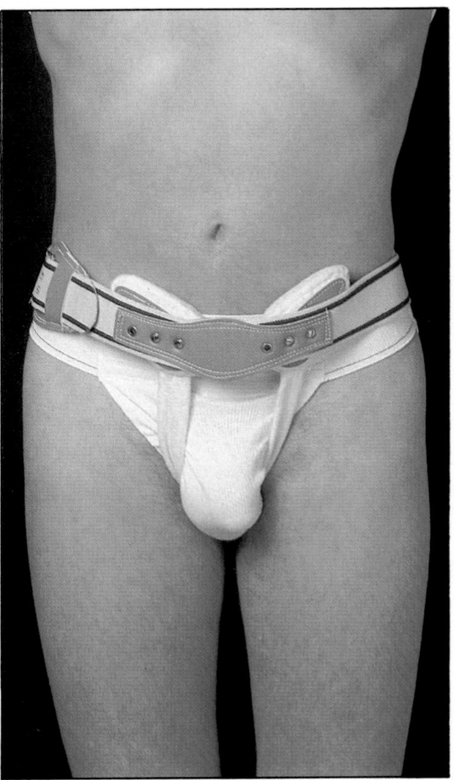

Truss: John Bell and Croyden

A truss for an inguinal hernia has a strap passing between the legs and a pad pressing on the area of the hernia.

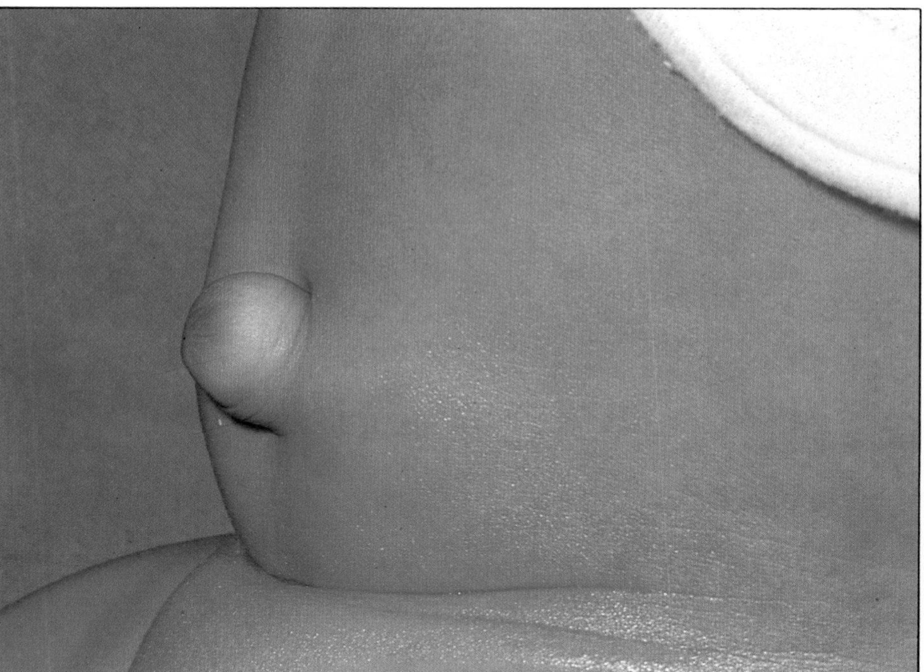

An umbilical hernia (at the navel) is common in babies. The swelling flattens easily; if it does not, consult a doctor. A para-umbilical hernia (near the navel) occurs in women.

Treatment

If there is a recognizable predisposition for a hernia, such as obesity, constipation, a cough, or difficulty in passing water, this should be treated first. Most hiatal hernias can be treated without surgery. Weight loss is probably the most important measure. To deal with the symptoms it is useful to avoid bending, use several pillows at night, avoid drinking just before bedtime, and take regular antacids to neutralize the stomach acids.

Surgery is contemplated only after these measures have failed and if the symptoms are very severe. Surgery can be performed, through either the upper part of the abdomen or the chest wall, to repair the weakness in the diaphragm. Nowadays, however, it is quite rare to have to operate on a hiatal hernia.

Treatment for inguinal hernias involves either wearing a truss or surgical repair. A truss is a special belt with an extra strap that passes between the legs to prevent it from riding up. It has a specially designed pad that presses on the area of the hernia, preventing it from bulging out. It can be uncomfortable to wear and can also be dangerous, because it may allow the hernia (which contains part of the intestines) to bulge and then press on the neck of the herniated intestinal sac, making strangulation more likely. This will usually happen if the hernia has not been fully pushed back before the truss is put on.

By far the best form of treatment for an inguinal hernia is surgery. This may be performed in order to prevent strangulation in the future; because the hernia is uncomfortable and is preventing the patient from working; or because there is strangulation (as an emergency condition).

The surgery is very simple and is generally performed under a general anesthetic. However, it can be performed under a local anesthetic if the patient is thin and the hernia is small, or if the patient is unfit for a general anesthetic. The thin sac of peritoneum is carefully removed and tied off at the neck, after all its contents have been returned to the abdominal cavity. In a child this is all that would be done, but in an adult the defect in the muscle wall of the abdomen is repaired. Usually a strong, nonsoluble thread is used, such as nylon, and the defect is darned. When the scar tissue has formed around the stitches (about three months after the operation), the area should be as strong as normal.

After an operation for a hernia, it takes some time for the muscle wall around the region of the hernia to become strong again. The length of time this takes varies, but it is probably around three months. After this there is no reason why a person who has had a hernia repair should not lead a completely normal life, including doing a job that requires heavy lifting.

A hernia operation does not guarantee that there will never be a recurrence of the hernia. However, the chances of this happening are very small, and if it does happen, a second operation can always be performed. If a hernia does return, consult your doctor for advice.

Heroin

Q How can I warn my children about the dangers of heroin addiction without encouraging them to experiment with it?

A Heroin addiction is such a serious and dangerous matter that you would be justified in doing your best to make them properly alarmed about it. Tell them that their life expectancy is likely to be limited to 25 years if they play around with the drug. Most young people respond to this approach. It is usually the maladjusted, antisocial, or insecure young person who finds the drug scene attractive, and in this case a parent's best course of action is to go to the family doctor for advice.

Q Is there any chance of being given heroin in the hospital and becoming addicted?

A No. Heroin is not used in the US; morphine is given to relieve severe pain instead. This drug is less addictive than heroin, and medical staff know exactly how much can be safely taken.

Q I happen to know that my teenage son has been smoking cannabis, and I'm concerned this may lead him to experiment with hard drugs like heroin. Am I right to worry?

A Yes, there is evidence to show that some hard drug users started by smoking cannabis. This is not in itself an addictive drug (although it may cause a mental dependence). However, if it is taken as a social activity, especially by young people, and if any of the people your son smokes with has a strong influence on him and is attracted by hard drugs, there is a chance of both of them progressing to heroin.

There are various signs to look for if you suspect someone of taking heroin. Their arms are likely to be scarred with tracks where the needle has been inserted in veins. Their pupils are likely to be small, like pinpoints, even in dim light. They may have empty syringes, burnt matchsticks, spoons, and other unexpected items in their room—all signs of taking the dose or fix.

Everyone should be aware of the dangers of heroin, which is the most addictive of the hard drugs.

Heroin is the drug produced from morphine, which is made from raw opium.

This substance has been used since prehistoric times as a medicine and as a narcotic (stupor-inducing) drug. However, it was not until 1803 that the active ingredient was isolated from raw opium and named *morphine* after the Greek god of dreams, Morpheus. Morphine then became the most widely used narcotic drug in medicine, but it was soon discovered to be addictive.

The introduction of heroin

Heroin (also called diamorphine) was first made from morphine at a London hospital. It was introduced in 1898 as a treatment for severe coughing and as a remedy for morphine addiction. It was found to be more potent than morphine and had the advantage of only acting for about two hours. It also made patients less prone to constipation and vomiting than morphine.

Unfortunately it later became clear that heroin only cured morphine addiction because it substituted itself as an addictive drug in its own right. In time it established itself as the most popular addictive drug with those who took drugs for kicks. To combat this, many countries banned its production even for medical purposes. The first country to do so was the United States in 1924, even though

The opium poppy (below) is the source of heroin. From the poppy comes opium, and from this comes morphine. Morphine is processed into heroin (inset)and is dark brown to pure white in color.

Eric Crichton/Bruce Coleman Ltd. Inset: Colin Ramsey/MC

Q How many doses of heroin does a person have to take before they are addicted?

A Remarkably few. Obviously the exact number will vary from person to person and with the size of the injection (fix). The generally accepted quantity of heroin necessary to produce addiction is 60 mg (one grain), taken over a period of two weeks. This means very few fixes. Heroin is so dangerous exactly because it is impossible to say exactly when dependence will set in.

It is fatal for someone to say "I'll try it once," because if the experience is pleasant and apparently harmless, he or she will probably take it again. From then on there is a real danger of addiction setting in. The only answer is not to touch the drug at all.

An addiction to heroin can be established in as little as 24 hours if the drug is taken in regular small quantities.

Q If I happen to be around when someone has taken what I think is a heroin overdose, what should I do?

A Because you often can't be certain which drug has been taken, doctors recommend the following first aid steps for any suspected drug overdose.

Call an ambulance without further delay. Tell them that someone has taken an overdose. Stay with the person until help arrives. If possible, find out how long ago the overdose was taken. If the person vomits any pills, keep them to give to the emergency medical technicians when they arrive.

If you have been trained in CPR, you might consider performing it. Heroin suppresses respiration, and can cause cardiac arrest, coma, or death. Although there is an antidote for heroin overdose, the person must be first tightly strapped down, as upon revival, they are usually uncontrollable and dangerous.

When the ambulance arrives, give the medical technicians any pills, syringes, or substances that could give a clue to the drug taken.

Rex Features

Continual heroin injections into a vein may cause its eventual collapse.

most illegal heroin used was black market heroin made from smuggled opium and morphine, rather than being stolen from legal medical supplies.

In 1953 the British government tried to prohibit the manufacture of heroin for medical purposes but lost the resulting battle against determined medical opinion. Today heroin is still available in Britain for medical purposes and in carefully controlled prescription doses to registered addicts, but it is not exported.

Uses

In those countries where heroin is used for medical purposes its principal use is for pain control. This includes pain that cannot be treated with morphine or that accompanies certain terminal diseases. It is superbly effective in these cases.

If the drug is needed to ease the pain of serious injuries, it will be given in carefully controlled doses tailored to the patient's exact needs, and there will be no danger of addiction.

The only circumstances in which morphine or heroin addiction might accidentally occur would be if someone was injured when they were days away from a hospital, for example, on an expedition to a remote area. If more than the stated dose was given for too long a period, it is possible that physical dependence could be established.

Heroin addiction

It is not quite clear why heroin is the favored drug of the addict, the person who begins by taking the drug for pleasure rather than for medical reasons.

Its effect is no different in essence to that of morphine; indeed, heroin is changed by the body into morphine once it is taken. However, there are a couple of probable reasons for its popularity.

First, heroin acts quickly, giving an instant, dramatic high, and once established it also satisfies the addict's craving without any delay. Second, it is less bulky than morphine and is therefore easier for those concerned in smuggling or trafficking illegal supplies to store or carry. However, on the streets where it is known by a variety of names such as H, smack, or horse it is usually mixed with other substances, such as dried milk or baking powder, to make it more bulky.

There are various ways of taking heroin. It may be smoked, sniffed like cocaine, or—most commonly—injected into the body with a syringe, first into a muscle, and later, as tolerance builds up, into a major vein, usually in the arm. Injecting makes the drug work more quickly and efficiently than when it is sniffed, but it has some considerable drawbacks.

With continual injections into the same vein, the skin becomes hardened and scarred and the vein eventually collapses. If the needle is not properly sterilized and is shared with other users, the addict may contract diseases such as hepatitis (see Hepatitis), AIDS (see AIDS), and jaundice (see Jaundice).

So what does the addict get from heroin? After the injection he or she quickly experiences a strong feeling of well-being and contentment. The extent of this high varies with the purity of the heroin and the emotional state of the addict before the fix. Generally, however, the more desperate the person's mood is beforehand, the greater the corresponding high will be.

Within a very short period of time the heroin user will become physically addicted to the drug. In theory the actual quantity needed to produce addiction is 60 mg (one grain) taken within a two-week period. In practice the amount is different for each person (the larger the body size, the more of the drug is needed to create the same effect), but essentially it boils down to remarkably few fixes during a two-week period causing addiction.

Long-term problems

As tolerance to the drug increases, so do physical and mental dependence. This means that the body becomes used to its effects and requires larger quantities to get high. As physical dependence increases so does the mental dependence that goes with it. The addict's physical and mental condition soon begin to suffer. Muscles waste away, the face looks old and sallow, the appetite fails, the liver does not function properly, and there are aches and pains, insomnia, constipation, memory failure, and impotence.

The addict loses interest at home and at work. Unemployment often follows, and the need to find money to buy expensive black market supplies of the drug often leads to crime.

The death rate among addicts is high; their average life expectancy has been estimated at 25 years. The actual causes of death are likely to be various, not only overdose of the drug itself, but also suicide, and diseases caused by sharing an infected needle.

The cure

The most popular method of treatment is with the heroin substitute methadone, which prevents physical withdrawal symptoms and produces no euphoria. Another drug (clonidine) can also be used. The minimum dose that is required to avoid withdrawal symptoms is first established and then gradually reduced until no longer required. A sudden withdrawal of heroin is painful but generally not life-threatening.

Withdrawal symptoms vary greatly depending on the size of the doses. They begin between four and six hours after the last fix and are at their most severe for about 10 days. They then become less unpleasant, but a complete cure may take from three to six months. Even when the physical unpleasantness is over, the former addict is likely to need a period of adjustment to life without the drug and this usually involves psychotherapy (see psychotherapy).

Preventing drug addiction

To well-adjusted people it is obvious that heroin, or any other sort of addictive drug, is simply not worth the limited short-lived release it brings from life's ongoing problems and pressures. Unfortunately it is rarely enough to point this out to a young addict, or to any potential drug addict. Those who resort to drug-taking just do not have this commonsense attitude, because they are in the process of being driven to drugs as a means of escape from the real world, and their own problems, insecurities, and inadequacies.

Therefore preventing addiction can mean tackling personality problems, first by identifying them and then by taking the appropriate action. This often involves skilled psychiatric counseling over a prolonged period.

Stages of heroin (or morphine) withdrawal

Time since last injection*	Symptoms
4–6 hours	The addict begins to feel nervous and distressed. This is often as much mental as physical
8–14 hours	Restlessness and anxiety increase. Frequent yawning, running eyes and nose, and heavy sweating
14–24 hours	Above symptoms, only worse
1–3 days	Pupils dilate, and the flesh is cold to the touch with waves of goose bumps passing over the body (this is the actual cold turkey stage, although the slang term applies to withdrawal as a whole). There is also likely to be fever, vomiting, diarrhea, profuse sweating, loss of appetite, inability to sleep, fast breathing, muscle cramps, and pains in the back of the legs and abdomen. Involuntary (uncontrollable) twitching of the muscles (kicking the habit) will occur. The body temperature increases, blood pressure rises, and blood sugar increases. The symptoms are usually at their height between days two and three
4–10 days	Gradual dying down of the symptoms
3–6 months	Complete recovery can be achieved but will probably require psychiatric help; symptoms include weakness, insomnia, and severe anxiety

*Actual times vary greatly depending on the size of the dose.

Raw opium, which is manufactured into heroin, oozes from cuts on an opium poppy seed head.

Bruce Coleman Ltd.

Herpes

Q I suffer quite badly from cold sores, and I worry in case they turn into shingles. Can this happen?

A Both cold sores and shingles are caused by herpes viruses. Shingles are caused by the herpes zoster virus and cold sores by the herpes simplex virus. However, there is no connection between the two, and one kind of herpes will not develop into the other kind.

Q My mother-in-law has shingles. I want to keep my children away from her in case they catch it. My husband says this is nonsense. Who is right?

A You are both right, in part. Your children cannot catch shingles from your mother-in-law, but they could catch chickenpox, if they have not already had it. This is because the same virus that causes chickenpox causes shingles. Shingles is only considered contagious when there is an outbreak of active lesions. Chickenpox is a mild illness, and one attack usually confers lifelong immunity.

Q I often get cold sores. Should I refrain from sex during an outbreak in case I give my partner genital herpes?

A Genital herpes, a type of herpes simplex, is related to the herpes simplex virus that causes cold sores. However, although around 10 percent of cases of genital herpes are thought to be caused by the cold sore virus, this only seems to be the case after oral sex.

Q I have genital herpes, and I'm terrified as I've heard that this is the first sign of cervical cancer. Is this true?

A You don't have to worry unduly. Statistically it has been shown that women suffering from genital herpes have a slightly higher risk of developing cervical cancer, but no more than that. The best way to set your mind at rest is to make sure you have a cervical smear test (Pap smear) every six months to one year.

Herpes are painful blisters that erupt on the skin in clusters or bands. Although there is no actual cure, and the symptoms will eventually disappear, there is much that can be done to ease the discomfort.

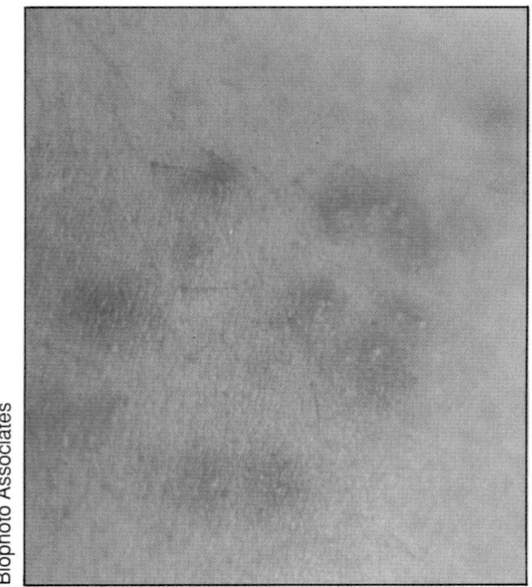

Biophoto Associates

In an attack of shingles, the blisters erupt in a characteristic band. This is signalled by fever and pain.

There are two distinct varieties of herpes virus. The first and more serious kind is called herpes zoster, and is commonly known as shingles (see Shingles). The second kind, called herpes simplex, is divided into two types: the type that affects the upper part of the body, particularly the nose and mouth (see Cold sores), and genital herpes.

Causes

Shingles (herpes zoster) is caused by the chickenpox virus (varicella), which lies dormant in the body after a childhood attack of chickenpox (see Chickenpox). It is not known how the virus is reactivated. Genital herpes (herpes simplex), caused by a different virus, is usually spread by sexual contact with an infected person.

Symptoms

The onset of an infection of shingles (herpes zoster) is signalled by a fever and sharp pain in the affected nerves. The pain of shingles can be anywhere on the body and is described as being similar to the pain of a broken rib, blood clot, or heart attack. It is followed by the eruption of the characteristic rash of blisters on one side of the chest only. The blisters eventually dry out and form shingle-like scabs.

An infection of genital herpes (herpes simplex) seems to recur at times of physical and emotional stress and, in women, around menstruation. The herpes, or blisters, that appear in and around the genitals and the anus, and on the upper thighs and buttock area, often rupture to form open sores.

Treatment

There is no actual cure for either of the herpes viruses as yet, so treatment can only concentrate on relieving the discomfort of the symptoms, which will eventually clear up on their own.

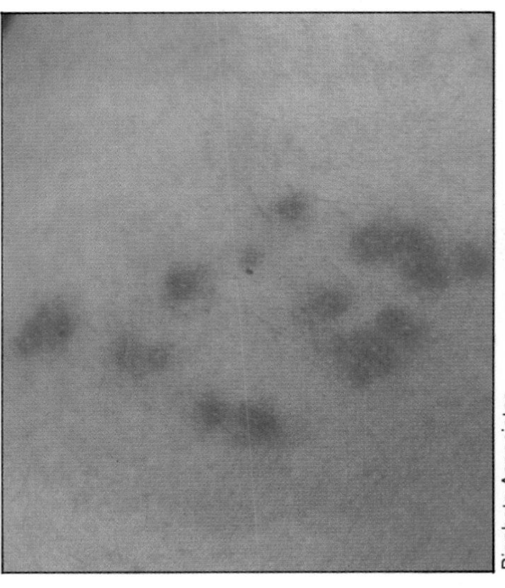

Biophoto Associates

The same patch of skin, a couple of days later. Distinct blisters have developed; these dry out and form scabs.

Painkilling drugs are often prescribed for shingles, and an anesthetic gel for genital herpes. Blisters are covered with a protective ointment or an antiseptic powder to keep them free of infection. The doctor may prescribe corticosteroid ointment and antibiotic preparations, and the antiviral drug acyclovir may also prove helpful.

Outlook

Once the symptoms have cleared up, shingles is unlikely to recur. Genital herpes, which lasts from a week to a month, can flare up from time to time. However, the first attack is usually the most severe, and many people find that the interval between attacks becomes longer and longer. When all the sores have healed, the virus is dormant.

Hiccups

Q Whenever I get nervous I always seem to start hiccuping, which can be kind of embarrassing. Why does this problem happen?

A Some people get hiccups when they are nervous because the state of anxiety sets off abnormal impulses in the brain center that controls breathing, or in the phrenic nerve controlling the movement of the diaphragm at the base of the chest. To prevent the problem try sucking on hard candy or chewing gum in situations that are likely to cause anxiety. This may stop hiccups from developing.

Q I have heard that for some people hiccups last for years. Is this really possible?

A Yes, it is. The world record for nonstop hiccups is held by a man from Iowa who started an attack of hiccups in 1922 and still had it decades later. However, this is a very rare occurrence.

In cases of prolonged hiccups, which can cause severe muscular weakness and also great mental distress, sometimes the only solution is surgery to remove the part of the nerve that is generating the problem. This involves some loss in breathing efficiency but not enough to be a threat to life.

Q Are there any exercises that you can do to help get rid of the hiccups?

A One good exercise is to lie on the floor and bring your knees up to your abdomen. Then hold them there for a second or two by gripping the backs of your thighs. The exercise puts pressure on the diaphragm, which makes abnormal movements during hiccups, and it may help to normalize breathing.

Q Can hiccups ever be contagious?

A Not in the way that you can catch a cold from someone who is infected, but there are some infectious diseases that have hiccups as one of their symptoms, i.e., mild cases of encephalitis lethargica (inflammation of the brain), which is caused by a virus.

Everyone has their own personal remedy for hiccups. However, what causes hiccups and can they be dangerous?

When a person breathes in and out normally, air flows smoothly in and out of the lungs in time with the up-and-down movements of the diaphragm (a tough sheet of muscle at the base of the chest cavity that separates the contents of the chest from the abdomen; see Diaphragm). In addition the muscles that lie between ribs (the intercostal muscles) contract and relax at the same time (see Breathing).

How a hiccup happens

A hiccup happens when the normal sequence of events is disturbed. As a person breathes in, the diaphragm contracts and flattens out as the lungs expand and fill with air.

At the same time a flap of tissue called the epiglottis, which prevents food from getting into the airway during swallowing, opens as it should. So does the glottis, the gap between the vocal cords (see Vocal cords).

A hiccup is a continuing spasm of the diaphragm muscle. This starts an unconscious gulping of air, during which the epiglottis and the glottis both snap shut.

The typical hiccup sound is produced as air is forced rapidly through the vocal cords and then cut off. Then the glottis and epiglottis open, the diaphragm relaxes and curves upward, the intercostal muscles relax, and air is breathed out.

Anything that irritates the diaphragm or its nerve supply can cause a hiccup, whether it is hot or cold foods or drinks, spicy food, eating too quickly, eating too much, drinking alcohol, gulping cold air, or taking vigorous exercise right after a meal. Less commonly, hepatitis, surgery, or pregnancy can also cause hiccups.

However, sometimes they seem to begin for no obvious reason and many babies seem to get hiccups after almost every feeding, even if they have no gas. Just what it is that triggers the hiccup reaction is still a mystery.

It is certain that in hiccups one of two nerve mechanisms are at fault. It could be that the nerve impulses sent out by

This remedy is supposed to work by making a person breathe in carbon dioxide, which influences the nerves that cause hiccups.

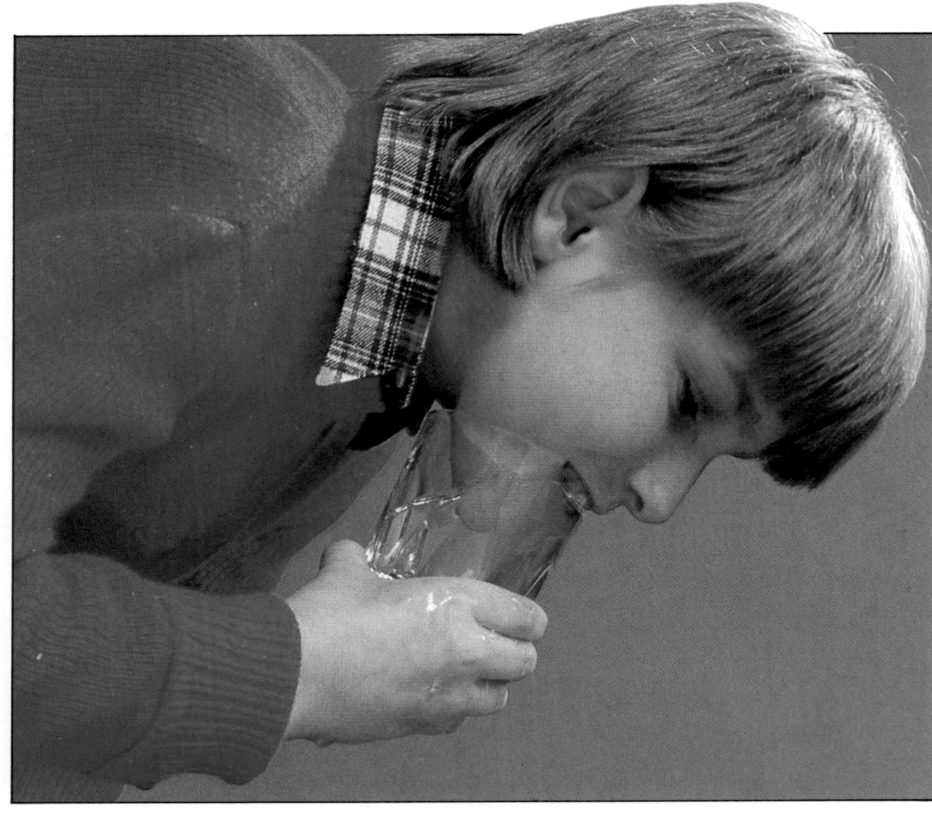

Drinking from the wrong side of a glass is another popular cure for hiccups.

the area of the brain that controls the rhythmical activities of breathing are disturbed. Alternatively imprecise impulses may be sent out by one of the two phrenic nerves that originate in the neck region of the spinal cord and specifically regulate the diaphragm.

It is not known why stomach problems trigger these impulses. The phrenic nerve sends many branches to the esophagus (the tube that takes food from the back of the throat to the stomach; see Esophagus), which explains why swallowing certain foods or taking in air in an odd way can cause hiccups, but there are very few branches of the nerve to the stomach itself.

Remedies

Young babies often get hiccups; it is best to ignore these unless they go on for as long as an hour, in which case a teaspoon of warm water can be given to the baby.

There are many home and folk remedies for hiccups. Popular cures include holding the breath, sucking on a lump of sugar, sipping very cold water, and drinking out of the wrong side of a glass.

All these ideas are thought to work because they distract the nervous system and so stop the hiccup rhythm. The other time-honored remedy is breathing in and out with the nose and mouth inside a paper bag. This is thought to be effective because carbon dioxide builds up in the air breathed in, which depresses the activity of the nerves in the brain that are responsible for causing hiccups.

Because the phrenic nerve is long and extends to many internal organs, its activity can sometimes be disturbed by serious diseases (see Nervous system). So hiccups can sometimes be one of the symptoms of peritonitis (an inflammation of the membrane that lines the abdominal cavity), disease of the kidneys, heart trouble, or the growth of tumors in the neck (which press on the nerve and make it send out impulses that can cause bouts of hiccups).

Medical treatment

Hiccups are only a case for medical treatment if they are associated with some other symptoms that suggest that there is something seriously wrong. If they go on for so long that the person feels tense and exhausted, the underlying cause requires treatment.

Some cases of hiccups defy treatment, but with severe cases a doctor will usually try a sedative drug such as chlorpromazine or thorazine.

How hiccups happen

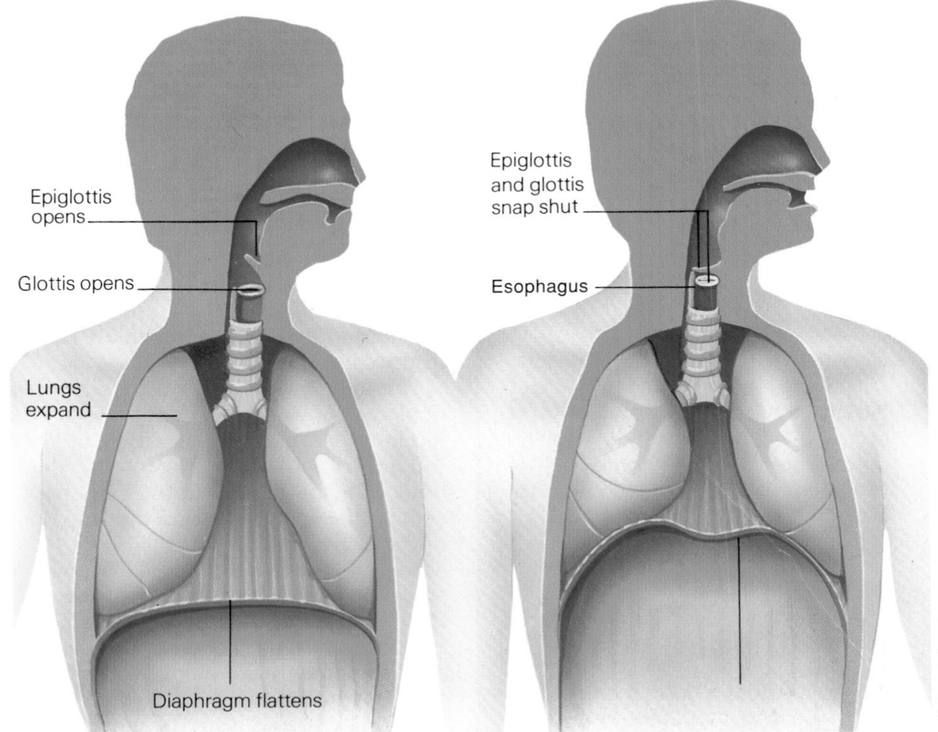

When a person breathes normally, the diaphragm flattens. The glottis and the epiglottis open, drawing in air, and this enables the lungs to expand.

When a person hiccups, the diaphragm starts to twitch. Air is forced past the glottis and epiglottis, which snap shut—resulting in the well-known hiccup sound.

Hip

Q **Why is it so easy for young children to do the splits, but almost impossible for most adults unless they have trained as dancers?**

A The reason is that children's ligaments and muscles are much more elastic than adults'. However, as any ballet dancer will testify, if the ligaments are kept supple by constant exercise, then there is no reason why it should not be possible for adults to retain the mobility of childhood.

Q **My six-year-old son is complaining of aching hips. Are these just growing pains?**

A Some of the uncertain pains of childhood are described as growing pains. However, as far as we know, they are not connected with physical growth but are psychologically caused by a need for affection or by problems in growing up. If pain is present in a particular part of the body, then it must have an underlying cause, even if this is just a mild infection. Make sure that your son has plenty of rest and take him to see your doctor as soon as possible, just in case something is wrong.

Q **Why is it that elderly women seem to break their hips so frequently?**

A In old age all the bones in the body become more brittle. The hip is likely to be broken in a fall because it is often the part that hits the ground first and so bears the whole weight of the body. Broken hips are a real problem in the elderly, not just because of the damage, but because they involve a prolonged period of immobility, which can diminish an old person's zest for living. So it is important for old people to take extra care.

Q **My mother is very overweight, and I am afraid that this is putting too much strain on her hips. Am I right?**

A Yes. Being overweight affects many internal organs, but the hips are particularly vulnerable because they have the task of bearing most of the body's weight.

The hips are designed to bear the weight of the body and enable a person to stand, walk, or run. Although they are very strong, problems still arise, especially in the very young and the elderly.

Camera Press

The versatility of the hip joint is especially obvious in young children.

The hip is the biggest joint in the body. It has two main functions: to carry the considerable weight of the trunk, and with the help of the spine, to enable a person to walk upright.

The description ball and socket is particularly appropriate in the case of the hip joint because here a large hemispherical projection at the top of the thighbone (the femur) fits into a cup-shaped socket (the acetabulum) in the iliac bone of the pelvic girdle.

Smooth movement is insured by the shiny cartilage that covers the head of the femur and lines the acetabulum. Lubrication is provided by the synovial fluid secreted by the synovial membranes that surround the joints (see Joints). These membranes form the inner layer of the tough fibrous capsule that makes a hermetic seal around the joint. This seal is very strong and airtight. The capsule is thin at the back of the joint but very thick at the sides and the front of the body, where the greatest pressure is exerted on the hip. Several accumulations of fatty tissue, which lie inside the tight seal provided by the capsule, pad the inside of the joint and act as shock absorbers.

Added stability is provided by a set of ligaments that bind the head (top) of the femur to the pelvic girdle, crisscrossing over one another to maximize their strength and to prevent the ball from slipping out of its socket. Of these the iliofemoral ligament, toward the outside of the joint, is thought to be the strongest in the body. For both walking and standing, it is essential that the thigh does not move further back than an imaginary straight line drawn vertically down the side of the trunk. This constraint is provided by the ligaments. When the leg seems to be pulled back beyond this line—for example, before kicking a football—it is the whole pelvic girdle that moves, not the hip joint.

If a person stands and moves the legs into different positions, it can be seen how many actions the hip joints allow. These movements are made possible by the muscles that lie over the ligaments. The action of pulling the knee up toward the head involves bending, or flexion, of the hip. Such a movement is brought about by two main muscles: the psoas major, which runs from the base of the spine across the front of the hip to the femur; and the iliacus, a flat, triangular muscle that is attached to the pelvis at one end and to the femur at the other. These two muscles are assisted by others in the thigh.

Straightening a bent leg is called extension. To perform this action the outermost and biggest buttock muscle, the gluteus maximus, is used, plus a group of muscles at the back of the thigh called the hamstrings (see Hamstring injuries). It is these muscles that are actually at work when a person is standing still.

Moving the leg out sideways is called abduction, and bringing it back again is known as adduction. The first of these movements involves two of the muscles that lie beneath the gluteus maximus; these are the tensor fascia lata, which joins the pelvis with the femur, and the sartorius, the longest muscle in the body, which runs from the pelvic girdle to the knee.

The pulling power between the pelvis and the femur needed for adduction is provided by a group of muscles including the adductor longus, adductor brevis, and adductor magnus. Many of these muscles are also used to allow the leg to rotate, although this movement is limited by the binding of the ligaments.

Congenital dislocation

Because of its complex structure, the hip is extremely stable compared to its counterpart, the shoulder. This stability means that in adult life, dislocation of the hip is a very rare injury. Paradoxically it is not only the most common hip problem of childhood but also the most common site of joint dislocation at birth.

Examination of the hips is carried out as a routine precaution immediately after the birth of every child. The baby is placed on his or her back, with the legs wide apart, and held firmly by the feet. If the hips are dislocated, the doctor will hear a deep clicking sound as he or she bends the child's knees and hips. The sound comes from the head of the femur as it goes into its socket. When the baby's legs are extended, another click will be heard as the femur disengages.

The doctor will also place his or her hand so that the thumb is on the baby's groin and the middle finger is on the projection of the thighbone. If the head of the femur is easily moved out of its socket, then the doctor will suspect that the hip is potentially unstable, or irritable. If this is the case, these tests are followed by X rays to check the diagnosis.

Nowadays the treatment for a congenital dislocation of the hip is extremely effective. Usually the infant is put into a plaster splint that keeps the legs wide apart so that they are in a froglike position. After a few months the joint is X-rayed again to check progress and in most cases the splint is then removed. Whether or not the baby has to stay in the hospital during this period depends on the domestic circumstances of the family. The child can be taken care of at home if this is possible.

If the hips are not dislocated but are irritable, the doctor may advise the mother to keep a very thick cloth diaper on the baby so that the legs are kept wide apart until the ligaments and muscles around the joint have developed enough strength to overcome the problem naturally.

The ability to do splits so easily is lost unless muscles are trained for it.

Sue Dandre

Diseases and injuries

Problems may arise in the hip joint later on in childhood due to diseases that

Muscles that move the leg

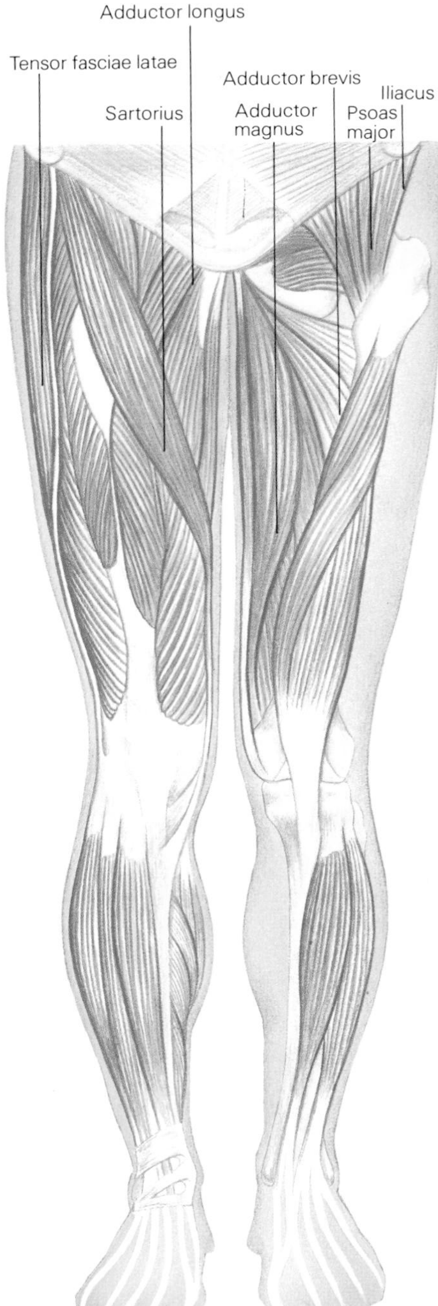

How ligaments stabilize the hip joint

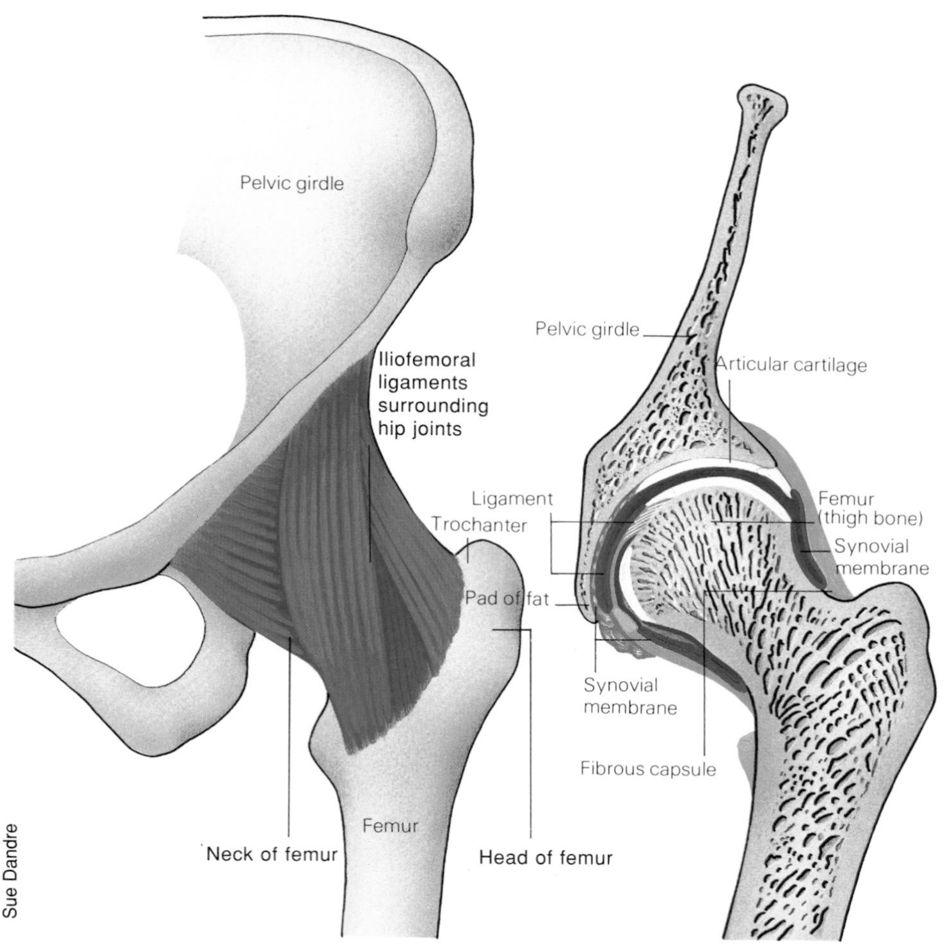

cause inflammation of the synovial membranes or, rarely these days, as a result of tuberculosis (see Tuberculosis). An unusual, but serious, hip condition, much more common in boys than girls, is Perthes' disease (see Perthes' disease). With this condition, for some unknown reason, the bony tissue in the head of the femur begins to disintegrate. The child will complain of aching or of sharp pains in the hip—and possibly in the knee on the same side, too—and he or she may have difficulty in walking. With early X-ray diagnosis and rest in bed, often for several years, the condition corrects itself and the bone grows back normally. However, if it is not treated in the early stage, it can lead to a permanent deformity of the joint. For this reason alone it is most important that any child who complains of hip pains is seen by the doctor, who will arrange for X rays.

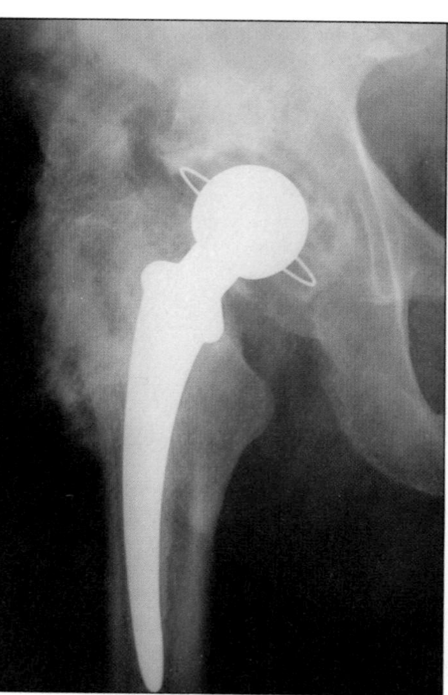

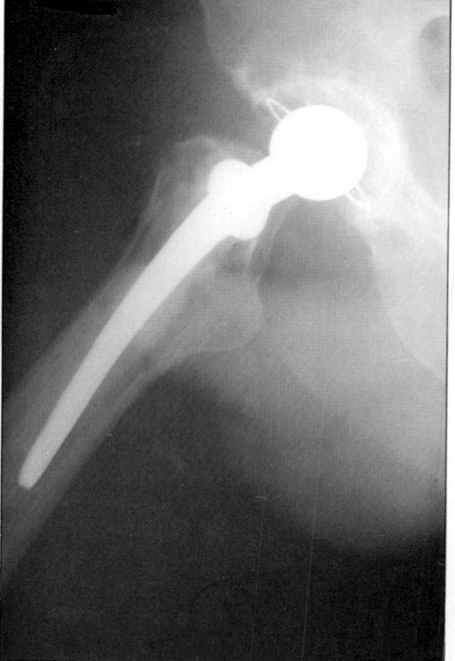

A hip replacement allows full movement of the patient's leg. The new joint is made of stainless steel and titanium.

Accidental injury to the joint is most common in old age and often follows heavy falls. The most likely place for the bone to break is across the neck of the femur. Symptoms of hip fracture include unbearable pain on walking, bruising, swelling, tenderness, or deformity of the hip. In cases of suspected hip fracture, call an ambulance first, then check for signs of shock or internal bleeding. You should not attempt to move the patient or splint the bone unless it is absolutely essential, for example if the patient is in the middle of the street.

Because of the great weight the hip joint has to bear and the many muscles that surround it, the most usual method of treatment is orthopedic surgery in which metal pins or plates are used to keep the bones in place (see Orthopedics).

After pin and plate surgery, although the patient is allowed out of bed a few days after the operation, he or she will not be permitted to put any weight on the joint until the surgeon is satisfied that the fracture has begun to heal properly. One of the problems of hip surgery is that the blood vessels may be damaged so that there is insufficient supply to the fracture for mending to take place. The worse the break, and the older the patient, the more likely it is that such problems will arise.

If a fracture at the head of the femur fails to mend properly, bone grafting may be recommended for a young patient, or the replacement of the joint by a metal substitute. Although such operations may mean long hospital stays and initial immobility, they are often the most effective form of treatment.

Hives

This skin complaint is one of the most common allergy symptoms. Fortunately attacks of hives are usually temporary and fleeting, and they often clear up without treatment.

Hives, also known as urticaria, has several similarities to insect bites or stings, though it may vary in appearance from small spots to large reddish welts. The skin becomes red and often feels burning and itchy.

It may appear in patches on areas of the skin that have been exposed to a substance the sufferer is allergic to, but it can appear on almost any part of the body. It also has the odd habit of appearing in one place, disappearing for no apparent reason, and then reappearing elsewhere.

Causes

Outbreaks of hives are almost always caused by an allergy (see Allergies). This may be an allergy to something that comes into direct contact with the skin, like wool or a hairy plant; to a food; or occasionally to a chemical in the environment.

Among the food allergies, eggs, strawberries, and shellfish are common culprits, but other allergens include animal fur, house dust mites, silk, perfumes, pollens, aspirin, penicillin, and red and yellow food dyes. Exposure to heat, cold, or pressure can cause hives in some people; a heat rash from a hot bath is also a form of hives.

Hives can also appear, with or without a simultaneous allergic cause, at times of emotional stress.

As with other allergies (see also Hay fever), the body's defense mechanism, the immune system, reacts toward the allergen as if it was a dangerous organism (see Immune system). In trying to neutralize the enemy, it releases histamine, which produces the allergy symptoms.

Treatment and outlook

The most important task is to identify the allergen and then try to avoid it, but this is not always very easy. Fortunately the attacks are usually short-lived, often clearing up without the need for treatment. Persistent hives is treated with antihistamine preparations.

Giant hives, or angioneurotic edema, is a particularly severe form of hives. Large swellings appear in such places as the lips, eyelids, back, and throat. This condition requires treatment with drugs.

The arm (below) shows hives in their most common form. The patient (right) has giant hives, a rare form.

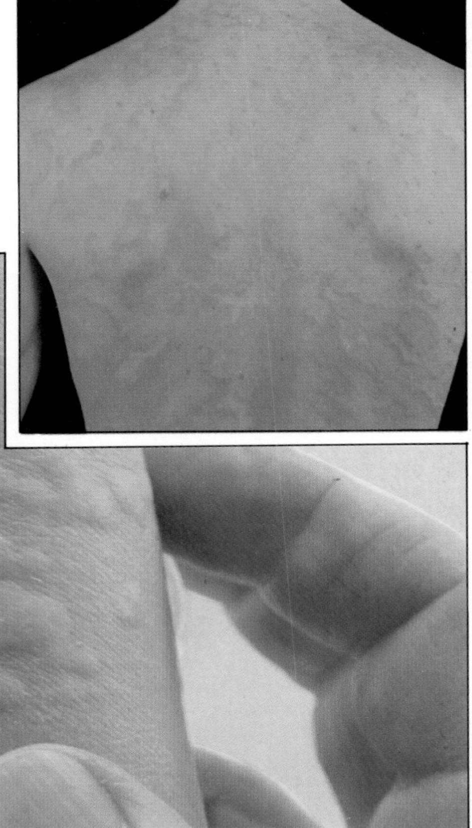

C James Webb

Q Is it possible to catch hives from someone?

A No, you can't catch hives. You could pick it up from contact with a plant or animal, but only if you were allergic to the animal's fur or some chemical in the plant. Fur and plants are just a few of the many allergens that can cause an allergic reaction.

Q My little brother loves strawberries but he gets an awful rash when he eats them. Could this be hives?

A It's possible. Quite a lot of people get hives from eating strawberries, and this may be due to an allergy.

The only answer is for your brother to avoid eating strawberries, though he might try eating one or two in a year's time just to see if his allergy is still as strong. However, if he gets severe hives, the doctor should be consulted before he tries this.

Q Whenever I sunbathe I break out in hives. I am going on vacation soon; is there any medicine I can take with me to prevent this?

A Although the rash and itching from sunburn are caused by histamine being released into the tissues in and around the skin, it would not be a good idea to use an antihistamine cream to deal with it. It might give temporary relief, but antihistamines are very potent drugs and it is possible to develop an allergy to them. The best answer is not to expose yourself too quickly to bright sunlight—however much you want to develop a good tan.

Q I suffer from hives and I'm worried that I may pass the condition on to my children. Does it run in families?

A Allergic complaints do tend to run in families, though there is no obvious pattern in the way they are passed on. However, hives is not a dangerous ailment (except in rare severe cases) so parents should not be too worried about a child developing it.

Hoarseness

Q **My son goes to a football game every weekend and comes home hoarse. Could this do him lasting damage?**

A He could develop swellings on his vocal cords if he gets continually hoarse. These are known as vocal nodes, and if they persist they might require surgery. Meanwhile if he frequently loses his voice for several days on end, you should take him to a speech therapist, who will probably advise him to speak quietly and stay away from football games for a while.

Q **Is it bad for me to sing while I am hoarse?**

A If you want to stop the hoarseness from getting worse, you should not sing or shout, or even cough or laugh until the problem clears up.

Q **Can hoarseness be a sign of cancer?**

A Yes, it can. The immediate symptom of cancer of the larynx is hoarseness, followed by discomfort and an irritating cough. It is worth anyone's while being aware of this, because if the diagnosis is made within a few weeks, it is possible to cure the condition with radiotherapy (the bombardment of the area with radioactive rays; see Radiotherapy) without the need for an operation. An ENT doctor normally examines the vocal chords by doing a laryngoscopy (see Endoscopy).

Hoarseness can also be an early sign of cancer of the lung, or the thyroid. It can also be caused by reflux (see Heartburn).

Q **I get hoarse sometimes for no apparent reason. Could it be caused by my smoking?**

A Not generally, but if you smoke heavily this will make voice loss or hoarseness more likely if you strain your voice, for example, from shouting or from coughing if you catch a cold. The greatest danger, however, is cancer of the lung or throat, not to mention that it can aggravate bronchitis or make you more susceptible both to artery and heart disease (see Smoking).

Hoarseness is almost always no more than a temporary discomfort, provided that the vocal cords are not continually aggravated by shouting.

How hoarseness happens

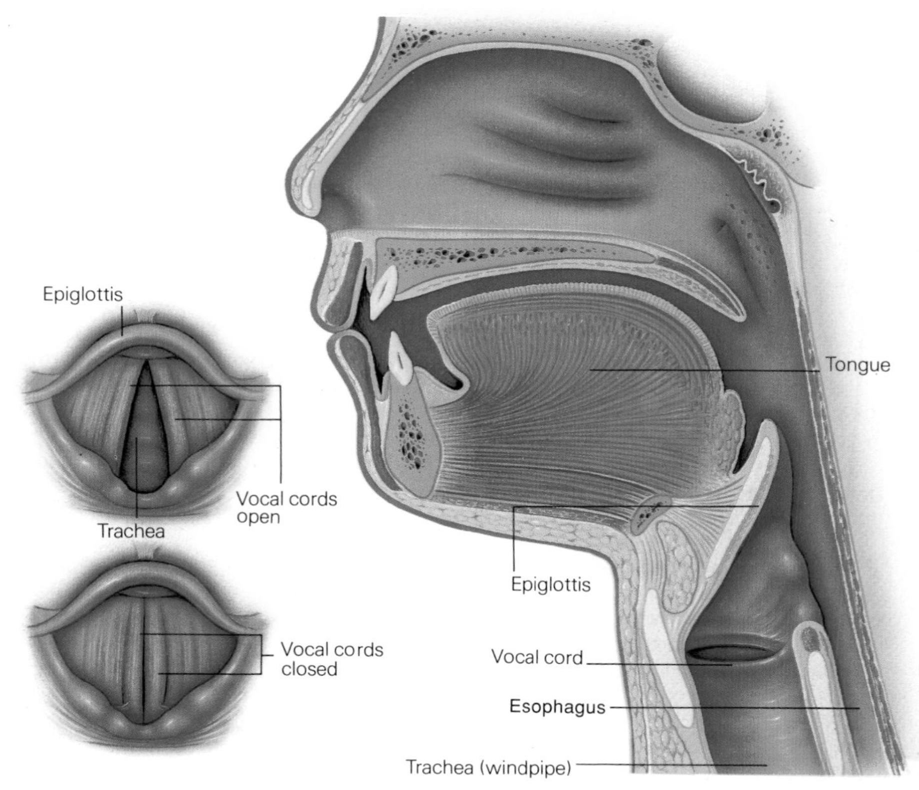

Incorrect breathing, strain from shouting, and a cold or the flu make the vocal cords close, resulting in hoarseness.

All sound is produced by vibration, a rapid to-and-fro movement. For example, the strings of a guitar vibrate to produce sound. With the human voice the vocal cords—a set of pliable, sheetlike membranes—vibrate to create sound. The vocal cords are situated in the larynx, part of the passage between the back of the mouth and the lungs (see Vocal Cords). The vibration is powered by air being breathed out. If something prevents the cords' smooth vibration, then hoarseness results.

Common causes

The most common causes of hoarseness include strain on the vocal cords caused by incorrect (very heavy) breathing, the forcing of the voice, or tiredness of the muscles in the larynx (see Larynx).

Any person who makes excessive demands on his or her voice on a regular basis—for example, people such as stage actors, teachers, or factory managers—are likely to suffer from this complaint. A smoky, dusty, or dry atmosphere can make the problem worse. Hoarseness can also occur with a cold or the flu. Here, the larynx and vocal cords become infected and are tender.

Continued, excessive strain on the vocal cords may bring chronic hoarseness that can last three weeks or more. An even worse situation occurs when vocal nodes form. These are swellings on the vocal cords that can cause a particularly harsh hoarseness or even complete voice loss.

Treatment

Hoarseness caused by strain is curable by resting the voice, avoiding smoky atmospheres, and by taking speech or voice therapy. The same regime applies in the treatment of vocal nodes, although long-standing nodes will need surgery.

Hodgkin's disease

Q My uncle has Hodgkin's disease. Is it possible to catch it from him?

A There is absolutely no risk of catching Hodgkin's disease directly. However, it has long been suspected that a viral infection in susceptible individuals may have something to do with starting off the process.

Q A friend of mine who has Hodgkin's disease often has infections. Is this normal?

A Yes. There is a definite tendency for people to suffer from unusual infections that they might not otherwise have had because their immune system isn't working properly. Doctors call this situation immunosuppression.

Q I have a cousin who has been diagnosed as having a non-Hodgkin's lymphoma. What does this mean?

A This odd-sounding name is used to describe tumors that come from the lymph tissue but are not actually Hodgkin's disease. The treatment for both is similar, but different medications are used in its treatment.

Q My doctor has told me that there is a slight possibility I may have Hodgkin's disease, and he is sending me for tests that involve surgery. Is it necessary to have this done?

A Doctors must perform certain tests to establish the presence of Hodgkin's disease because its symptoms may mimic infections that give rise to either lymph node swelling or tumors that are not Hodgkin's disease. A small piece of abnormal tissue is removed from the site so that it can be looked at under a microscope. The appearance of the disease is very characteristic. To obtain a piece of tissue, a small operation must be performed.

Q Is Hodgkin's disease painful?

A No. Lumps caused by cancer are usually painless.

Hodgkin's disease is one form of cancer that responds to treatment, which often leads to a complete cure.

Hodgkin's disease is a form of cancer (see Cancer) that arises in the lymphatic system, which is responsible for defending the body against infection (see Lymphatic System, and Blood). Although the disease can occur at any age, for unknown reasons it is most common at ages 15–30.

Hodgkin's disease is classed as one of the malignant lymphomas. This group includes Hodgkin's lymphoma and the group of non-Hodgkin's lymphomas. The distinction between the two is made by microscopic examination of the tumor tissue. Hodgkin's lymphomas contain a unique cell type called Reed-Sternberg cells. The distinction is important as it affects treatment.

How common is the disease?

Malignant lymphomas are the sixth most common cause of cancer in the United States with just under 60,000 cases a year. Some 15 percent of people with malignant lymphomas have Hodgkin's disease.

Lymphomas are becoming more common especially among the elderly and in people with AIDS (see AIDS). They were the first type of cancer to be effectively treated by chemotherapy and the experience gained has helped in the search for non-surgical treatments for other cancers.

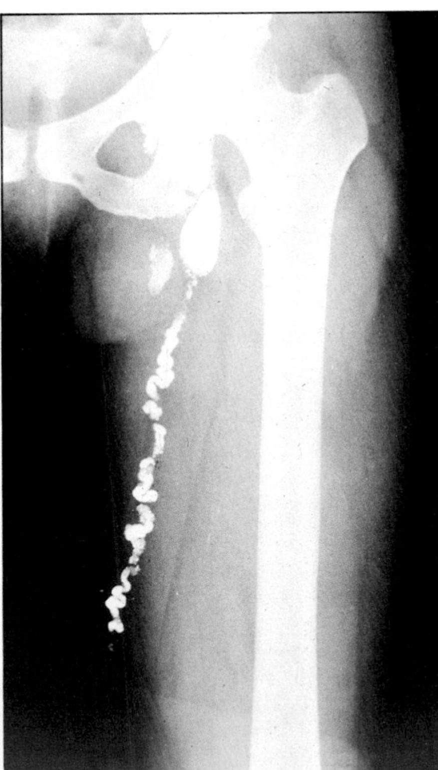

Ken Moreman

Causes

In the USA, Hodgkin's disease is more common in males than in females. Most cases occur in people in their 20s, and to a lesser degree, in people in their 60s. It occurs more frequently in people in the higher socio-economic groups, from small families, and is significantly more common in first-born children than in others. There is a distinct relationship with higher education. By contrast, in developing countries, Hodgkin's disease peaks during adolescence. The disease is very rare in Japan.

Hodgkin's disease runs in families and is 10 times as common in a brother or sister of an affected person, if of the same sex, than in the general population. This fact ties in with the observation that affected people in the same family usually have a similar pattern of tissue types on testing. These facts suggest that both genetic and environmental factors are important in determining the cause of the disease.

There is strong evidence to suggest a connection between Hodgkin's disease and the Epstein-Barr virus, which causes glandular fever (See Infectious mononucleosis). Hodgkin's disease occurs significantly more often in people with a history of infective mononucleosis than in others. Most significant of all, the complete DNA sequence (genome) of this virus is found within the malignant cells of about half of all people with Hodgkin's disease. Because the disease presents itself in different ways, there are probably several causes which interact in different ways with genetic, immune, and environmental factors.

In Hodgkin's disease the lymph nodes in areas such as the groin (left) swell. The binucleate (two nuclei) Reed-Sternberg cell shown in the center of the slide below is evidence of the disease.

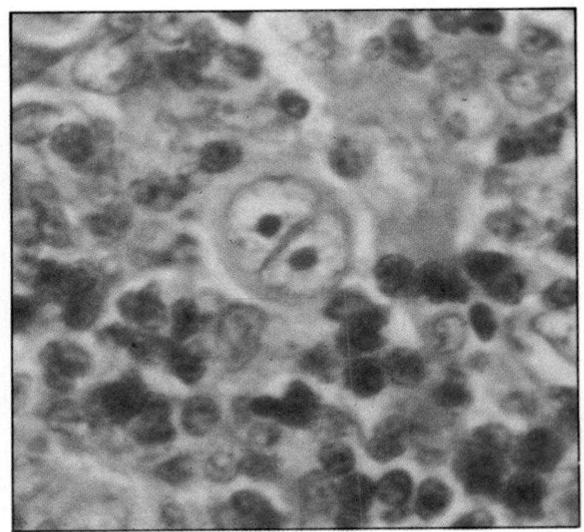

Ken Moreman

Hodgkin's disease affects the lymph tissues, which are composed of lymph cells (lymphocytes), a type of white blood cell. These cells are found in the blood and bone marrow and are grouped together in the lymph nodes in the neck, armpits, groin, chest, abdomen, liver, and spleen. In Hodgkin's disease the lymph cells increase in number, and the affected nodes become enlarged. One group of lymph nodes, usually in the groin or neck, is affected first, and then the disease spreads through the other groups of nodes until the whole lymphatic system may be involved.

Symptoms

Normally there are no symptoms apart from the swelling of the lymph nodes. However, sometimes there is fever, night sweating, weight loss, and tiredness, indicating that the disease has become widespread. These symptoms are more common in people over age 40. Untreated Hodgkin's disease will get progressively worse and become malignant rapidly.

A small proportion of people with Hodgkin's disease have severe symptoms. These include drenching sweats at night, a particular pattern of fever, and severe weight loss. Two additional and remarkable features are total body itching which may be extremely unpleasant, and pain at the sites of affected lymph nodes just after alcohol has been drunk. This is the only time in which lymph node enlargement in Hodgkin's disease is painful.

Treatment and outlook

Once Hodgkin's disease has been diagnosed by a biopsy (see Biopsy), further tests are done to assess the spread of the disease. This important test is called staging. Several methods of examination are used including a clinical examination for lymph nodes that can be felt. Normal lymph nodes are so soft that they can't be felt. The most important investigation, however, is lymph node biopsy, in which nodes are removed surgically for laboratory examination by a pathologist.

A special X ray called a CT scan (see Scans) is used, in which the lymphatic system is outlined by injecting an X ray dye into a lymph vessel in the foot. CT scanning is also used to identify all sites at which lymph nodes are affected. This is especially important in finding affected nodes in the center of the chest. Conventional X ray examination is liable to miss these. A laparotomy (surgery in which the abdomen is opened to search for signs of disease; see Laparotomy) may be performed; the lymph nodes in the abdomen are examined, the liver is biopsied, and the spleen is then removed. Laparotomy is not as common today because chemotherapy can reach lymph nodes throughout the body. The outcome is no longer affected by whether or not a laparotomy has been done.

Treatment depends on the extent of the disease. If it is not widespread, then the lymph nodes involved will be treated with radiotherapy (see Radiotherapy), which kills the abnormal cells but has less effect on the normal cells. More widespread disease is treated with cytotoxic (cell-killing) drugs, which have a similar effect.

Forty years ago people with Hodgkin's disease often died. Today, many are cured and most remain healthy for a long time.

A patient undergoes radiotherapy to treat Hodgkin's disease. The illuminated discs over his chest indicate the areas to receive radiation. This form of treatment is very successful in killing abnormal cells.

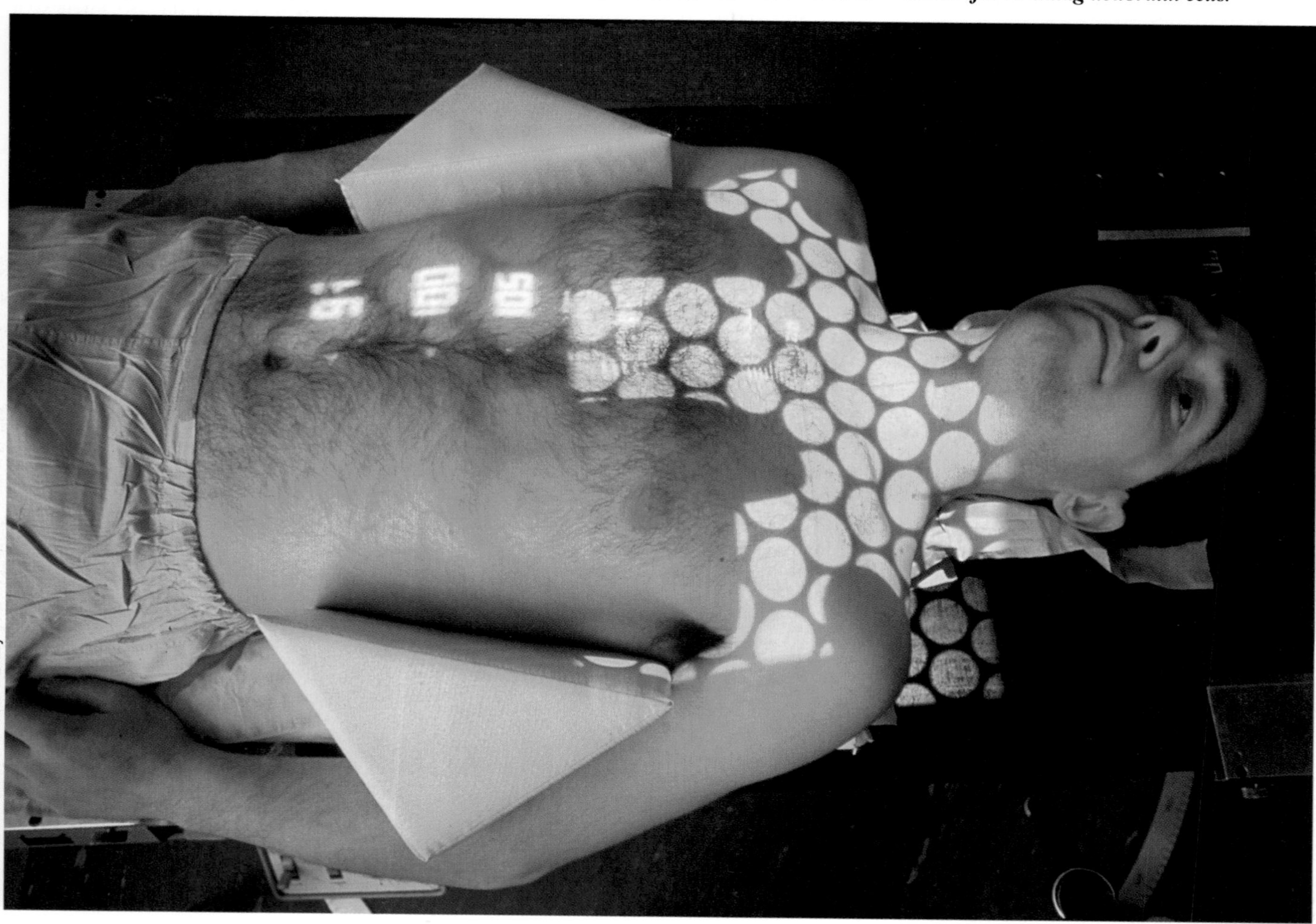

Martin Dohrn/Science Photo Library

Holistic medicine

Q I am interested in holistic medicine, but is it safe?

A Some therapies, such as acupuncture, herbalism, and hypnotherapy, can be dangerous in the wrong hands, and it is always important to make sure that you see a reliable practitioner.

Q What is the best way to find a reliable practitioner?

A The best way is word of mouth. However, always follow your own instincts, and if you do not feel comfortable with someone, they are not the therapist for you. Many practitioners offer a short initial consultation free of charge. As with any doctor, you should always ask about their training and experience. Umbrella organizations will send you a list of people practicing in your area, but bear in mind that these organizations vary in their reliability. Your doctor may also be able to recommend someone.

Q How should I choose the right therapy for me?

A The safest approach is to err on the side of caution. Consider carefully your complaint and the available options. Compare the suggested treatments and approaches of several types of practitioners. For example, hypnotherapy works through the mind, massage on the body. It is always safest to tell your doctor what you are doing and why, in case you have a serious concern that could be easily treated.

Q I hear many terms used to describe nonconventional forms of medicine. Do they all mean the same thing?

A Holistic medicine is sometimes called alternative because it is an alternative to conventional medicine, complementary because it is used alongside conventional medicine, traditional because it has developed from ideas and practices that predate conventional medicine, or natural because it doesn't use high-tech machinery or synthetic medications. By and large, however, all these terms refer to the same thing.

Holistic medicine includes a wide variety of therapies, such as acupuncture, hypnotherapy, and massage, but they all share a common approach.

Holistic medicine, also called holistic or comprehensive health care, aims to treat the person as a whole. This means first that an individual is treated on all levels, physical, mental, and spiritual, and second that each person is considered individually so that two people with the same symptoms might be prescribed entirely different remedies. Conventional medicine, on the other hand, deals with diseases and tends to see these as cut and dried; a particular medication, for instance, should always be used to treat a particular complaint.

Holistic medicine starts from the basic principle that the body has powers to heal itself and that disease is not something that attacks from outside the body, but is a helpful sign that something is wrong. Symptoms are not suppressed. Instead the body's own healing powers are stimulated so that the body's equilibrium or its homeostasis (a constancy in the internal environment of the body, naturally maintained by adaptive responses that promote healthy survival) is restored. Quite a few sensing, feedback, and control mechanisms function to carry out this steady state. Key control mechanisms include the reticular formation in the brainstem and the endocrine glands. Some of the functions controlled by these homeostatic mechanisms are the heartbeat, blood pressure, body temperature, electrolytic balance, respiration, and glandular secretion.

It may sound as if an alternative approach may be too unscientific to deal with such major sections of the body when they are temporarily out of balance, but many people have absolute faith in the ability of the holistic approach to cure whatever ails them.

What the treatment is like

You will be asked a wide range of questions about your health and your current state of mind, some of which you might think have no bearing on your immediate health complaint. A homeopath (see Homeopathy), for instance, might ask you what kind of food you dislike, what you dream about, and whether you feel the cold or whether you cry at the smallest

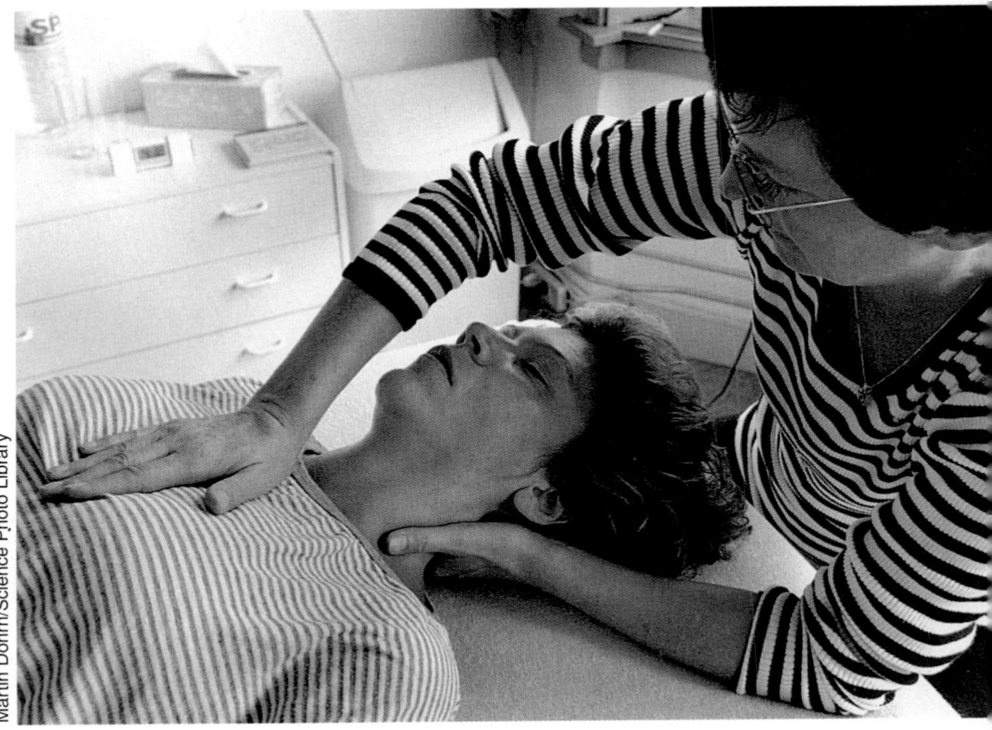

Martin Dohrn/Science Photo Library

Here a woman is receiving reiki therapy, a therapy used to treat psychological and emotional problems. The therapist lays hands softly on any of 20 specific parts of the body, releasing pent-up emotions.

slight or any sad situation; for example, seeing television reportage of starving children in a war-torn country. They will also take detailed notes on your family's health, previous social history, and then gradually build up a picture of your health.

Some holistic practitioners use conventional methods of diagnosis such as blood and urine testing, but most have their own particular methods. For example, in chiropractic therapy, a form of spinal manipulation to relieve lower back pain, the practitioner will concentrate on one or two vertebrae of the spine. He or she will also use X rays to assess the main problem.

A nutritional therapist might test a clipping of your hair for mineral deficiencies and then determine a diet that is rich in those deficiencies for you to follow as part of the treatment.

Other methods used include iridology (see Iridology). In this treatment, therapists examine the irises of your eyes to determine what is wrong with you. In kinesiology, the practitioner carries out a series of systematic tests on certain muscle groups to ascertain the strength of your muscles. Kinesiology is perhaps best known for diagnosing allergies, but it has a wide range of other applications, too. Kinesiological balancing can help with immune dysfunction, back pain, learning difficulties, anxiety and phobia states, nutritional deficiencies and food sensitivity, and sports fitness and injury. The theory behind kinesiology is that the body is thought to recognize and react instantly to foods and chemicals, which in turn affect the way muscles work.

Sometimes holistic treatments can take longer to work than conventional treatments. It is important to realize this before you begin treatment since you may begin to doubt its success if you feel no immediate improvement. You may find that you need to receive treatment on a weekly basis to start with, and perhaps every two weeks as you improve, and then less frequently. You will always be asked your opinion about the results, however, and you will make many more of the decisions about your treatment than you do when consulting a conventional doctor.

After the initial treatment you may feel worse before you feel better, but this is considered good and a sign that your body's own healing powers are getting to work. Sometimes, particularly in homeopathy, you may work backward through your illness from the more serious symptoms to the minor ones.

You may notice a temporary increase in your body's elimination systems, such as sweating, urination, and so on, as the toxins are cleared. Or you may feel tearful or even angry as negative emotions are released. On the other hand, many people notice an immediate feeling of overwhelming relief and say they come away from treatment sessions feeling as if they could climb mountains. These are all signs of improvement in the balance of your body's mechanisms.

The aim of holistic medicine is long-term improvement in health and well-being. As well as receiving treatment people are encouraged to do all they can for themselves. The term self-help is appropriate in this case. For this reason advice on diet and lifestyle are almost always part of the treatment, and many therapists teach people things they can do at home. A hypnotherapist might suggest you try regular self-hypnosis, an aromatherapist might give you oils you can use in the bath, and a reflexologist might show you where to massage your own feet or hands whenever you feel a particular symptom returning. Most of all, a therapist will help you understand your illness and ensure you take a positive part in the healing process.

Self-treatment without training is sometimes possible but should always be undertaken with caution. A little knowledge can be a dangerous thing in certain circumstances. Some vitamin and mineral supplements are dangerous in large doses and several herbal remedies or aromatherapy oils should not be used during pregnancy. In all cases proper help from a trained therapist is going to be more effective.

Who it can help

Life-threatening and acute conditions, such as a heart attack, advanced cancer, serious infectious diseases, or conditions requiring surgery, are best dealt with by conventional medicine. Apart from that, however, there is no disease that cannot be treated to some degree by holistic medicine. This is not to say that such treatment will guarantee you a cure; nothing can do that.

You can combine conventional and holistic treatment but you should always tell your therapist because in some cases it is not advisable to combine different

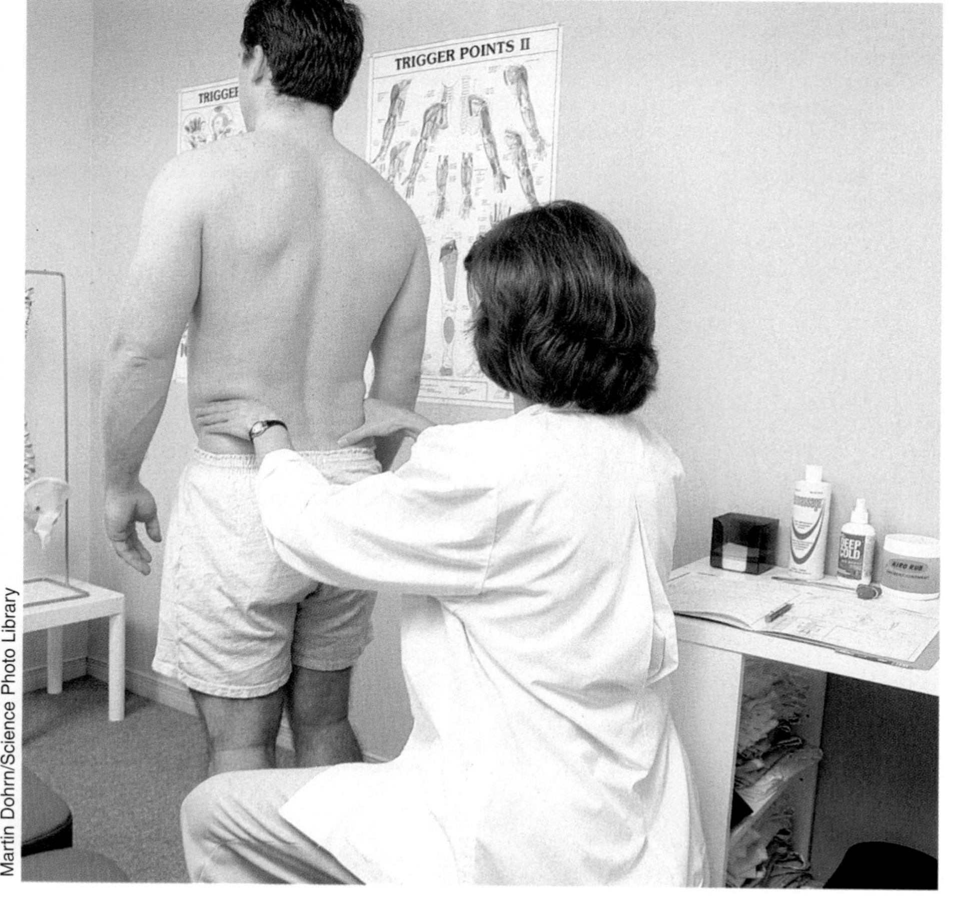

Martin Dohrn/Science Photo Library

The chiropractic technique analyzes and treats the whole body through the spine. The practitioner can manipulate and align by hand any minor displacements of the spinal column and bones.

Rex Features

The Alexander technique aims to correct poor posture and body movement by teaching patients to stand and move efficiently. It can reduce back pain and other disorders.

methods of treatment, as in taking a prescribed medication and herbal treatments at the same time, for instance. Conventional treatment does make your holistic therapist's job more difficult, but an experienced holisitic therapist will not try to persuade you to stop the course of conventional treatment if you are pleased with it.

Whether or not you tell your doctor about your holistic treatment is a personal decision. Many doctors can be very skeptical about its benefits, but this small-minded attitude is changing.

Practitioners of holistic medicine claim that it is particularly good for chronic diseases, such as arthritis or multiple sclerosis (MS), which conventional medicine is unable to help, because it may well improve the sufferer's quality of life. It is also suitable for all those minor problems that you would not bother a doctor with, but that nevertheless detract from your wellbeing, such as headaches, loss of appetite, or fatigue.These are seen by holistic practitioners as early warning signs, and they take such indications seriously. You do not have to have anything wrong with you to visit a holistic practitioner because one of the main tenets of holistic medicine is preventative health.

Pets can also be treated by holistic methods. There are veterinarians who specialize in alternative treatments.

Does it work?

Because holistic treatment varies so much from patient to patient and because successful treatment depends both on the rapport between patient and therapist and on how much self-help the patient is willing to undertake, it is very difficult to conduct scientific trials on holistic medicine. What do you compare with what, for instance, and what do you give as a placebo?

However, there have been trials on the major therapies, such as acupuncture. At the same time scientists are rediscovering the value of herbal remedies in their search for new medications. The chart (overleaf) gives an idea of the status of some of the different therapies. New therapies are being developed all the time and while these may not have been extensively tested, this does not mean that they will be any less effective for you. One problem with the newer therapies, however, is lack of regulation, which does makes it more difficult to find reliable help.

According to a 1986 survey a third of people using holistic medicine said they thought they had been cured of their ailment, half said they believed that their condition had improved, and three-quarters said that they would definitely use this form of medicine again

Holistic medicine is certainly growing in popularity.According to a recent major survey, one in three US adults used some form of holistic therapy in 1990, which was a much higher figure than previously recorded. In the UK, where laws on nonconventional treatments are less restrictive than in the US, growth has been even greater, with consultations increasing at the rate of 10–15 percent a year, five times more than conventional medicine.

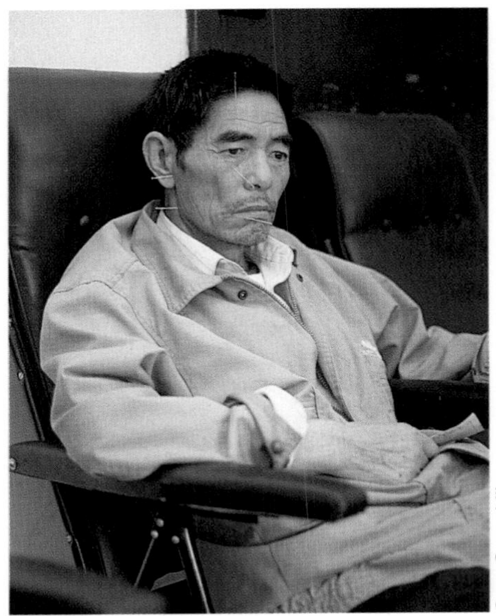

Sam Greenhill

The acupuncturist inserts needles into appropriate points in the patient's skin to restore health. This traditional Chinese therapy can also induce anesthesia.

Some examples of holistic therapies

Name	Description of treatment	How it is said to work	Where it comes from	History	Respectability
Acupuncture	Fine needles inserted all over body	Energy channels called meridians are stimulated and unblocked	China	Started at least 4,500 years ago and officially recognized in China today	Not properly explained by Western science but much research in its favor
Alexander Technique	Retraining of posture and the way every part of the body is held	Frees mental and physical tension	Australia	Developed by Frederick Alexander last century, originally to help himself	In harmony with current understanding of anatomy and physiology
Aromatherapy	Plant essences taken internally, vaporized, or diluted in oil, and used for massage	Physiological effects from chemicals in the essences, plus psychological ones from the aroma	France	Arose from the perfume industry this century	Little research but very popular. Internal use largely in France. Other uses said to be good for pain relief and relaxation
Herbalism	Tablets, tinctures (alcoholic solutions), lotions, or teas made from plants (and sometimes from animal sources in Chinese herbalism)	Physical, mental, and spiritual effects from the herbs	Worldwide	One of the oldest forms of medicine. Suppressed from the Middle Ages onward in the West as male-dominated types of treatment took over	Some people are concerned that practitioners and remedies are not centrally regulated
Homeopathy	Tablets of ground-down plants, minerals, metals, and other substances but so diluted as to be undetectable scientifically	Substances used that in larger doses would produce effects similar to those the patient is suffering from but in such minute doses stimulate the body's natural defenses (something like vaccination)	Germany	Discovered by a doctor early last century. Opposed by American Medical Association until 1930. Incorporated into UK National Health Service	Not scientifically explained. Research has shown a homeopathic effect, but only a few of the 2,000 or so remedies have been tested
Hypnotherapy	A state of deep relaxation is induced	In this state the mind can be reprogrammed to avoid bad habits, whether physical, mental, or spiritual, and disturbing buried memories can be recovered and resolved. Also used for pain relief and psychosomatic illness	Europe	First used medically in 18th century and later by Sigmund Freud at the beginning of this century	History one of checkered respectability but now approved by American and British Medical Associations. Regulation of practitioners very patchy
Osteopathy	Massage and manipulation of muscles and joints	Frees mental and physical tension	United States	Developed by Dr. Andrew Taylor Still in the last century	Most widespread natural therapy in the U.S. with all practitioners trained doctors as well. Only natural therapy to be regulated by law in the UK
Reflexology	Foot (and sometimes hand and ear) massage	Points on feet (and hands and ears) are connected by energy channels to rest of body and the massage corrects the energy flow (similar to acupuncture)	The East	Earliest traces date from some 5,000 years ago. Spread to Europe in the Dark and Middle Ages and rediscovered in America early this century	Lack of research but anecdotal evidence in its favor

Homeopathy

Homeopathy, the principle of like curing like, is gaining popularity among patients and doctors alike, both as a curative and a preventive technique.

Homeopathy is the name given to a system of medicine that was established in Germany at the end of the 18th century by Dr. Samuel Hahnemann. The term *homeopathy* comes from two Greek words meaning similar to the disease. Hahnemann based his theory on the principle that like is healed by like. He reasoned that to cure an illness, a medicine that could mimic the diseased state would stimulate the body's natural defense mechanisms against the illness. For example, while a homeopath might use an onion because it makes the nose and eyes run just as they do in hay fever (see Hay fever), the onion itself does not give the patient hay fever. Orthodox medicine incorporated this same principle in its use of vaccinations, in which a small dose of bacterial or viral substance is injected into the patient to promote the formation of antibodies (elements that defend the body against further infection).

In the United States, homeopathy is practiced by medical doctors, who have completed extra studies in the subject after their regular medical training, as well as osteopaths, and other licenced health-care providers, such as nurse practitioners, dentists, and even veterinarians. Currently, there are approximately 3,000 homeopathic practitioners throughout the United States. According to a 1993 study, approximately one percent of Americans used homeopathy and 4.8 million visits were made to homeopathic practitioners in 1990.

A 1995 survey of family physicians in the Chesapeake region found that 27 percent of respondents considered homeopathy a legitimate practice, while a further 60 percent were interested in homeopathic training. In addition, two grants for research in homeopathy, including a

A bouquet of common plants that are used in homeopathic remedies.

Bill Petch

Q I have an appointment with a homeopathic practitioner and would like to check on her experience. What questions should I ask?

A Generally you should ask if the practitioner specializes in homeopathy, and whether the person practices its classical form. You also need to ask where he or she was trained, how long he or she has been practicing, and finally whether he or she is board-certified in homeopathy. If you are happy with the answers, go ahead!

Q What sort of homeopathic remedies should I keep in my first-aid box at home?

A Some homeopathic druggists produce a kit for first-aid purposes in the home. Common remedies for stings and rashes, for nerve strain and tension, and for colds on the chest are included. However, there are always several different remedies for any ailment, and it is helpful if the choice is narrowed down according to the specific symptoms in each case.

Q I've heard that homeopathy can help treat animals. Is there any truth in this?

A There are 200–500 homeopathic veterinarians in the US, and there are claims that farm animals have been treated successfully. One such veterinarian in the UK treated half of a herd of cattle to prevent mastitis (infection of the udder) while the other half acted as a control group. The homeopathic group stayed healthy and the untreated group developed mastitis.

Q My whole family goes to a homeopathic doctor. What would happen if one of us developed, say, appendicitis?

A The practitioner would refer the patient to a surgeon without delay. In the US, homeopaths are trained doctors who have also studied homeopathic medicines. As scientists, they recognize that there are situations that need the help of orthodox medicine, including the use of conventional medications.

Bill Petch

Many of the more than 2,000 homeopathic remedies are made from plants.

clinical trial on the homeopathic treatment of mild traumatic brain injury, were awarded recently by the National Institutes of Health Office of Alternative Medicine.

In Europe, homeopathy is an integral part of everyday health care. At present, 40 percent of Dutch, 39 percent of French, 20 percent of German, and up to 37 percent of British physicians use homeopathy. It is fully reimbursable under the French social security system, the German national health insurance system, and the British National Health Service. Homeopathy is widely used in India, Mexico, South America, and the former Soviet Union. The world market is estimated at between one billion and five billion dollars.

These are indications that what was once considered to be fringe medicine is now almost mainstream medicine.

The basis of homeopathy

The theory of homeopathy is based on the assumption that a healthy body has the resources to protect itself against illness, stress, and all the side effects of the environment, and to repair itself if it is temporarily overwhelmed. In effect, homeopathists regard symptoms as the body's way of restoring health. Homeopathists believe their medications stimulate, not suppress, the body's healing mechanism. Clinical trials have indicated positive results for conditions, such as hay fever, migraine headaches, gastritis, and flu.

Purpose

Homeopathy differs from orthodox medicine in that it does not regard a disease or an illness as a definable state that is exactly the same for any two people, since each person responds to a disorder in an individual way that is characteristic of his or her physical type, personality, emotions, and environment.

For example, one person may catch every virus that is circulating during a winter season, but another person may not be affected at all. Therefore there is no one homeopathic medicine for, say, the flu, but rather a choice of remedies to suit the range of individual responses and unique requirements.

Homeopathic prescribing is very precise; whether you have a tickle in your throat or not, dislike heat, enjoy sweet foods, or cry easily, all of these factors and others will make a difference to the medicines prescribed. Homeopathic physicians claim to treat the whole person rather than the disease in isolation. The

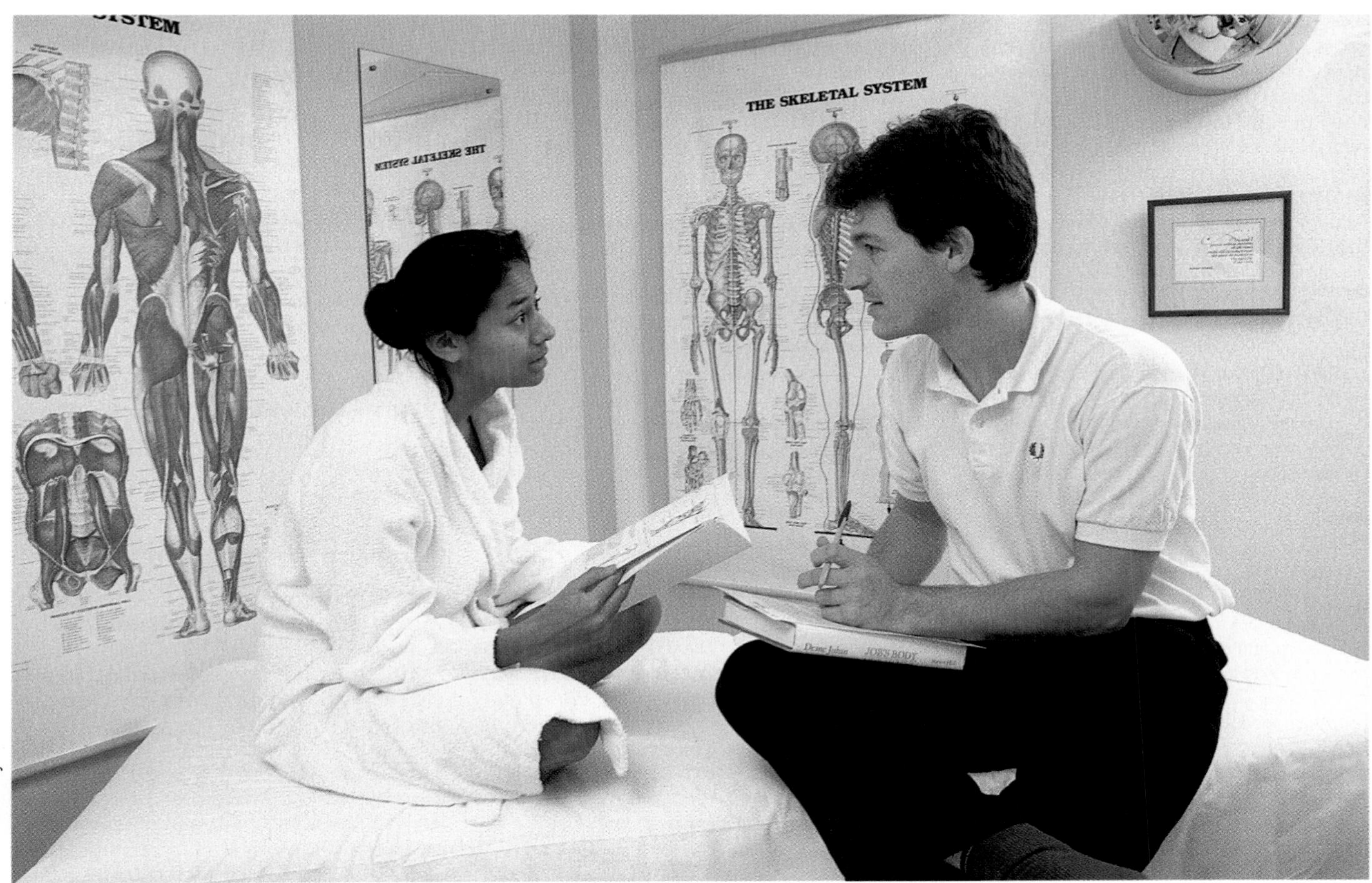

John Walmsley

The homeopath asks questions about a patient's environment, preferences, and lifestyle, so that a whole picture of the person's lifestyle and current state of mental and physical health is built up. This helps the practitioner to correctly prescribe a remedy to suit the individual.

patient is seen as an integrated organism who is struggling with a harmful influence, rather than, say, a case of cystitis. The homeopathic approach is to help the patient throw off the illness by strengthening his or her natural defenses.

How homeopathy works

Homeopathic medicines are specially prepared in accordance with the *Homeopathic Pharmacopeia of the United States* (HPUS). A total of 1,300 medicines are catalogued in the HPUS, of which 75 percent are made from plants, and the remaining 25 percent from minerals, or animal sources, such as lachesis (a snake venom) and apis (from the bee). These medicines are considered very safe. As a result, some 95 percent are available over-the-counter (OTC)

While he was testing his original remedies, Hahnemann made a very remarkable discovery: the healing effect of a remedy increased if the amount of the substance present in the medication was decreased. This discovery is incorporated in the preparation of doses of different strengths, a process called potentizing. It can be continued almost indefinitely, and each successive potency contains less of the original substance: homeopaths use potencies that are dilutions in which only the most minute trace of the original substance remains. Because less and less of it is left in the medicine, any toxic effects are eliminated.

This is very important because many of the remedies would be poisonous if taken in large doses. Since there are no poisonous or toxic agents involved, there are no adverse side effects. Consequently homeopathy, whether it is effective or not, is an intrinsically safe form of treatment, provided that the patient recognizes the occasions when treatment with conventional medicine is required and acts accordingly.

Many doctors tend not to accept that tiny doses of medications make any real difference to the health of the body or that they are sufficient to treat powerful diseases. They may be very skeptical of the whole concept of homeopathy. You can listen to their opinions and those of the homeopath and make up your own mind on which treatment you prefer.

Initial consultation

The homeopathic doctor will want to take a detailed case history and will ask the patient questions that may at first seem unrelated to the illness.

You will be asked about many things, including reactions to heat and cold, whether sweet foods are preferred to savory ones, and many other small details. The homeopath tries to build up an image of the whole person, his or her characteristics, and way of life. The object is to match symptoms and reactions to the effects created by the medicines in the *Materia Medica*, a book that contains details of over 2,000 different remedies.

In the course of the interview or during subsequent treatment, the homeopath may diagnose the constitutional remedy, one particular medicine to which the patient is particularly sensitive because it so well matches the personality and physical type. A course of this remedy mobilizes various responses that improve general health.

Homeopathic treatment

Homeopaths prescribe only one remedy at a time to assess the effect of each one.

The potency of the medication depends on a number of factors, including the patient's age and health, how deep-seated the illness is, and whether it is acute or chronic (including asthma, depression, headache or migraine, allergy, dermatitis or eczema, arthritis, and high blood pressure). The dosage varies widely, from once a month in chronic cases to several times a day in more acute cases.

Remedies in the home

Many common afflictions can be managed at home if you choose the right remedy. Here are a few successful natural remedies for you to keep in the medicine cabinet. Remember all remedies should be handled with respect. If symptoms persist, or for more serious accidents, you should always consult a homeopath or doctor.

- Take up to three tablets a day for not more than three days in a row
- Tablets for children or animals can be crushed into a powder-like form between two spoons to make the substance easier to swallow
- Avoid food, drink, cleaning teeth with toothpaste, or smoking tobacco for at least 20 minutes before and after taking a remedy
- Avoid handling the tablets. Tip them into the container lid and drop them under your tongue so that they dissolve. Do not crunch or swallow them.

Arnica Heals physical trauma, such as shock, bumps and bruises, sprains or aching muscles. Lessens jet lag and aids recovery after childbirth or surgery.

Aconite The first remedy to take for fear or shock, for example, after an auto collision. It also helps recover from chills and a feverish cold.

Ledum Good for treating wounds, bee or wasp stings, swollen insect bites, dog bites, or accidents with nails.

Hypericum Good for treating painful cuts and lacerations, crushed toes or fingers squashed in car doors, and for falls that affect the base of the spine.

Nux vomica Treats indigestion and hangovers caused by overindulgence in rich food and drink.

Chamomilla These are teething granules that are used to calm fractious teething babies.

Urtica An ointment that soothes minor burns and irritating sunburn.

Calendula This is an antiseptic healer for grazes, small cuts and septic wounds. Dilute three drops of the lotion in a cup of water to use.

Treatment is changed or suspended when there is an improvement in the condition of the patient. However, it often happens that symptoms get worse for a short time before they get better; sometimes the symptoms of a previous illness can recur.

Homeopathic physicians claim that powerful modern medications often suppress illness and drive the condition deeper into the system. As the defenses are strengthened by homeopathic treatment, old symptoms recur when the illness is eliminated. Although it may seem temporarily that the patient is getting worse, an overall improvement in health is believed to be taking place. After the first consultation subsequent visits to the homeopath take place every two to four weeks until improvements occur.

Taking the preparations

Homeopathic preparations are dissolved on the tongue rather than swallowed and stimulants such as coffee should be avoided because they may diminish its effects. Homeopathic medicines, at least in the lower potencies, are completely safe and no ill effects will arise if the remedy chosen is not quite right, but it is also possible that there will there be no significant improvement and you will have to ask the homeopath to reconsider the prescribed remedy.

Homeopathic medicines are carried in most national drugstore chains. They are less expensive than conventional medicines, costing an average $3–7 per bottle. In 1995, retail sales of homeopathic medicines in the US were estimated at $201 million, growing at a rate of 20 percent a year, according to figures from the American Homeopathic Pharmaceutical Association.

Ailments that respond to homeopathy

premenstrual syndrome
myalgic encephalomyelitis (ME)
depression
behavioral difficulties in children
cystitis and thrush
migraine
menopausal problems
eating disorders
glue ear
sinusitis
irritable colon syndrome
continual coughs and colds
hay fever
asthma
eczema

Tinctures can be used to make lotions for skin care and mouthwashes for dental purposes.

Homeopathy and good health

Homeopathic treatment may benefit your general health as well as treat specific diseases and illnesses. It is most popular for curing allergies such as hay fever. It may also prevent the development of many illnesses that usually occur only when natural resistance is at a low ebb.

Homeopathy can also be used in conjunction with standard medications if necessary, for example, with antibiotics.

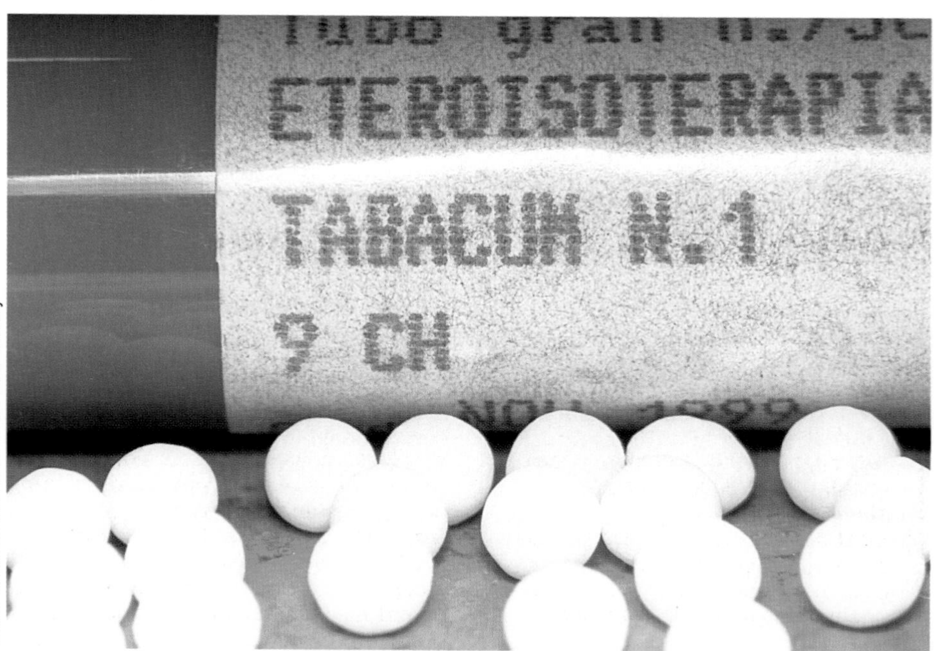

Klaus Guldbrandsen/Science Photo Library

Homeopathic remedies may help to cure addictive habits like smoking, which are dangerous to a person's health.

Homesickness

Q At what age is it reasonable to expect my daughter to spend time away from home without becoming homesick?

A It depends very much on the child. Some children may be ready for the occasional night away from home at seven years old if they stay in a familiar household and show signs of being independent. Some might not want to venture away for the night until age 11 or older. There is no point in pushing your daughter, you will only make her unhappy.

Q Is it possible to prevent homesickness in my child by encouraging independence from an early age?

A Of course independence should always be encouraged, but you must tailor it to a child's needs and sensitivity. Sometimes a child appears to be more independent than he or she really is. If a child is sent away from home when too young, the experience of homesickness may leave a scar and be stronger in subsequent situations, even when the child is much older. You can help by encouraging the idea that staying away is a treat and something to look forward to.

Q I am thinking of sending my child on a foreign student exchange, using an agency. How can I make sure that my child adjusts to living in a foreign country with a strange family?

A A good agency will try to match the families, ages of children, interests, and hobbies. Check that yours is doing this. Tell the agency as much as you can about your child, and be honest, because that is the only way you will get some degree of accuracy in matching. It is no good saying that you have an extrovert, cooperative child when he or she is really a loner. Take your child to a restaurant serving the food of the country to be visited and explain about its customs. Point out that most people find new surroundings strange at first. If possible take the child to visit the country before he or she goes to stay there alone.

Many people experience homesickness at some time in their lives. However, there are ways of easing the miserable feelings that can afflict children and adults alike when they are away from familiar home surroundings.

John Walmsley

A trip away from home may seem like an exciting idea at first, but as the departure date approaches, insecurity may set in.

Homesickness may be caused by loneliness, insecurity, or anxiety about being in a seemingly unfriendly place, but there is no doubt that it is a distressing experience, for adults as well as for children.

When people long for home, what they are missing most is its familiarity. A person may be in a hotel bedroom in a foreign country, for example, and have a sudden desire for his or her own room at home with its well-loved books and ornaments. Suddenly there is a yearning for the safety and security that these things symbolize. A hotel room, no matter how luxurious, seems strange and unfriendly.

If the mood continues a person may begin to feel isolated and lonely. The hotel room starts to seem like a prison and the outside world is threatening. The next move might be toward the whiskey bottle or the first plane home, in other words depression or panic sets in.

This is a fairly extreme example, but it does give some idea of what people can suffer. Homesickness is not confined to the lonely young business executive traveling for his or her company. A working parent may feel terrible pangs on finding him- or herself at a conference. He or she may worry about how their partner is coping alone at home and about the children. These can be the triggers of an agonizing kind of homesickness, since it may be mixed with feelings of guilt about having left loved ones behind.

Relieving homesickness

There are ways in which homesickness can be prevented or relieved. If a person suffers from it, there are measures that can be taken even before leaving home: friends, colleagues, and relatives can be asked if they know of anyone who can be contacted at the new destination. There is no need to be shy and reticent; most people are glad to have news of their friends far away from someone who has seen them recently. They may also be proud to show visitors their hometown, too. Friends in a strange place are half the battle against homesickness.

Carrying a photo of the family and phoning home regularly can help to relieve pangs of homesickness. It is reassuring to hear familiar voices, especially when they assure a person that all is well with the family and that things are running smoothly at home.

There is no reason why a person must stay in a hotel room alone. It is a positive step to watch television in the hotel lounge and to talk to some of the other

John Walmsley

When on holiday in a foreign city, consult a guidebook and explore the sights, rather than sitting in your hotel room alone.

guests; they may be having similar feelings, and it is possible to cheer each other up. A drink at the bar can be a good idea, too. Even if it is only a soft drink, at least there will be the company of other people. Letters home can be therapeutic; they will be much appreciated at the other end and will give a traveler the feeling of being in touch.

There is a whole world to explore outside the hotel. Cities have parks, museums, art galleries, movie theaters, and shops. It is always nice to go hunting for souvenirs and presents to give to family and friends back home. On country visits the scenery can be admired and the fresh air taken in with a long, rambling walk.

The homesick child

Children are even more vulnerable to homesickness than adults because they are more dependent on their familiar surroundings and family. A small boy may beg to be allowed to stay overnight with a friend. He gets his wish and then at 11:30 P.M. there is a phone call from the friend's mother to say that Johnny cannot get to sleep and wants to come home. Why should this happen, after all the pleasurable anticipation? Exasperating as it may be, there is a good reason. The child has slightly overestimated his ability to cope with his first night away from home. A minor incident may have made everything go wrong: perhaps he was tired by the excitement; perhaps a television program upset him; or perhaps he had had a bad day at school. Any of these could be sufficiently disturbing to make the child think that he would really like to be in his own bed more than anywhere else in the world, at least on this particular night.

Another possible cause of homesickness in a child is a basic insecurity about the family and home situation. The parents may have quarreled lately or they may seem to favor a younger child. Perhaps a grandparent has died recently or there is some other reason why the child is anxious to stay at home just in case something worse happens.

Children in this position usually resist going away from home, but there may be times when they cannot refuse a trip, for example, an invitation to stay with relatives or a school trip. The child may hide his or her doubts about going, and the unhappiness only appears a couple of days into the trip. This problem is not easy to solve, but there are ways to help a child; some are listed below.

How to help your child avoid homesickness

- Give your child a photo of the family; you can tell him or her it is to show his or her hosts, but it is really for reassurance
- Lend him or her something of yours—a pen, a comb, or a scarf. It will act as a link with you
- Let the child take a favorite toy, book, or game
- Pack a cheerful postcard in the child's suitcase so that he or she will find it when unpacking
- Write a short note and send it to the child's destination so that it greets him or her on arrival. Write frequently afterward
- Inform any accompanying adult of the habits, fears, and dislikes of your child, such as wanting a light on at night, for example

Homosexuality

My son is 18 and, as far as I know, has not shown any interest in girls. Does this mean that he is a homosexual?

A No. Since you do not say that he has had any close relationships with men, it seems far more likely that he either has a comparatively low sex drive, which creates no particular problem in itself, or else he is a little shy and keeps his relationships to himself.

Q My 12-year-old son has told me that he was touched in the shower by an older boy. Is there any chance that he will be affected by the experience?

A It is highly unlikely. To begin with he told you about the experience so he probably does not feel guilty about it, only puzzled. Many boys experiment sexually at that age, and the experience is usually shrugged off.

Q Is lesbianism (female homosexuality) as common as male homosexuality?

A No. In the United States up to 12 percent of all women have had at least one lesbian experience, but only 1 or 2 percent (mostly unmarried women) regard themselves as entirely lesbian. This compares with the 4 percent of men who say they are exclusively homosexual.

Q I have found out that my son has had at least one homosexual affair. Can this be a passing phase, and, if not, should I try to cure him?

A It can be a passing phase. Some young men try out—and reject—homosexuality very dispassionately; others accept it. But most attempts at curing them are likely to fail. Parents may blame themselves, often without reason, for their son's behavior. This can lead to conflict, so relations should be strengthened with the help of a family therapist who can be contacted through your doctor. Religious organizations may be able to help you improve your communication skills and capacity for empathy and compassion.

When a man's sexual response is to a member of his own sex, he is called a homosexual. A homosexual woman is called a lesbian. Homosexuals (or gays) of both sexes often have problems that need sympathetic understanding.

Any behavior between two people of the same sex that results in sexual arousal can be called homosexual behavior; it does not have to lead to orgasm. Kissing and caressing between men, for example, can thus constitute homosexual behavior.

Defining a homosexual is more difficult, because many men who have had occasional homosexual encounters regard these experiences as purely incidental and do not consider themselves to be homosexual. The American sex researcher Alfred Kinsey devised a scale that could be used to estimate the extent of the homosexual impulse. Using this scale a recent survey showed that about 30 percent of adult American males have had at least one homosexual contact, but only about 4 percent claim to be exclusively homosexual.

A number of research studies have shown that some homosexuality occurs purely as a result of special circumstances. Most prison inmates, for example, are heterosexual—they are inclined toward the opposite sex—both before and after their imprisonment, yet homosexuality in prison is commonplace.

An investigation of male athletes at universities found that 40 percent had engaged in at least two homosexual acts that reached orgasm during the last two years, yet only 8 percent of them regarded themselves as homosexual.

The absence of opposite sex contacts—in prisons and single-sex boarding schools, for example—and the close body contact of certain one sex groups—such as athletic clubs—may thus encourage homosexual experiments without producing exclusive homosexuality.

Causes of male homosexuality

Research indicates that four main factors contribute toward producing male homosexual behavior. There may be a

Demonstrations like this draw attention to society's attitude toward gay people and may help to change perceptions.

Rex Features

small genetic (inherited) predisposition, but this has not been proven, and it is not known whether this produces homosexuality directly. Irregular levels of sex hormones during the development of the child in the uterus have also been cited as an influence.

Family upbringing may have an effect by failing to produce a strong sense of being male in the growing boy, by inducing guilt about early heterosexual contacts, or by blocking initial heterosexual behavior. Finally, experiences outside the family may also encourage homosexual behavior.

Homosexuality in women

An estimated 2 percent of women in the United States are thought to be homosexual and an additional 8–10 percent are believed to have had one or more lesbian contacts in their lives. The cause of female homosexuality is still not certain, but experiences during adolescence seem to be a major contributing factor.

Bisexuality also occurs among female and male homosexuals, with the two sexes attracted to both homosexual and heterosexual relationships. The term *bisexual* also refers to hermaphrodites, people who have internal and external physical characteristics of both sexes.

Living in a heterosexual world

Because homosexuality occurs in a minority of people, homosexuals are usually under pressure in a number of ways, even in more liberal societies. They are under social pressure to conform in the same way as any group that diverges from the accepted norm. They are also under pressure from parents who see a homosexual child's behavior as a failure that reflects on their upbringing. They are also the victims of prejudice from people who incorrectly regard male homosexuals as sex maniacs and child molesters.

Even though homosexual behavior is legal in certain countries, the threat of blackmail is still very real, especially for people in positions of responsibility or in the public eye. Over and above these constraints there is the fact that homosexuality is a problem for many of those who practice it, in that it restricts their sexual, emotional, and social life to a minority of possible relationships.

Coming to terms with these pressures and difficulties often has to be achieved during late adolescence, when growing-up problems are already at their most intense. Many homosexuals, in fact, never do admit their homosexuality. Twenty percent of male homosexuals marry and less than a third tell their wives about their homosexuality before marriage. The picture, however, is gradually changing. Movements such as Gay Liberation and the Campaign for Homosexual Equality, and a growing tolerance toward different sexual patterns, have done much to allow those with either a partial or a total leaning toward homosexuality to come to terms with their situation.

Parents and partners

It is nevertheless in the realm of family relationships that there are naturally the greatest problems of acceptance. Parents who realize that their child is a homosexual may find adjustment difficult, while a wife who becomes aware of her husband's homosexual leanings may find the revelation particularly painful. However, special counseling services are now available in many areas of the United States and Europe, for example, for homosexuals, their parents, and their partners. A family doctor can advise on how to contact such counselors. Religious organizations may also offer advice and help to homosexuals and their families.

Today the ethics of trying to alter homosexual behavior are questioned by many therapists, who refuse to attempt this unless the individual is deeply disturbed by his or her behavior and totally motivated to change. Success is more often achieved with younger homosexuals who had their first encounter after 16 years of age, who have had some enjoyable heterosexual activity, and who are still certain of their own sense of being male or female. It is generally regarded as preferable to help the individual come to terms with his or her sexual status rather than to try and change it.

Young people who discover they are gay can lead a very lonely existence. Gay clubs and pubs like this provide them with a meeting place and a fuller social life.

Colin Ramsey/MC Library

Hookworms

Q I am going to India this summer. Is there any way I can avoid catching hookworms?

A Parasitic infections, such as hookworm disease, are common in the tropics. Avoid walking barefoot, especially near lavatories. If you do put yourself at risk, wash your feet well immediately, as it takes only five or 10 minutes for hookworm larvae to penetrate the skin.

Q I went on vacation to Africa last summer and have had an upset stomach ever since. Could it be hookworms?

A It sounds as though you may have picked up an infection on your travels. You should see your doctor to arrange for a laboratory test on your feces. Appropriate treatment can then be given.

Q My sister has been treated for hookworms. Should I be treated as well?

A If you were both exposed to the infection, it is likely you were infected too, and you may develop symptoms in the future. You should see your doctor to arrange for a laboratory test, and then he or she can treat you accordingly.

Q I had hookworms three years ago. Could I still be infected?

A Left untreated, hookworms usually disappear after about two years, although they can live up to five. Provided you have not been reinfected and have no symptoms now, it is unlikely that any of the worms have survived.

Q After a year in the tropics, I have got hookworms and now anemia. How can the anemia be treated?

A First the hookworms must be treated, as the worms' presence in the intestine upsets digestion. Iron tablets should be taken with a high-protein diet to allow the body to make up more blood cells and to treat any malnutrition that may exist.

Hookworm disease occurs in tropical and subtropical climates. Once detected it is easily cured.

Hookworms are small parasitic worms. Infection with a few hookworms is not serious, but if large numbers establish themselves, severe disability may follow; this is called *hookworm disease*. There are two species of hookworm, *Necator americanus* and *Ancylostoma duodenale*. About 25 percent of the world's population is infected with hookworms.

Causes, symptoms, and dangers

Hookworm disease is caused by parasites that enter the body through the soles of the feet and travel through the bloodstream to the lungs. From there they are coughed up and swallowed, and so reach the small intestine. The eggs of the hookworms are expelled in the feces; anyone who goes barefoot in the tropics therefore runs the risk of infection.

Hookworms are more likely to be acquired when the soil is damp enough for larvae to survive. The risk is greatest in areas in which human feces are commonly deposited on the ground. The worms affect anyone whose bare skin comes in contact with soil containing larvae, and this is most likely with children and those whose work involves close contact with soil. The duties of military personnel commonly expose them to hookworm infection.

Eggs released in the feces hatch in the soil, releasing larvae that, under suitable conditions, grow and molt on the third to fifth day after deposition. After this time the larvae are in the infective stage and are capable of penetrating the skin. When the larvae pass through the skin, they cause an itchy, slightly raised rash at each entry site. This is known as ground itch. Occasionally the rash may ulcerate (the skin may lose its surface covering and become infected; see Ulcers). It may also be possible to see twisting tracks under the surface of the skin that indicate the routes taken by the larvae.

Although most cases of infection occur by skin penetration, people may be infected with *A. duodenale* by consuming larvae on contaminated food.

Life cycle of hookworm

After passing though the skin and traveling for a time within the thickness of the skin, larvae remain in the tissues for a variable period. Eventually they encounter small blood vessels, and break through

How hookworm disease occurs

Hookworms enter the host's body, traveling to the intestine where they suck blood.

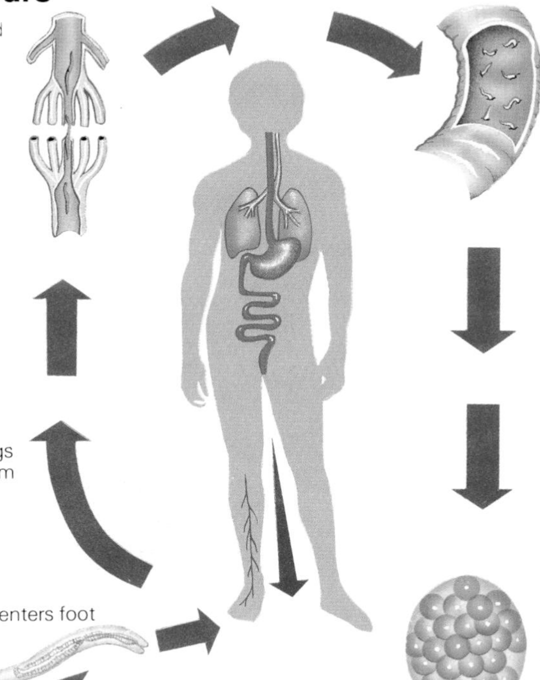

Bernard Fallon

into the bloodstream. Once in the blood those that find themselves in veins are carried almost immediately to the right side of the heart, and from there are taken by the circulatory system to the lungs (sse Blood). Here, for the first time, they enter capillaries—the smallest blood vessels. These capillaries are very thin-walled and are situated in the walls of the tiny air sacs of the lungs (the alveoli). The growing larvae pass through the walls of the capillaries to enter the alveoli (see Lung and lung diseases). From there they make their way up the air passages and out through the voice box (larynx) into the back of the throat, where they are swallowed. The passage of larvae through the lungs may cause a brief inflammation of the lung tissue known as pneumonitis.

Once in the intestine the larvae grow into young adult worms 0.3–0.5 in (8–13 mm) long and 0.3–0.6 mm thick. At the mouth end they have hooks or cutting plates that they use to attach themselves to the mucous membrane lining of the intestine. It is this feature that gives the worms their popular name. Each male has a single testis, but the females have paired vaginas leading forward and backward to open into the oviducts. After copulation each *A. duodenale* female produces about 25,000 eggs per day. *N. americanus* females produce about 10,000 eggs per day. These eggs have a characteristic appearance under the microscope, and can be readily identified in the stools.

Symptoms

The presence of larvae and young adult worms in the bowel may cause flatulence, sickness, diarrhea (for several weeks), vomiting, and abdominal pain, which is often worse after meals. The worms feed on blood, each adult taking in from 0.1–0.4 ml of blood every day. This is an insignificant amount in a light infection in which only 40 or so worms are present. In heavy infections of over 250 worms, however, there may be severe iron deficiency anemia, which may even cause death in children. Such anemia is especially serious in malnourished children; there are still areas of the world in which the infection rate with hookworms is virtually 100 percent.

The time between infection and the laying of new eggs is between four to six weeks, so symptoms in someone making, say, a short business trip to a tropical or subtropical country do not appear until after the traveler has returned home. Hookworm disease may not be suspected, which is why those who develop an intestinal infection should inform their doctor of their trip.

In the tropics hookworm disease is a serious problem for people who are already anemic, and the consequent fatigue and inability to fight off other infections may have fatal results.

Diagnosis

The definitive method of diagnosis of hookworm disease is the finding of the characteristic eggs in the stools. A sample is suspended in saline (salt) solution and a drop placed on a microscope slide. This is then covered with a slip of thin glass and examined.

Another feature of the infection that can help in the diagnosis is the tendency for worm parasites to cause a sharp rise in the numbers of a particular type of white blood cell (known as an eosinophil leucocyte). This cell contains many granules that readily take a red dye (known as eosin), and the cells can easily be identified after such staining. A rise in the number of eosinophils is known as an eosinophilia, and it is a feature of hookworm disease and other worm infections. The extent of the eosinophilia is usually a rough indicator of the number of worms present. It is greatest at the time of tissue invasion by the larval or adult worms, when the migration of infecting larvae is occurring. Once the infection is fully established, however, the blood levels of eosinophils tend to fall. These cells are also found in large numbers around worms in the tissues.

Treatment and outlook

Treatment entails taking a three-day course of tablets or powders of an anthelmintic drug, such as mebendazole. There is a 95 percent cure rate after the first course, but for very heavy infections the treatment must be repeated.

Hookworm disease is totally curable, but there is a risk of reinfection in tropical and subtropical climates, particularly where there is substandard sanitation.

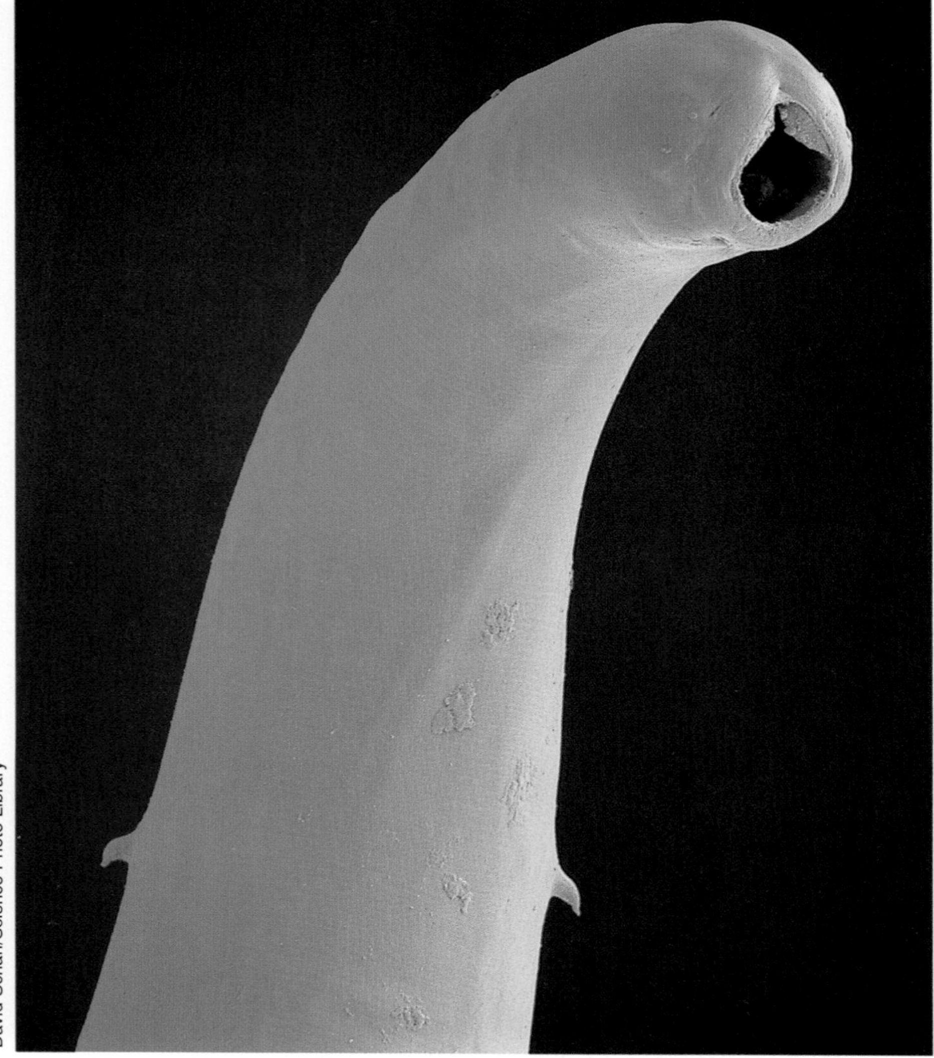

David Scharf/Science Photo Library

The head of a hookworm has toothlike structures that allow it to cling to the host.

Hormone replacement therapy

Q **I have read that HRT can protect women from heart disease. Is this true?**

A Yes. There is clear evidence that shows that HRT affords substantial protection against coronary heart disease in postmenopausal women.

Q **I believe that I can have estrogen by three monthly injections so that I don't have to keep taking tablets. Is this true?**

A Yes, it is possible to have implants of estrogen that can last for months.

Q **I have just started HRT, and my hot flashes are much better. How long should I continue the therapy?**

A You should continue for a year, and your symptoms will almost certainly improve. If you or your doctor decide that you should continue the treatment for more than a year, the risks and benefits need to be discussed.

Q **Can HRT keep a woman fertile after normal childbearing age?**

A No. Not only have the ovaries stopped producing the hormone estrogen, but they have also stopped producing eggs. HRT is designed to replace the estrogen but does nothing to replace the eggs, so it has no effect on fertility.

Q **Will HRT make sexual intercourse easier after menopause?**

A Yes. HRT certainly helps to lubricate the walls of the vagina, and it therefore makes intercourse easier. Many women also find that their desire for intercourse is increased on HRT.

Q **Is there any reason I should not have HRT?**

A Some women experience leg cramps, nausea, fluid retention, and tender breasts. There are also increased risks of blood clotting and cancers of the uterus and the breast.

Hormone replacement therapy (HRT), also known as estrogen replacement, aims to relieve the troublesome effects of female menopause by giving the body the estrogen no longer secreted by the ovaries. However, what are the pros and cons of this treatment?

Zefa

Hormone replacement therapy can help older women to enjoy an active life.

Hormones, which are usually given by mouth, are used to replace the body's natural hormones when one of the endocrine glands, the glands responsible for secreting hormones, has stopped working properly (see Endocrine system). However, there are two glands whose secretions eventually fail in all women, and these are the ovaries. The decline and eventual cessation of estrogen secretion by the ovaries, or to be more exact the ovarian follicles, is responsible for menopause (the change of life; see Menopause).

Estrogen and menopause

As the secretion of estrogen by the ovaries fails, usually between the ages of 45 and 55, there are a number of effects on the body, some of them obvious, others less so. First the monthly periods stop. Second the woman may experience the well-known symptoms of hot flashes and night sweats (see Hot flashes).

Without estrogen the mucous membrane lining of the vagina atrophies (becomes both dryer and thinner). The effect may be very uncomfortable, and may cause older women to lose pleasure in their sex life.

Osteoporosis (reduction in bone density; see Osteoporosis) tends to start after menopause, resulting in fragile bones that break easily. This fragility is related to the loss of estrogen activity, but there are almost certainly other factors involved that have not yet been identified.

The presence of estrogen in the blood of women before menopause seems to have the great advantage of protecting them from heart attacks, which are a common cause of death in men in the same age range. This protection is lost after menopause.

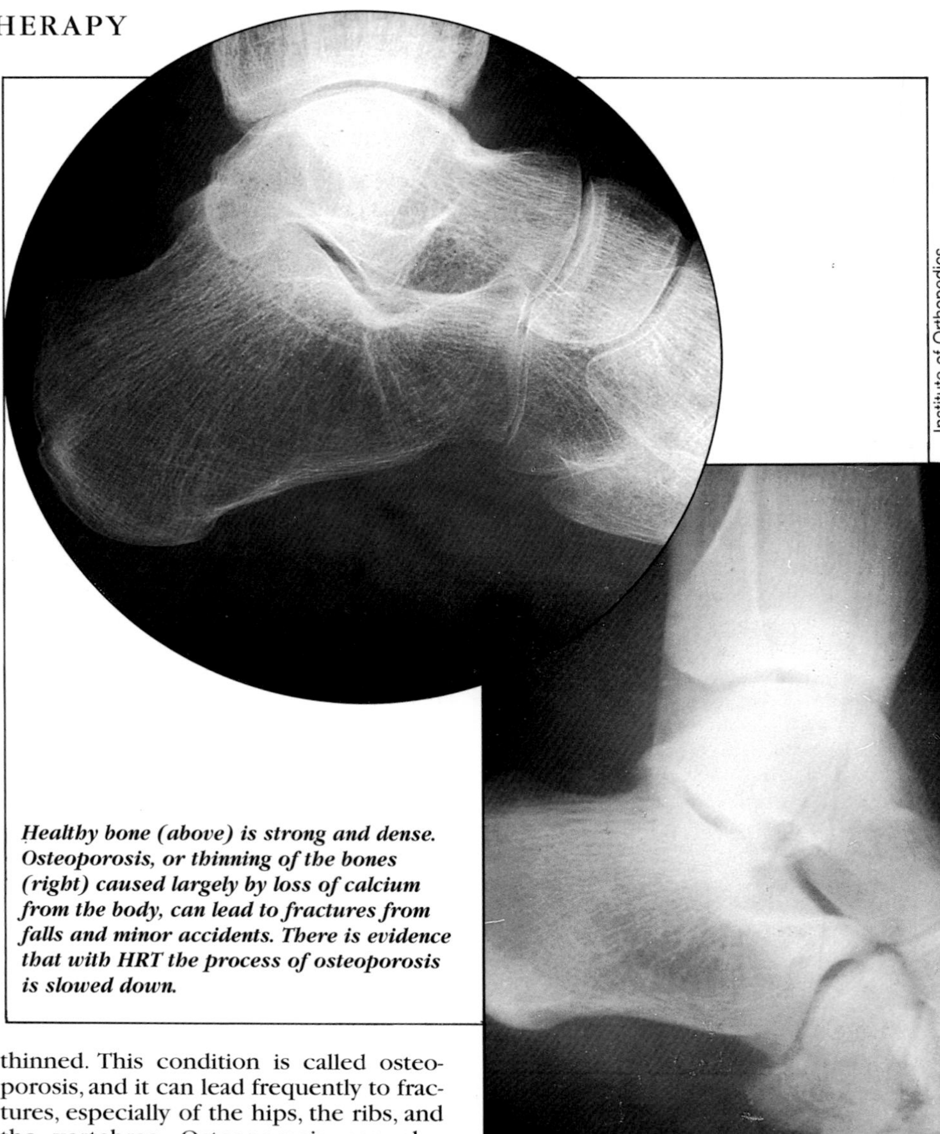

Healthy bone (above) is strong and dense. Osteoporosis, or thinning of the bones (right) caused largely by loss of calcium from the body, can lead to fractures from falls and minor accidents. There is evidence that with HRT the process of osteoporosis is slowed down.

Institute of Orthopedics

Benefits of HRT

Several symptoms associated with menopause can be relieved by HRT. The most widely recognized symptom is hot flashes, which occur in about 80 percent of women within three months of menopause. Among these women, 85 percent will experience hot flashes for more than one year, and 25 to 50 percent for up to five years.

Hot flashes will frequently occur at night and interrupt sleep; the resultant sleep deprivation can lead to chronic fatigue, depression, and poor concentration. The reason for hot flashes is not well understood, but they are known to be relieved by estrogen therapy in about 95 percent of cases. However, hot flashes are seldom so severe that they require therapy, and most women find that they stop in time without resorting to hormonal treatment.

Thinning of vaginal tissue is another symptom of menopause, which can result in poor vaginal lubrication, vaginal itching and burning, pain on sexual intercourse, and increased rates of urinary tract infections. These symptoms can also be relieved by HRT or by the application of estrogen-containing creams to the vagina.

Osteoporosis

Osteoporosis, or thinning of the bones, is a major problem in older women. Bone is a living, active substance; old bone is constantly reabsorbed and replaced by newly generated bone, which is dependent on the presence of estrogen.

When estrogen is deficient, bone continues to be reabsorbed but it cannot be generated adequately. This leads to an imbalance and the bones become thinned. This condition is called osteoporosis, and it can lead frequently to fractures, especially of the hips, the ribs, and the vertebrae. Osteoporosis can also cause pain (particularly in the lower back), loss of stature, and various deformities. Post-menopausal women are not the only ones to suffer from the condition: sedentary or immobilized people or patients confined to bed for lengthy periods may also contract osteoporosis.

There are approximately 150,000 hip fractures in the United States each year in women over age 65, many of which are extremely debilitating, and about 40 percent of women have osteoporosis of the vertebrae by age 80, often leading to vertebral fractures.

In addition to low levels of estrogen, risk factors for osteoporosis-related fractures include a history of fractures in a woman's mother, advanced age, and cigarette smoking.

The best way to prevent osteoporosis and related fractures is by hormone replacement therapy. Studies have shown that there is a 35 to 50 percent decrease in the rate of osteoporotic fractures in women who have taken estrogen for at least five years after menopause. It is not yet clear for how long women should continue HRT to derive optimal benefit in regard to osteoporosis.

Heart disease

Heart disease is the leading cause of death in women over age 60. Although menstruating women have remarkably low rates of heart disease, the incidence increases rapidly after menopause, suggesting a protective role for estrogen.

Several large studies have addressed the ability of HRT to protect against postmenopausal heart disease. The largest of these involved 48,000 women and found that those who took estrogen were half as likely to have major heart disease.

The reasons for estrogen's protective effect are not completely understood, but one contributing factor is its effect on cholesterol, a natural substance widely distributed in the body. Estrogen therapy can raise a woman's HDL (high-density lipoprotein) cholesterol ("good" cholesterol) and lower LDL (low-density lipoprotein) cholesterol ("bad" cholesterol). A high level of LDL cholesterol in the blood is implicated in some cases of atherosclerosis, in which the artery walls become thickened, resulting in reduced blood flow and possibly heart disease.

Questions have been raised as to whether estrogen is as beneficial when taken with another hormone called progesterone, which is how it is currently prescribed. Most studies on the effect of HRT on heart disease and cholesterol have examined estrogen therapy without progesterone. Recently, several smaller studies have demonstrated similar effects in women who take estrogen combined with progesterone. A large study of 1250 women published in November 1996 showed similar effects with or without progesterone in combination with estrogen.

Risks of HRT

HRT was first used in the 1970s but quickly went out of favor when many women on HRT were diagnosed as having endometrial cancer (cancer of the mucous membrane lining the uterus). Studies since that time have demonstrated that women taking unopposed estrogen (i.e. estrogen without progesterone) are more than twice as likely as women not taking the drugs ("control" women) to develop endometrial cancer.

However, this is not the case when estrogen is used in combination with progesterone, as it is prescribed today. Several studies have shown that there is no increase in endometrial cancer or precancerous lesions in women who take both estrogen and progesterone. Therefore, today's HRT usually consists of both types of hormone, except for those women who have had a hysterectomy (surgical removal of the uterus) and who therefore run no risk of developing endometrial cancer.

Breast cancer

Many women are reluctant to take HRT because they believe it will increase their risk of breast cancer. A 50-year-old woman has a 10 percent probability of developing breast cancer and a 3 percent probability of dying from it. The corresponding risks of heart disease for women are 46 and 31 percent, respectively.

It has long been hotly debated whether estrogens increase the risk of breast cancer. Many studies have addressed this question but scientists have not been able to draw any conclusions so far. About one third of these studies show a decreased risk of breast cancer in women taking HRT, one third show an increased risk, and one third show no difference.

However, most of the trials have shown that in women with a family history of breast cancer (i.e. breast cancer in a mother, sister, or daughter), HRT does in fact increase the risk of breast cancer, possibly by as much as two- or threefold.

Balancing the risks

How can a woman use this information to make an informed decision about hormone replacement therapy? Essentially she must weigh the risks and benefits for her. For example, if she has risk factors for heart disease, such as hypertension and high cholesterol levels, but no family history of breast cancer, HRT would probably be of benefit to her. However, if there is a family history of breast cancer, a woman may decide not to have HRT to avoid the possibility of adding to her own risk of breast cancer. HRT may well be the right decision for a woman whose mother had severe osteoporosis.

A woman also needs to consider which diseases she fears most. For example, many women are profoundly afraid of breast cancer and are unwilling to take any medication that may increase their risk of the disease.

The issue remains quite complex. In addition to considering the risks and benefits of HRT, a woman needs to be aware of the emotional impact of taking medication every day for the forseeable future. She may also wish to address the physical and emotional feelings she may experience during HRT.

For and against HRT

HRT can help to prevent

- Osteoporosis
- Heart disease
- Dryness of the vagina
- Hot flashes and night sweats
- Depression, weepiness, fatigue

Disadvantages of HRT

- Possible nausea, leg cramps, fluid retention, tender breasts
- Risk of thrombosis (clotting of blood in arteries or veins)
- Risk of cancer of breast and uterus

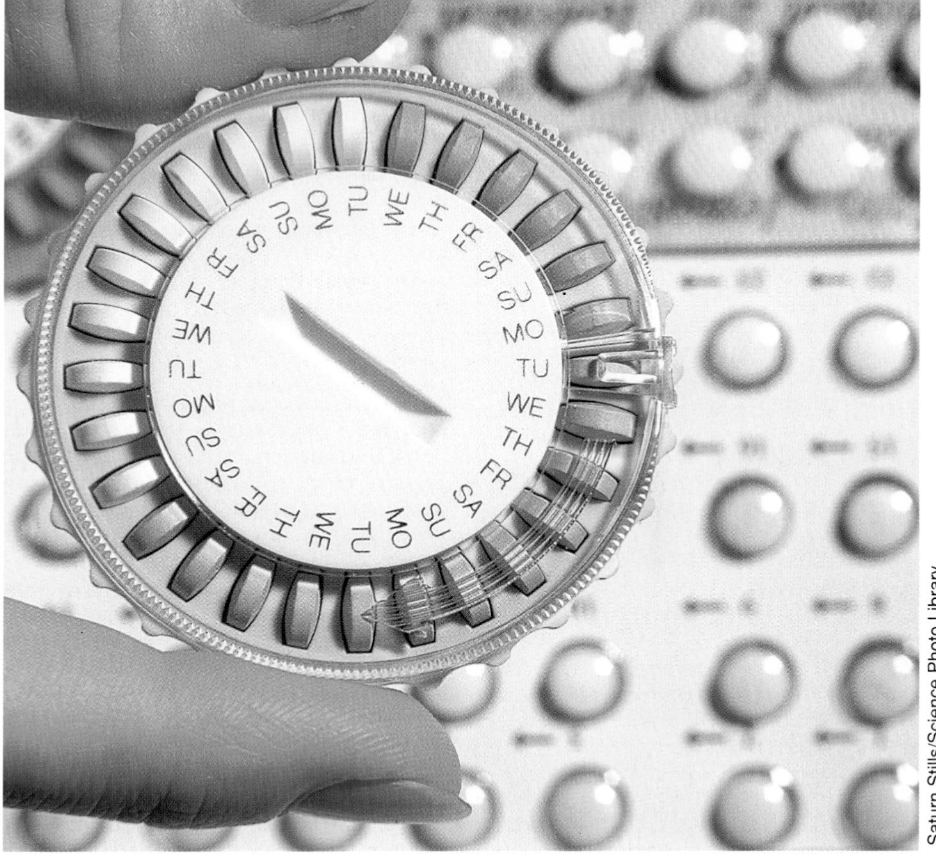

Saturn Stills/Science Photo Library

Combined estrogen and progesterone hormone replacement therapy involves taking one or other of the hormones in pill form daily on a monthly cycle that imitates the menstrual cycle. The pills are often dispensed in a circular pack marked with the days of the month.

Hormones

Q **My face is developing wrinkles. Can hormone creams really help before this goes too far?**

A Although some beauticians claim they do, there is a risk of dangerous side effects that outweighs any benefit. It is possible for the hormones to be absorbed by the blood vessels in the skin and carried in the bloodstream to other parts of the body. The best advice is therefore to avoid such hormone preparations. You can, however, take good general care of your skin with other commercially available creams.

Q **Is it true that morning sickness in pregnancy is caused by hormones?**

A Morning sickness is one of the early symptoms of pregnancy, and it coincides with a big upsurge in the ovaries' production of the hormone progesterone. This hormone helps to bring about physical changes in the uterus lining that prepare it for nourishing the fetus.

The effects of progesterone may produce feelings of nausea and also tenderness of the breasts. These discomforts pass when the placenta takes over much of the hormone production. This will occur about 14 weeks after the beginning of the pregnancy.

Q **Since having treatment for problems connected with her thyroid gland, my wife is much easier to live with. She is calmer and more even tempered. What could have brought about this total change?**

A The thyroid hormones, of which your wife was probably producing an excess, have many physical effects on the body and also emotional ones. Many people who produce too much find themselves in a state of jumpiness or overanxiety, and this is not helped by the fact that the sufferers know they are not reacting normally. Once this problem has been dealt with, not only are the physical symptoms relieved, but also the emotional problems are often brought back into balance.

The correct balance of hormones in the body is essential to physical health. So what are hormones, and why are they so important to a person's well-being?

The body's chemical messengers

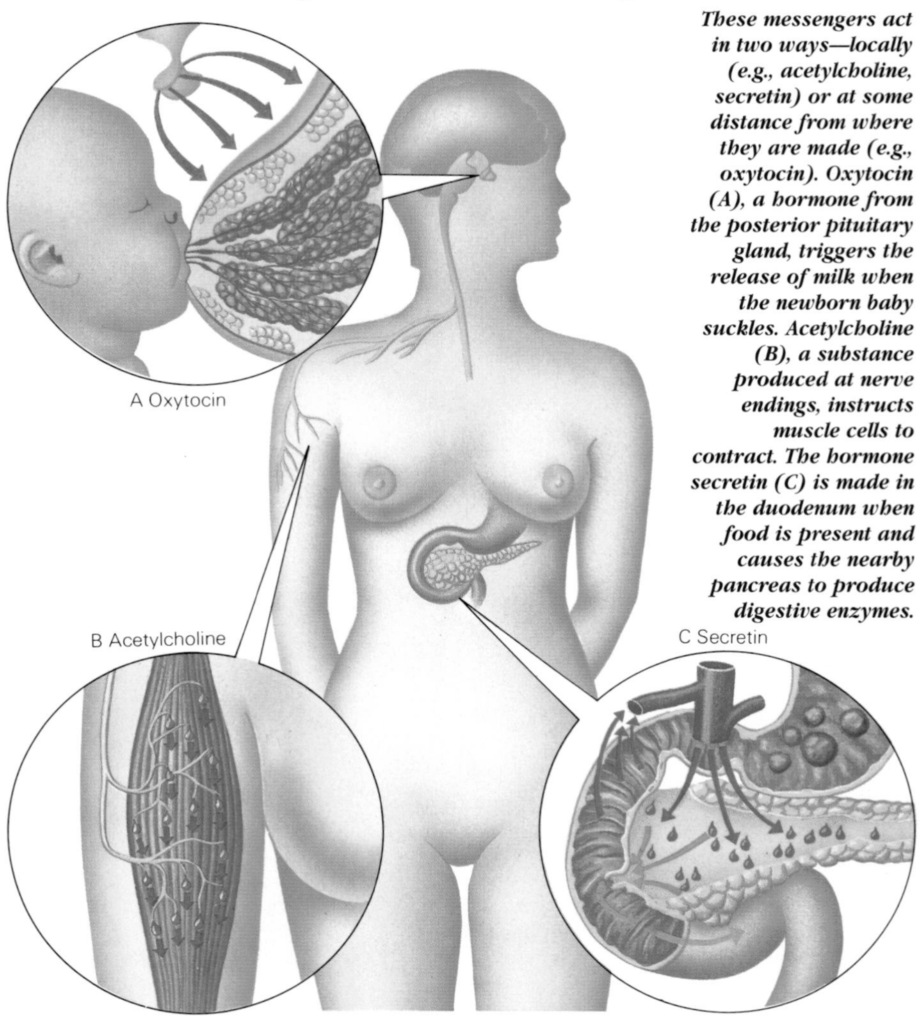

These messengers act in two ways—locally (e.g., acetylcholine, secretin) or at some distance from where they are made (e.g., oxytocin). Oxytocin (A), a hormone from the posterior pituitary gland, triggers the release of milk when the newborn baby suckles. Acetylcholine (B), a substance produced at nerve endings, instructs muscle cells to contract. The hormone secretin (C) is made in the duodenum when food is present and causes the nearby pancreas to produce digestive enzymes.

Hormones are the body's chemical messengers. Unlike nerve impulses, which carry information around the body in the form of electrical charges, hormones are made and released in one part of the body, and are circulated in the blood to other body cells (known as targets) where their effects are brought about. The organs largely responsible for making and releasing most of the body's hormones are the collection of ductless or endocrine glands, so called because they discharge their products directly into the blood and not via a tube or duct.

How hormones work

Compared with nerves, hormones tend to act slowly and also to spread their activity over a much longer time. Not all hormones act so slowly, but many of those that do are involved in fundamental activities such as growth and reproduction. In general hormones tend to be concerned with controlling or influencing the chemistry of the target cells: for example, by determining the rate at which they use up food substances and release energy; or whether or not these cells should produce milk, hair, or some other product of the body's metabolic processes.

Because they have the most widespread effects, the hormones made by the major endocrine glands are known as general hormones; these include insulin and the sex hormones. The body makes many other hormones that act much nearer to their point of production.

One example of such a local hormone is secretin, which is made in the duodenum in response to the presence of food (see Digestion). The hormone then travels a short distance in the blood to the nearby pancreas and stimulates it to release a flood of watery juice containing enzymes (chemical transformers) that are essential to the digestive processes.

Other examples of local hormones, or transmitters, include the substance acetylcholine, which is made every time a nerve passes a message to a muscle cell, to tell it to contract.

Proteins and steroids

All hormones are active in very small amounts. In some cases less than a millionth of a gram is enough for a task to be carried out.

Chemically hormones fall into two basic categories: those that are proteins or protein derivatives; and those that have a ring, or steroid, structure. The sex hormones and the hormones made by the outer part or cortex of the adrenal glands are all steroid hormones.

Insulin is a protein, and the thyroid hormones are manufactured from a protein base and are protein derivatives.

When each hormone reaches its target, it can only go to work if it finds itself in a correctly shaped site on the target cell membrane. Once it has become locked into this receptor site, the hormone does its work by stimulating the formation of a substance called cyclic AMP (adenosine monophosphate). The cyclic AMP is thought to work by activating a series of enzyme systems within the cell so that particular reactions are stimulated and the required products are made.

The reaction of each target cell depends on its own chemistry. Thus the hormone insulin triggers cells to take up and use glucose, while the hormone glucagon, also made by the pancreas causes glucose to be released by cells, and to build up in the blood, to be burned off as energy-giving fuel for physical activity (see Pancreas).

After they have done their work, the hormones may be either rendered inactive by the target cells themselves, or carried to the liver for deactivation, broken down, and either excreted or used to make new hormone molecules.

Controlling the system

The whole system of hormone production and use in the body is very complex and is often likened to an orchestra whose conductor is the pituitary gland. Lying at the base of the brain and connected to it by a short stalk, the pituitary gland is divided into two parts. The front portion (or anterior pituitary) secretes many hormones that exert their influence by stimulating other endocrine glands to release their products. These are the trophic (or stimulating) hormones. They include the thyroid-stimulating hormone that triggers the release of thyroid hormone; the adrenocorticotrophic hormone that stimulates the adrenal cortex to make cortisol (an important hormone that helps measure the function of the pituitary and adrenal glands; see Adrenal Glands); and the sex hormones—the follicle-stimulating hormone that controls the release of hormones by the ovaries and testes, and the luteinizing hormone that triggers the output of testosterone in a man and progesterone in a woman.

Other hormones made by the anterior pituitary exert their influence directly and include the growth hormone, which acts on cells throughout the body to promote normal growth and cell replacement. Prolactin stimulates milk production and inhibits menstruation while a woman is breast-feeding.

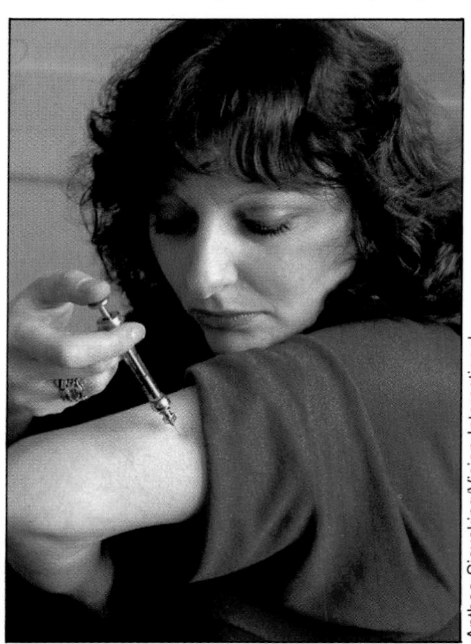

Anthea Sieveking/Vision International

Injections of the hormone insulin are used to control diabetes.

The posterior part of the pituitary gland makes two important hormones—the antidiuretic hormone, which travels to the kidneys and helps to maintain a correct fluid balance within the body; and oxytocin, which triggers the let-down of milk from the breasts once a newborn baby starts to suckle.

These posterior pituitary hormones are interesting because their release is directly controlled by nerve impulses generated in the hypothalamus (the part of the brain to which the pituitary gland is attached).

The only other hormones directly controlled by nerve impulses are adrenaline and noradrenaline, which are made and released by the inner medulla of the adrenal glands. It has been found, however, that there is an important, if less direct link between the nerve cells of the hypothalamus and the secretions of the anterior part of the pituitary. Special nerve cells in the hypothalamus make so-called releasing factors, which must act on the cells of the anterior pituitary before they can send out their hormones.

Effects on emotions

The strong link between the brain and the pituitary goes a long way toward explaining why there is such a definite connection between the hormones and the emotions. Many women find, for example, that if they are anxious or upset, the timing of their periods may be altered. The levels of the same hormones —estrogen and progesterone—that control the periods can also have profound effects on a woman's moods.

The sudden fall in hormone levels that happens just before menstruation is thought to play an important part in creating the symptoms of what is called premenstrual tension, while the high hormone levels midcycle are thought to give many women a sense of well-being. It may not be an accident that this is the time at which women are most fertile and most responsive sexually. However, hormone levels can also be altered by emotional factors. During sexual foreplay, for example, it is thought that levels of estrogen and progesterone rise as a direct result of pleasurable impulses to the brain. Conversely the very thought of having sexual intercourse with someone who is physically repulsive is, literally, a turn off because it inhibits hormone production.

At the end of her reproductive life—at menopause—a woman may experience great emotional ups and downs. This is partly because her ovaries stop responding to the follicle-stimulating hormone and so stop making estrogen and progesterone. These changes of mood may also be due to psychological factors. Similarly, the sudden withdrawal of hormones from the system after a woman has given birth may have emotional effects similar to those of menopause.

Hormones can be found in a huge range of preparations, from the contraceptive Pill to the ointments used to treat eczema (see Eczema). However, taking hormone preparations does have its dangers. If a doctor recommends these drugs, it is important that he or she also points out the potential dangers; they must be used with care and, of course, exactly as prescribed.

Hormone-related disorders and their treatment

Hormone	Disorder	Symptoms	Treatment
Growth hormone	Too little	Failure of growth, often linked with failure of sexual maturity	Administration of growth hormone (see Growths)
Growth hormone	Too much	Excessive growth in childhood leading to very long limbs (gigantism). In adults causes acromegaly—excess growth in skull, feet, and hands; enlarged larynx; deepening of voice; thickened skin	Treatment of gland by radiotherapy (see Radiotherapy) or by removal of part of gland (the other pituitary hormones may then need to be replaced)
Prolactin	Too much	Periods stop; breasts may produce milk and be tender; infertility	Drug treatment to reduce production
Antidiuretic hormone	Too little (or kidneys fail to respond to hormone produced)	Production of large quantities of very dilute urine (diabetes insipidus)	Synthetically produced hormone usually given as a nasal spray. Hormone then absorbed into blood
Thyroxine	Too much	Weight loss; large appetite; excess body heat; periods may stop in women. One form (Graves' disease) also causes popping eyes	Antithyroid drugs; radioactive iodine by mouth to destroy cells that are overproducing; surgery to remove part of gland
Thyroxine	Too little	Overweight; loss of appetite; general body swelling. Lassitude; constipation. In infants produces condition called cretinism, associated with failure of physical and mental development	Replacement of missing hormones at carefully controlled doses needed for life. It is now widespread practice in the United States to screen newborn infants for cretinism so that problem can be dealt with as soon as possible
Parathormone	Too much (usually due to tumor)	Passing a great deal of urine; kidney stones; indigestion; feeling of malaise	Removal of tumor
Parathormone	Too little	Muscular spasms; convulsions; lassitude; mental disturbance	Administration of vitamin D pills that mimic the action of the missing hormone
Hormones of adrenal cortex (e.g., cortisol, aldosterone)	Too much	Muscle wasting and weakness, leading to thin limbs but obese trunk. Fragile bones and blood vessels; purple stretch marks on skin. Diabetes; high blood pressure (Cushing's syndrome)	Drug treatment to block cortisone production. Where only one adrenal gland is involved, it is removed. Usually both are involved as a result of a tumor in the pituitary or elsewhere
Hormones of adrenal cortex	Too little	Faintness; nausea; vomiting; loss of weight; low blood sugar; increased pigmentation on skin (Addison's disease)	Cortisone pills taken for life at carefully controlled dosage
Adrenaline	Too much	Episodes of palpitations; fright; raised blood pressure; fast pulse, leading to permanently raised blood pressure; pale face or occasional flushing	Removal of adrenaline-secreting tumor (usually found in the adrenal medulla)
Insulin	Too little	High blood sugar that may lead to loss of weight, thirst, and passing large quantities of urine (diabetes mellitus; see Diabetes)	Diet is the cornerstone of treatment, with a reduction in the amount of sugar. This may be supplemented by antidiabetic tablets or insulin injections
Male sex hormones	Too little	Failure of growth and sexual development or, in adulthood, impotence and infertility	Replacement of missing hormones by monthly injections
Female sex hormones	Too little	Failure of growth and sexual development; menstrual periods do not start. Later in life, menopause (a normal event) due to reduced hormone levels	Replacement of hormones by pills

Hospices

Q My husband has been told he has terminal cancer. Could he be cured in a hospice?

A Unfortunately this is unlikely. Hospices are not designed for curing people; rather they try to make life easier for those who are beyond cure. What they can do is relieve the uncomfortable symptoms of illness and provide care and support. The change of atmosphere and gentle treatment gives many patients a new lease on life.

Q Is it difficult to get a very sick or terminally ill person a bed in a hospice?

A There are fewer hospice beds than there are people who might benefit from being in one. The doctor in charge has to decide which patients are in greatest need after consulting with their doctors and families. However, the pain-relieving therapy offered by a hospice can be provided at home, either by a doctor, a visiting specialist, or the patient's family.

Q I have the choice of sending my dying uncle to a hospital or a hospice. What is the difference between them?

A Hospices are usually more friendly and informal than hospitals. They are much smaller; most have between 12–20 beds. The staff have more time to spend on each patient, giving them relief from pain and support for emotional and spiritual problems. Hospitals exist to preserve life and cure disease, while hospices aim to relieve the suffering of those who have little or no chance of cure.

Q My father has cancer and is in terrible pain. Will a hospice be able to do anything for him?

A Yes. Hospices specialize in caring for patients suffering from cancer by using powerful painkilling drugs. They adjust the medication so that the patient remains alert and does not develop a tolerance to the drug. The drugs are then administered whenever the patient is in pain.

The goal of medicine is to preserve life, but unfortunately treatment cannot always be successful. Hospices are places where terminally ill patients are cared for and offered pain relief and emotional and spiritual support.

Caring for the dying and terminally ill calls for special skills. Hospices are designed to look after such patients, especially those suffering from cancer and for whom there is little or no real chance of cure but who still need medical treatment to relieve pain and to bring them physical and mental comfort.

What is a hospice?

Hospices are the oldest kind of medical institution, dating back to the time when monks and nuns cared for the sick and dying in cloister hospitals. Although they had little to offer in the way of healing medicines, they did provide spiritual guidance and simple human contact.

Hospices today do have powerful, effective medicines for relieving pain, and they also try to provide the kind of informal, friendly atmosphere that is often hard to find in a busy modern hospital.

Hospices are small: few have more than 30 beds. Almost all of the staff have a special vocation for this kind of care. They are trained not only to care for their patients' physical needs, but also to anticipate the emotional and spiritual problems and fears that confront people who know they may not have long to live.

Some of the longest established hospices are run by religious orders with the help of doctors, but hospices are now becoming part of the secular hospital plan. This new development has been due largely to the efforts of doctors who felt that modern medicine was not doing enough for those who could not be cured but needed special care.

The work of hospices is sometimes described as terminal care, though most medical staff prefer to describe it as continuing care. The reason for this is that not all terminally ill patients die in the hospice itself, and many of them live

Hospices are not depressing places; they give great comfort to those in pain.

Courtesy of St. Joseph's Hospice

longer than might have seemed likely when they first arrived.

Medical treatment

Most people admitted to a hospice are suffering from cancer and have had all the medical treatments available for combating the disease. Not all forms of cancer cause pain (in fact, only about 50 percent of cancer patients experience any pain), but hospice medical staff are specialists in pain relief. They give drugs that relieve physical pain while trying not to impair the patient's mental faculties. Pain specialists do not attempt to fight the disease itself; rather they try to check its most unpleasant symptoms.

Pain from the most severe cancer can be controlled with potent narcotic painkillers that relieve pain but do not make patients tolerant of the drug so that they need ever-increasing amounts. The dose of drugs is tailored to each individual patient's needs, and once the ideal dose has been achieved most patients are substantially, if not totally, pain-free and also still have their mental faculties intact.

Some are quite able to walk about, take part in occupational therapy, or even leave the hospice. Indeed some patients only come to a hospice for a short stay; once they have been stabilized on their treatment they can return home where they can easily be cared for by their family and family doctor.

A classic medication for relieving cancer pain is a mixture known as the Brompton cocktail, which is named after the Brompton Hospital in London where it was reputedly first devised. The cocktail consists of morphine, cocaine, and alcohol, and though this generally makes patients pain-free and carefree, it has largely been replaced by simpler medications, such as morphine and water, that cause less stimulation and mental clouding. Morphine causes constipation, so patients are often given a laxative medicine too. Should the morphine cause nausea, an antiemetic drug is given until the ideal dose of painkiller has been worked out by trial and error.

Similarly a patient who feels very anxious might be given an antianxiety drug. However, the general policy in hospices is to keep medication to the minimum necessary to insure that patients are comfortable.

Unlike some hospital wards where patients may have to ask for painkillers before being given them, hospice patients are maintained on just enough medication to prevent their pain recurring. This helps patients keep their minds off their disease because they are free from pain, and thus more relaxed, and less anxious.

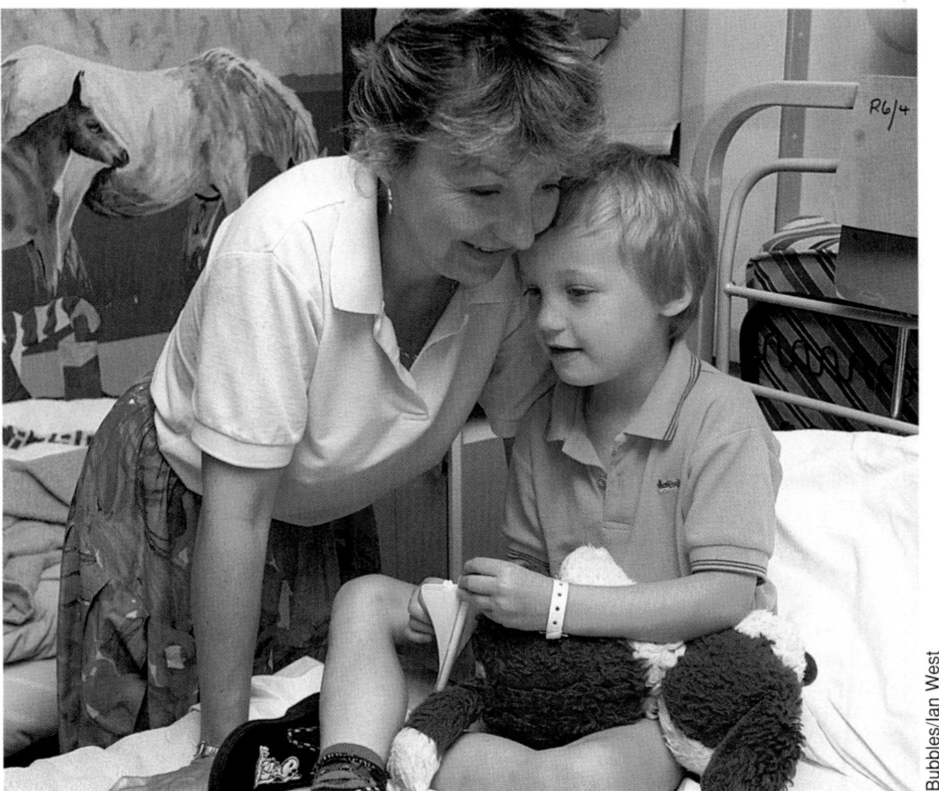

Bubbles/Ian West

Hospices care for terminally ill children as well as adults, and all patients are given expert nursing in a cheerful environment. The patient and his mother seen here are portrayed by models.

Emotional and spiritual care

As well as feeling physical pain, many patients are understandably distressed by the knowledge that they are soon likely to die. They may be worried about their family, they may want to settle their financial affairs, or they may be concerned about the effect bereavement will have on their spouse or children.

Hospice staff try to help their patients with this kind of mental anguish by making the atmosphere of the hospice as informal and homelike as possible and by being ready to spend time listening to the patients and talking with them. Although staff in a large general hospital might want to offer similar care, they often find it difficult because the work schedules and layout of the standard hospital give little opportunity for this kind of intimate contact with patients.

Families and children are encouraged to visit their relatives, and patients who do not have to be bedridden are encouraged to keep themselves active if they want. Hospice staff make an effort to meet and talk with a patient's family to discuss their relative's condition and to identify any hidden worries they may have. Again, this is what hospital doctors and nurses try to do, but it is much easier in a hospice because there are generally more staff and because emotional and spiritual care is made as much of a priority as physical care.

Not just a place to die in

Most patients who are admitted to hospices have no hope of being cured and are likely to die within months, if not weeks. Many do die in the hospice. However, a small number of patients return home to die. Some doctors prefer patients to do this if possible, not only because there is still a shortage of hospice beds, but also because patients often feel more comfortable in familiar surroundings. Once their drug regimen has been worked out, it is as easy for them to be looked after at home as in a hospice.

Although patients are beyond the help of surgery, radiotherapy, or anticancer drugs, some do seem to respond very positively to the hospice and thereafter to home treatment. A few patients live much longer than previously expected, and many who are physically and mentally exhausted by their disease and by the side effects of anticancer therapy will feel physically and mentally much better from the care they receive in the hospice. Those who do die in the hospice, on the other hand, will often feel happier for having been allowed to die with peace and dignity.

Hospitals

Q My eight-year-old brother is in the hospital unable to move because his broken leg is in traction. How can I help to relieve his boredom?

A The only answer is to make sure he is always busy. Schoolwork should continue in any case even if he is not in tip-top health, and it might be a good idea to ask a teacher from his school to visit him. This may help to convince him of the importance of not falling behind the rest of his grade. When he's not learning, he can be reading, drawing, or writing letters. There are also all the usual pastimes, such as board games, video games, checkers, and chess, that he could play with the other children. Hospitals usually have a supply of these, but they also make useful presents to a child in a hospital. If you really think your brother is becoming desperate, it's certainly worth having a word with the occupational therapist; staff have many patients to attend to, and they cannot notice every problem. Mention your brother's boredom in a tactful way, and he's bound to receive extra help in his efforts to keep occupied.

Q My five-year-old daughter has to go into the hospital for an adenoids operation and is absolutely terrified. How can I calm her down?

A Telephone the head nurse of the children's ward and explain the situation to her. She will probably invite your daughter to visit the ward before going into the hospital so she can see all the fun that goes on. You should explain to your daughter that hospitals are places where people get better and that although she may be away from you for a short time, you will visit her and there will always be a nurse to look after her. Try not to worry too much about her yourself, because even the most terrified children settle in eventually; sometimes there are tears when they have to go home. Lastly don't forget that hospitals are likely to have arrangements for mothers of very young or particularly upset children to actually live in for all or part of the child's stay.

Modern hospitals are more than just places where the sick are treated; they are universities, scientific research stations, laboratories, and welfare organizations all in one. So how are they organized?

The modern hospital, where a wide range of medical activities take place, is a comparatively recent development. It was not until the early 1800s that the larger hospitals began having medical schools attached to them and started to regard medical research as a necessary part of their work.

Until the 20th century hospitals were generally supported by charity. In the earliest forms (during the Middle Ages, between 800–1500) they were primarily religious institutions, more often than not attached to monasteries or convents and run by monks or nuns.

In the 18th century municipal hospitals operated by the civil authorities began to appear, particularly in the UK. In the US various small private hospitals were operated by churches and by individual physicians, but it was not until 1751 that the first public hospital, the Pennsylvania Hospital in Philadelphia, opened through the efforts of Benjamin Franklin and the Philadelphia physician Thomas Bond.

From the mid-19th century onward, the number of hospitals, particularly in the US, greatly increased, principally because of the discovery of anesthesia and antiseptic surgical techniques. During the 20th century the demand for hospital services expanded further with the spread of prosperity and the introduction of various forms of hospitalization insurance.

Types of hospitals

Early hospitals often grouped all patients in a single ward, regardless of disease. Notable exceptions were mental asylums, quarantine centers, and the tuberculosis sanitoriums that were developed in the late 19th century. Although advances in treatment have made most of these special institutions unnecessary, others have developed to treat certain types of patients or illnesses. Separate hospitals that take advantage of modern specialized techniques and equipment (and are usually associated with research and teaching institutions) exist for women and for children, and for the treatment of such disorders as cancer and eye disease. The modern general hospital may be an urban medical center with 1,000 or more beds and may comprise several specialized hospitals; or it may be a 10- or 20-bed hospital serving a community of a few thousand with general medical, surgical, and maternity care.

Modern hospitals can be divided according to their sponsorship as well as their type. The majority of hospitals in the US are short-stay, nonprofit institutions operated by community or religious groups. Public general hospitals are

Children are usually fearful of their first hospital stay, so it's best to bring along their favorite toys.

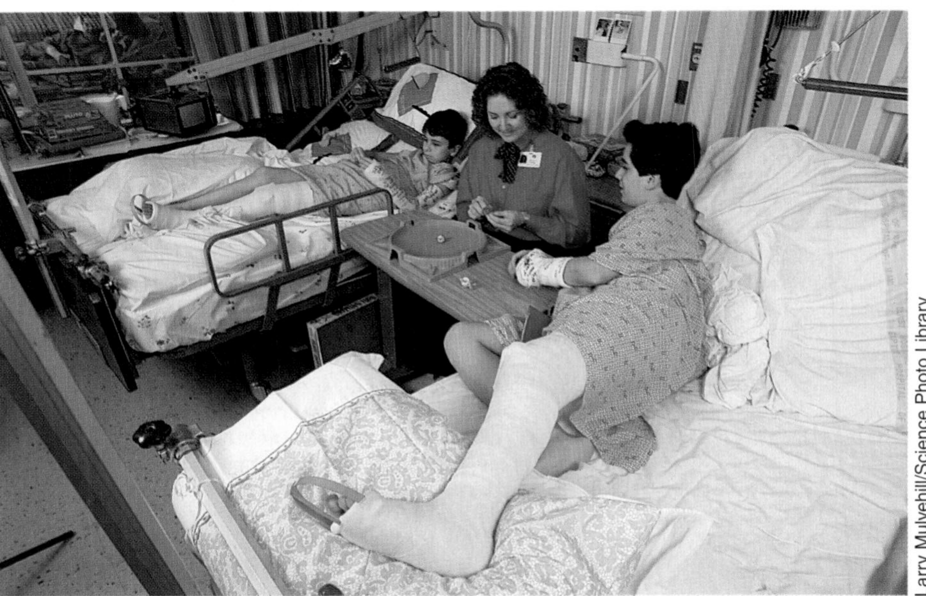

Larry Mulvehill/Science Photo Library

Q **I was dissatisfied with some of the treatment my mother recently received in the hospital. How should I go about complaining?**

A Write to the administrator of the hospital and ask for details of the complaints procedure. Every hospital has its own system for dealing fairly and efficiently with complaints, and the American Hospital Association has a Patient's Bill of Rights. Like any complaint yours will be best received if it is fully and carefully presented, with supporting evidence. It is always a temptation to name names or bring in personal feelings about people when making a complaint, but it's best to avoid this, confining your remarks to professional conduct.

Q **If a doctor comes to my bed and wants to examine me in front of a group of students, can I refuse?**

A You are describing a situation that mainly occurs in a hospital affiliated with a medical school. You ought to be informed before you go in that your case may be of interest for teaching purposes, and if you make no objection it is usually assumed that you will not mind students looking at you. However, doctors and nurses do understand that some people have mixed feelings about this, and if you object to being examined in front of students, all you have to do is say so, firmly but pleasantly. Doctors are used to this happening and you should not be treated any differently.

Q **I got fed up with being in the hospital after a recent minor operation, and so I discharged myself. Does this mean the hospital will no longer look after me?**

A No. If you discharge yourself against medical advice, the hospital will ask you to sign a form saying it is no longer responsible for your condition. This just means that if things do go wrong you cannot sue the hospital. However, if you became ill another time the specialist in charge of your case would usually agree to take you in.

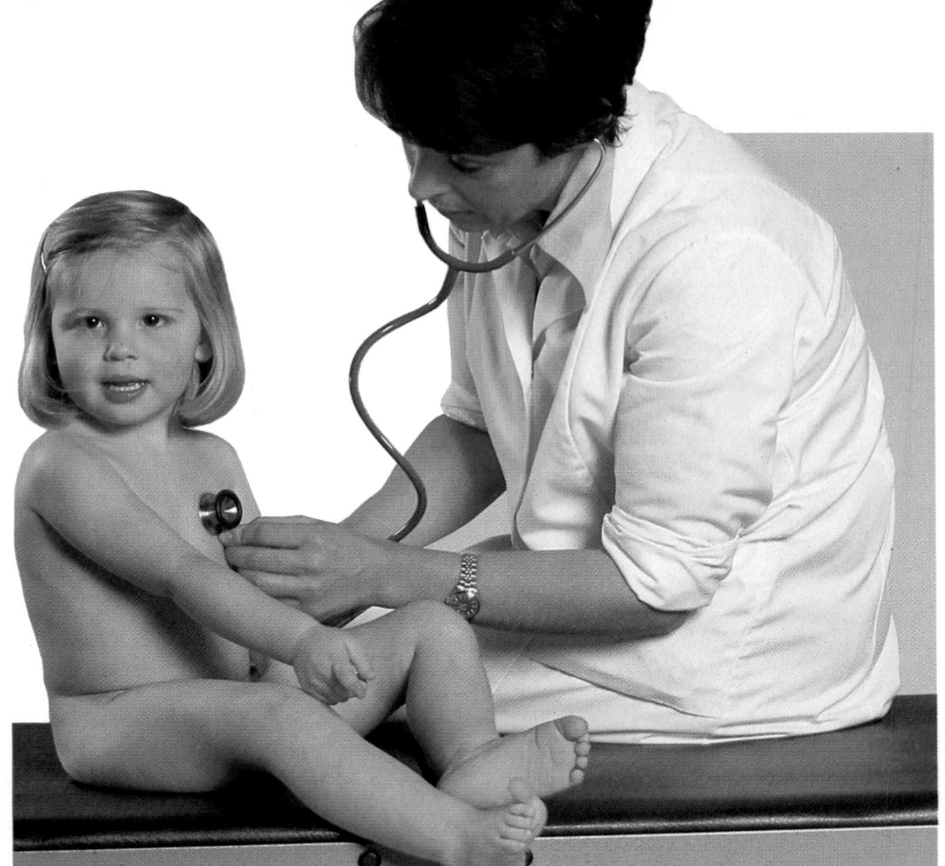

Transworld Features

To avoid worrying children about any tests, explain to them beforehand what the doctor is going to do.

operated by federal, state, and city governments, and a growing number of hospitals are operated as profit-making institutions.

Hospital facilities

In the 20th century the custodial care of chronic and incurable invalids has been undertaken largely by nursing homes; hospitals concentrate on caring for the acutely sick and injured and on outpatient services. A modern general hospital, even of moderate size, is a complex institution. In addition to its purely medical functions, the hospital must also provide shelter, heat, food, and other services to its patients and staff. A substantial area of a hospital building is given over to boiler rooms, laundries, kitchens, cafeterias, linen rooms, and storerooms. The medical services require space for laboratories, X-ray and other diagnostic equipment, a pharmacy, an emergency room, operating rooms, delivery rooms for obstetric cases, a pathology laboratory, nurses' stations, a morgue, and accommodations for various types of treatment, such as physical and occupational therapy. Patients' accommodations include wards, semiprivate (two to six beds) and private rooms, isolation rooms, nurseries, special nurseries for premature babies, and lounges and waiting rooms. The hospital administration must have offices for accounting and record keeping. Many sizable hospitals include schools of nursing that require a variety of dormitory, classroom, and laboratory accommodations.

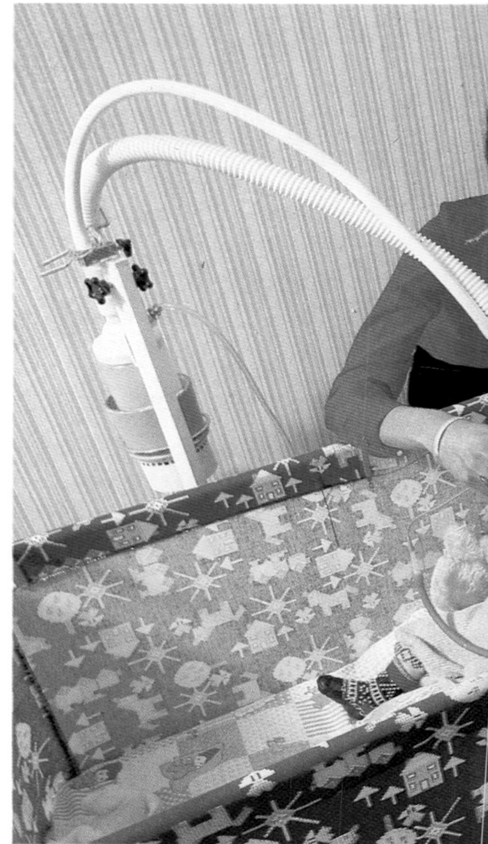

If your child is going into the hospital ...

DO
- Tell the truth; let the child know he or she will be in the hospital for a while
- Visit the child as often and for as long as possible
- Tell the nurses about special food likes and dislikes, and about any fears the child has
- Mention your child's nickname to the ward nurse
- Ask frequently about the child's progress; staff don't mind

DON'T
- Bring in candies and cakes without asking the head nurse
- Rush away without saying goodbye; sudden departures upset and frighten children
- Forget to bring the favorite toy, blanket, or book
- Pretend that painful treatment is going to be painless; the child may end up feeling betrayed

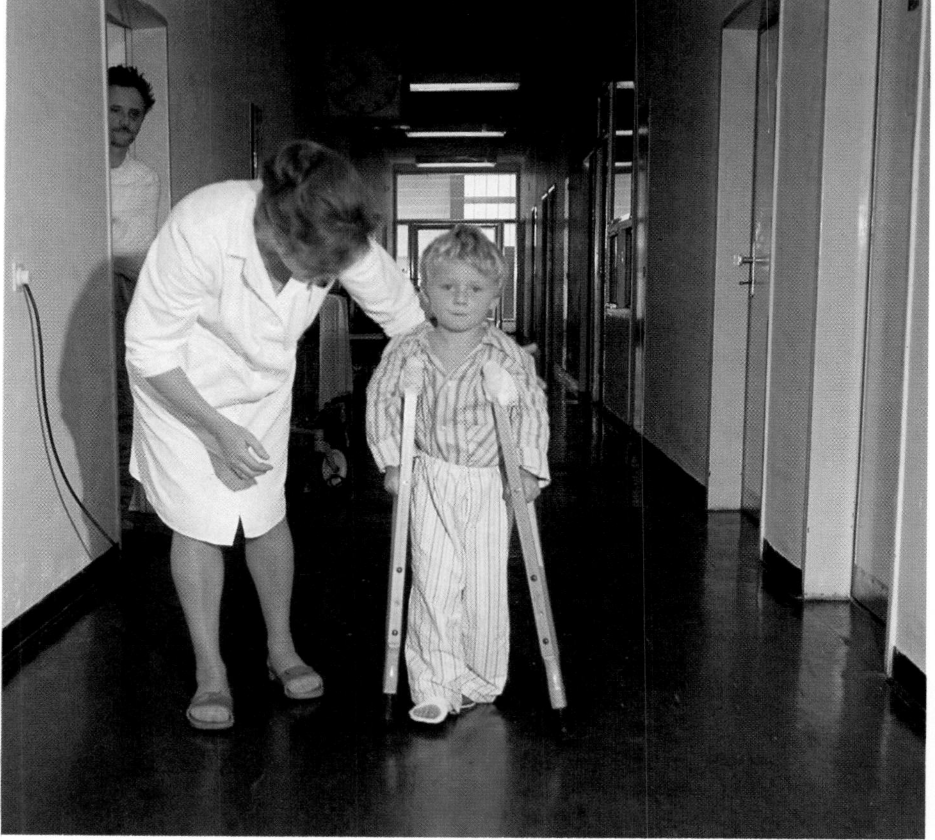
Zefa

Nurses are very helpful and understanding in their treatment of young patients who are on the road to recovery.

Transworld Features

Mothers whose babies are born prematurely are encouraged to take an active part in their care.

Hospital administration

Although hospitals can operate under a wide variety of administrative arrangements, the organization outlined below is typical of numerous nonprofit community hospitals.

The board of trustees of the hospital, made up of prominent citizens of the community, has general control of the hospital finances, policy, and operations. It also appoints members of the medical staff and the chief executive officer, who supervises all phases of the hospital's operation.

The medical staff in most hospitals is self-governing and is delegated by the board of trustees to supervise the medical services rendered to patients. The medical staff, through its executive committee or medical board composed of practicing physicians, makes recommendations on the quality of medical care in the hospital. Physicians practicing within the hospitals may be in private practice, affiliated with group practices, or on the full-time hospital staff. The chief of the medical staff has administrative responsibility for the medical staff and is in charge of selecting and training interns and residents during their postgraduate training. Frequently each specialized staff or department, such as that for surgery, obstetrics, or neurology, has its own chief.

The nursing staff, which is the largest group of staff in the hospital, is administered by a director who assigns nurses to various duties and who may also direct the hospital's school of nursing.

Hospital services

With the spread of hospitalization insurance in the US, and notably since the introduction of Medicare and Medicaid in the mid-1960s, demand for hospital services has grown at an unprecedented rate.The most dramatic increase has been in demand for ambulatory or outpatient care services. In 1962, 99 million outpatient visits were made to hospitals in the US; by the early 1980s the number had climbed to more than 270 million.

The increased need for outpatient services has stimulated community planning of health programs and new hospital-sponsored facilities, such as neighborhood health centers and satellite clinics to treat drug addiction and alcoholism. Within the hospitals new emphasis has been placed on social service counseling, ambulatory care, and formalized patient and community education programs, as well as on outpatient psychiatric care.

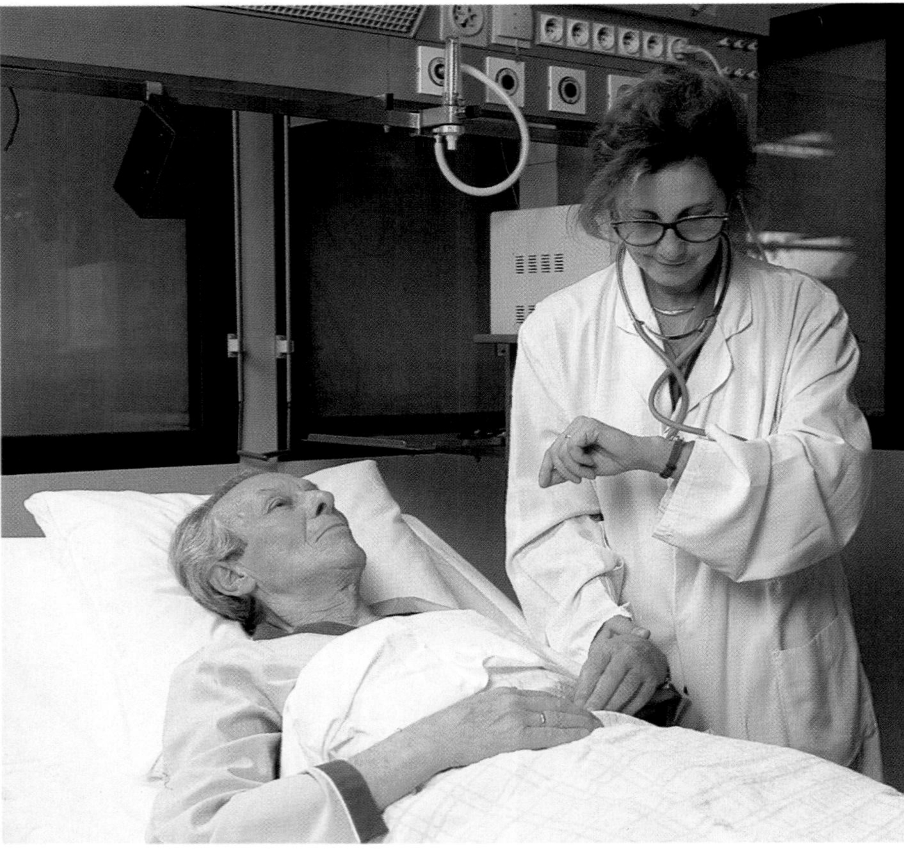

John Greim/Science Photo Library

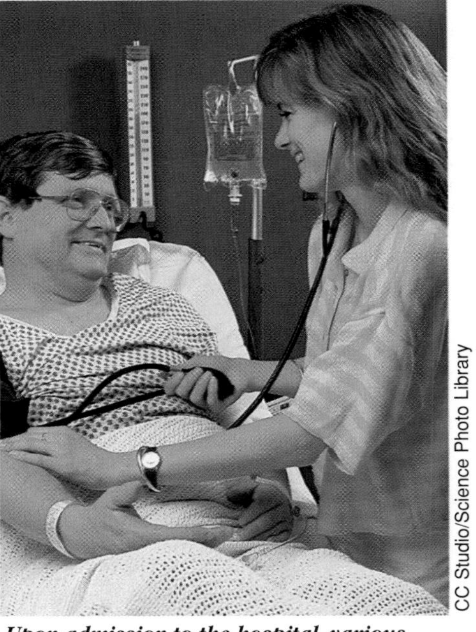

CC Studio/Science Photo Library

Upon admission to the hospital, various preliminary tests are performed. These include taking the patient's pulse (left) and blood pressure (above).

Hospital staff and their roles

The various ranks of doctors	The most senior hospital doctor is a department head. In the US this person leads a team composed of attending physicians, residents, and interns
Pathologists	Hospital laboratories help doctors with their diagnoses. Here samples of blood, urine, feces, and so on are examined. Specialties include hematology (blood); biochemistry (the chemistry of living organs); morbid pathology (causes of death); and surgical pathology (the study of tissues removed at operations)
Nursing staff	At the top of the ladder, a director of nursing oversees the activities of the entire nursing staff and assigns nurses to their various duties. Each ward in the hospital is run by a head nurse who supervises the work of the staff nurses. There may also be student nurses, as well as nurses' aides, either paid or voluntary, who generally help out. In some hospitals there are specially trained children's nurses
Therapists	The various therapists, each with different uniforms, carry out important backup treatments. Radiotherapists, acting on instructions from a senior doctor, operate the machines that give radiation dosages, usually to combat cancer. Physical therapists generally help patients regain fitness and use of limbs after, for example, severe strains or breaks. Occupational therapists help to retrain people for the activities of normal life and also try to provide mental stimulation for convalescent patients
Medical social workers	Trained social workers are attached to hospitals to deal with patients' social problems
Ancillary staff	House keepers, orderlies, technicians, engineers, and other vital staff

Hospices

Nowadays hospitals offer terminal care facilities to help patients and their families cope with death and dying. Following the ideas of the British physician Cicely Saunders, director of the St. Christopher's Hospice in London, the United States hospices attempt to help patients to die with dignity. The patient makes his or her own decisions about pain relief, can keep his or her possessions (including pets) nearby, is allowed to have visitors at any time, and can choose to die at home. Some hospices also offer teams of therapists who provide bereavement counseling to family members (see Counseling).

Rising hospital costs

Two main factors have caused recent hospital costs to climb at more than twice the rate of inflation. One is the cost of new equipment needed for organ transplants, renal dialysis, cancer radiation therapy, and many other rapidly changing treatments. Adding to the expense are modern diagnostic equipment and the burgeoning numbers of tests that physicians require for a complete diagnosis.

The greatest expense, however, is the huge staff needed to operate a hospital, which accounts for 54 percent of the costs. With a ratio of three or more staff members for every patient and close to 3.7 million full-time equivalent personnel, U.S. hospitals expended more than $324 billion in 1992, up from $153 billion in 1985. (The figure for full-time equivalent personnel includes all full-time employees and half the number of part-time employees.)

The cost of health care in the United States in general rose to $820 billion in 1992 and over 1 trillion in 1995. This figure constitutes 12.2 percent of the gross national product, making health care the largest single industry in the United States. More than 90 percent of all medical bills were paid for by insurance.

Inner-city hospitals

In the late 1970s and early 1980s, many municipal hospitals in the United States ran up large deficits and had to cut back services or in many cases close down. Their financial distress was due to the flight of wealthier patients to private hospitals, especially in the suburbs, and to more use of emergency units by the so-called medically indigent—those people who were above the income level for Medicaid but could not afford private insurance. In New York City, the hardest hit, the 17 public hospitals had an annual deficit of $125 million ($93 million from the inability to collect for outpatient services).

Statistics

By 1993 the American Hospital Association registered 6,467 hospitals, providing some 1,163,000 beds. Almost 36 million patients were admitted that year.

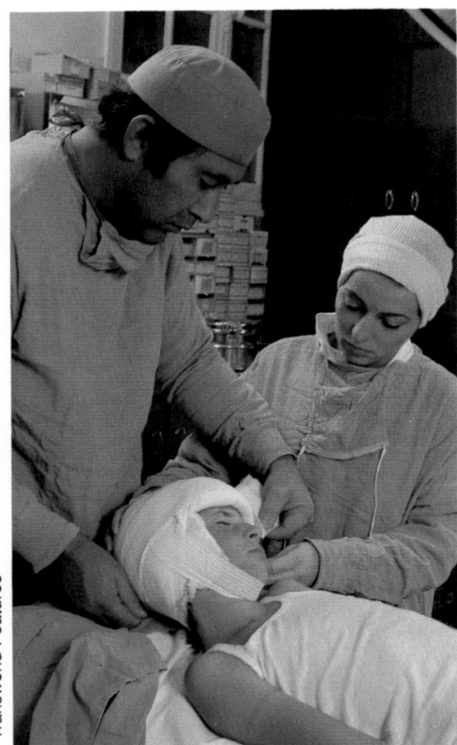

Transworld Features

Emergency rooms are equipped with modern equipment, and staff are prepared to deal with all kinds of crises.

A Patient's Bill of Rights

1. The patient has the right to considerate and respectful care.
2. The patient has the right to and is encouraged to obtain from caregivers relevant and understandable information concerning diagnosis, treatment, and prognosis. Except in emergencies when the patient lacks decision-making capacity and the need for treatment is urgent, the patient is entitled to the opportunity to discuss and request information related to the specific procedures and/or treatments, the risks involved, the possible length of recuperation, and the medically reasonable alternatives and their accompanying risks and benefits.
Patients have the right to know the identity of physicians, nurses, and others involved in their care. The patient also has the right to know the immediate and long-term financial implications of treatment choices, insofar as they are known.
3. The patient has the right to make decisions about the plan of care prior to and during treatment and to refuse a recommended treatment or plan of care to the extent permitted by law and hospital policy and to be informed of the medical consequences of this action. In case of such refusal, the patient is entitled to other appropriate care and services that the hospital provides or transfer to another hospital. The hospital should notify patients of any policy that might affect patient choice within the institution.
4. The patient has the right to have an advance directive (such as a living will, health care proxy, or durable power of attorney for health care) concerning treatment or designating a surrogate decision maker with the expectation that the hospital will honor the intent of that directive to the extent permitted by law and hospital policy.
Health care institutions must advise patients of their rights under state law and hospital policy to make informed medical choices, ask if the patient has an advance directive, and include that information in patient records. The patient has the right to timely information about hospital policy that may limit its ability to implement fully a legally valid advance directive.
5. The patient has the right to privacy. Case discussion, consultation, examination, and treatment should be conducted so as to protect each patient's privacy.
6. The patient has the right to expect that all communications and records pertaining to his/her care will be treated as confidential by the hospital, except in cases such as suspected abuse and public health hazards when reporting is permitted or required by law. The patient has the right to expect that the hospital will emphasize the confidentiality of this information when it releases it to any other parties entitled to review information in these records.
7. The patient has the right to review the records pertaining to his/her medical care and to have the information explained or interpreted as necessary, except when restricted by law.
8. The patient has the right to expect that, within its capacity and policies, a hospital will make reasonable response to the request of a patient for appropriate and medically indicated care and services. The hospital must provide evaluation, service, and/or referral as indicated by the urgency of the case. When medically appropriate and legally permissible, or when a patient has so requested, a patient may be transferred. The institution to which the patient is to be transferred must first have accepted the patient for transfer. The patient must also have the benefit of complete information and explanation concerning the need for, risks, benefits, and alternatives to such a transfer.
9. The patient has the right to ask and be informed of the existence of business relationships among the hospital, educational institutions, other health care providers, or payers that may influence treatment and care.
10. The patient has the right to consent to or decline to participate in proposed research studies or human experimentation affecting care and treatment or requiring direct patient involvement, and to have those studies fully explained prior to consent. A patient who declines to participate in research or experimentation is entitled to the most effective care that the hospital can otherwise provide.
11. The patient has the right to expect continuity of care when appropriate and to be informed by physicians and other caregivers of available and realistic patient care options when hospital care is no longer appropriate.
12. The patient has the right to be informed of hospital policies and practices that relate to patient care, treatment, and responsibilities. The patient has the right to be informed of available resources for resolving disputes, grievances and conflicts, or other mechanisms available in the institution. The patient has the right to be informed of the hospital's charges for services and available payment methods.

The collaborative nature of health care requires that patients, or their families/surrogates, participate in their care. The effectiveness of care and patient satisfaction with the course of treatment depend, in part, on the patient fulfilling certain responsibilities. Patients are responsible for providing information about past illnesses, hospitalizations, medications, and other matters related to health status. To participate effectively in decision making, patients must be encouraged to take responsibility for requesting additional information or clarification about their health status or treatment when they do not understand information and instructions.
Patients are also responsible for ensuring that the health care institution has a copy of their written advance directive if they have one.
Patients are responsible for informing their physicians and other caregivers if they anticipate problems in following prescribed treatment.
Patients should also be aware of the hospital's obligation to be reasonably efficient and equitable in providing care to other patients and the community. Patients and their families are responsible for making reasonable accommodations to the needs of the hospital, other patients, medical staff, and hospital employees. Patients are responsible for providing necessary information for insurance claims and for working with the hospital to make payment arrangements, when necessary.
A person's health depends on much more than health care services. Patients are responsible for recognizing the impact of their lifestyle on their personal health.

1992 by the American Hospital Association

Hot flashes

Q I am 51 years old and still having periods regularly. I have been having hot flashes for about four months. Is this the change of life?

A The change of life, or menopause, is when the periods stop. So you have not yet reached menopause. However, hot flashes sometimes start before the periods stop.

Q I am 56. My periods stopped three years ago, but I have never had any hot flashes. Am I normal or is something wrong?

A There is no need for you to worry; about 20 percent of women never have hot flashes during menopause.

Q I have been waking up the last few nights feeling hot and sweaty. Could this be hot flashes? I am 52.

A Yes, it could. However, if it has only been happening for a few nights, and you ache all over as well, it could be the flu or some other infection. If it continues see your doctor.

Q Can men get hot flashes as well as women?

A Yes, they can. However, although men may slow down in many ways as they age, they do not undergo a change of life in the same way that women do, so their hot flashes have another cause.

Q If women are told they should stop taking the contraceptive pill when they reach 35, why are they given the same hormones when they reach menopause?

A The hormones are not exactly the same, although they are similar. The Pill is about 10 times stronger than HRT, and can be dangerous to women over age 35 who smoke (see Oral contraceptives). HRT replaces hormones that the body no longer makes after menopause. The hormones in the Pill change the level of hormones the pituitary gland is already releasing.

The majority of women experience hot flashes during their change of life. Many suffer in silence, thinking there is little that can be done for them; in fact, medical help is available to help them cope with the problem.

Colin Ramsey/MC Library

Hot flashes can be acutely embarrassing to the sufferer, especially if the skin becomes moist or drenched in sweat.

The term *hot flashes* is used to describe a sensation of heat that is felt spreading all over the upper part of the body and up the neck to the face.

Hot flashes most commonly affect women at menopause (the change of life; see Menopause). In fact, about 80 percent of women experience hot flashes within three months of menopause, which may occur before the woman reaches the age of 40 or not until her late 50s. In most women menopause happens between the ages of 45 and 55, with the average age being 51.

There may be very little to see externally during a hot flash, although blotchy red patches may appear on the skin. Hot flashes may last from only a few seconds to half an hour, and sometimes the skin becomes moist or drenched in sweat. A cold feeling with some shivering may follow, and this is sometimes accompanied by dizziness, palpitations, and occasionally fainting.

A hot flash is unlike a blush, which produces a milder, warm feeling that spreads over the face and neck. Menopausal hot flashes range from those that are very mild and pass quickly to those that are very distressing and occur several times throughout the day and night. Sometimes they can become continuous over many hours at a time, sleep may be disturbed, and the sufferer throws off the sheets and blankets to try to cool down.

Causes

At menopause the ovaries cease the production of estrogen and stop releasing eggs. Menstruation (monthly periods) ceases and the body has to adapt to a new hormone balance.

Until menopause, estrogen is secreted by ovarian follicles in response to FSH (the follicle-stimulating hormone) that is released by the pituitary gland at the base of the skull. The follicles gradually run out of estrogen and wear out, so that when menopause is reached, the ovaries no longer contain any of these follicles.

Because there are no follicles to respond to the FSH, there is a much higher level of FSH in the body. This can lead to hot flashes because the small blood vessels in the skin become more easily dilated. This leads to an increase in skin temperature, and at times a reddening of the skin. Overstimulation of the sweat glands may also occur.

However, although changes in hormone levels are thought to be responsible for hot flashes, it is possible to have them with perfectly normal hormone levels for several months, or even years, before the periods begin to alter.

Other women may have a hormone deficiency and yet have no hot flashes. There is a 20 percent possibility that the hot flashes will persist despite HRT (see Hormone replacement therapy). HRT may be used to correct other symptoms due to menopause, such as dryness of the vagina, which makes sexual intercourse painful and difficult.

Some women notice that some forms of stress bring on hot flashes. They are likely to be more irritable and to get upset and cry more easily than usual. Simple day-to-day tasks that previously caused no problem become difficult and can even lead to a sense of confusion.

Other causes

There are other, very different causes of hot flashes, which can occur in men as well as women.

The feeling of turning hot and cold with sweating and shivering, especially during the night, occurs with many infections that produce a fever.

Another less common cause of hot flashes is a skin complaint called rosacea, which produces a ruddy discoloration of the forehead, nose, cheeks, and chin.

Occasionally a growth, called a carcinoid tumor, can occur in the stomach or intestine. The tumor produces excessive amounts of a hormone called serotonin, which affects different body organs and causes symptoms such as asthma, loud rumblings in the abdomen, and diarrhea, as well as hot flashes that affect the whole body, including the arms and legs.

Treatment

Some women's menopausal symptoms are very mild and transient. They require no treatment other than encouragement to accept the natural changes that are taking place and to watch their weight. A reasonable amount of exercise helps to safeguard good health, particularly at the time of menopause. Walking, swimming, gardening, and similar activities are all very beneficial to the system.

However, if the flashes are more severe and frequent, a woman should see her doctor so that a proper diagnosis can be made and treatment can be given if necessary. The doctor may refer her to a gynecologist for a specialist opinion if he or she is in doubt about the treatment.

Hormone replacement therapy may be considered. Hormones are usually given to replace the body's normal ones if one of the glands responsible for secreting hormones stops working. During menopause estrogen is no longer being produced, and if this is causing problems, such as severe hot flashes, the woman may be given replacement estrogen or progesterone.

A doctor may prescribe a progesterone pill, an estrogen patch, or a combination of both. Sometimes estrogen cream is applied to the vagina, but this may not control severe hot flashes.

A doctor may advise against hormone replacement therapy if the woman has a family history of cancer of the uterus or of the breasts. There is still debate over whether estrogens increase the risk of breast cancer, and studies so far have not been able to provide any conclusions. However, hormone replacement therapy has been shown to increase the risk of breast cancer in women whose mother, sister, or daughter have suffered from the disease.

It is now thought that it is safer for the two hormones, estrogen and progesterone, to be combined in one treatment (see Hormone replacement therapy). Several studies have shown that there is no increase in cancer of the lining of the uterus (called endometrial cancer) in women who take take both estrogen and progesterone.

The drawback of the cyclical use of these hormones is that it leads to the shedding of the lining of the uterus each month, and so it may not be acceptable to a woman who has stopped having periods and now faces the prospect of having them again in exchange for losing the hot flashes. However, when both hormones are taken every day, most drawbacks are limited to spotting for about a year.

Coping with hot flashes

- When you feel a hot flash coming on, it is best to stop whatever you are doing and sit down quietly. If the hot flashes are very mild and do not last long, there may not be time to do anything more. If, however, you are one of the unlucky ones whose hot flashes are severe and last more than a minute or two, undo any tight clothing if possible, especially a high collar. If you are in a hot room or with a lot of people, try to get out into the fresh air
- If you are driving a car or working with dangerous machinery and your hot flashes tend to make you feel faint or dizzy, you should stop the car or move away from any moving parts of the machine
- The discreet use of a small fan might be helpful, unless this would make you feel more embarrassed. It is worth remembering that unless your hot flashes are severe, it is unlikely that anybody else will notice your discomfort, since the face seldom looks as hot and wet as it feels to you
- If you are very uncomfortable at night, take a warm shower or bath before going to bed. Use only the lightest sheets and blankets and avoid nylon material altogether
- If night hot flashes are severe even after hormone replacement treatment, tell your doctor. He or she may be able to prescribe a suitable sedative to take when you go to bed
- Tell your partner how you are feeling so that he can understand your problem; he may be able to help you to relax

Outlook

It is difficult to predict just how long hot flashes will continue, because various factors are involved and they differ from one woman to another. Usually hot flashes will diminish in their severity and number within two or three years of menopause (from the time the periods stop completely).

The treatment time for the use of hormone replacement therapy is initially one year. As long as there is medical supervision, with follow-up examinations and tests, there is little risk of serious side effects and symptoms should diminish considerably during this time.

Occasionally hot flashes in women persist into their 60s. More intensive treatment can usually bring even these under control, although it may be necessary to continue with the hormone replacement therapy for years if it is considered suitable for the patient.

Humidifiers

Q I am suffering from headaches after recently starting work in a new office. The air is very dry: could the headaches have anything to do with the humidity level?

A The lack of moisture in the air in your new office may be causing your eyes, nose, and mouth to dry up, and this could lead to headaches. However, headaches can be caused by many things, so if they persist, consult your doctor. If you want to check whether the atmosphere at work is too dry, the relative humidity can be measured by an instrument called a hygrometer, which isn't expensive. At 68°F (20°C), which is the usual office temperature, the relative humidity should be around 50–60 percent.

Q My home has central heating and the air seems very dry. Will it help if I have lots of plants, since I have heard that they increase the amount of humidity in the air.

A Plants need water as much as animals do. So although a warm, dry atmosphere will make leaves release water into the air by evaporation, the plant will need this water to be replaced if it is to survive long. Green plants may therefore make a room look tropically humid, but they have to be regularly watered if they are to survive in a centrally heated room. Dry air can be harmful to some broad-leaved tropical plants that need to have their leaves kept moist. Whether or not you choose to keep plants, you should keep a saucer or bowl of water next to the radiator to increase the relative humidity of the air.

Q I have an open fireplace that I sit in front of every night. My skin is very dry and chapped. What can I do about it?

A The air near a fireplace gets very dry because of the intense heat. It is not a good idea to sit directly in the line of the heat; your skin is dried out because moisture is being sucked from it. Move back, spray a mist of water into the air, and use a moisturizer.

Although it is not possible to change the outside air if it is too dry or too humid, humidifiers can help to insure that the air in homes and offices is just right. Their use also helps to maintain general health.

Water is an essential ingredient of the air that we breathe. We cannot see it or smell it, but it makes up about 4 percent of the atmosphere. Too much or too little water in the air can play havoc with our health and well-being.

How much moisture?

The ideal humidity for human health and comfort is between 45-65 percent of the maximum amount of moisture the air can hold at a particular temperature. This is what is known as relative humidity.

The warmer the air becomes, the greater its capacity for holding water. So in hot, dry climates or in overheated rooms where the relative humidity falls much below the ideal because the air is thirsty and draws moisture from the body, a person may suffer from dry eyes, dry mouths, sore throats, headaches, and chills. In a very hot, tropical climate, on the other hand, where the relative humidity may be as much as 95-100 percent, a person may feel uncomfortable because the air is so laden with moisture that it cannot evaporate the perspiration from the skin. Because perspiration is the body's way of maintaining a constant temperature, the body quickly becomes overheated.

An electrically operated humidifier will prevent the air from becoming too dry.

Controlling humidity levels

There is obviously not a lot that can be done to change the humidity of the outside air if it does not suit us. However, a great problem today, when many people live and work in artificially heated environments, is to keep indoor humidity at the right level.

Central heating and air-conditioning—if they are not supplemented with some kind of humidifying process—dry out the air and can easily bring the relative humidity down to undesirable levels. People who work in offices or factories where the relative humidity is less than 50 percent tend to suffer from more colds and flulike symptoms. People who suffer from asthma or bronchitis often feel much worse; they usually feel best when the relative humidity is about 65 percent. Rheumatic sufferers may appreciate dryer air with a relative humidity of around 40-50 percent.

How humidifiers work

There is a wide range of humidifying equipment, but the most simple homemade device is a saucer of water placed near a fireplace or a heater. Small water containers, which can be hung unobtrusively over radiators, can be purchased. There are also electrically operated humidifiers that use a fan to draw dry air in and charge it with water stored in a tank in the machine. This type of humidifier can sometimes be attached to the domestic water supply so that the tank does not have to be refilled by hand.

There are also humidifiers built into air-conditioning and heating systems. Once the air has been filtered and heated or cooled, it is passed through or over water. A device called a humidistat controls the amount of water that the air can take up.

For excessively humid environments dehumidifying machines can be used to dry the air. They work by refrigerating the air; the air cools, it loses its capacity for holding water and the water condenses in the machine. In the home the simplest way to reduce high humidity is to increase the air temperature and encourage the air to circulate with the help of a fan or a convection heater put on cold.

Huntington's disease

Q My grandfather is mentally active and enjoys playing chess. However, he sometimes makes involuntary twitching movements. Is it possible he has Huntington's disease?

A Probably not. Although the onset of Huntington's disease is gradual, it usually begins between the ages of 35–50. Also one of the characteristic features that his family would soon notice is mental deterioration. It sounds as if your grandfather is in the peak of mental health.

Q Should all the relatives of a person who has Huntington's disease be tested to see if they will develop the condition in later life?

A It is difficult to answer this question. Individual advice from a skilled medical geneticist is needed in each case (see Genetic Counseling). A positive test result in a young relative of a sufferer means that he or she will develop the disease. Such knowledge could be devastating to a young person, and many people would simply prefer not to know. If a member of the family wants to have a child, however, a test is very important. The geneticist will probably require samples from other members of the family, even if they are not told the results, so that a pattern of inheritance can be established and an accurate risk assessment can be made.

Q I am trying to get pregnant, and my family has a history of Huntington's disease. How is prenatal diagnosis of this condition carried out?

A At about the fourth month of pregnancy, tiny samples of fetal tissue are removed from the womb using the technique called chorionic villus sampling (CVS). Special tests on the sample, which take several days to perform, can identify the DNA on the fourth chromosome. If the baby is found to carry the gene for Huntington's disease, the mother may be offered a termination of the pregnancy if this is a legal option. You should ask your doctor for information on genetic counseling.

Huntington's disease is a rare hereditary disorder that progressively affects the nerves. Its symptoms do not appear until middle age, and there is no cure.

Huntington's disease (also called Huntington's chorea) is an autoimmune condition affecting the nervous system that causes involuntary twitching movements of the arms, neck, and face. Walking is also difficult, and because the brain is affected, there may be speech defects and severe emotional disturbances. Loss of memory and dementia usually follow. Little can be done to treat the symptoms, and there is no way of halting the progress of the disease, which inevitably leads to total incapacity during its terminal stages.

Hereditary defect

The cause of Huntington's disease is a defective gene on the fourth chromosome. The gene is dominant, so if a parent has the disorder there is a 50/50 chance that each of his or her children will have the disease. Symptoms of the disease do not appear until middle age, but now that the gene defect has been identified it is possible to test children and young adults with a CT scan (see Scans) to see if they are carriers. The test is 95 percent accurate, and a positive result means that the person will develop the disease in later life.

Once symptoms begin to appear, the patient gets progressively worse over a period of about 15 years. Among the distressing aspects of the disease are the mood changes in the patient, which resemble manic-depressive psychosis. Deep depression can lead to suicide in up to one in ten cases. Antipsychotic drugs, such as the phenothiazines, may be used during the manic phases to minimize violent behavior, and antidepressants, such as the tranquilizer imipramine, are used to combat depression. Patients often need care in a psychiatric hospital in the later stages of the disease.

If either member of a couple has a history of Huntington's disease in the family, he or she should seek genetic counseling before deciding to have children.

Daily Telegraph Colour Library

Hydrocephalus

Q My baby's head is an odd shape, as if the top of the skull were coming up to a point. Could this be a sign that he has hydrocephalus?

A This does not sound like the shape of head found in hydrocephalus. Often odd head shapes have no special significance, but occasionally it may be that some of the bones of the skull have joined together too early. A particularly pointed skull may result from this. It is most likely that as long as your child's head is of normal size and he has no other symptoms, then all is well. However, if his head is growing very fast and the forehead is very large in relation to the rest of the face, then a doctor should see him.

Q I had meningitis when I was a child. Is there a danger that I could develop hydrocephalus later in life?

A Hydrocephalus following meningitis will develop soon after the meningitis if it is going to develop at all. If some years have passed since your attack of meningitis, it is unlikely that you will get any more trouble from it.

Q My five-year-old boy is bright and lively and seems perfectly well, but his head is large. Could he possibly have hydrocephalus?

A No. It is not likely that he has hydrocephalus unless there was an increase in his head size when he was younger. Some people just have bigger heads than others. The important thing is that your son sounds extremely healthy.

Q I have one child with hydrocephalus. What is the chance of having another child with it?

A If you have had one child with hydrocephalus or spina bifida (see Spina Bifida), the chance of having another child with one of these defects increases to about one in 40. After two such children the chance increases yet again to one in eight and after three the chance is one in four.

The word* hydrocephalus *means, literally, "water on the brain," and it refers to an excessive buildup of fluid in and around the brain. With modern surgical techniques very effective treatment is now possible.

Cerebrospinal fluid is a clear, watery fluid that flows around the meninges (the membranes that cover the brain) and spinal cord and through the brain's ventricles (cavities). The fluid has a cushioning effect that helps to protect the vital brain tissue from injury. The fluid is made continuously from the blood by specialized cells of the choroid plexus in the brain ventricles. Unlike the heart ventricles, which have names, the brain ventricles have numbers. The numbering goes from the topmost to the bottom, and the first and second ventricles (known as the lateral ventricles) are the largest (see Brain).

The fluid flows from the lateral ventricles through a narrow hole into the small third ventricle and then through an even narrower channel, the cerebral aqueduct, into the slightly wider fourth ventricle. From here it escapes through holes in the roof of the ventricle into the fluid-filled spaces (cisterns) that surround the brain stem at the base of the brain. The fluid then flows up over the top of the brain (the cerebral hemispheres) and is reabsorbed by special outgrowths, called arachnoid villi, on the arachnoid meninges, one of three membrane covering the brain (see Meningitis).

Hydrocephalus, which is a rare condition, occurs when something interferes with the circulation of the cerebrospinal fluid. The effect this has on children depends on whether the bones of the skull have joined together before the pressure inside begins to rise.

In young children, whose skull bones have not joined together, the increased pressure forces the bones apart and the head increases in size. In older children and adults, the increased pressure cannot do this and the expanding fluid presses on the brain, causing progressive damage.

Causes

Various conditions affect the circulation of cerebrospinal fluid (see Spinal Cord). Some conditions are congenital (present at birth) though not necessarily inherited. Other causes may be acquired later in life.

Hydrocephalus is divided into obstructive hydrocephalus, where there is something that obstructs the circulation of the fluid, and communicating hydrocephalus, where there is something wrong with the reabsorption of the fluid by the arachnoid membrane.

Obstructive hydrocephalus

The more common variety of the disease is obstructive hydrocephalus, and it may occur in either adults or children for a host of reasons.

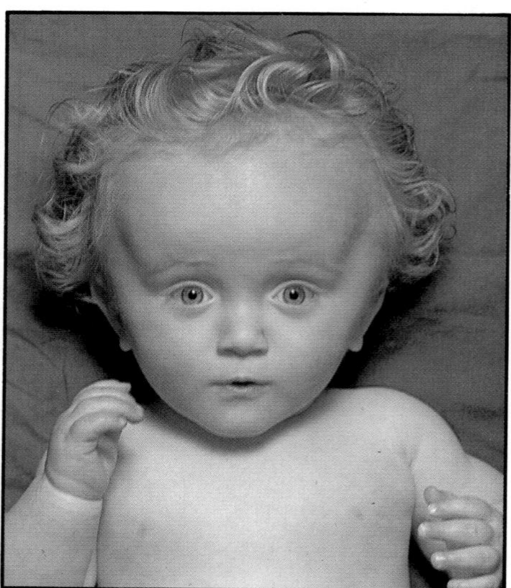

This child suffering from hydrocephalus has a very distinctive skull shape with a prominent forehead and a small face in relation to the rest of the head.

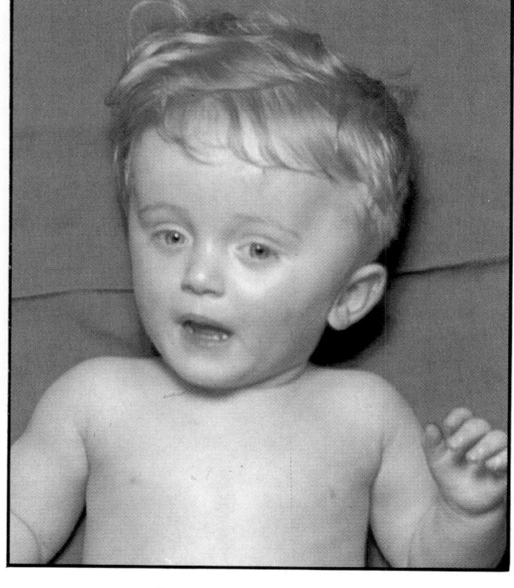

After treatment to drain off the excess fluid in the brain, the child's head has returned to a normal size, with the face in proportion to the rest of the head.

Arnold-Chiari malformation

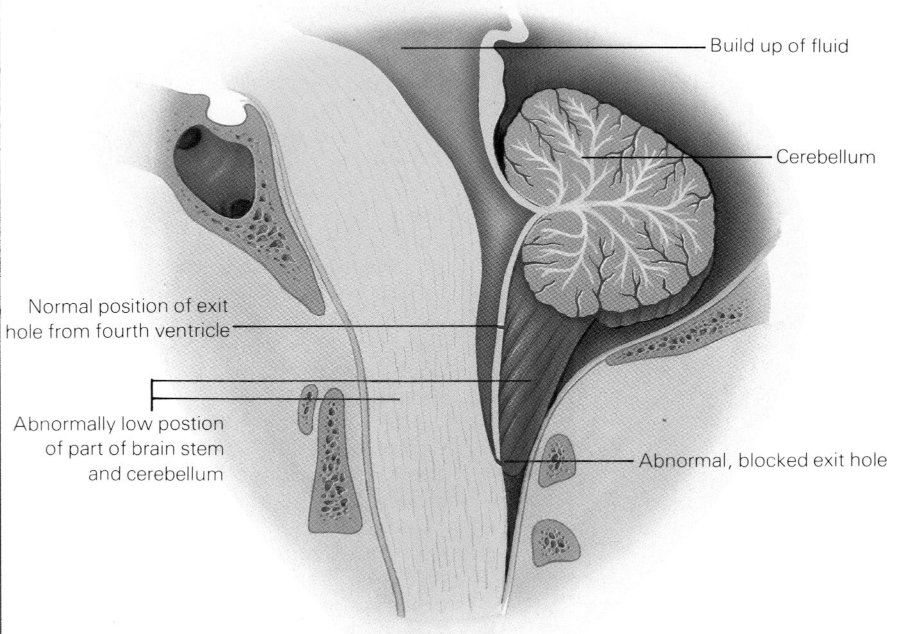

Top picture shows the flow of cerebrospinal fluid around a normal brain. Above: an abnormally developed cerebellum and lower brain stem have obstructed the normal flow and caused a buildup of fluid in the brain.

Mike Courteney

An obstruction anywhere in the circulation of the cerebrospinal fluid means that the fluid will dam up behind the obstruction, gradually increasing the pressure in the brain and squeezing the delicate tissues inside the skull.

Children born with spina bifida (a congenital defect of the spine) may also have an abnormality of the spinal cord in the neck or brain (meningomyelocele) and an abnormality of the structure of the lower brain stem and lower part of the cerebellum (the area of the brain in charge of balance and coordination). This is known as an Arnold-Chiari malformation, and it has the effect of blocking off the exit hole at the bottom of the fourth ventricle, thus causing hydrocephalus.

Another less common congenital abnormality is called a Dandy-Walker cyst. In this case the exit holes from the fourth ventricles do not form at all, the ventricle balloons out into a large cyst, and the cerebellum therefore cannot form properly.

In other congenital hydrocephalus cases there may be an obstruction or a failure in the formation of the cerebral aqueduct, and this causes the third and lateral ventricles to swell up. If there is a collection of abnormal blood vessels or a swelling in one of the cerebral veins near the narrow cerebral aqueduct, these may press on the channel and block it off.

Sometimes obstructive hydrocephalus is caused by an acquired condition. For example, a tumor growing within the brain may press hard enough on the cerebral aqueduct or third ventricle to block the outflow of cerebrospinal fluid.

Very small tumors or benign cysts can cause considerable hydrocephalus if they are in particular places and block aqueducts or exit holes.

Communicating hydrocephalus

Communicating hydrocephalus can be caused by a congenital abnormality of the arachnoid membrane, in which it has not developed sufficiently to reabsorb the cerebrospinal fluid.

Other causes of communicating hydrocephalus include infections of the meninges by bacteria (meningitis) and bleeding into the space around the brain (subarachnoid hemorrhage). In both these cases fibrous scarring occurs that prevents the proper reabsorption of the cerebrospinal fluid.

Communicating hydrocephalus may also be a complication of head injuries that result in small hemorrhages.

Symptoms in children

The most noticeable change that occurs in children is an increase in head size; the bones of the skull normally join when a child is six to ten years old, so head expansion with hydrocephalus mainly occurs in younger children.

Children's head size varies enormously, and if a child's head is large it does not necessarily mean that he or she has hydrocephalus. If hydrocephalus is the cause, the growth of the head will be much faster. The shape of the skull will be distinctive, the forehead prominent, and the face conspicuously small in relation to the rest of the head. The eyes are also pushed down so that a setting-sun face is seen, with the whites of the eyes visible above the colored irises.

If the condition is not treated it can lead to double vision or even blindness. If the hydrocephalus is rapidly developing it may cause mental deterioration, paralysis, and stiffness of limbs.

Symptoms in adults

Hydrocephalus cannot cause an increase in head size once the bones of the skull have finally joined together; this means that as the ventricles expand the brain gets squashed against the unyielding skull.

Progressive mental deterioration is a prominent symptom and may take the form of dementia (deterioration of mental faculties) and deterioration of intellectual functions and memory.

As the pressure in the skull increases, damage to brain tissue becomes obvious because the patient has difficulty walking. The retina may swell at the back of the eye and this can be seen by a doctor using an ophthalmoscope.

There is a particular form of hydrocephalus, called normal pressure hydrocephalus, that occurs in older people. As the ventricles expand the brain shrinks away and the pressure does not rise consistently. This causes a fairly rapidly developing dementia with walking difficulties and incontinence that appear out of proportion to the degree of dementia.

Dangers

Many of the symptoms of hydrocephalus can be reversed or arrested by treatment, and the earlier it is started the less risk there is of lasting damage to the brain.

If the increased pressure is put on the brain and its nerves for too long, irreversible damage occurs.

Diagnosis

Diagnosis is made using a CT scan (a form of X-ray scan linked to a computer that enables the fluid-filled cavities of the brain to be clearly seen). The CT scan involves no risk to the patient and is a painless procedure (see X rays, and Scans).

The scan will show up small tumors and cysts so that the cause of the hydrocephalus may be obvious from the scan.

Further special X-ray investigations of the neck may be necessary if there are congenital abnormalities, such as the Arnold-Chiari malformation, which may need correction.

Occasionally special studies are done (using the CT scan and injected marker dyes) of the pattern of flow of the cerebrospinal fluid. These studies show those cases where the hydrocephalus is due to defective absorption of the fluid by the arachnoid membranes.

Treatment and outlook

In most types of hydrocephalus surgical treatment is necessary. The ventricles can be drained by the insertion of a tube between the ventricles and the spaces at the base of the brain if there is an obstruction in the fourth ventricle or a narrowing of the aqueduct (this is called the Torkildsen procedure).

In other types of hydrocephalus, including most of the congenital sorts and normal pressure hydrocephalus, the cerebrospinal fluid is drained from the ventricles into the bloodstream or the peritoneal cavity in the abdomen.

A valve is necessary to prevent the flow from going the wrong way. This may be one of two types: the Spitz-Holter or the Pudenz-Heyer.

A small hole is made in the skull and a tube is inserted that runs from the ventricles to either the jugular vein or the abdomen. These shunts, as they are called, often have to stay in place for the rest of the patient's life.

The outcome of cases of hydrocephalus after treatment varies considerably. It is mainly dependent on what caused the hydrocephalus in the first place, whether damage to the brain occurred before the hydrocephalus was discovered, and whether there were any other congenital abnormalities.

A child with a shunt in place has a good chance of developing normally in terms of mental ability if there has been no other brain damage. Hydrocephalics who have undergone treatment can go to college, hold down good jobs, and live a normal life just like other people.

A small hole is made in the skull and a tube is inserted that runs from the brain, through the jugular vein to the heart, where the excess fluid on the brain is absorbed into the bloodstream.

The Spitz-Holter shunt operation

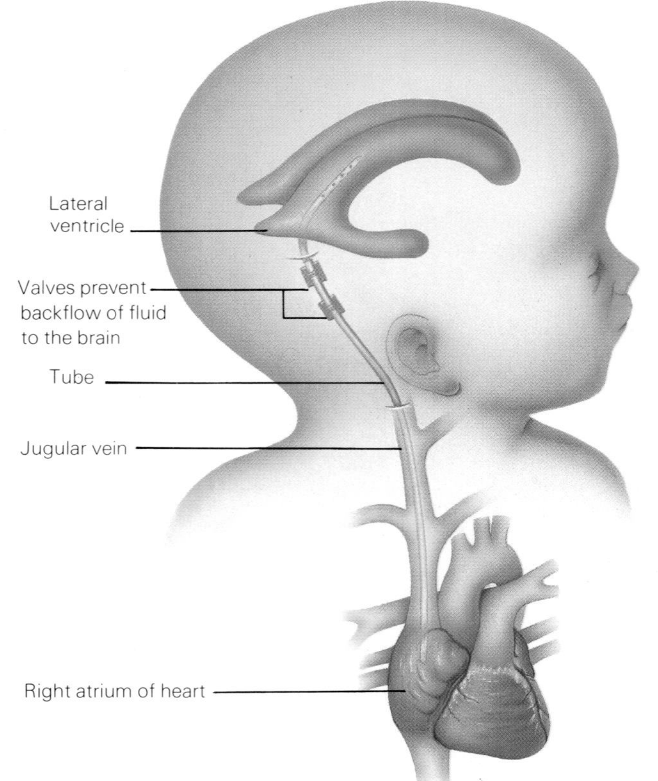

Mike Courteney

Hydrotherapy

Q Would hydrotherapy help the arthritis in my hip?

A When arthritis is so severe that the joint is limited in movement and ordinary exercises are impossible, then hydrotherapy could help. If you think you need hydrotherapy, ask your doctor who may refer you to a center where the treatment is available.

Q I can't swim and I'm terrified of the water, so how could I have hydrotherapy?

A In the first place you do not need to swim, and in the second place, if you ever needed treatment you would probably overcome this fear to receive help. Remember too that a therapist is with you in the pool, so it is no more dangerous than getting into a very big bathtub.

Q Is everyday swimming a form of hydrotherapy?

A Swimming is a very efficient form of exercise, especially since body weight is supported by the water, but this is not the same as hydrotherapy. First the water temperature is much cooler, and second the exercise in swimming need not be related to a specific movement of a joint or the action of one particular group of muscles.

Q With so many sick patients using a hydrotherapy pool, isn't there a risk of diseases spreading?

A Patients are very carefully screened before being recommended for hydrotherapy, and everyone showers or bathes before entering the pool. The water is kept under strict supervision by the hospital bacteriologist so there is no risk of diseases spreading.

Q My aunt has had a stroke and has lost the use of one arm. She is now having hydrotherapy. Will this help?

A Yes. Hydrotherapy helps restore muscle power and, where muscles are permanently damaged, reeducates other muscles to take over their function.

Hydrotherapy is the form of physical therapy in which patients are immersed in warm water. This allows them to exercise without pain and thereby aids recovery from a variety of complaints.

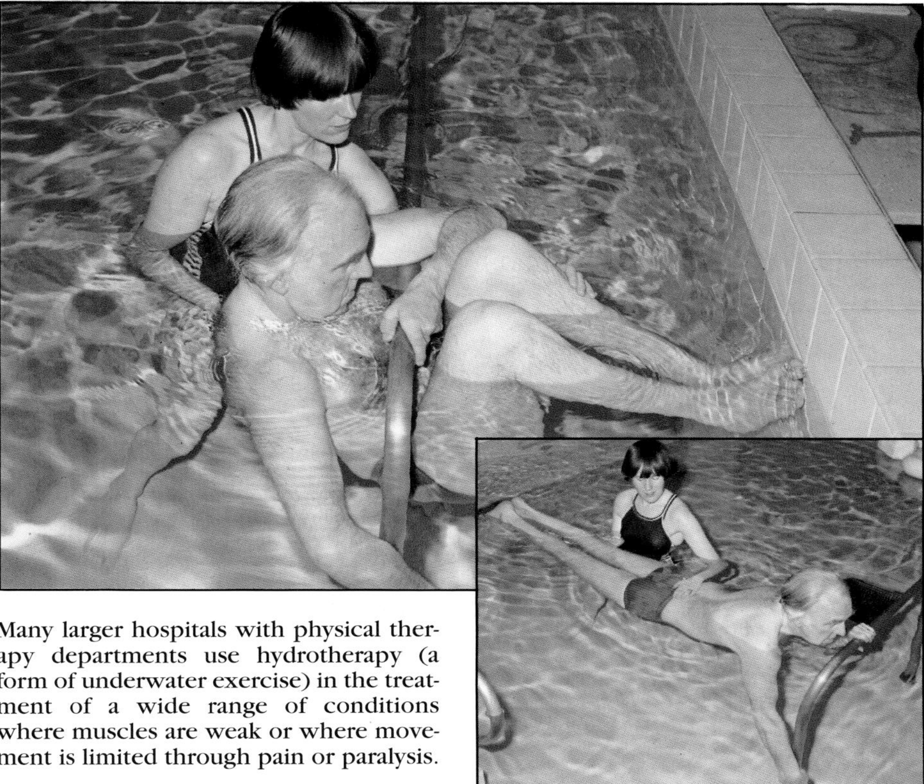

To strengthen the back, the patient— aided by the therapist—holds on to a special handlebar and curls himself into a ball by pulling his knees up toward his chest. He then brings his legs down and stretches them out behind.

Many larger hospitals with physical therapy departments use hydrotherapy (a form of underwater exercise) in the treatment of a wide range of conditions where muscles are weak or where movement is limited through pain or paralysis.

Hydrotherapy treatment

Treatment is given under the supervision of a hydrotherapist, in a pool that looks much like an ordinary swimming pool. However, a hydrotherapy pool has several modifications, such as mechanical hoists for lifting patients in and out of the water, walking bars, and special handles, all of which are designed to help people who find it difficult or painful to move. Unlike an ordinary swimming pool, the water in a hydrotherapy pool must be at body temperature to be effective. In some pools special water, such as water from natural hot springs (with its own claims for healing), is used to provide buoyancy and warmth.

Patients are immersed in warm water for three main reasons. First, because gravity is abolished the body floats and the limited power in the muscles can be amplified to produce larger movements of a particular limb. Second, the warmth of the water produces heat, which can help to relax muscles and to ease pain. Third, the resistance to movement in the water can be used as a basis for a set of gentle, graded exercises.

How treatment is given

Like any other form of exercise treatment, the amount needed varies depending on the condition of the patient. Usually patients can only take between 15–30 minutes of the hot water at one session; therefore treatments tend to be daily for three or four weeks. Some chronically ill patients need treatment for much longer, especially those making a slow recovery from neurological illness, and may have hydrotherapy twice daily.

The patient changes into ordinary swimwear and then either has a full body shower or walks through a disinfectant trough and straight into the warm water; the entries into the pool are designed for easy access. He or she then goes through a planned program of exercises with the hydrotherapist, using floats, paddles, or

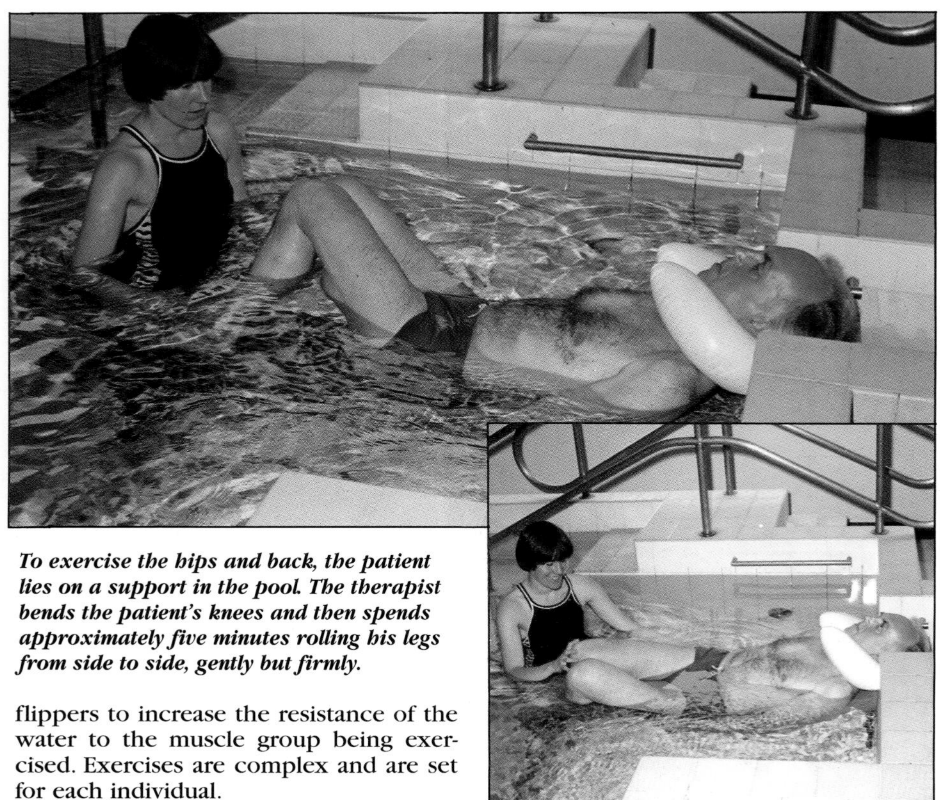

To exercise the hips and back, the patient lies on a support in the pool. The therapist bends the patient's knees and then spends approximately five minutes rolling his legs from side to side, gently but firmly.

flippers to increase the resistance of the water to the muscle group being exercised. Exercises are complex and are set for each individual.

The pool is often used for walking exercises for people with weak legs and for all types of rheumatism in the joints to help the range of movement. In addition to exercises, water jets fitted into the pool may also be used to provide a massage effect on the areas of the body that need treatment.

After the treatment is over the patient may be given a cold shower to cool off or may be wrapped in a pack of dry towels to cool gradually. In some centers hot and cold showers are used to improve a patient's blood circulation.

How hydrotherapy helps

Following hip or knee surgery, or when there is severe arthritis, hydrotherapy can be very helpful and has proved to be a valuable part of the treatment.

After an operation the muscles around a joint tend to waste, and some may have been weakened by the cutting effects of the surgery. Movement against gravity is painful, so being immersed in warm water makes that movement much easier. The water tends to lift the limbs up, and this action helps to improve joint movements and get the joints back into proper working order.

In a condition known as ankylosing spondylitis—a form of spinal arthritis—there is a progressive inflammation of the spinal vertebrae, and movement becomes very limited as the spine becomes fused. Hydrotherapy is extremely valuable to restore movement. In other forms of arthritis normal movement can be so painful that exercising the arthritic joint is impossible without the aid of hydrotherapy. The hip joint is most commonly helped in this way.

In neurological conditions, although hydrotherapy does not affect the course of the illness, it can increase muscle power and mobility. For example, in diseases where there is progressive weakness or paralysis, hydrotherapy allows movement in joints that are otherwise unable to move.

When muscle power is recovering, as in the condition called Guillain-Barré syndrome (see Guillain-Barré syndrome) where there is temporary paralysis, hydrotherapy encourages the patient and helps promote muscle strength. In addition to strengthening muscles hydrotherapy also plays an important part in the reeducation of muscles to take over the function of damaged muscles after a stroke.

Exceptions

Although hydrotherapy can usually help conditions when there is some pain on

Lying in the position shown above, the patient does several trunk flexes to strengthen the back muscles. Starting with the legs straight, the knees are brought up to the chest and then down.

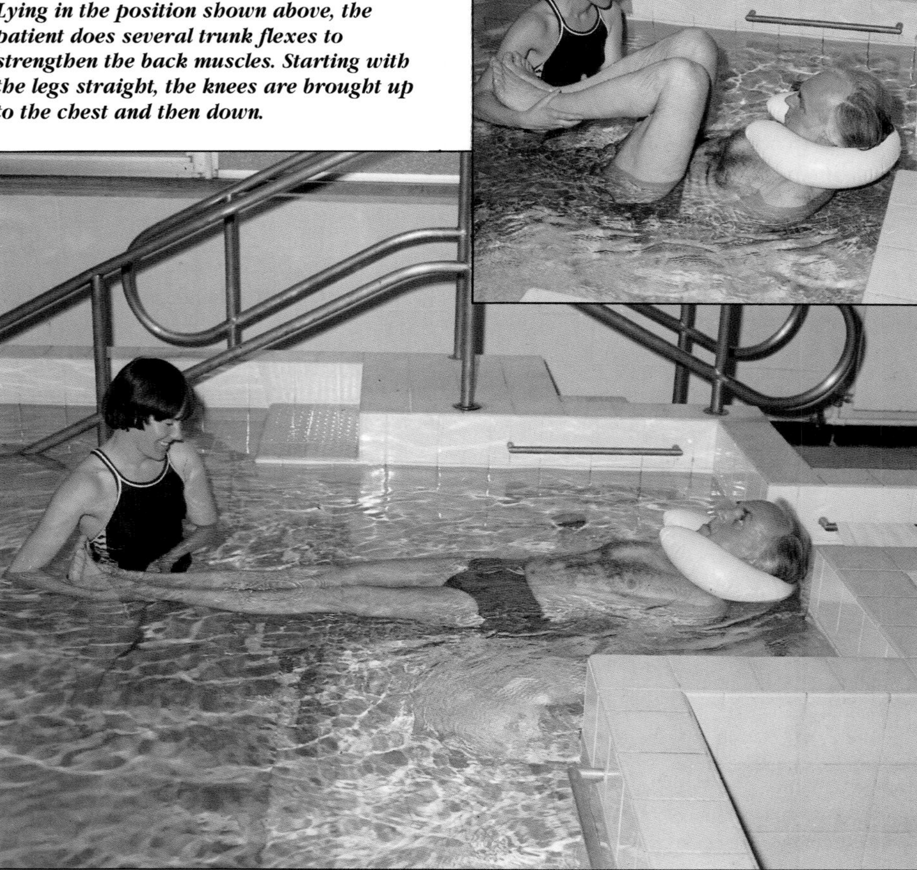

How hydrotherapy can help

Condition	Symptoms	Treatment	Outlook
Frozen shoulder	Stiffness; pain; lack of movement	Kneel on pool floor so that affected shoulder is covered. Hold float out at arm's length. Slowly push down against water, then raise arm up to shoulder level	Warmth of water relaxes joints and eases pain. Maintains muscle strength and increases range of movement
Hip replacement	Stiffness after an operation; muscle weakness and wasting	Lie on side, supported by floats, with affected hip uppermost. Bring knee up toward chest. Stretch leg out to the front, then down and back, keeping knee straight	Encourages maximum range of movement. Restores muscle power
Back injuries	Pain; stiffness	Float on back, holding on to bar at side of pool. Keeping knees straight, bring legs down into standing position, pushing against the water	Warmth of water eases pain. Muscles supporting back are strengthened
Osteoarthritis of the knee	Pain; muscle wasting; knees giving way	Stand in pool. Bring knee up to water surface. Then push foot down against water. Attach float to foot for increased resistance	By strengthening the quadriceps muscles, the knee gets more support and walking is easier. Warmth of water eases pain

movement, or weakness, unfortunately some people are unable to benefit from this form of treatment.

A patient who is incontinent cannot be placed in the water for reasons of hygiene. Although the bacteriology experts stress that there is little or no risk of infection, the situation would not be acceptable to other pool users. However, in some centers dealing with paraplegic patients, the water is specially treated to deal with the possibility of incontinence.

People who suffer from high blood pressure are unsuitable for treatment, because hydrotherapy raises the blood pressure. Also patients with skin diseases or those who are allergic to the chlorine put in the water to keep it clean will not be able to use the pool.

Some patients also have a tendency to faint easily or to have fits. However, the hydrotherapist is always there and the pool is supervised carefully in case this happens, so these patients need not necessarily be excluded from treatment.

Outlook

In its most simple form, hydrotherapy is no more than underwater exercises, and in its most complex form, it is a scientific development of physical therapy. Although its success depends very much on the condition of the individual patient, in the centers where it is used as part of the treatment of orthopedic and neurological conditions, it is of proven value.

To encourage a full range of movement and to restore muscle power, the patient lies on his side, supported by floats and holding on to the bar. Helped by the therapist, he first pulls his knees up to his chest then brings his legs down and back.

All photos taken courtesy of The Royal National Orthopaedic Hospital

Hygiene

Q My daughter is allergic to some soaps. How can she keep clean?

A First she should try a nonperfumed, mild soap. Allergies are often caused by an additive (such as the scent) in the soap, rather than the soap itself. If this does not work, the doctor will prescribe a cleansing cream that contains no soap.

Q My child is being taught personal hygiene at school, but surely this is my responsibility?

A Yes, it is your responsibility, but schools also have a responsibility to their pupils, some of whom have parents who do not bother to educate their children in this way. It might help to have a chat with your child's teacher so that you can compare notes about the points you stress to your child.

Q My neighbor says I should keep raw meat away from cooked food. Is this true?

A Yes. There may be bacteria on raw meat, and if you handle it the bacteria may be transferred to your hands. If you happen to be near other food, for example, bread, cakes, or salad ingredients, there is a chance you may handle them before you wash your hands. Cooking kills bacteria, but your bread, cake, or lettuce will, of course, be eaten as they are. Equally flies, which are notorious carriers, could transfer bacteria from raw meat to other foods if they are left next to each other. So your neighbor's suggestion really is a sensible precaution against the spread of bacteria.

Q I know that people should wash their hands after going to the bathroom, but just how important is it to do this every time?

A It is important enough to insist that it be a regular part of the routine for every member of your family from an early age. Bacteria can be transmitted to the hands from even the smallest trace of urine or feces.

Hygiene is the means by which people can maintain good health and lessen the risk of infection. Learning and practicing the basic rules of hygiene are therefore essential to protecting the health of every member of the family.

Tom Belshaw

Possibly the greatest ever advance in standards of hygiene in most developed countries was the introduction of safe water supplies and sewage systems during the 19th century. Some doctors think that this did even more to combat the spread of infectious diseases than the great advances in vaccination.

However, many countries are still without a safe water supply for the majority of the population. Diseases, spread through contaminated water, remain a fact of life for countless people, however dedicated they are to keeping their homes clean. Cholera and typhoid are probably the most serious of the diseases associated with unsanitary living conditions.

Those lucky enough to have access to clean and sanitary water cannot, however, relax their standards. Dangerous germs, such as bacteria, can lurk in the most modern of homes if the basic rules of hygiene are not respected. Homes with young children need particularly high standards, because children are exposed to an abundance of germs.

A healthy life

Keeping the home clean is just the beginning. Hygiene extends to every aspect of life. Like so many health precautions, its benefits can be reduced to nothing if a person drinks excessively or smokes. A healthy, balanced diet also helps to keep the body free of disease, and regular exercise, combined with relaxation, will reinforce the good effects of all the other basic efforts to maintain health.

Once young children are over fears they may have had about bathing, and are old enough to do so without close supervision, let them enjoy themselves in the bath as much as they possibly can without making a mess. If they can link bath time with fun and games, you will find it easier to teach them the basics of personal hygiene.

Personal hygiene

Clothing should always be kept clean. Underwear should be changed everyday, and clothes should never be worn once they become dirty. It is important to make sure that clothes fit well—which means not too tightly. This applies particularly to shoes, because if they are badly fitting, they can cause foot problems that last for the rest of the wearer's life.

Corns, bunions, and ingrown toenails are usually caused by very tight shoes, and high heels can create back problems. The fundamental rule when buying shoes should be comfort, not fashion. Wearing uncomfortable shoes for a short time is unlikely to cause damage, but this can be difficult to explain to the teenager who is determined always to wear the highest of heels or the most pointed toes, dismissing healthy footwear as dowdy.

Luckily modern shoe fashion offers a wide range of styles, and it is now much easier to find stylish shoes that are also comfortable. If your children are unwilling to accept comfortable shoes, it is worth reminding them of the thousands of people who need frequent, often painful, treatment by podiatrists, all because they are slaves to fashion.

The right fabrics

Although modern advances in clothing technology have meant easier washing and fabric care, it is now clear that synthetic fibers can be unhealthy—especially for women, because they can lead to vaginal infections.

Natural fibers, such as wool or cotton, can breathe, whereas artificial fibers tend to leave the body hot and clammy—an ideal environment for bacteria. Always choose cotton underpants, particularly for wearing with nylon stockings. Those who are prone to vaginal infections may find that these cease if they stop wearing tights altogether; stockings with an open or cotton gusset, can also help.

Keep a child's interest alive while you cut his or her nails by playing interactive counting games with the fingers.

Tom Belshaw

Washing

Keeping the body clean is vitally important. The hair should be washed at least once a week, probably twice or more in city environments. Aside from the more obvious benefits, this will help to prevent head lice infestation, a much more common problem than many people realize. The lice are usually caught from other human carriers rather than from dirty or unhygienic living conditions. If you or your children get head lice, the scalp will feel irritated, and scratching can spread infection to new sites. Special lotions and shampoos are available over the counter to deal with the problem.

Dandruff (loose flakes of skin from the scalp) can be helped by regular washing with an antidandruff shampoo.

Ears should be gently washed with warm water to remove wax. Any large buildup of wax should be dealt with only by the doctor, because the ear is a delicate organ that should never be poked or scraped with any rigid object.

Blemishes

Pimples and acne are common complaints for teenagers. They are not necessarily caused by dirty habits, but anyone who suffers in this way should be extra scrupulous about general cleanliness because the pimples can become infect-

Tom Belshaw

A baby's toys and clothes must be clean. Cloth diapers must be soaked in a disinfectant prewash and washed in the hottest water.

Children may not like washing their hair, but you can soothe some fears by using a nonstinging shampoo and trying to keep water away from their faces when rinsing.

ed, aggravating the condition. A helpful approach is to keep reminding the teenager that the skin will almost certainly clear after a few years. Meanwhile mild acne can benefit from washing with a gentle, nonperfumed soap. Serious cases require medical advice (see Acne and pimples).

Acne sufferers should avoid makeup and wearing wool next to the skin. The pimples should not be picked, because this can spread infection and cause scarring. The hair should be kept well washed and brushed back from the face.

Commonsense precautions

Always cover the nose and mouth when coughing or sneezing to prevent the thousands of germ-bearing droplets from spreading onto other people or food. Teeth should be brushed at least twice a day (and preferably after every meal) for three minutes using a medium-hard brush held at a 45° angle to the gums. The only effective motion for brushing is a circular, up-and-down one (see Teeth and teething).

Hands should always be washed after visiting the bathroom. Bacteria from the feces or urine can be transmitted through toilet paper onto the hands.

Nails should always be kept clean because bacteria can be harbored underneath them. Feet should be washed daily and dried carefully between the toes. If all these practices are followed regularly, the body will stay clean and fresh. Some people may wish to use a deodorant on the underarms, but this is usually unnecessary if daily washing takes place.

The genital area needs to be washed with soap and warm water at least once a day. Douching for women is not necessary because the vagina has its own delicate self-cleaning mechanism, which can be disturbed by harsh douching or vaginal deodorants. This can lead to vaginal infection and abnormal discharges. If you are worried about a discharge and think you may have an infection, this will not be helped by washing and should be treated by a doctor. Tampons and sanitary napkins should be changed at least three times a day, and tampons should only be used during menstruation.

Men should gently clean the penis, including under the foreskin, and wash the genital area before lovemaking.

Cystitis

Urinary infections, particularly cystitis (a painful inflammation of the bladder area; see Cystitis), are often caused by a bacteria from the anus being transmitted to the urethra opening. A woman should wipe herself from front to back after going to the bathroom and keep the whole area very clean.

Hygiene and the baby

If a baby is bottle-fed, all bottles, nipples, and spoons should be kept sterilized. There are special sterilizing units on sale for this purpose.

Terry-cloth diapers need to be soaked for an hour in a solution of cold water and a diaper cleaning agent. They should then be washed on the hottest setting of the washing machine. If a washing machine is not available, the diapers should be boiled for 15 minutes and then washed in the hottest possible water—using rubber gloves of course.

Food

Food should be eaten within 24 hours of any sell by date, and food that seems even slightly suspicious should be thrown away. This also applies to bulging, swollen cans but not to dented ones.

Precooked meats—pies, ham, or luncheon meat, for example—should be covered and refrigerated immediately. Any food cooked at home should be quickly cooled and refrigerated if it is not to be eaten at once. Frozen meat, particularly poultry, should be thoroughly thawed before cooking, because salmonellosis (a severe kind of food poisoning caused by the salmonella bacteria) can be caught from meat not properly cooked.

Salad ingredients should be washed under running water, and fruit should be washed or peeled before eating.

A refrigerator is an important aid to hygiene, but it should be remembered that it does not kill germs—it only stops them from multiplying.

Pets

Animals can be a source of infection. All pets should be kept healthy, because some animal illnesses can be passed on to humans. Cats and dogs can infect humans with ringworm (see Ringworm), which is a fungus infection; it is also possible to catch roundworm from dogs.

Any bite or scratch caused by an animal should be held under running water immediately and then dabbed with an antiseptic. If the animal was wild, carefully note its behavior and go to the doctor immediately (see Rabies). Take the child to the doctor if there is any inflammation or a fever after a scratch or bite, and keep children away from any sick animal.

Vermin such as rats or mice, in addition to other kinds of infestations, are best dealt with by the local public health department. Vermin droppings can contaminate food, so take action right away.

Tom Belshaw

Always make sure you wash fresh fruit before eating it. And encourage children to do the same.

On vacation

Going abroad may mean you need to take extra precautions, although most Western countries now have high public health standards. Remember that traveler's diarrhea—usually taken to mean any kind of diarrhea caught when abroad—can often be the result of too much wine rather than bad food.

Drink bottled water if in any doubt about the cleanliness of the water supply, and always make sure that water for babies is boiled before drinking. Do not eat in restaurants that look unhygienic.

If you are on a camping vacation and do not have access to a refrigerator, always eat fresh or cooked meat the day you buy it. Be careful about how you dispose of trash; burn it if there are no trash cans available on the campsite.

Make sure you are immunized according to the regulations for any country you visit; for example, against cholera and typhoid.

Learning about hygiene

Children learn best by example, so it is pointless telling your child to observe rules that you do not bother with yourself. Explain why the rules are important.

Certain rules should be made from an early age, particularly the washing of hands before meals and after going to the bathroom. Your child should have a daily bath, but if this is not possible, make sure that there is daily washing of the hands, face, feet, and genitals.

Hygiene and the community

However hygiene-conscious you are, you may still be at risk of infection if the water and sewage systems in your area are not properly maintained.

Simple plumbing problems within the home, such as a leaking toilet cistern, can be easily solved by a plumber, but if something goes wrong with the drains or external sewage pipes, then you should call in the public health department. If you are connected to the town's water supply, then this supply is usually the responsibility of the local public health department.

Those who live in private rented accommodation will need to arrange with their landlord for repairs of internal plumbing or improvement of unhygienic

If your child has a cold or the flu, teach him or her to cover both the nose and the mouth with his or her hands when sneezing.

Q Where do food poisoning germs live? I want to know which places I should clean most regularly.

A The bacteria that cause food poisoning live in house dust, on the human skin, on raw meat, and even in cracks in tabletops. They can also be picked up from dishcloths and cloth napkins, or from kitchen equipment such as wooden spoons.

From this it should be clear that the only foolproof approach is to insure overall cleanliness in your kitchen. Dust and wipe regularly. Wash your hands and wrists before preparing food. Use clean dishcloths. Wash all cooking implements and dishes thoroughly. Cook meat as soon as possible after buying it. Unfreeze meat fully before cooking it; cooking kills bacteria, but they can survive in a partially frozen area.

Q I can't help noticing how some of the local children have foot infections, and I'm worried my son will catch one, too. How can I prevent this?

A There are two main infectious foot conditions—athlete's foot (in its mild form, split skin and soreness between the toes) and verrucae—warts on the sole of the foot. The trouble with them is that they are caught most easily where people go barefoot, typically in changing rooms. For this reason there is not much you can do to keep your son from catching them.

If there is an epidemic of athlete's foot among your son's friends, try to persuade him to stay away from the swimming pool for a few weeks. Verrucae (see Verruca) are much less common, and people usually do not worry about them until they happen. If he does catch athlete's foot (see Athlete's foot), this may indicate that he is vulnerable to the fungus that causes it. With this in mind you could give him a suitable antifungal powder (available from drugstores) to use everyday in his shoes and socks.If a family member does have a foot infection, you should make sure that he or she uses a separate towel and bath mat and does not run around the house in bare feet.

Hygiene in the bathroom

Do

- Keep everything scrupulously clean. All surfaces, handles, and faucets should be washed with a powerful cleaner or bleach at least once a week
- Clean the toilet bowl, washbasin, and faucets at least once a day if someone in the family has a stomach upset or diarrhea
- Make sure everyone in the family has their own washcloth and towel. If someone has a foot infection (such as athlete's foot), make them use a separate bath mat and wear slippers as soon as they step out of the bath

Don't

- Leave leaking outlet pipes to drip or delay before calling the plumber if the bath or sink outlet starts smelling foul
- Allow children to neglect washing their hands after visiting the bathroom

Hygiene in the kitchen

Do

- Wash hands before touching food, and make sure that any cut or sore is covered by an adhesive bandage
- Keep food covered and away from flies. Use a fly spray if flies are a nuisance
- Wash all salad ingredients very thoroughly
- Wash saucepans thoroughly
- Use liners in kitchen wastebaskets and trash cans
- Soak dishcloths, mops, and floor cloths in solutions of bleach once a week
- Use clean cloths for drying dishes
- Use paper towels for mopping up

Don't

- Keep the trash can near the kitchen door; this encourages flies to make trips between it and any food left out in the kitchen

conditions in the kitchen or bathroom. New homes as well as old ones can suffer from condensation or mold (each a potential health risk), however clean the occupants may be.

People also have the right to report stores, cafés, or restaurants that they believe fall below public health standards. Although there are frequent spot-checks of such places and the rules governing them are strict, public health inspectors cannot be everywhere at once.

If you see suspicious-looking food on sale, or if a store is selling food later than its do not use after date, report it to the local inspector. Just because you are observant enough not to buy these goods does not prevent another person from making a mistake.

Keeping hygiene in perspective

Try not to turn the home into a battleground in the campaign against bacteria. The rules of hygiene should not take over or interfere with family life; rather, they should be a part of it.

It is also worth remembering that the most hygienic person is bound to catch some type of infectious disease now and then.The occasional bout of diarrhea does not mean that a person is dirty, irresponsible, or careless.

Household pets are not a health hazard as long as they are clean and kept free of fleas, if necessary by spraying.

Tom Belshaw

Hymen

Q **If her hymen is not broken, does this mean that my daughter will not be able to use a tampon?**

A Hymens vary in the extent to which they cover the vaginal entrance, and they also vary in their elasticity. In many cases it is quite possible to use a tampon without damaging the hymen. It is incorrect to say that only women with sexual experience are able to use tampons successfully.

Q **Can a girl be born without a hymen? I am sure I never had one.**

A Although most women do have a hymen, some are born without one. Because the hymen has no biological function, its absence does not create any physical problems.

Q **Is it possible for a woman to reach old age without her hymen breaking?**

A A woman rarely reaches old age with her hymen intact, since most women will have experienced sexual intercourse. Also the hymen may tear as a result of physical exercise and sometimes for no apparent reason.

Q **If my hymen were to break naturally, would this mean I was no longer a virgin?**

A No. Unless you have had sexual intercourse, you are still a virgin even if your hymen is broken. The unbroken hymen as proof of virginity is only a myth, but unfortunately it has caused a lot of anxiety for many women.

Q **I have heard that it is possible to have an artificial hymen made. Is this true?**

A It is possible for a doctor to stretch a piece of tissue across the vagina, but this is a very unusual practice. It may be done in places where for social or cultural reasons it is essential for blood to be present after intercourse. This is an unfortunate consequence of the myth that links virginity with the presence of an intact hymen.

The belief that an unbroken hymen is proof of a woman's virginity is based on nothing more than a myth; a woman very rarely has a hymen that completely covers the entrance of the vagina.

The hymen, also known as the maidenhead, is a thin membrane that partially covers the entrance to the vaginal canal. It is named after the Greek god of marriage, *Hymen*.

The hymen has no known physiological function but has achieved great importance in almost all cultures as a sign of virginity. However, hymens come in all shapes and sizes, and there is no way in which a hymen can be a reliable indication of virginity.

The membrane is usually thin, punctured by holes, and can easily be broken by strenuous physical exercise such as running and horseback riding. Heavy petting, masturbation, or the insertion of tampons can also cause a rupture.

Although the condition of the hymen is no proof of virginity, very often the hymen is broken during the first experience of sexual intercourse.

Bleeding

When the hymen is first torn, there can be some pain and slight bleeding. However, both of these only last for a short time and rarely cause much discomfort. If a woman has a thick hymen and is worried about pain during her first experience of sexual intercourse, her gynecologist can show her how to stretch the hymen with her fingers so that it will be less of a potential problem.

Problems

On rare occasions the hymen forms a complete barrier, and this can cause problems because it may restrict the menstrual flow. When this happens the hymen can be removed by a simple operation called a hymenectomy, which causes very little pain.

Sometimes this operation is necessary if the normally thin and flexible hymen is thick and fibrous and resistant to penetration of the penis during sexual intercourse. On the other hand if the hymen is so elastic that it stretches rather than tears during sexual intercourse, it may need to be removed from a pregnant woman before her child is born.

Pregnancy

Contrary to popular belief an intact hymen does not prevent pregnancy. A sperm that comes into contact with the genital area, perhaps as a result of heavy petting, can travel through a hole in the hymen and up into the vaginal canal.

Unruptured and ruptured hymens

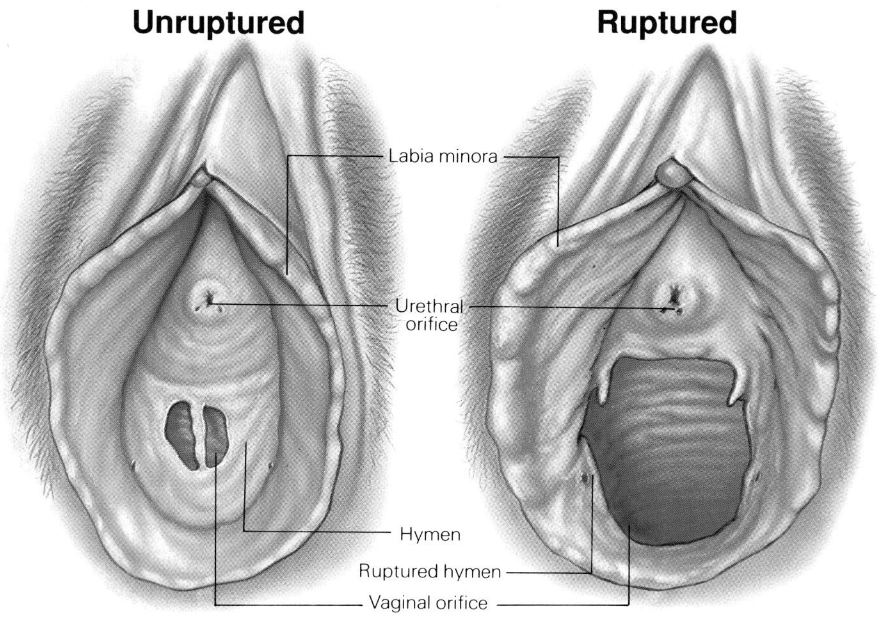

Hyperactivity

Q My five-year-old son has just been admitted to a child psychiatric unit. He is hyperactive and I just can't cope anymore, so my doctor thought it was for the best. Have I failed as a mother?

A You have not failed. This is one of the most distressing problems any parent has to cope with. Normal methods of control are ineffective for a hyperactive child. The staff in the psychiatric unit will find ways of modifying his behavior, and you will be told how to put their methods into practice when he comes home. The break will give you a chance to renew your strength, and you may well find your son improved when he returns.

Q My toddler is into everything, always asking questions, wanting to copy everything I do, and touching things that I have forbidden him to touch. I am quite worn out by the end of the day. Is he hyperactive and does he need treatment?

A Your toddler sounds like a normally energetic and intelligent boy. It is a tiring time for mothers, but toddlers do grow out of this stage and he should soon learn not to touch things that you have forbidden him to touch. If he willingly spends more than a few minutes playing with something, he has a normal attention span. The hyperactive child cannot concentrate on anything for more than a few moments, because he is continually distracted by the slightest thing. However, if you are still worried, talk to your doctor.

Q Can a nice quiet baby grow into a hyperactive toddler?

A This is very unlikely. The hyperkinetic syndrome, which is a disorder of development that usually occurs without any other mental or physical disorders, does not often develop in older babies; the hyperactivity is usually present right from the start and the baby is very restless from an early age. It might be possible for the hyperactivity to develop in an older child if it is associated with some other disorder.

A hyperactive child is never still but constantly rushes around everywhere, impulsively starting one activity and then immediately abandoning it for another. It is quite exhausting for the parents, but fortunately treatment is available to calm such children.

Hyperactivity is one of many symptoms that may be present in children with certain psychiatric problems. It can also be connected with conditions such as brain damage, epilepsy, autism (mental disability that is characterized by self-absorption), and childhood schizophrenia (disintegration of the personality).

However, most people think of hyperactivity as a condition unconnected to other disorders, with overactivity as the main feature. This is known as the hyperkinetic syndrome or attention deficit disorder. It is relatively rare and affects four times as many boys as girls.

Parents of a hyperactive child have a lot to contend with. As well as being overactive, the child is often aggressive and finds it difficult to form relationships with other children. He or she may be destructive and have sudden bursts of rage if thwarted, but a hyperactive child's moods swing so suddenly that rage and aggression can be quickly followed by expressions of joy or misery. The child's concentration is so poor that he or she rarely does well in school.

Causes

Overactivity may be caused by a disorder such as autism, in which case there will be other symptoms as well. However, it may be the only symptom, as in attention deficit disorder.

Doctors are divided over what causes the hyperkinetic syndrome. It is thought that it could be the result of an organic brain disorder or that there could be a genetic link. Some therapists believe it to be a family problem, which can only be dealt with by seeing the family as a whole and working out what aspect of the relationship might be causing the child's hyperactivity.

Some studies seem to indicate that there is a link between hyperactivity and certain factors in a child's diet. The chief

A hyperactive child needs encouragement to improve his or her concentration. If he or she is concentrating on one activity, the surroundings need to be as free from distraction as possible. He or she may also find it difficult to form normal relationships with other children.

Alex Bartel/Science Photo Library

Tom Belshaw

It is important to recognize that the child is not just being willful and disobedient. If necessary ask for professional help. Psychotherapists often deal with the whole family as a unit.

culprits are thought to be food additives, such as artificial colors (particularly the yellow substance tartrazine), flavorings, antioxidants, and nitrite preservatives.

Symptoms

Most hyperactive children are overactive as babies, but the symptoms become most obvious when they start to walk. At this point the parents become aware of the disorganized way in which such a child constantly tears around.

The main symptom that becomes obvious as the child grows older is a complete lack of concentration and a very short attention span. The child is often of below average intelligence and is late in starting to talk. He or she is often very clumsy, even when not being deliberately destructive, and his or her mood changes with bewildering rapidity.

The hyperactive child rarely gets along well with other children. He or she cannot concentrate long enough to join in games and is often very aggressive.

At school the hyperactivity continues. The child has difficulty in learning to read and often has perceptional problems, for example, finding it hard to tell left from right and to understand spatial relationships.

Dangers

The main worry for the parents of a hyperactive child is that he or she will harm him- or herself. The impulsive thoughtlessness of the hyperactive child means that he or she is capable of dashing into the road or tumbling out of a window.

Aggressive behavior with other children means that the child has to be carefully watched in case he or she hurts them. Babies in his or her own family may be at risk—particularly if the child becomes jealous of the parents' attention to the baby, feeling that they are more impatient with him or her and more loving toward the less demanding baby.

Another less tangible danger is that of relationships within the family deteriorating, and the child's parents being angry as if he or she were being deliberately naughty. The hyperactive child needs love coupled with firmness, not punishment. The more secure the child feels at home, the better able he or she is to cope with social pressures caused by inability to get along with other children and learning problems at school.

Treatment

Hyperactivity responds well to drug treatment. In some cases tranquilizers are used with good results. Amphetamine-based drugs, such as methylphenidate, that have a stimulating effect on adults, often have the reverse effect on children, so these may be prescribed for their tranquilizing effect. Black coffee may be used in a similar way to calm a hyperactive child, whereas it would normally keep an adult awake. (A doctor should always be consulted before this is given.)

Treatment with drugs is carefully monitored by the doctor because they may have side effects, and it is sometimes necessary to try out several different drugs before the best one is found. A doctor may also recommend that foods containing certain additives be avoided.

Behavior therapy may be used to try and improve the child's attention and concentration (see Behavior therapy). If the child suffers from anxiety, then psychotherapy, often involving the whole family, may help. In any case parents will generally need help themselves in learning how to handle their child.

Outlook

The hyperactive child tends to become calmer as he or she grows older, and the overactivity has almost always ceased by the time the child reaches adolescence. However, what may happen at this stage instead is that the overactivity is replaced by underactivity and lethargy, and the child will now need help to develop drive and initiative.

Because the child has been unable to build relationships with friends, the antisocial problems often remain and need to be dealt with. Learning also continues to be a problem, and remedial lessons may still be necessary.

Hypersensitivity

Q My two children disturbed a wasp's nest while they were playing in the yard and both of them got stung. My son collapsed and had to be rushed to the hospital, but my daughter was not badly affected. Why should they react so differently? Can anything be done to protect my son if he is stung again?

A Your son is one of the very few people who are hypersensitive to wasp venom and he experienced anaphylactic (severe allergic) shock when he was stung. Your daughter reacted differently for one of two possible reasons.

First, she may not be prone to developing a hypersensitivity to wasp venom. Alternatively she may be prone but has never before been stung by a wasp; hypersensitive reactions usually only appear on the second and subsequent contact with the provoking substance. If the second explanation is correct, your daughter will have been sensitized (made sensitive) by her first contact with wasp venom and could suffer from anaphylactic shock if she is stung again. Your doctor can find out whether she is now hypersensitive by scratching her skin with a minute quantity of venom and observing the reaction. Your son and possibly your daughter may benefit from a set of desensitizing injections. You you should consult your doctor.

Q Can hypersensitivity appear at any time of life, or is it always present from birth?

A A tendency to develop certain types of hypersensitivity is present from birth and tends to run in families. These hypersensitive individuals tend to suffer from a skin condition called atopic eczema, caused by hypersensitivity to certain foods, when they are young. They may also suffer from hay fever or asthma.

However, hypersensitivity also appears in other people, often because they are continuously exposed to something that can cause a reaction. This means that the environment can play as large a part as heredity in the development of hypersensitivity.

Hypersensitivity is an exaggerated reaction of the body's defense system to basically harmless substances that may have been inhaled, eaten, drunk, injected, or simply in contact with the skin. Fortunately medical treatment can improve this condition.

Hypersensitivity means virtually the same thing as allergy (see Allergies). Most people are either never troubled by hypersensitive reactions or are sensitive to only one or two substances. A few people, however, seem predisposed to develop hypersensitive reactions to a wide range of substances (see Total allergy syndrome). These people are called atopic, and the disorder tends to run in families. Hypersensitive reactions vary from mild irritation to a very rare dangerous state of shock called anaphylaxis.

Sweet pea pollen

London Scientific Fotos

Pollen from the sweet pea (above) and many other plants can make the summer months a misery for those hypersensitive people who suffer from hay fever.

Symptoms

The best known hypersensitivity to substances in the air is hay fever (see Hay fever), which is frequently caused by grass or tree pollen. Therefore the symptoms of a runny nose, eye irritation, and sneezing may occur only at certain times of the year.

A number of other substances, such as house dust, animal fur, and fungal spores, can cause symptoms similar to hay fever. Asthmatic attacks, characterized by wheezing and breathing difficulties, are caused by similar inhaled substances (see Asthma). One of the most common causes is the house dust mite that is found everywhere in the home.

Almost any food can cause a hypersensitive reaction, but the most common offenders are milk, eggs, shellfish, fruit, nuts, and wheat. Food hypersensitivity can cause a wide range of symptoms—from diarrhea and vomiting to asthma, hives, or a scaly skin condition called atopic eczema (see Eczema) that appears on the face, chest, hands, forearms, and behind the knees.

Bee and wasp stings are painful and annoying at the best of times, but for the one-in-a-thousand person who is hypersensitive to the venom of these insects, a sting can have serious consequences. In very rare cases the victim may have difficulty breathing, turn pale, and feel faint. This condition is called anaphylactic shock, and urgent medical attention is always required.

Drugs that may cause serious hypersensitive reactions include penicillin sulfonamide antibiotics, barbiturate sleeping pills, and especially aspirin. One of the most common symptoms is a measleslike rash affecting the whole body. In more serious cases a drug hypersensitivity can cause an anaphylactic state of shock similar to that occurring with insect bites. It can also cause damage to the liver, kidneys, heart, and blood cells.

House dust mite

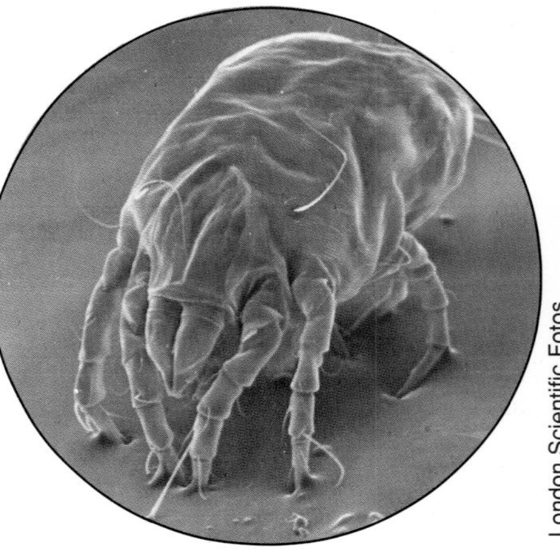

London Scientific Fotos

The tiny house dust mite, which is found in most parts of the home—especially in damp mattresses—is a common cause of asthmatic attacks in certain people.

Another kind of hypersensitivity is contact dermatitis, which is a skin condition that develops in reaction to a substance in contact with the skin. Common offenders include metals such as nickel in jewelry, chemicals found in cosmetics or encountered at work, elastic, and adhesive dressings. In such cases the skin becomes red and itchy in the area in contact with the substance.

Causes

Hypersensitive reactions occur as a result of some defect in the body's immune system. The immune system's job is to fight infection, which it does by producing substances called antibodies. These neutralize harmful foreign substances (antigens) that enter the body.

In hypersensitive people the process is directed against harmless substances (known as allergens) and histamine is released into the body. This causes inflammation, itching, and also the escape of fluid from the blood vessels into surrounding tissues, causing them to swell.

Sometimes antibodies and allergens combine and attract white cells in the blood, called polymorphs, that release enzymes (chemical transformers) that can damage the tissues.

In some types of drug hypersensitivity, the drug itself is not recognized as a foreign substance. However, it may provoke the formation of antibodies when it combines with proteins already in the body, such as proteins on the surface of red cells. The body's defenses may then attack and destroy the red blood cells, and this can lead to a form of anemia.

Why certain substances can be harmless to some people but cause a hypersensitive reaction in others is not fully understood. In individuals with skin sensitivity to scratch tests, an inherited defect is thought to cause an excess production of the antibody immunoglobulin E (IgE), which is responsible for anaphylactic shock reactions. In other cases continuous exposure to high concentrations of a substance may eventually cause a hypersensitivity to that particular substance.

A recent theory suggested that the tendency to develop hypersensitive reactions is caused by a breakdown in a mechanism that normally prevents potential antigens from entering the body tissues.

Diagnosis and treatment

Many types of hypersensitivity can be diagnosed by a skin prick test. Hypersensitivity to a food may be obvious—for example, vomiting and diarrhea whenever a person eats shellfish. If the offending food is unknown, however, the doctor can provide lists of special diets that eliminate various foods. The cause of contact dermatitis may be obvious if it happens when a certain piece of jewelry or other material is worn next to the skin. In cases of doubt the doctor can discover the identity of the offending substance by testing the skin's reaction to various chemicals found in the home or at work.

Some types of hypersensitivity can be relieved by drugs or desensitizing shots. Desensitization is most effective against grass and tree pollens, but may be given for house dust and house dust mites and wasp and bee stings. It is not effective in cases of food hypersensitivity.

Anaphylactic shock, which only occurs very rarely in reaction to a drug or insect sting, requires urgent medical attention. An adrenaline injection together with antihistamine relieves the attack.

Tom Belshaw

Almost any food or drink can cause a hypersensitive reaction in a person, but the most common offenders are milk, fruit, eggs, nuts, wheat, and shellfish.

Avoidance

In the case of food hypersensitivity or contact dermatitis, avoidance is fairly simple, but hay fever and asthma sufferers may have more difficulty. Asthma sufferers sensitive to house dust or mites should avoid activities such as cleaning out dusty attics and should use synthetic materials rather than feathers in pillows and comforters, because these are less likely to harbor house mites.

The chances of an infant developing a food allergy can be considerably reduced by breast-feeding rather than bottle-feeding for at least the first three months, and by not giving certain other foods, such as eggs, nuts, and shellfish for the first six months of life.

Hypnosis

Q Can a person be made to do anything when he or she is put under hypnosis?

A No. However, by suggesting to a hypnotized person that he or she is in a situation where a generally wrong action is permissible, it appears to be possible to persuade the person into at least minor antisocial acts—especially if there is already a hidden desire to perform that action anyway! Evidence exists, however, that some part of a hypnotized subject's brain is still alert and watching over the person even in a deep trance.

Q A few years ago I watched a hypnotist at a club making people perform seemingly impossible feats of physical skill. Do people ever hurt themselves doing this?

A Yes they do, which is one of the reasons why hypnotism as a form of entertainment is discouraged nowadays. However, such feats are sometimes performed in demonstrations given by medical hypnotists, in which only other professionals are involved.

Q Will being hypnotized make me give up smoking permanently?

A This can never be guaranteed, but a class in hypnotic suggestion can do much to help a suitable subject break the habit. After the habit is broken continued abstinence is up to the individual.

Q What does posthypnotic suggestion mean?

A This involves commanding the subject under hypnosis to perform an action after the hypnotic trance is over and the person is in a normal alert state or even asleep. This phenomenon is extraordinary in that the subject is sometimes completely unaware of the action until the time comes to perform it, which may be some time after the hypnotic trance is concluded. However, it is almost impossible to make a subject perform an action that is deeply against his or her will.

Hypnosis used to be a popular stage entertainment, but today it may be used in hospitals as an aid to pain relief and by psychologists as a means of relieving certain psychologically based disorders.

Deeply relaxed under hypnosis, this woman is responding well to the methods of the behavioral psychologist who is treating her fear of spiders.

The hypnotic trance is now generally regarded as no more than a state of great suggestibility, yet its value as an aid to modifying behavior or reducing pain makes it far more important than a mere variety act in the theater.

The word *hypnosis* is derived from the Greek word *hypnos*, meaning "sleep," since it was originally thought to be a form of artificial sleep. Nowadays, however, it is known that this is incorrect, for the brain wave pattern of a hypnotized person is the same as that of someone who is fully awake. Nevertheless a hypnotic state seems to be a very different one from that of fully conscious life.

Signs of hypnosis

People under hypnosis can seem more open to suggestion than they normally are; indeed they often show annoyance if the hypnotist tells them to plan some activity of their own when under hypnosis. Their attention focuses completely on the hypnotist, even when no command has been given to do so. They seem able to fantasize easily and to believe the impossible, for example, that an animal is talking to them.

They also have a greater ability to take on particular roles: for example, acting out situations in which they are drunk, are a member of the opposite sex, or have returned to their childhood. Finally there is the unexpected ability of hypnotized people to block sensations of pain on command. Hypnosis is, in fact, sometimes used to anesthetize a patient before certain medical procedures or minor operations in cases where a chemical anesthetic is deemed undesirable.

Techniques

A hypnotist who is an entertainer may fix the person to be hypnotized (the subject) with a piercing stare while making various hand movements; this elaborate technique is unnecessary, although it can work very well.

A more preferable technique requires the subject to sit comfortably on a chair or lie on a couch. He or she is then encouraged to relax completely and asked to follow carefully what the hypnotist is saying: this could be a request to pay attention to the sensations coming from, say, the left hand, which should be reported to the hypnotist. As soon as the subject feels any movement in the thumb or any of the fingers, the hypnotist will issue an instruction to raise it.

Slight movement occurs eventually and the person lifts the fingers. The hypnotist then suggests that the hand and arm are getting lighter and will rise steadily to touch the subject's forehead and that, as it rises, the subject will become sleepier. When the hand touches the forehead, some degree of hypnotic trance will have been induced.

Subjects for hypnotism

To start with, only those people who are willing and cooperative can be hypnotized. It is almost impossible to hypnotize people against their will. It is also a mistake to think that only those who are weakminded make good subjects.

Some people are unable to be hypnotized even with their cooperation over hundreds of trials. About 5 percent of the population can be placed in a deep hypnotic trance without any difficulty. Many others can reach a deep trance after a number of sessions, and the majority of people will pass into a light trance under favorable circumstances.

There is also evidence that susceptibility to hypnosis tends partly to run in families. Those with a fondness for reading, music, nature, or an involvement in religion make especially good subjects.

Uses

Hypnotism is practiced nowadays for two basic reasons, for entertainment and as a therapeutic technique. Hypnotism as a stage or club act is, however, falling into disuse, partly because in many countries there are laws forbidding or restricting its use as a form of entertainment due to the dangers that can arise, and partly because

The psychologist here is helping the subject to break her habit of smoking by hypnotic suggestion, in this case that the taste of cigarettes is horrible and that she dislikes them intensely.

it seems to be frowned upon by the theatrical profession itself.

In the wrong hands there are two kinds of dangers associated with hypnosis. There can be a lack of competence in the hypnotist that can lead to difficulties in controlling or ending a hypnotic state induced in a subject. In addition there can be ethical difficulties. While it is not easy to make someone do something under hypnosis that they would not do in their normal state, it is possible to make a hypnotized person believe that he or she is in a situation where normally undesirable behavior is allowable. Hence the decline of hypnotism as an act.

In the therapeutic situation, however, hypnotism can be used not only to reduce or eliminate pain under some circumstances, but also to help discover the nature of buried conflicts and problems or to help a person to remember forgotten experiences that might be important emotionally. It can also be used to modify such habits as smoking or eliminate undesirable speech mannerisms. Another use is to achieve the deep relaxation necessary for curing phobias, fears, and compulsions by behavior therapy (see Behavior therapy).

Certain physical ailments and conditions that are thought to have psychological causes—such as some forms of asthma, stomach upsets, or limb paralysis—can also be relieved through the use of hypnotic suggestion.

Sensations under hypnosis

Feelings during and after hypnosis vary according to the depth and purpose of the hypnosis. People who have gone into a deep trance report almost mystical experiences, such as feeling at one with the universe or gaining wisdom beyond words. Other people remember nothing. In lighter trances most people report a feeling of well-being and relaxation afterward, even when what has taken place under hypnosis has involved considerable emotional upheaval.

Hypnotic drugs

Q Is there a danger in mixing my sleeping pills with a nighttime alcoholic drink?

A Yes. The effects of alcohol add to the effects of all sedatives and therefore to take both can produce excessive sedation, which may be dangerous. A (small) bedtime drink taken by itself may be the best form of sedative although of course, the regular use of alcohol can have its own dangers.

Q Are sleeping pills dangerous if they are taken by children?

A It is vital that all drugs, but especially sleeping pills, are kept out of reach of children. Because of their small body size, children can be killed by even very small overdoses of sleeping pills. There are occasions when a mild sleeping pill is needed for a short period to correct a difficult sleep pattern in a child, but the dosage prescribed should be very carefully observed.

Q Are there some sedatives that make you too drowsy to drive?

A Yes. Most of the commonly used sedatives cause significant drowsiness, lasting for some time after the person appears to have woken from sleep. For this reason anyone taking these drugs should take care not to drive when under their influence.

Q Is it a bad thing to keep taking sleeping pills for years and years?

A Yes. Through careless prescribing in the past many people became addicted, particularly to barbiturates. The problem is that over a period of time the effects of a certain dose diminish so that a larger dose is required to have an effect. Also the type of sleep induced by sedatives is not as refreshing as natural sleep, so it is better to use sleeping pills only for a limited period while steps are taken to find out the cause of the insomnia and treat the condition.

Some people have difficulty in sleeping, and taking one of the hypnotic drugs (sedatives and sleeping pills) can aid rest. However, it must be prescribed and taken with care.

Sleep difficulties are common, and there is a great demand for drugs that will help those who suffer from such problems. Hypnotic drugs are a broad category of sedatives (see Sedatives), tranquilizers, and anti-anxiety agents. Although no sedative-hypnotic drug produces normal sleep, some induce sleep that is nearer to natural sleep than others. However, some difficulties in sleeping are not likely to be helped by purely sedating drugs at all.

Different types of hypnotic drugs

There are various types of calming and sleep-inducing drugs available, but they all tend to have side effects to some degree.

Chloral derivatives: Chloral hydrate was one of the earliest drugs to be used specifically as a hypnotic. The original chemical is not used much now, but chloral is the main ingredient in a drug called dichloralphenazone, which is widely prescribed in pill form and is especially useful to elderly people. Chloral hydrate itself can irritate the stomach and even the milder dichloralphenazone has to be avoided by people who have peptic ulcers or delicate stomachs. This group of drugs can be addictive when mixed with alcohol.

Barbiturates: Although once used widely, barbiturates have now been almost overtaken by safer, less addictive drugs; they are now used mainly in injections to produce general anesthesia.

Barbiturates are significantly habit-forming, even addictive, with prolonged hangover effects: those who take them are not at their best for most of the morning after a barbiturate-induced sleep. Overdoses are also dangerous (see Overdoses).

Benzodiazepines: These are safe, even when a large overdose is taken. Considering how well they work, they have remarkably few side effects although they may cause nightmares. However, even the benzodiazepines can be habit-forming, and if they are withdrawn there may be a recurrence of sleeplessness.

Other hypnotics: A mixed group of non-barbiturates has largely been replaced by the benzodiazepine group. One drug that was popular some years back was a mixture of a hypnotic, methaqualone, and a sedative antihistamine, diphenhydramine. It was potent and effective but very dangerous if an overdose was taken.

On the rare occasions when children need a drug with some hypnotic effect, the most useful are the sedative antihistamines, including promethazine and trimeprazine. Chlormethiazole is a safe hypnotic drug for elderly people.

How hypnotic drugs work

The reticular activating system is the part of the brain that is responsible for cycles of sleep and wakefulness. This system is a widely spread network of brain cells and their nerve fibers, which lace up and down the brain stem (see Brain), controlling the amount of electrical activity in the brain. Some drugs, such as the barbiturates, suppress the activity of considerable areas of the brain, causing hypnotic effects at low doses and complete general anesthesia at higher doses. CNS (central nervous system) depressants, such as alcohol, opiates, antihistamines, and sedatives also have the same effects. Other drugs, such as the benzodiazepines, do not produce general anesthesia even at very high doses.

Dangers and side effects

The barbiturates are particularly liable to cause hangovers, and it is dangerous to drive until their effects have completely worn off because coordination and the reflexes are significantly suppressed.

The benzodiazepines were introduced as drugs that would cause very little of a hangover effect. However, one of them, nitrazepam, does have this side effect, lasting for up to 20 hours after it is taken.

Another serious side effect occurs in people with chronic chest complaints; many of the hypnotics, especially the barbiturates, interfere with their breathing during the night, often to a serious extent, and so it is best for sufferers to avoid the use of all hypnotics.

Some people are allergic to certain drugs in the hypnotic group. It is not usually possible to predict which one will cause the allergic reaction, but if a person has a reaction to one drug in a particular group of hypnotics, he or she will probably be allergic to similar drugs.

Barbiturates can make people—especially the elderly—feel confused, and this can be dangerous because it can lead to accidents. Another problem, again especially of barbiturates but also of chloral derivatives, is interaction with other prescribed or over-the-counter drugs. It is important for a doctor to know if a patient is taking a hypnotic drug before prescribing any others.

Hypnotic drugs, their uses and possible side effects

Group	Drug	Uses	Possible side effects
Barbiturates	Phenobarbital	Sleep-inducing and anticonvulsant, for routine and preoperative sedation, and seizures (see Epilepsy)	Addiction, hangover, interference with breathing, allergy
	Pentobarbital	Sleep-inducing, used in hospitals for anesthesia	As for phenobarbital
	Secobarbital	As for phenobarbital	As for phenobarbital
Benzodiazepines	Diazepam	Sedative, sleep-inducing, treatment of anxiety, anticonvulsant	Hangover, habit-forming
	Triazolam	Sleep-inducing	Drowsiness, headache, amnesia
Chloral derivatives	Dichloralphenazone	Sleep-inducing	Nausea, allergy (both rare)
Sedative antihistamines	Promethazine	Sleep-inducing (for children), travel sickness	Dry mouth
	Trimeprazine	Sleep-inducing (for children), premedication for operations (for children)	Dry mouth
Imidazopyridine derivatives	Zolpidem	As for benzodiazepines, but nonaddicting	Drowsiness, dizziness, poor coordination, heart palpitation, nausea

*In all cases prescribed dosages should always be adhered to, and medical supervision is essential to control any side effects

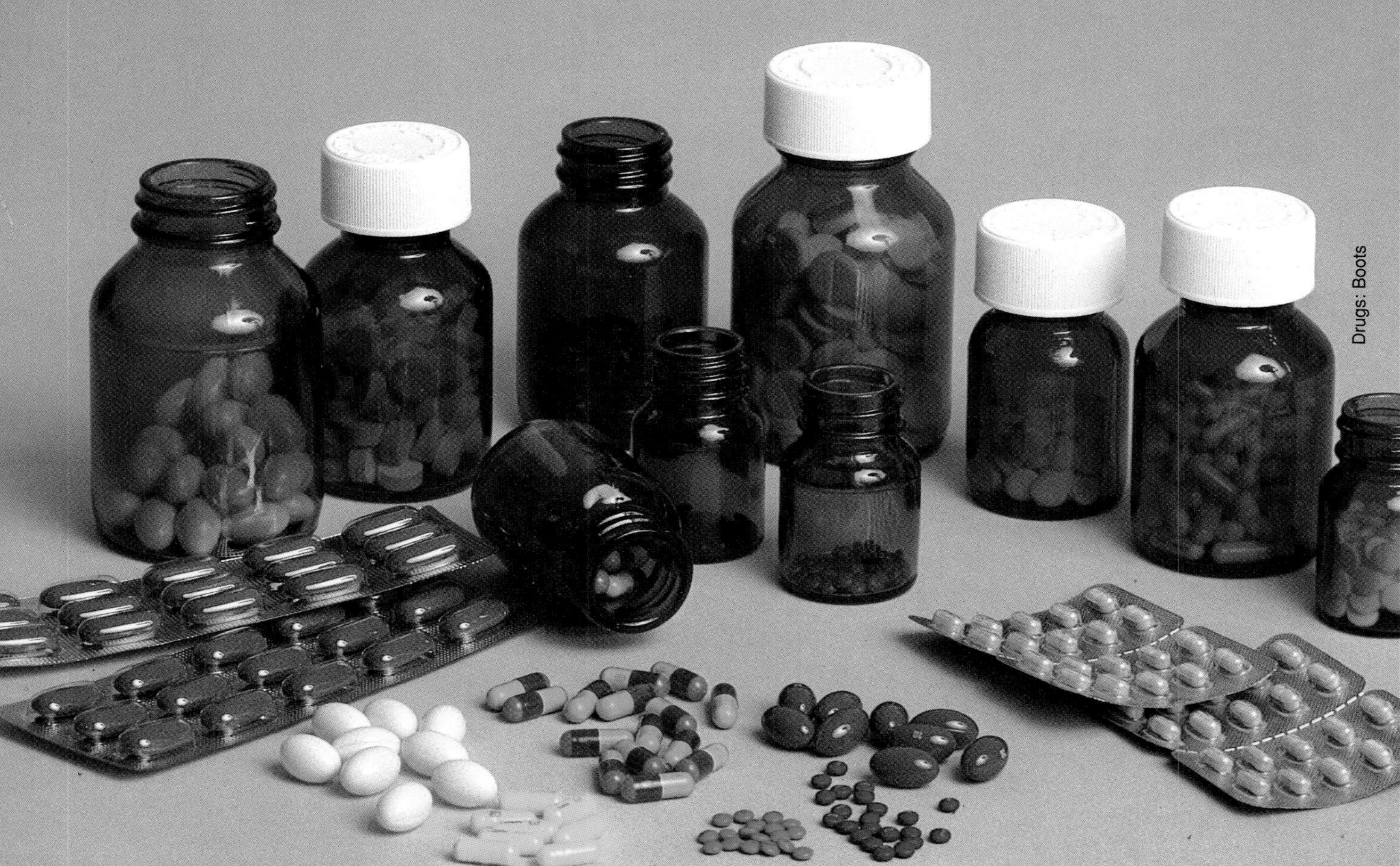

Drugs: Boots

Hypochondria

People who suffer from an exaggerated concern about their health are described as hypochondriacs. However, hypochondria should always be taken seriously, because it is a sign of emotional disturbance. Specialist help may be needed to uncover and deal with the real causes.

Q Is hypochondria always a sign of some underlying emotional disturbance?

A The simple answer is yes. A better way of putting it is to describe hypochondria as a state of mind that leads to anxiety about, and preoccupation with, one's health; the cause of this state of mind is always some underlying emotional disturbance.

Q My uncle has a not very serious ulcer that he has exaggerated way out of proportion. Would he be called a hypochondriac?

A This is one way in which hypochondria can develop, but it usually means that the patient had a tendency to be overconcerned with his health even before he or she becomes ill. However, it is necessary to realize that the symptoms of hypochondria are no less genuine than those of an illness itself.

Q Is it true that women are more prone to hypochondria than men?

A No. Men and women are equally liable to hypochondria, for example, if they feel unable to cope after being laid off work, or have suffered an emotional shock, such as the loss of a loved one. Events such as these can cause both men and women to become both introspective, and to worry unduly about their health instead of trying to cope with the situation.

Q My husband says I'm a hypochondriac because I like to read about medical subjects. Is this true?

A An interest in medicine often leads people to become doctors or nurses, but people can also be interested in medicine without either wanting to join these professions or being called hypochondriacs. Learning about medicine can lead to a healthier life. However, one should guard against reading about medical subjects out of an exaggerated interest in one's own health, since this may indicate hypochondria.

A key factor in hypochondria is a family background in which the need to take care of one's health was overstressed. Early exposure to chronic illness in one or both parents or grandparents, or deaths of near relatives, can also have a profound effect on a developing child, who might grow up with a fear of illness or death. Excessive interest in keeping fit may be another subtle factor; although it may be very important to exercise regularly, there is a limit to the amount of time that needs to be taken up this way.

Anxiety and depression

There are a number of psychiatric disorders that are commonly found to be associated with hypochondria. The first is an anxiety state, the unpleasant apprehension that something awful is about to happen. This is accompanied by a number of changes in the body's functions: increased heart and breathing rates and excessive sweating, especially of the palms of the hands and under the arms. Appetite may be lost or, in some people, it may increase dramatically. Either diarrhea or constipation may occur. Sleep may be disturbed, dizzy feelings may be experienced, and fainting might occur. In women there may be changes in periods, which can become infrequent or irregular. Hypochondriacs focus on any of these anxiety-produced symptoms, which are thought to be due to a feared disease such as cancer or heart disease.

Depressive states are a second contributing factor. Usually these arise following some unhappy event, such as a serious illness in the sufferer or a loved one, or possibly a breakdown of an important relationship. Occasionally there may be some long-standing emotional conflict that has not been resolved but that continues to smolder deep in the mind. Again, bodily functions may be disturbed, usually slowed down in some way, and this leads to further feelings of depression or anxiety. In severe depressive states delusional thoughts may develop so that the person's fear of cancer becomes a belief that he or she actually has cancer.

Obsessions and hysteria

Obsessional states can occur through family environment or the tendency may be inherited through the genes. Persistent thoughts arise that something has gone wrong in the body, and the person tends to ruminate over it. Often repetitive movements or habits develop; these are sometimes described as rituals and may be related to numbers, such as touching the doorknob six times before turning it. Alternatively a patient may become obsessed with the belief that he or she has a particular disease. This may

be related to deep guilt feelings about events that happened in the past.

Hysterical states (which may be partly genetic) become evident when a person is under stress. Ordinary bodily feelings or symptoms of simple ailments are exaggerated. There may be a strong feeling that everything is out of control, so that the person develops an intense fear that his or her health, or even life, is threatened.

Psychotic disorders

Illnesses such as schizophrenia and manic depression (more properly called bipolar disorder; see Manic depression) are well-known psychotic disorders in which hypochondria can appear. Symptoms may be bizarre or grotesque and the patient may imagine that his or her body is crawling with insects, filled with mold, shrinking, or swelling up. Increasing interest in the body's functions may lead to severe introspection or even complete withdrawal from all outside activities.

Finally some accident victims may develop a persistent belief that their injuries have left them with some permanent disability or handicap, even though their recovery has been complete. This is more common with patients with some preexisting psychiatric illness.

Hypochondriacs visit their doctor with a wide range of complaints. These can include changes in bodily functions affecting the heart or bowels; pains in the arms, back, or legs; or loss of sight or hearing. Although the symptoms may be really felt, they are usually evidence of some unresolved emotional disturbance.

Symptoms

Hypochondriacs tend to have many different symptoms, sometimes one after another, or even all at the same time. Alternatively there may be one continuous single symptom that is the sole center of attention. Usually the description is so graphic that a diagnosis of hypochondria is likely, particularly when there are complaints about the various functions of the body.

Dangers

Sometimes it is difficult to discover symptoms that might be due to a serious physical illness, because they are hidden behind the anxiety caused by imaginary symptoms. A full examination must be made and doctors must be continually on guard in case the patient does actually develop a real illness.

Treatment

Simple reassurance by the doctor might help in the early stages, but it is generally only the doctor who feels reassured by negative clinical findings. Hypochondriacs are often unable to accept such findings and reassurance, and they remain convinced that they have some dreadful disease and that the doctor is not telling them the truth. The use of tranquilizers and antidepressant pills are usually of no substantial help.

In hypochondria, as in all illnesses, it is the cause and not the symptoms that must be treated. The family doctor is probably in the best position to help the patient initially, but it may be necessary to call in specialist help. A psychiatrist or psychotherapist could help to discover and deal with the underlying psychological or emotional disturbances, and therefore help to cure the patient.

However, sometimes severe hypochondria has to be accepted as a state of mind that must be endured by the patient, by his or her relatives and friends, and by the doctor. Fortunately the passage of time often creates changes in the patient's life that reduce the intensity of hypochondriacal feelings, and this brings relief.

Outlook

If hypochondria is recognized early enough, it may be possible to bring about a satisfactory resolution, but in more severe cases the outlook is poor. Although it can safely be said that no one ever dies from hypochondria, the depression can occasionally become so profound that there is the possibility that the sufferer may contemplate suicide; this must be kept in mind and all preventive measures taken. For most hypochondriacs, however, the symptoms gradually lessen and many reach a ripe old age.

Hypoglycemia

Q **My mother is planning to go on a sugar-free diet. Will this reduce her blood sugar to a dangerously low level?**

A No, but serious malnutrition can cause hypoglycemia. This is because there is a lack of calories generally, not because the diet is specifically short of sugar. In a normally well-nourished person, a diet low in sugar is probably quite beneficial. The body is designed to extract sugar from a whole range of foods, and it is a good thing if it is allowed to do so naturally.

Q **My brother has diabetes that is treated with pills. Can he get hypoglycemia?**

A Yes, he can. Some of the pills that are used to treat diabetes work by stimulating the pancreas to produce more insulin. This means that excessive doses can produce hypoglycemia.

Q **Why does drinking on an empty stomach make me feel so rotten?**

A Intoxication is one possible reason, but hypoglycemia is another. The latter condition occurs because the large amounts of sugar in most alcoholic drinks is quickly absorbed into the blood, producing a lot of insulin that rapidly disperses it. However, if you eat as well as drink, additional sugar can be drawn from the food, giving the excess insulin something to work on so that the blood sugar level is maintained.

Q **A friend of mine has spells of dizziness and fainting whenever she is under pressure. Could this be hypoglycemia?**

A This is possible. Emotional difficulties are, in some cases, thought to produce symptoms of hypoglycemia. In particular this affects women who are especially tense or who are under emotional strain. Your friend should see her doctor, and if hypoglycemia is diagnosed, the doctor may recommend a diet that is high in protein and low in carbohydrates, to be eaten in small servings at regular intervals.

Hypoglycemia is a low level of blood sugar that causes disorientation and eventually unconsciousness. Diabetics are prone to it after taking insulin, but it is uncommon in most other people. It can be effectively controlled.

Our bodies digest the carbohydrates we eat (see Starches) into fuel our body can use (e.g. glucose, see Digestion). Excess fuel is stored in the liver as glycogen. When we need more energy, the glycogen is converted back to glucose. Hormones secreted by the pancreas control the levels of glucose and glycogen (see Pancreas). Too much glucose in the blood stimulates the pancreas to secrete insulin to make the liver store more glucose as glycogen (see Insulin). Too little glucose stimulates the pancreas to secrete glucagon to make the liver convert more glycogen back to glucose. Hypoglycemia occurs when the glucose level drops below normal.

Causes

Diabetics suffer from a lack of insulin (see Diabetes) and so have too much glucose sugar in their blood (hyperglycemia). If they take too much insulin or eat irregularly, and so fail to balance their sugar and insulin intake, they are prone to hypoglycemia. Hypoglycemia is also a feature of a rare condition called Addison's disease, where the adrenal glands do not produce enough cortisone. An underactive pituitary gland will also produce hypoglycemia, as will an enzyme deficiency (enzymes are the body's chemical transformers) in children, or a sensitivity to fructose or galactose (carbohydrates in fruit, honey, and milk). Occasionally the pancreas, which contains the insulin-secreting cells, may develop a tumor that leads to overproduction of insulin. Finally, drinking alcohol on an empty stomach may cause a hypoglycemic state.

Hypoglycemic symptoms—dizziness, slurred speech, and palpitations—can occur when a person drinks on an empty stomach.

Symptoms and dangers

Since the brain depends on glucose in the blood to work properly, hypoglycemia affects the nervous system. There is a general feeling of being unwell and of anxiety and panic. Speech may be slurred and behavior irrational. Walking is unsteady and there is sweating and palpitations.

Unless the level of blood glucose rises, the patient will eventually become unconscious. This is more frequent in diabetics.

Treatment

Diabetics must take sugar by mouth as soon as symptoms occur. They must learn to balance their food intake with insulin injections. People should eat something solid before drinking alcohol.

In all other cases a doctor should be consulted to check blood sugar levels.

Susan Griggs Agency

Hypothalamus

Q **My husband's head was injured in an accident at work. Now he has to take hormones. Why is this?**

A There is a delicate connection between the hypothalamus and the pituitary gland, which lies at the base of the skull (see Pituitary gland). This connection can be easily severed in an accident, leading to the problem of an underactive pituitary; this is probably what happened to your husband. Because the gland is no longer receiving stimulation from the hypothalamus to release hormones, drug treatment with synthetic hormones is necessary. However, the other neurological activities of the hypothalamus, like the control of eating, drinking, and sleeping, are less likely to be affected by head injuries.

Q **My friend is turning into a really heavy drinker. Could this affect his brain?**

A Unfortunately, yes. Alcohol is known to inhibit the release of hormones from the posterior pituitary. One of the results of this is a loss of water from the kidney that gives rise to dehydration and thirst after drinking, a problem that many people have noticed from time to time. Also really heavy drinking depletes the brain of thiamine (one of the B vitamins), and this produces small hemorrhages in the hypothalamic region of the brain.

Q **My 16-year-old son is always lounging around the house—he only seems to eat and sleep. Could his hormones be at fault in some way?**

A This is very unlikely. Your son's behavior sounds just like that of a typical teenager. The unfortunate few people who suffer from disease of the hypothalamus overeat so much that they suffer from gross obesity. When they sleep it is often difficult to wake them for much of the time. Withdrawn and confused behavior with occasional outbursts of violence may also happen in cases of disease of the hypothalamus, but fortunately this is rare.

Many life-maintaining processes, including eating, sleeping, and drinking, are all under the control of one small area of the brain—the hypothalamus.

How the hypothalamus controls body temperature

The hypothalamus receives information about the body's temperature in two ways: the heat of the blood passing through it and the messages from the temperature sensitive nerve endings in the skin surface.

One region of the hypothalamus is sensitive to an increase in body heat and another reacts to a decrease. The nerve pathways from these regions pass through the spinal cord via the autonomic nervous system and control a number of bodily activities, such as sweating, which increase or decrease the temperature of the body.

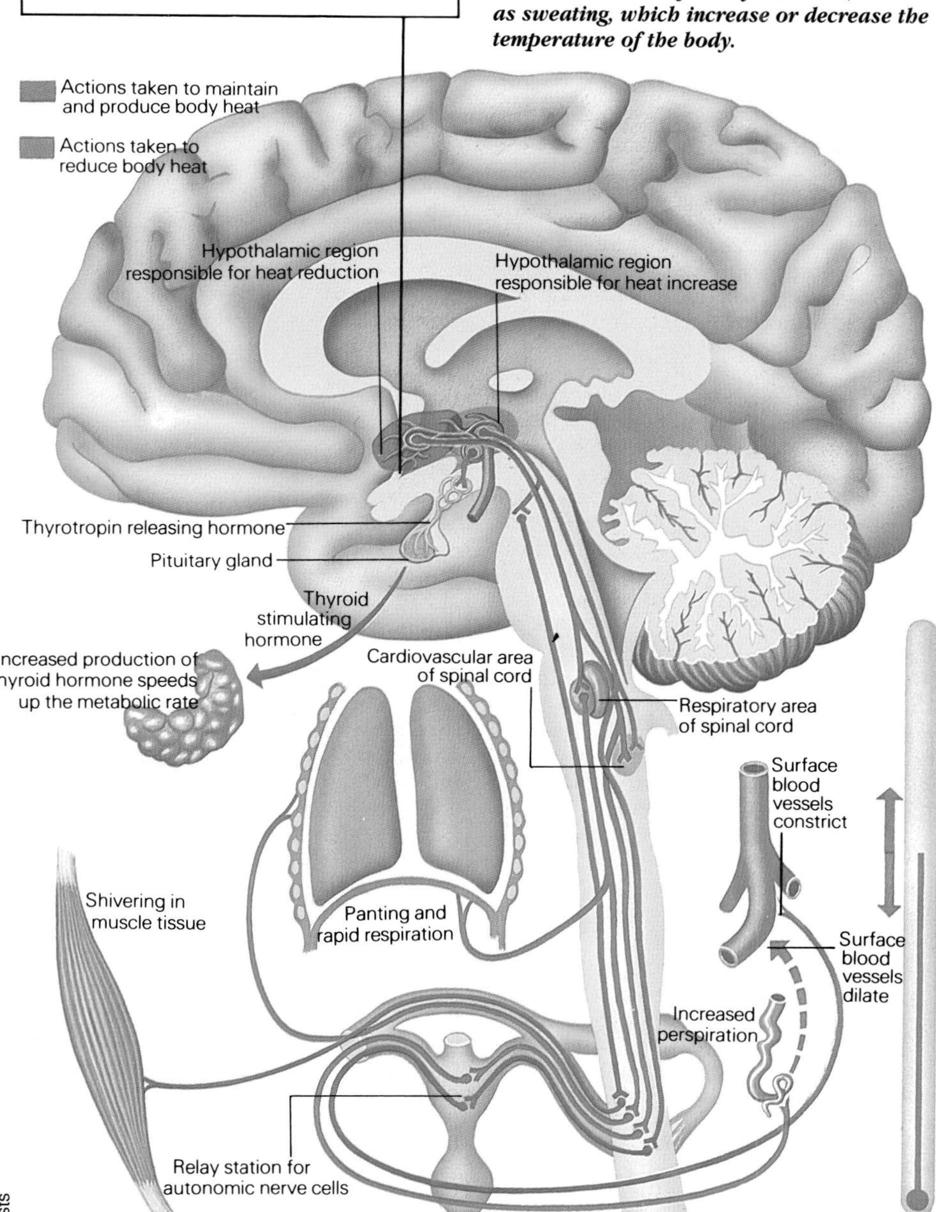

Venner Artists

Trevor Wood Picture Library

Although the food looks delicious, it is the hypothalamus that actually controls a person's appetite and thirst.

The hypothalamus lies at the base of the brain under the two cerebral hemispheres (see Brain). It is immediately below another important structure in the nervous system, the thalamus, which acts as a telephone exchange between the spinal cord and the cerebral hemispheres (see Nervous system and Thalamus).

The hypothalamus is a collection of specialized nerve centers that connect with other important areas of the brain, as well as with the pituitary gland. This is the region of the brain concerned with the control of such vital functions as eating and sleeping. It is also closely linked with the endocrine (hormone) system (see Endocrine system and Hormones).

Exerting control

The hypothalamus has nervous pathways that connect with the limbic system, which is closely connected with the smell centers of the brain. This portion of the brain also deals with memory, and abnormalities here may cause memory loss.

A vital function of the hypothalamus is temperature control. Temperatures are caused by substances that act directly on the hypothalamus. In the case of serious head injuries when the hypothalamus is affected, high temperatures of over 105°F (40.5°C) may result for long periods.

Another connection is with the reticular activating pathways, which run up and down the central core of the brain and spinal cord (see Spinal cord). The reticular activating formation is concerned with sleeping and waking. The condition called narcolepsy, in which a person falls asleep suddenly at any time and cannot be roused, is usually due to disease of the hypothalamus.

As if this were not enough, the hypothalamus is also the controlling center for both appetite and thirst. Although problems in this area are rare, one of the more common is gross obesity due to massive overeating; there is also usually excessive sleeping. This is called the Pickwickian syndrome after a fictional character.

The control of thirst and water balance is handled separately. The hormone that deals with loss of water from the kidneys is called antidiuretic hormone (ADH) (see Excretory systems). This is secreted from the posterior part of the pituitary gland, which is actually separate from the anterior part of the gland. The posterior part of the pituitary is actually part of the hypothalamus, and the two are connected by the pituitary stalk. The receptors that measure the concentration of the blood (and therefore help the hypothalamus decide how it should be organizing the body's water balance) are found in the hypothalamus itself. Disorders may result from abnormal retention of water by the kidneys (excessive ADH activity) or from a loss of ADH secretion (this is called diabetes insipidus). This condition may also result from head injuries where the pituitary stalk has been damaged.

There is no doubt too that the hypothalamus is concerned with the control of behavior and emotion. Withdrawn and confused behavior with some aggressive outbursts may happen in cases of disease. Sexual overactivity may also occur.

Links with hormones

Apart from its role in the nervous system, the hypothalamus is an integral part of the endocrine system. The hormone ADH is actually formed in the hypothalamus and then passes down the specialized nerve cells of the pituitary stalk to be released from the posterior part of the pituitary gland.

However, the anterior part of the gland is anatomically separate, and most of the important interactions occur between the hypothalamus and the anterior pituitary. It is really a little endocrine system of its own. Hormones—called inhibitory, or releasing, factors—are produced in the hypothalamus and carried to the pituitary in blood vessels that flow down the pituitary stalk.

The hormone TSH (thyroid-stimulating hormone) or thyrotrophin, produced by the anterior part of the pituitary, stimulates the thyroid to release thyroid hormone. In turn the production of TSH is stimulated by the thyrotrophin-releasing hormone (TRH) from the hypothalamus.

Similar systems exist to stimulate the release of corticotrophin, which controls adrenal activity, and FSH (follicle-stimulating hormone) and LH (luteinizing hormone), which stimulate the ovaries and the testes (see Glands).

The anterior pituitary also produces two hormones that act directly upon the tissues. Growth hormone is one of these. It is essential for normal growth and is also involved in the control of blood sugar. Growth hormone seems to be controlled by two factors, one of which stimulates release, while the other inhibits it (see Growth).

In contrast the hormone prolactin—which stimulates lactation (milk production) and inhibits menstruation—seems to be largely controlled by a substance called prolactin inhibiting factor, which restrains rather than stimulates secretion.

All of these releasing and inhibiting factors are simple chemicals and the formulas for many of them have been figured out. Today they can be made and used not only to test pituitary function but occasionally for treating patients.

One of the most fascinating developments in this field has been the realization that some of these compounds, particularly somatostatin (which affects growth hormone release) and TRH, are actually widespread in the nervous system and act as transmitters.

Diseases of the hypothalamus are rare. Tumors may occur in that area, and infection of the nervous system in the form of encephalitis or meningitis may also affect the function of the hypothalamus.

In a similar way head injuries or surgery may cause problems that are difficult to treat. It is possible that some of the small benign hormone-producing tumors that are known to occur in the pituitary actually result from overstimulation by the hypothalamus.

Hypothermia

Q My grandmother lives alone and often doesn't bother cooking. Are there foods she should eat to keep out the cold?

A Unfortunately not. Having hot food and drinks, although good for people's morale, makes very little difference to the outcome once hypothermia has set in. Make sure that this does not happen: check that her home is always adequately heated and that she is warmly dressed when it is cold outside.

Q I have heard that certain operations involve cooling the person's body. Isn't this dangerous?

A By making the body very cold the level of metabolism (the body's life-maintaining system) is lowered, and the amount of oxygen required is reduced. This means that breathing or circulation may be reduced for a short time without damaging the brain. The first operations for open heart surgery were performed on patients in a hypothermic state. The technique is no longer used—it has been replaced by other methods. Brain surgery is still sometimes performed under hypothermic conditions, but the patient is always carefully monitored (see Freezing).

Q Is exposure the same thing as hypothermia?

A The word *exposure* is used to mean hypothermia that has been caused by exposure outdoors to wind, snow, or water, whereas the term *hypothermia* is much more precise. It applies to the cooling of the body and can happen indoors too, usually to elderly people or small children.

Q Can you tell if you have got hypothermia, or does it just creep up on you?

A You will certainly know it if you become cold rapidly. The danger occurs if you are outdoors and have had too much to drink or are under the influence of drugs. Then your normal protective mechanisms will not be working well and you will be more at risk.

Hypothermia—a subnormal body temperature—causes needless deaths every year, so preventive measures are vital for those most at risk: the very old, the very young, and those who take part in outdoor activities.

The medical definition of hypothermia depends upon what is considered to be the normal body temperature. This is around 98.6°F (37°C), which is the temperature of the heart at the center of the body, but the temperature of the skin or in the mouth can fall very much lower than this. Therefore, in the case of a subnormal temperature, the routine method of measurement is very inaccurate. So doctors have to measure the temperature in the rectum. If this is below 95°F (35°C), the person is considered to have hypothermia.

What happens in the body

When the body loses heat its automatic reaction is to try to generate more by shivering. At this stage the person just feels uncomfortable and miserable, but as he or she gets colder, lethargy and drowsiness increase. Soon all shivering stops. When this cooling-down process happens slowly, victims are less likely to shiver than when the cooling is rapid. However, whatever happens, their condition is potentially serious.

If cooling continues mental confusion follows, then an overpowering desire to sleep, and finally a coma. This usually happens when the body temperature approaches 89.6°F (32°C). When the temperature drops to around 86°F (30°C), the hypothalamus (the organ situated below the brain; see Hypothalamus) loses its temperature-regulating ability, cell activity and breathing rate slow down, and the oxygen supply to the cells diminishes. The normal heartbeat is replaced by a condition called fibrillation, when the heart muscles ripple but do not actually pump blood.

The temperature at which fibrillation occurs is critical, because this marks the time when blood circulation stops, and unless something is done, the victim dies. Infants and children develop fibrillation at much lower temperatures than adults, sometimes as low as 69.8°F (21°C).

Spectrum

A baby's skin area is large in relation to total body size and so heat is easily lost. Babies taken out in wintry weather must be dressed warmly.

Tom Belshaw

Elderly people should be visited regularly to insure that they are keeping warm. Mittens will help keep their hands warm.

People at risk

There are two groups of people most at risk from hypothermia: those who are unable to defend themselves against heat loss with the normal protective reflexes of the body and those exposed to a harsh environment.

Old people living alone sometimes find it difficult to take care of themselves. During cold snaps it is not unusual for them to sit in a chair and hope to keep warm because they are indoors, rather than to get up and switch on the heat; they may simply lack the will or motivation to do this or, in some tragic cases, they may not be able to afford the cost of fuel. Their inactive state also prevents the body from shivering.

Very small babies are also at risk. Their bodies do not have a mature temperature-regulating mechanism, so they are unable to shiver. They have a large surface area of skin in proportion to their body volume, so their bodies act as very good radiators of heat.

The body's normal protective mechanism includes shivering and constriction of the blood vessels running to the skin, so that radiation of heat from the body is stopped. This constriction of blood vessels takes place over the entire surface of the body, with the exception of the head. The blood vessels running to the face and scalp cannot be constricted in response to cold, so however cold the victim, heat loss from the head will continue. When vigorous movement is not possible, because the victim is either very old or very young, shivering does not occur. As a result heat loss is more rapid than normal. Matters are made worse when the victim is deeply unconscious. This rapid heat loss also happens to people who are intoxicated with alcohol or drugs, particularly barbiturates (see Barbiturates).

Exposure to the elements is another way in which people may develop hypothermia. Climbers, walkers, and divers in cold water are particularly at risk. In divers the rate at which heat is conducted away from the body by water is over 100 times greater than air of the same temperature. This heat loss is greatly increased if the wind is blowing or if the water is rough. When boats capsize, death often results not from drowning but from exposure.

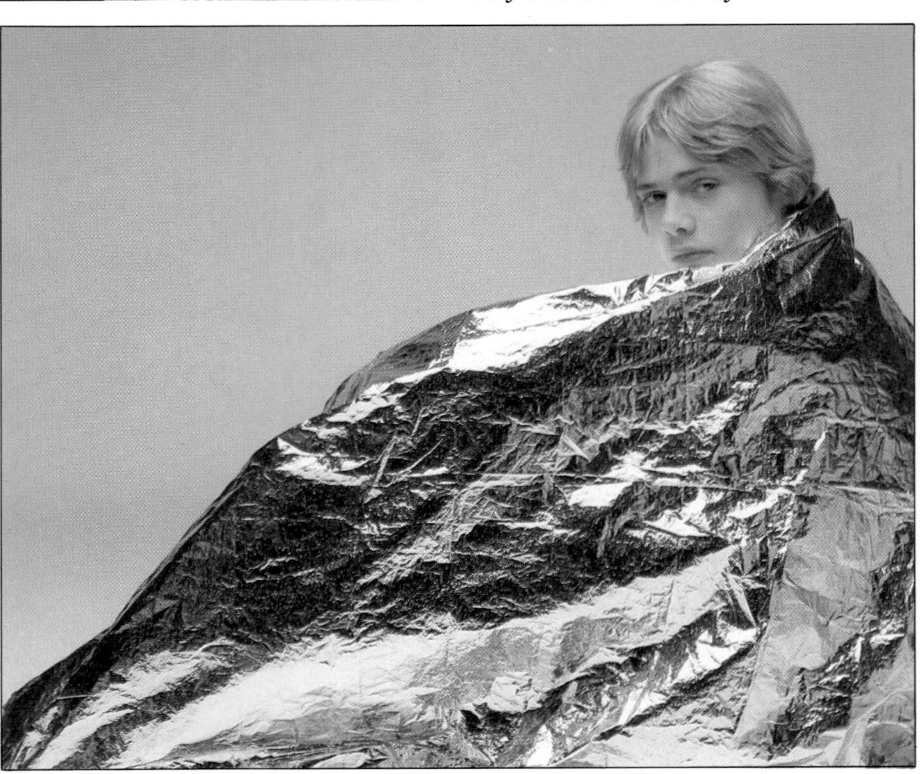

People suffering from exposure are covered by a space blanket. This has aluminum foil on both sides that reflects body heat back to the body.

Mike Hill

How to avoid hypothermia

In old people
- Reorganize your home so that in winter you can live in fewer rooms
- Keep your home warm and well insulated
- Wear warm clothing, especially wool and wool blends
- Make sure you eat and drink enough
- Try to keep active
- Make sure that someone knows you are on your own

In babies
- Dress them warmly in winter
- Keep rooms warm
- If they kick off blankets, put them in a sleeping bag; for toddlers, use sleepers with attached feet

When walking or climbing
- Before setting off check the weather forecast
- Wear protective clothing
- Take advice from experts
- Tell people where you intend to go
- If you get lost stay where you are, try to build a shelter, and wait for help
- Try to keep dry

During water sports
- Wear an officially approved life jacket
- For diving in cold waters, wear a wet suit and protect extremities
- Wear wool or fleece next to your skin, then a windproof jacket

How to help a victim
- Seek medical help. Hospital treatment may be necessary
- Remove wet clothing and dry the victim's body
- Cover victim with blankets and give them a well-wrapped hot water bottle
- Do not give hot food, drinks, or alcohol if a victim appears seriously ill

A brisk winter walk can warm an elderly person, but thick clothing must be worn.

Treatment
There is a good deal of medical argument about the correct treatment, but the ideal procedure would appear to be for all conscious patients to be rewarmed actively, while unconscious ones should be rewarmed passively. Active rewarming means immersing the patient in hot water at a temperature of 104°F (40°C), which is obviously carefully tested first. This type of treatment is used for the patient who becomes hypothermic rapidly, for example, as a result of exposure to the elements.

In old, frail, or unconscious victims, the bathtub treatment is not such a good idea, and insulation with a space blanket—made of heat-reflecting aluminum foil— and then warm woolen blankets is preferable. The patient is then left in a room that has a temperature of 95°F (35°C) to recover. It may take many hours or even days for the rewarming process to be complete.

Hot food or drinks, although comforting, contribute very little, and in seriously ill patients they are better avoided because of the risk of vomiting. Alcohol produces less peripheral dilation than it was previously thought, and the euphoria it produces may be beneficial.

Dangers
Cold kills. This message cannot be emphasized enough. A cold spell in winter, together with a heating failure, could put an elderly person's life in danger. This is why older people living alone should be regularly visited by some caring outsider if they have no close relatives.

Another danger of hypothermia is that a victim may seem to be dead, and efforts to resuscitate him or her may be abandoned too soon. There are many stories of how severely hypothermic victims have survived up to one and a half hours after their heartbeat and breathing appeared to have stopped. This is especially true when barbiturates or alcohol are involved.

Hysterectomy

Q Is it possible to conceive after a hysterectomy?

A This is very rare—so rare that if it does occur, it is reported in the press. What happens is that the fetus grows inside the abdominal cavity instead of in the uterus (see Ectopic pregnancy).

Q After a hysterectomy what happens to the blood a woman normally loses every month? Does it still appear and then build up inside her?

A When a woman has a period she loses the lining of the uterus together with some blood that has built up behind it. After a hysterectomy, since she no longer has a uterus, she no longer has its lining and therefore no blood is produced that needs to be shed each month.

Q I have been told I must have a hysterectomy. Will I get a backache afterward?

A There is no reason why the operation should cause a backache, unless you develop a urinary infection at the time of the operation. If you do the condition can be treated by antibiotics.

Q Do all women who have had a hysterectomy gain weight?

A After the operation women are less active for a few weeks and therefore require fewer calories. Provided they are aware of this and do not eat to build up their strength, they should not gain any weight.

Q If my ovaries have to be removed when I have a hysterectomy, will I be given artificial hormones?

A This must depend on whether you have any problems without these hormones and on what advice your doctor gives.

Q Will I still have pleasure during sexual intercourse after a hysterectomy?

A Yes! There is absolutely no need to worry about this.

Hysterectomy is the removal of a uterus that is diseased, misplaced, or malfunctioning. By improving a woman's general health, it can also increase her enjoyment of life.

The words *hysteria* and *hysterectomy* both come from the Greek word *hystera*, meaning "the uterus." In ancient Greece the uterus was believed to be the source of many emotional or hysterical disturbances in women. Of course this view is no longer favored, but the reverse may sometimes be true: that nervous disorders may have an effect on the way the uterus functions (see Uterus). Women with anorexia nervosa (compulsive self-starvation), for example, often cease to have periods (see Anorexia and bulimia).

Because of the lingering association between the uterus and emotional instability, many women approach the idea of having a hysterectomy—an operation to remove the uterus, including the neck (the cervix) and the body (the fundus)—with great anxiety.

The operation may be very advisable because of a serious tumor in the uterus or associated tissues, or it may be suggested as a treatment for symptoms that are not always due to serious disease, such as heavy periods. In these cases only the woman concerned knows how incapacitated she is by her symptoms, and so she must decide whether or not she wants a hysterectomy.

The operation is becoming less common in the United States, because many of the conditions for which it used to be performed are being treated in other ways. For example, abnormal bleeding from an otherwise healthy uterus can often be successfully treated with hormone pills, and cancer of the cervix may be treated by radiotherapy (see Radiotherapy).

Hysterectomy is, if possible, avoided in women who have not completed their families. Because of this, and the higher incidence of disease of the uterus later in life, the operation is most commonly performed on women between 45–55.

During a woman's reproductive years the lining of the uterus is shed at regular intervals and so she has a period (see Menstruation). When she becomes pregnant the fetus grows in the uterus, so removal of this organ will put a stop to periods and pregnancies.

In subtotal hysterectomy the cervix is not removed. In total hysterectomy the entire uterus is removed (and sometimes the ovaries and fallopian tubes). Dotted lines show the usual extent of surgery. A prolapsed uterus is one of the conditions that may necessitate a total hysterectomy through the vagina.

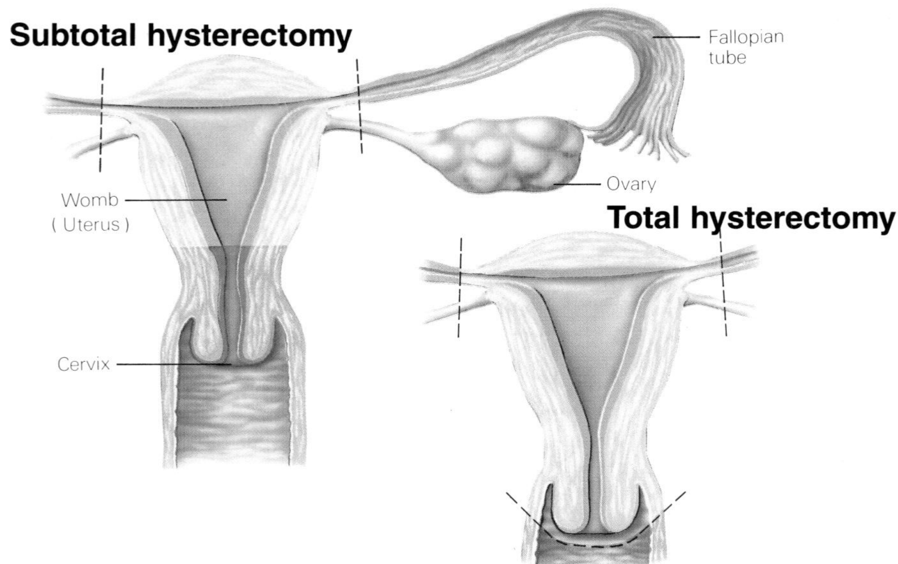

Frank Kennard

Different types of hysterectomy

Abdominal hysterectomy involves the removal of the uterus through an incision in the lower abdominal wall. In a vaginal hysterectomy the uterus may be removed through the vagina.

Abdominal hysterectomy gives the surgeon a view of all the pelvic organs, and

Tom Belshaw

A hysterectomy does not affect a woman's enjoyment of life.

their health can therefore be checked. The incision is larger than in a vaginal hysterectomy, which makes it easier to remove an enlarged uterus or one that is stuck in an abnormal way to other structures, such as the large intestine. The disadvantage of the method is that it leaves a scar on the lower abdomen.

The uterus is normally supported in the abdominal cavity by a floor of muscle and ligaments that are attached to the region between the neck and body of the uterus. These ligaments can become loose with age or childbearing, and the uterus tends to fall into the vagina. This is called a prolapse (see Prolapse). Sometimes this on its own causes discomfort, and at other times it also affects the large intestine and bladder, which are also pulled downward. If this becomes a severe problem, it may be treated by removing the uterus through the vagina and putting tissue and stitches in place to support the intestine and bladder in their correct positions. One advantage of having a hysterectomy vaginally is that there are no visible scars afterward.

Prolapsed uterus

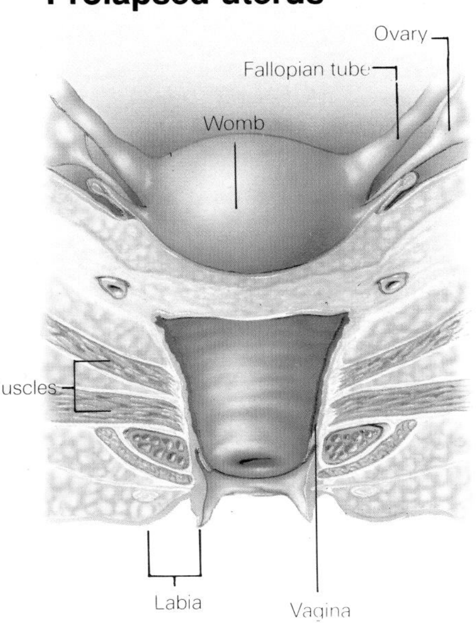

Removal of the entire uterus is called a total hysterectomy. Sometimes it is too difficult to remove the neck of the uterus, which is attached to the bladder, and this area is left behind. This operation is called a subtotal hysterectomy. When it is performed it is still possible for the woman to have very light periods and she should remember to have regular Pap smears for cancer of the cervix (see Cervix and cervical smears and Pap smear).

Infrequently the entire uterus together with the ovaries and tubes are removed. This procedure goes under the long name of total abdominal hysterectomy and bilateral salpingo-oophorectomy (TAH-BSO). When a woman reaches the change of life (see Menopause) it is in part because her ovaries no longer release their hormones; if a woman who has not reached menopause has her ovaries removed, she may experience the sudden onset of symptoms such as hot flashes (see Hot flashes).

Reasons for hysterectomy

The reasons for performing a hysterectomy fall into five main categories: removal of a normal uterus that is giving the woman heavy or frequent periods (called dysfunctional uterine bleeding) when other, simpler treatments have been unsuccessful; removal of the uterus because of a tumor in it or in a related structure, such as an ovary; for sterilization (but this is unusual unless the woman also has other problems related to her uterus); because of pain related to a woman's genital tract, as in a chronic pelvic infection that has not improved through other measures, such as antibiotics; and finally, because the uterus has prolapsed (slipped down) into the vagina, though a hysterectomy is not always needed to correct this condition.

What is involved

A hysterectomy is a fairly large operation that is only undertaken after much thought and several investigations, often including a D&C (see Dilatation and curettage), to determine that this is the best option for the patient.

The woman is admitted to the hospital a day before the operation. This allows time for her to be examined to check that she is healthy enough for an operation. It may be necessary to shave the patient's pubic hair, since the incision in the abdominal wall may go through this area. She will also be given an enema or suppositories to insure that her large intestine is empty and that it will not get in the way during the operation (see Enema).

The hysterectomy is performed under general anesthetic. During the removal of the uterus it is necessary to strip the bladder from the lower end of the uterus, and this often bruises it. To allow the bruising to heal quickly, it is sometimes necessary to rest the bladder for a day or two by passing a catheter into it and letting it empty continuously.

The intestines are also handled during the operation and may not function well for a few hours afterward. Until it regains its capacity to work normally, the patient is not given food, but fluids are given through an IV infusion (see Intravenous infusion). Within 24 hours of the operation most patients are out of bed and feeling much better.

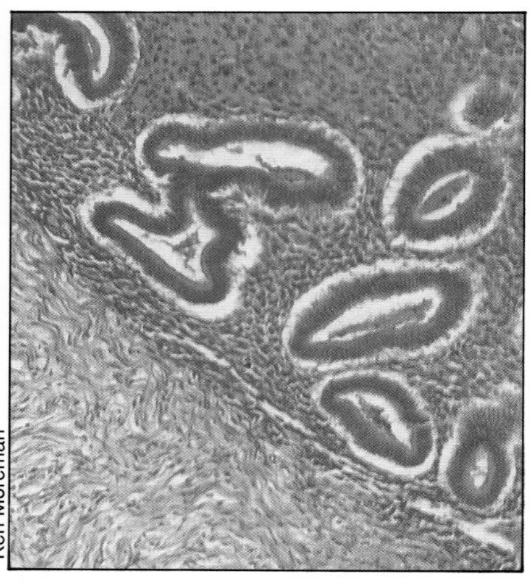

If the lining of the uterus (upper part of picture) is deposited, as it is here, on an ovary—a condition called endometriosis—a total hysterectomy may be needed.

Women who have had a hysterectomy are encouraged to get up and walk around soon after the operation. During the first six weeks of their convalescence, it is important that they avoid heavy lifting or housework to allow time for their tissues to heal without strain.

Many women find that they feel very tired during this time and some are slightly depressed. Both these problems pass as health is regained.

Women can resume their normal sex life once they have been examined by their doctor to check that the wound has healed—usually six weeks after the operation. Many couples find that sexual intercourse is more enjoyable after the hysterectomy because they no longer need to worry about an unwanted pregnancy.

Outlook

In the majority of cases women who have had a hysterectomy are left with normally functioning ovaries. Therefore those women who are prone to premenstrual tension may still have the same signs and symptoms, but without the accompanying period. At the appropriate age they may also experience some of the usual symptoms of menopause.

Most women who have a hysterectomy derive great benefit from it and feel much healthier within a few weeks.

Possible reasons for a hysterectomy

Reason for hysterectomy	Type of hysterectomy usually performed	Purpose of operation	Outcome (in all cases no further periods or pregnancies)
The uterus has dropped (prolapsed) from its intra-abdominal site into the front passage	Vaginal hysterectomy	During this operation it is possible to put stitches in the front wall of the passage to support the bladder and in the back wall to support the intestine. This may cure some intestine or bladder problems	Cure
Early stages of cancer of the uterus	Total abdominal hysterectomy and removal of the ovaries and tubes	To remove the growth and areas that a few malignant cells might have affected	Result will depend on many factors. Doctor's advice should be sought
Abnormal bleeding from an otherwise healthy uterus (dysfunctional uterine bleeding) not cured by drugs	Abdominal hysterectomy, usually leaving the ovaries	To remove the organ from which the bleeding came	Cure
Large fibroids (benign growths; see Fibroids) or fibroids causing symptoms such as heavy bleeding	Same as above	To remove the fibroids. Sometimes a larger abdominal incision is made to facilitate removal of very large fibroids	Cure
Rarely used form of sterilization	Abdominal hysterectomy, leaving ovaries	Removes the organ in which the fetus would grow. Stops sperm from meeting the egg	One recently reported ectopic pregnancy following a hysterectomy but extremely rare
Cancer of fallopian tubes—rare	Total abdominal hysterectomy with removal of ovaries & tubes	Removes the growth	So rare that survival rates are uncertain
Cancer of the ovary (area which releases the eggs)	Total abdominal hysterectomy and removal of the ovaries and tubes	Removes growth and areas to which small parts of growth may have spread	If early, patient may be cured. If the woman has not already gone through menopause, she will do so after the operation
Severe chronic pelvic infection that has not responded to antibiotics	Total abdominal hysterectomy; if possible, ovaries are left	Removes infected area that may have caused pain, especially during sexual intercourse	Usually curative
Tissue resembling the lining of the uterus may be deposited at abnormal sites (endometriosis)	As above; may rarely also involve removal of the ovaries	To remove this tissue	Usually curative

Hysteria

Q Is hysteria more common in women than in men?

A Yes, and there are historic reasons for this. In the past, almost total male domination left women with few resources for protest. Some women, when driven to distraction by mental and social restrictions, became hysterical as a form of release. Men had a better time of it and maintained the strong, silent approach. But it is important to remember that emotional outbursts are not what doctors now mean by hysteria.

Q Is there any connection between the words hysterectomy and hysteria?

A Certainly. As you know, hysterectomy is the operation to remove the uterus (in Greek, *hystera*). Plato taught that the uterus was desperate to produce children and if frustrated in this desire, became angry and caused all kinds of upsets, especially emotional instability. From this quaint idea rose the later concept of hysteria, which, obviously, could only happen in women.

Q My young son often works himself into a tantrum about silly things. Is he hysterical?

A No. Hysteria, in the medical sense, does not manifest itself in tantrums. Your son's behavior is probably consciously manipulative and designed so that he can get his own way with you. Temper tantrums are one of the few weapons available to a young child in the battle of wills with his or her parents. Ignore them if you can.

Q Is it true that hysteria can cause blindness?

A Yes. Very rarely a person can suffer from a type of apparent blindness, for which there is no physical cause. In such a case, the cause of the blindness is a serious psychological problem, usually a reaction to severe mental stress. Such blindness, called hysterical blindness, would prevent the person from having to do something that is profoundly against his or her inclination.

Hysteria is a severe psychological disturbance causing an upset of body function. Hysteria may involve a dramatic display of emotional disturbance, but in many cases the symptoms are even more alarming.

Zefa

Their unstable emotions make adolescents prone to hysteria. It can be sparked off at events such as discos and pop concerts.

The medical meaning of the term *hysteria* differs fundamentally from the sense in which the word is used in popular speech. Far from being an uncontrolled display of emotional disturbance that seems calculated to attract as much attention as possible, true hysteria commonly manifests itself in major bodily disturbances which are often viewed by the affected person with apparent indifference. Partly because of this confusion, and partly because of social disapproval of hysterical behaviour, many doctors prefer to use the term *conversion disorder*.

Historical perspective

Hysteria comes from the Greek word for uterus, *hystera*. The ancient Greeks believed that a woman's uterus became angry and hysterical if it was denied the exercise of its childbearing function—hence the idea that hysteria affects only women. This is one of Plato's concepts that we can happily dismiss.

In more recent times, hysteria was brought prominently to medical attention by the distinguished French neurologist Jean Martin Charcot (1825–1893), most of whose hysterical patients were women. In that era, the main cause of hysteria was the conflict between sexual or aggressive impulses and powerful social barriers. As a result hysteria was commonplace. Today, sexual and other restrictions have almost vanished and so true hysteria is comparatively rare, representing only about one psychiatric case in 10,000.

Conversion disorder may occur at any age but is most common in adolescents and young adults in the lower socioeconomic groups. It is still more common in women than in men; reported figures show that there are between two and five times as many cases in females as in males.

The meaning of conversion

Inner conflicts that cannot be fully faced or expressed verbally still demand an outlet, but in a form that is acceptable to the person concerned. Conversion provides a means of disguising the impulse from the person, so that it need not be confronted, but, at the same time, indicating or demonstrating to others, in a nonverbal way, that there is a need for special attention. As a result, unacceptable life situations may be changed, other people may be manipulated, and responsibilities may be evaded. These effects are called secondary gains of the conversion.

The conversion process occurs at an unconscious level so that the affected person may be unaware of the psychological basis of the resulting physical symptoms and is thus unable to control them voluntarily. The Diagnostic and Statistical Manual of Mental Disorders of the American Psychiatric Association (DSM-IV) lays down criteria for diagnosing conversion disorder. These require that there should be a loss of, or alteration in, physical functioning, and not simply a pain or a disturbance of sexual function. There must be a psychosocial stress apparently related to a conflict or need and related to the start or worsening of the symptom. And there must be unawareness by the person concerned of intention to produce the symptom.

Hysterical symptoms

These may take many forms, but among the most common are: loss of sensation in any part of the body, various paralyses, weakness, blindness, tunnel vision, deafness, abnormal forms of walking, epileptic-like seizures, and tics and jerks.

Dealing with a hysterical episode

In a child

If possible ignore the outburst. The cause is usually trivial, so beyond a swift appraisal to see if anything is physically wrong, allow the episode to burn itself out. Don't pick up the child and comfort him or her; this is exactly the sort of attention he or she is playing for. Once the child realizes that you're responding, the outbursts will become more persistent and more of a nuisance.

In an adult

It is helpful to try to calm the person down, but no attempt to talk things over should be made until calmness is restored. A quickly made cup of tea and a convincing show of firmness is often all that is necessary. Above all do not allow yourself to get excited. Instead make as little of the episode as possible, but praise the person's attempt at becoming calm.

Few people outside the medical profession have much idea of neuroanatomy and, as a result, the so-called neurological disorders produced by conversion hysteria usually do not correspond to any possible anatomical pattern. No nerve disorder, for instance, can cause total loss of sensation in a hand covered by a glove; sensory nerves are simply not distributed in this way. Nevertheless, "glove and stocking" anesthesia is one of the most common manifestations of hysteria.

In another pattern of hysteria that does not correspond to organic disease the person has a wildly staggering gait with body jerks and flailing arms, but does not fall down. People with hysterical blindness seldom bump into things and those having fits do not hurt themselves if they fall.

In spite of these apparently gross neurological disturbances, all tendon reflexes and neurophysiological tests are normal. Although insisting that they have a severe disability, people with hysteria often seem remarkably unconcerned. This is called *la belle indifference* and is a feature of the condition. Experienced doctors are wary of making a diagnosis of hysteria and will never do so without first carrying out a full neurological examination. They do this because genuine neurological disease is now more common than conversion disorder. To misdiagnose a patient as an hysteric can have serious consequences.

Treatment

Once the diagnosis of conversion hysteria is established the affected person can be safely treated by a careful exploration of the origins of the problem. He or she will be told firmly that the symptoms, however serious they may seem, are not an indication of organic disease and that they are likely to recover soon. Patients are never told that their symptoms are imaginary. This is likely to make matters worse.

Reassurance does nothing to solve the person's problems, however, and further conversions, taking either the same or different forms, are common, especially in those who have much to gain. So an energetic psychological investigation is needed to get to the root of the problem. Insight-oriented psychotherapy is commonly employed. This is a method in which the therapist and the affected person patiently explore the underlying conflict and the symbolism of the conversion symptom. It is commonly found that the symptom has been modelled on those of a person important to the patient, sometimes someone who has recently died.

Treatment should be provided early in the process because experience has shown that the longer a conversion symptom has persisted, the more difficult it is to deal with the problem.

Children may become hysterical when denied something they want. Ignoring the outbursts will discourage them from this type of behavior.

Bubbles/Loisjoy Thurston

Imagination

Q I often have the feeling that I have been in some place or situation before. Is this just a trick of my imagination?

A Many explanations have been put forward to explain this experience, which is called *déjà vu*. Some scientists think that it is a "trick" phenomenon, due to a mix-up of impulses in the brain. Others believe that it is the effect of a minute time lag in the transfer of information from one side of the brain to the other. Yet others think that *déjà vu* is due to a misrouting of memory signals in the brain. There is no evidence to confirm or deny any of these theories, nor the one held by some people that it is really a memory of a past existence.

Q My six-year-old daughter lies awake screaming at night because she imagines there is a "big bad wolf" in her room. What can I do to help her?

A This sort of behavior is a common problem in children who have vivid imaginations. Give your daughter a low-power night-light or leave her bedroom door open a little so that her room is not in complete darkness. Try to make sure she is as calm as possible before she goes to bed and has not been overstimulated by a scary television program or a book featuring wolves, ghosts, monsters, or any other "scary" creatures. Very often these nightmares are a passing phase, so your daughter is likely to outgrow them.

Q My 18-year-old sister is constantly imagining that everyone is criticizing her. In particular I seem to be able to do nothing right. Could she be mentally ill?

A Such imaginings can be a warning sign of mental illness so you should make sure that your sister sees a doctor as soon as possible. He or she will be able to tell if she is in need of psychiatric help. Your sister is unlikely to be able to express her feelings to you rationally since you are too close to her, and this helps to explain why she is so aggressive toward you and should have professional help.

Children often have vivid imaginations, but imagination can also play a major part in adult life. So what are its uses, and why does it sometimes mislead us?

The ability to imagine develops in the early years of life. By the time they are four or five, most children have the capacity to use their imaginations to play highly inventive games and to use both toys and household objects in an imaginative and creative way.

Play is one of the most important means by which a child can develop his or her imagination and is vital in the preschool years. By encouraging a child to use the imagination, a parent is providing him or her with the chance to widen mental horizons and to develop the skills of co-ordination and other related abilities.

The development of the imagination can give rise to many childhood fears—not simply fear of ghosts, monsters, and other supernatural beings but also fear of accidents, illness, and death. Parents should do all they can to disperse such fears, but if they persist to the extent that they hinder the child's emotional or physical development, then the child should see a doctor.

Imagination and intelligence

The brain is involved in the development and use of the imagination, and research has shown that of the two cerebral hemispheres of the brain (the large domes at the top of the brain), it is the right-hand one that is more involved with imaginative powers. The left side of the brain is concerned with thought and language, while three-dimensional, artistic, and musical abilities, which are associated with the imagination, are controlled by the right side.

As imagination is a function carried out by the brain, it might be logical to think that there is some link between imagination and intelligence. Many attempts have been made to find a connection between imagination—expressed through creativity—and intelligence, but it has been shown that there is no statistical link. It is

Parents should encourage children's already vivid imaginations so that they can develop mental and manual skills.

Daily Telegraph Colour Library

Zefa

Children can express their imaginations in a variety of ways. They may act out fantasies (above) or get involved in the world of magic and illusion (below).

just as possible to be highly creative and score poorly on IQ tests as it is to have a high IQ and low creativity.

Attempts have also been made to find a connection between imaginative thinking and personality. These studies showed that, in general, the more imaginative a person is, the more likely he or she is to be introverted and need plenty of solitude, although there were many exceptions. Powers of intuition and the ability to grasp abstract concepts were also more highly developed in the most imaginative and creative people tested. These people paid little regard to conventional behavior and felt less need to achieve acceptance by their peers.

Possible problems

The imagination can go wrong at times. Hallucinations are thought to be one aspect of faulty imagination. They can occur when the brain is deprived of sleep; in cases of mental illness; or they can be induced by drugs such as LSD. They are also common among people who have been deprived of sensory input to their brains—for example, by being kept in solitary confinement for long periods. They can take many forms—from the desert traveler desperate for water who "sees" an oasis, to the hallucinations of a sleep-deprived truck driver who sees imaginary spiders crawling over the windshield.

A misdirection of the imagination may be involved in a variety of emotional problems and mental illnesses. In a mild form, a child who is overanxious about school may project his or her anxieties into imagining that he or she is victimized by teacher or classmates.

Later in childhood, or in adult life, the imagination may run riot in an abnormal way during many types of illness. An anorexic girl who compulsively starves herself may imagine that she is fat for a whole variety of reasons, including fear of growing up and developing into a woman. Someone with a depressive illness may constantly imagine that they are being followed, or that they must wash because their hands are covered with imaginary germs. When a person is unable to distinguish between fantasy and reality they are probably suffering from some form of mental illness and they will need medical and psychiatric help.

The most serious derangement of the imagination is thought to occur in the mental illness of schizophrenia, perhaps the most serious of the common mental illnesses. The hallmarks of this disease are hallucinations—imaginary voices or figures—that may be heard or seen, together with delusions (imaginary feelings usually concerning some sort of persecution). Modern research suggests that schizophrenia is due to a chemical abnormality in the brain; it certainly responds to tranquilizers.

Zefa

Immune system

Q Can a person's state of mind affect their immune system by making them prone to illness?

A Not necessarily, but it is known, for example, that absenteeism from work due to illness runs hand in hand with depression or job dissatisfaction. Therefore people who become run down as a result of depression or dissatisfaction are more vulnerable to infection, possibly because the immune system is not working efficiently. So, generally speaking, people who are happy in their work and in their lives are more likely to be healthy.

Q Is it possible for a child to inherit immunity to any disease from its mother?

A Yes. There are some globulins that cross the placenta and so give the baby some protection for the first six weeks to three months of life while the immune system is still immature. An example of this is protection of the baby from infection from the measles virus. Of course if the mother hasn't suffered from the measles, she won't pass on the antibody created to fight the infection, and the baby will be susceptible to it.

Another important source of immunity is from globulins in the mother's breast milk. In certain societies it is the custom to breast-feed for long periods, possibly because its beneficial effects were observed in situations where there might otherwise have been higher infant mortality.

Q Is it possible for the body to be immune to anything?

A No. If your immune system is working well and you are healthy, you should be able to make antibodies to many infecting agents. However, this will not always prevent you from having the same illness on more than one occasion. Antibodies don't protect you from getting an illness again, but they do fight the illness faster if you do get it. Colds are a different matter: there are so many cold viruses that you can never be immune to all of them.

The body has its own internal defense system designed to protect itself from illness: the immune system. So how does it work, and why does it sometimes fail?

The immune system protects us from infection and invasion by all sorts of bacteria, viruses, and microbes. It has two major weapons to accomplish this.

The agents of the humoral (antibody) system are plasma cells, special kinds of white blood cells called B lymphocytes that secrete immunoglobulins (see Blood, Lymphocytes, and Plasma).

The cellular immune system works through a second kind of lymphocyte, the T cell, which migrates from the bone marrow (see Marrow and transplants) to the thymus (see Thymus) and then settles in the lymph nodes or circulates in the blood (see Lymphatic system). The T cells either kill invaders directly or act as helper cells.

People who enjoy life are less likely to become run down and so are generally less vulnerable to infection.

Sally and Richard Greenhill

B lymphocytes

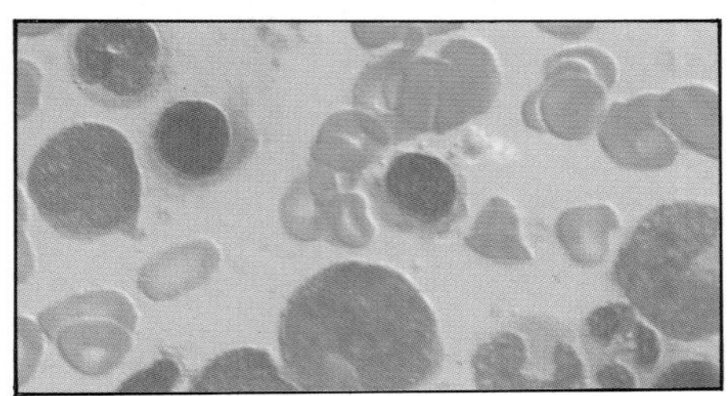

B lymphocytes, or plasma cells (above), produce immunoglobulins that enter the bloodstream to ward off attack by bacteria, microbes, and viruses. Like B lymphocytes, T lymphocytes (below), stored in the lymph nodes, are alerted to attack foreign tissue and viruses by helper cells, which carry messages of invasion to developing lymphocytes.

T lymphocytes

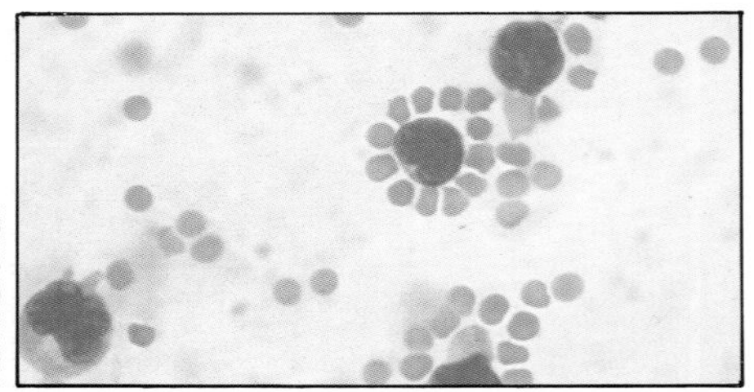

Ken Moreman

How immunity-producing cells function

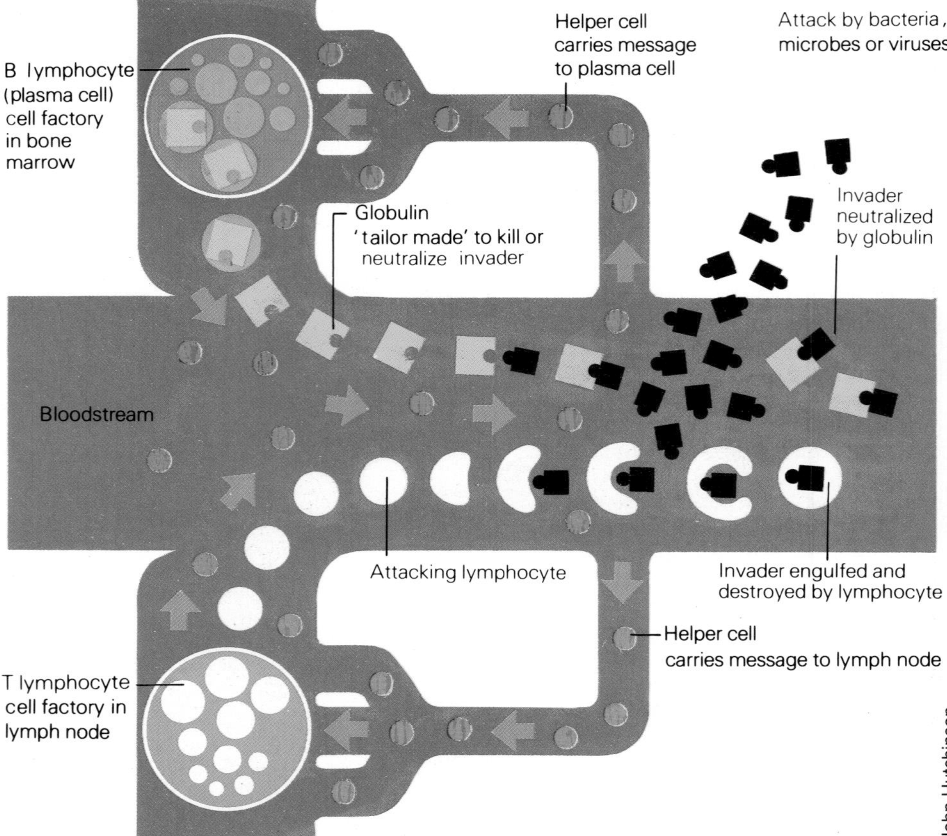

John Hutchinson

How immunity works

Immunity by B cells: The B cell makes substances called immunoglobulins (Ig). The globulin molecules consist of two long chains of amino acids (called heavy chains because of their large size) flanked by two shorter strands of amino acids, the light chains.

There are five classes of immunoglobulins; IgM, IgG, IgA, IgD, and IgE. The most primitive is IgM, which can be found in lower vertebrates. This is the globulin made by all B cells at first, some of them changing later to make one of the other classes. IgM is the largest globulin molecule and comprises 10 percent of the total plasma globulin concentration. IgM is the first antibody to appear after an infection starts and may assist B cells to remember invaders they have met before.

IgG is the most important globulin, comprising 80 percent of the total concentration. It plays the major role in neutralizing bacterial toxins and in coating the bacteria themselves so that they can be engulfed by other blood cells (see Bacteria). Being a small molecule it is able to cross the placenta and transfer a mother's immunity to disease to her baby.

IgA is the principal antibody in mucous secretions and is found in saliva, tears, and along the respiratory and intestinal tracts. It plays a first line role in defending the body against bacteria. The function of IgD is unknown, but it may help B cells to grow and develop. IgE is responsible for hypersensitivity in hay fever and hereditary allergic disease (see Allergies).

Immunity by T cells: The precursors of T cells migrate from the bone marrow to the thymus, where they are programmed for the number of antigens they will recognize. Leaving the thymus they settle in lymph nodes or circulate in the blood, where they constitute 70 percent of all lymphocytes. Some T cells are killer cells that directly attack bacteria and viruses. They also detect and destroy foreign tissue and so are responsible for rejecting transplanted organs. The same quality may protect us against cancer: T cells recognize developing malignant cells and destroy them before they spread (see Cancer).

Other T cells are thought to regulate B cell antibody production, either by increasing it (helper cells) or turning it off (suppressor cells).

What can go wrong?

Immunity in the system depends on the ability of B and T cells to recognize an invading bacterium or virus. If they do not recognize the invader, they will not go into action against it, and it will then be able to get to work in the body. Once the B and T cells remember an invader, they will attack and repel it, sometimes with the help of a vaccine (see Vaccinations).

There are a number of very rare inherited diseases, usually caused by abnormalities in the chromosomes, that result in a deficiency in production of globulin antibodies or of T lymphocytes or both. In certain instances one particular class of globulin is missing; for example, the IgG antibody is absent in a disease called agammaglobulinemia.

It is possible to survive severe deficiency of immunoglobulins because effective globulin from other people can be given to the person who needs it by injection, approximately once a month. However, a complete deficiency of white cells is more difficult to treat, and sufferers usually succumb to a viral infection very early in life.

The AIDS virus, HIV, acts on a particular type of T lymphocyte (T4), causing them to die and therefore crippling the immune system. No effective cure has yet been found (see AIDS), but scientific research in this area continues.

Immunization

Q Why do I have to be immunized against rubella before thinking about becoming pregnant?

A Infection with rubella (German measles; see Rubella) during the first three months of pregnancy often results in an abnormal baby. This is because the rubella virus gets across the placenta and invades the baby's tissues. The main strategy in the United States has been to immunize all children, regardless of sex, to prevent epidemics and thus reduce the risk of pregnant women to exposure. Women of childbearing age are handled individually and immunized if there is no chance of pregnancy in the very near future.

Q Why are three tetanus injections needed, spaced out in the way that they are?

A This is done to get the utmost antibody response; it is the level of IgG antibody that is so important. After the first injection at three months, very little change in antibody level occurs. However, after a second dose there is a very large increase, and after the third dose an even bigger one. Throughout a person's life subsequent injections of the tetanus toxoid will result in these very large increases in antibody response, so the injections are used as boosters (see Tetanus).

Q Can being immunized against a disease go wrong and result in actually giving you the illness it is supposed to protect you against?

A Yes. This happens only when a live, as opposed to a dead, virus is used. For example, the first form of smallpox vaccination discovered in Turkey over 300 years ago could itself cause smallpox. Later forms, however, were much safer. The measles virus used in vaccinations may be associated with a type of inflammation of the brain that can result in permanent damage to the patient. However, these side effects are extremely rare, and the odds are very much in favor of having a vaccination.

Immunization increases human resistance to certain infectious diseases by adding to the body's natural supply of protective antibodies.

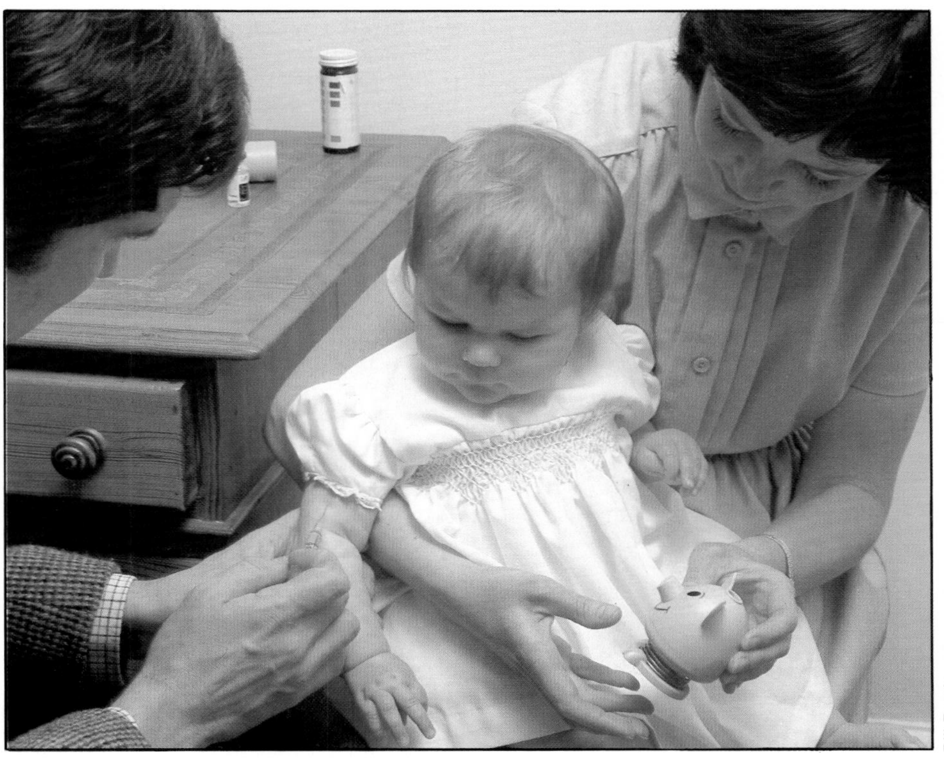

Bill Petch

Triple vaccine for diphtheria, tetanus, and whooping cough is given at two months, repeated twice in the first year, and again at 18 months and at four–six years old.

Immunization may be done either by injecting an antibody that has been made outside the patient directly into him or her (passive immunization) or by injecting an inactive form of the germ into the patient, thereby provoking an antibody response against further infection (active immunization). After passive immunization, protection against infection is immediate and gradually diminishes over the next three to four weeks. After active immunization, complete immunity does not develop for a month or so but in some instances is lifelong.

Passive immunization

Passive immunization is used regularly only in the prevention of tetanus (lockjaw). It is given to people who are seriously exposed to the risk of developing the disease, for example, from a cut from a garden rake. The object of the treatment is to supply the patient with an antibody that has been derived from another source. Horses have been used as reservoirs for this type of antibody since 1894, but more and more use is being made of human immunoglobulin (IgG). This has many advantages over horse globulin, the most important being that patients no longer have the allergic reaction to horse serum itself that was so common a few years ago. The disease caused by horse serum (known as serum sickness) developed within 36–48 hours of an injection and was characterized by a fever, aching joints, a rash, and sometimes by the appearance of protein in the urine.

It is important to remember that passive immunization, although it provides protection immediately after the injection is given, does not last long and in no way protects the patient against the possibility of subsequent infection. For this reason the antitetanus serum (passive immunization) is followed by an injection of tetanus toxoid (active immunization), unless the last injection of toxoid was given less than 10 years previously. (A toxoid is a harmful substance treated to destroy its harmful qualities but able to make antibodies when it is used in an injection form.)

Q Why doesn't the body become immune to some diseases?

A There may be a number of reasons for this, the most important being that the infecting germ is capable of changing its structure, or that it may exist in many different forms.

For example, the polio virus exists in three forms, and natural infection with one does not lead to immunity against the other two. The common cold is caused by a variety of different viruses, and it is very difficult to produce a vaccine against all of these.

Q Are flu shots effective against flu epidemics?

A There is a good deal of evidence to suggest that people who have been vaccinated against influenza are less likely to get it and that, if they do, their illness is less severe than in unvaccinated people. At the present time influenza is still regarded as a fairly trivial disease for healthy people, but for those who are elderly or sick, especially those with severe bronchitis, it is wise to have a flu injection before the start of winter.

Q When traveling abroad do I need to be vaccinated against smallpox?

A Smallpox was wiped out in 1975. There are now very few countries in the world that insist on a vaccination certificate. The last two cases of smallpox have both been in England, a country that does not require routine smallpox vaccination, and they resulted from laboratory accidents (see Smallpox).

Q Does my child have to be vaccinated against tuberculosis?

A No. There is no compulsion to have this vaccination at all and it is questionable whether it works. In the United States the approach to controlling tuberculosis (TB) is to identify, by testing their skin, people who have been infected and to treat them accordingly for the condition.

Active immunization

The earliest forms of protection against disease by immunization were practiced in Turkey over three centuries ago against *poxvirus variolae,* which caused the dreaded smallpox. The process was known as variolation and was first introduced into England in 1721. Inoculation was effected by scratching the skin of the patient with pus from the ulcers on the skin of a sufferer, thereby transmitting the infection. The disease transmitted in this way was usually less severe, and the patient survived infection to live with a permanent immunity to smallpox.

A much safer form of inoculation by injection of cowpox germs was introduced by an English country doctor, Edward Jenner, in the early 19th century. He noticed that farm laborers who suffered a mild disease known as cowpox—for it was from cows that the disease was contracted—developed a surprising resistance to smallpox. He reasoned that the cowpox germ was sufficiently similar in structure to the deadly smallpox germ for the antibody-producing system of the body to be fooled into making globulins that would kill both smallpox and cowpox germs. Jenner's method was so successful that the variolation method was banned in England in 1840.

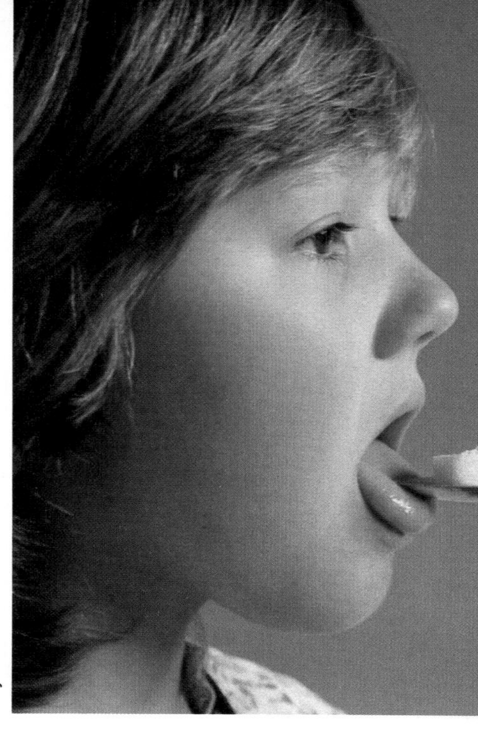

Ray Green

The widespread use of smallpox vaccination has led to one of the great success stories of medicine; the last time smallpox was seen as a natural infection was in 1975. Since then there have been only two cases, both in England and both the result of accidents in laboratories where

When the polio vaccine is given to a tiny baby, it is made into a syrup that is put into a dropper and squeezed into the baby's throat.

Camilla Jessel

Polio vaccine is given orally. For school-age children the vaccine is put on a sugar cube, which the child then sucks.

When vaccination and immunization procedures are performed

Age	Vaccine	Interval
During first year of life	Triple vaccine (DTP) for diphtheria, tetanus, and whooping cough (pertussis); oral polio vaccine (OPV); Hib for *Haemophilus influenza* b, a cause of meningitis	2 months
	DTP, OPV, and Hib	4 months
	DTP (OPV optional)	6 months
During second year of life	Measles, mumps, rubella (MMR)	Given at 15 months
	DTP and OPV	Given at 18 months; considered part of primary series
At entry to nursery or elementary school	DTP and OPV	Given together
Between 14–16 years	Adult tetanus booster and diphtheria	Repeat tetanus every 10 years for lifetime
Adult life	OPV Tetanus booster	During polio outbreaks only Every 10 years

strains of smallpox virus were kept for reference purposes. Since the disease has been wiped out, there is no further need for vaccination, and a certificate of vaccination is no longer necessary for people who travel abroad.

The principles of immunization by vaccination are now widely applied to a variety of infectious diseases. The injected material that is used to raise the antibody response and provide protection may be living or dead. In certain cases only a portion of it may be injected, for example, a protein derived from its cell wall. The live vaccines are made less vigorous by growing them in the laboratory for generations or by growing them in animals. The process by which the vigor of the vaccine is blunted is called attenuation. Live attenuated vaccines cause mild illnesses in the patient to whom they are given, and they are infectious.

Considering vaccinations

The decision to use vaccinations rests upon balancing the risks of the side effects of vaccination itself against the risks of suffering from the disease. Measles, for example, causes severe illness in one in every 15 patients, while the live and attenuated vaccine offers good protection and causes only a mild illness, sometimes with a rash in 10 percent of patients (see Measles). Mumps does not usually produce a severe illness and a vaccine is not as important as for other diseases (see Mumps).

Geographical location is also important. For example, it is not necessary to vaccinate against yellow fever or cholera in western Europe or Australasia, where both diseases are very rare.

Before long it should be possible to vaccinate against such diseases as syphilis, malaria, and even the common cold.

Diseases prevented by vaccination

The diseases most commonly prevented by vaccination include:

Diphtheria, tetanus, whooping cough: Vaccines are prepared from dead bacteria and given mixed together as a single injection known as the triple vaccine. The first is given at the age of two months. After six to eight weeks, another dose is given to boost the antibody response, and a third dose is given eight weeks after that so that all three injections are completed within the space of the first year of the child's life. The triple vaccine is repeated when the child is 18 months old and again when he or she enters nursery school. Ideally it is also given once again when he or she leaves school and starts work (see Diphtheria).

Polio: Polio vaccine is given by mouth and combines a mixture of three types of live attenuated virus. It gives good protection against the three types of naturally occurring polio virus (see Poliomyelitis).

Since this virus is live, it may cause mild symptoms such as abdominal discomfort, a fever, and diarrhea, but these are never a problem. The vaccine is given on a sugar cube at about the same time as the triple vaccine, with a booster when the child goes to elementary school. Outbreaks of polio still sometimes occur in Western countries, and it is wise to revaccinate during these outbreaks.

Rubella (German measles): Infection with German measles in the first three months of pregnancy frequently results in the birth of an abnormal baby. Immunization should be given before childbearing age to all girls who have not already contracted the disease; this gives them lifelong immunity.

Tuberculosis: BCG, or Bacillus Calmette-Guerin, is a strain of tuberculosis that infects cattle. Although BCG has been used to immunize against tuberculosis, it is questionable whether it works. BCG is not used in the United States (see Tuberculosis).

Meningitis: Hib conjugate vaccine (also called HbCV) gives protection against infection by *Haemophilus influenza* type b, which is the leading cause of bacterial meningitis (see Meningitis). It is given in three doses, ideally at two, four and six months of age.

Immunosuppressive drugs

Q If someone undergoes a transplant operation and is given immunosuppressive drugs, will that person be more prone to catching a disease or some type of infection?

A To an extent, yes. By suppressing the immune system to induce the body to accept a transplant, the natural defense mechanism against bacteria and viruses is also suppressed. Therefore as long as the patient is taking an immunosuppressive drug, he or she will have an increased chance of catching infectious diseases and special precautions are taken to prevent this from happening. This is an essential part of the treatment of transplant patients.

Q I've heard that patients on immunosuppressive drugs should be in germ-free environments. How can such an environment be maintained in someone's home?

A It probably can't be. However, patients who are being nursed at home are not on very big doses of immunosuppressive drugs. When higher doses of drugs become necessary and the immune system is completely suppressed, patients are very much at risk of infection and they must then be admitted to the hospital where a germ-free environment can be maintained. There are certain centers that specialize in this form of treatment for such patients.

Q Will a person who has had an organ transplant have to take immunosuppressive drugs for the rest of his or her life?

A Yes. The dose required to maintain immunosuppression may be quite small, particularly if the tissue typing (matching a tissue) has been extremely good. Generally, however, patients with a tissue transplant that has a blood supply (this excludes corneal and cartilage transplants) do need to take immunosuppressive drugs for the rest of their lives so that the effects of immunosuppression can be maintained.

Immunosuppressive drugs are used extensively in the treatment of cancer and other serious conditions, and to prevent rejection after transplants. Control of side effects is continually improving.

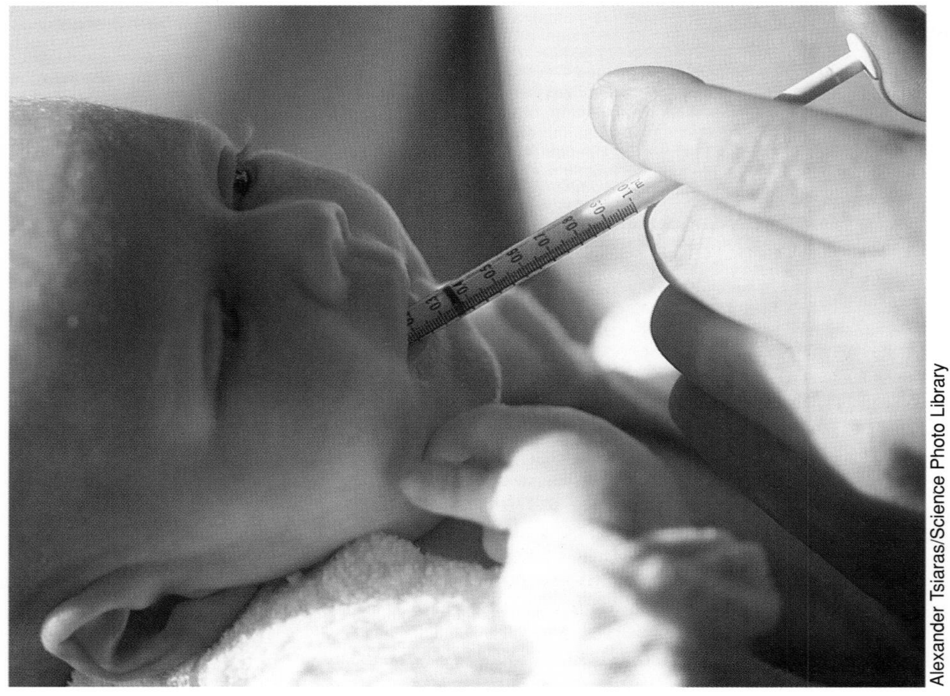

Alexander Tsiaras/Science Photo Library

Here a baby is being given cyclosporine orally through a syringe following his heart transplant operation. Cyclosporine is an immunosuppressive drug that is used to prevent the tissue rejection that may occur following organ transplant.

Drugs that affect the workings of the immune system—the system that normally protects the body from disease (see Immune system)—are termed immunosuppressive drugs. Most of them have been developed from the toxic (poisonous) medicines that were originally used to kill cancer cells, especially leukemia cancer cells (see Leukemia). Because of their potential cell-killing action, they are also known as cytotoxic drugs.

When they are administered in small doses, the cells are suppressed rather than killed—this is called immunosuppression. A large dose might be used to treat cancer, while a smaller dose may be used to treat the recipient of transplanted tissue to prevent rejection of the foreign tissue by the body's immune system. These immunosuppressive drugs may also be used to treat an unusual group of diseases in which the immune system seems to be attacking the body itself: these are called auto-immune diseases (see AIDS).

How they work

Immunosuppressive drugs work by disrupting the production of protein in the body by deoxyribonucleic acid (DNA) and messenger ribonucleic acid (mRNA) so that the cells stop dividing (see Cells and chromosomes). The cells that are most affected will be those that are dividing at the highest rate, such as cancer cells (see Cancer).

Unfortunately there are other cells in the body that also divide very fast, and these include the cells of the bone marrow and the hair follicles. Because of this the unwanted side effects of these drugs can include hair loss, anemia, and a higher susceptibility to infection.

Some immunosuppressive drugs interfere with cell division by allowing themselves to be incorporated into proteins that make up the cells. They do this by convincing the DNA and mRNA that they are the natural raw material from which protein is made. Once these abnormal raw materials are mistakenly built into protein, the resulting chemical fails to work properly and the cell dies. Drugs that work in this way are called antimetabolites, because they stop the body's normal metabolism and protein-building from taking place.

A number of naturally occurring substances damage the enzyme systems essential for normal cell division. So some immunosuppressive drugs are derived from common plants, for example, periwinkle or the autumn crocus; still others are derived from fungi. An early example of a fungal product that was lethal to rapidly dividing cells was penicillin, though in that case the cells were bacteria rather than body cells (see Penicillin). Penicillin has no toxic effect in normal doses on our own body cells.

A recent addition to the armory is the fungal product cyclosporine, which has created enormous interest because of its ability to diminish the immune response without making the patient ill. This drug has now revolutionized the field of transplant surgery by further reducing the body's tendency to reject transplanted tissue (see Transplants).

Uses

Immunosuppressive drugs are used extensively in cancer treatment. They slow down the rate at which cancer cells divide, and this forms the basis of their use in the treatment of tumors (see Tumors). Most of the immunosuppressive drugs in use today resulted from a search for medicines that controlled leukemia. With modern methods of administering these drugs in the form of cycles of treatment, there are some types of leukemia that can now be treated and cured.

Immunosuppressive drugs are also used when a tissue has been transplanted. Foreign tissue is recognized by the body and destroyed by lymphocytes (a type of white blood cell; see Lymphocytes). By suppressing the activity of lymphocytes, the transplant survives longer. Cyclosporine selectively suppresses T lymphocytes and has proved of enormous value in improving the survival of transplanted tissue.

Immunosuppressive drugs are used in the treatment of immune diseases. In certain rare instances disease is caused by the immune system turning against the body itself, a so-called autoimmune disease. There are many examples of this type of disease, though perhaps the best known is rheumatoid arthritis, which is thought to be at least partly autoimmune in origin (see Rheumatoid arthritis). Immunosuppressive drugs may help both in improving the symptoms and slowing down the progress of these types of disease. Other autoimmune diseases include systemic lupus erythematosus, scleroderma (see Scleroderma), and a certain type of anemia (acquired hemolytic anemia).

Autumn crocus

Elaine Keenan

Immunosuppressive drugs are composed of a variety of different substances. Some are derived from plants such as the autumn crocus (above) and periwinkle; others from fungi, like penicillin or cyclosporine.

Problems

As well as the problems of unwanted side effects that immunosuppressive drugs create, there are some additional difficulties. Because these drugs work by suppressing the immune system, patients who are taking them are much more susceptible to disease. They are therefore vulnerable to diseases that a person with a fully functioning immune system would not be likely to catch.

Patients may become infected with unusual germs that are often resistant to the commonly used antibiotics. These germs are notoriously difficult to isolate, but in most cases a diagnosis can be made and then followed up with the appropriate antibiotics and careful observation. The risk of developing cancer when the immune system is suppressed is also being recognized.

The future

The future of these drugs undoubtedly lies in the hands of the biochemists. It is they who are carrying out work, often in small innovative companies, to find a drug that will suppress only the part of the immune system that is required, without doing damage elsewhere in the body. Developments so far are encouraging, and there can be little doubt that these drugs will be found in due course. It is just a question of time and continuing research.

One possible target for immunosuppression is the adhesion molecule. This refers to a group of molecules that are found on the white blood cells and on the endothelial cells lining the blood vessels. They are used by the white blood cells to get out of the blood and into the tissues. Because different adhesion molecules are used by different white blood cells, it is possible to block the movement of specific types of white blood cells into the tissues. One area of investigation is attempting to develop drugs that will block the use of specific adhesion molecules by the white blood cells.

Another area of research involves the cytokines. These are mediators produced by cells that affect the function of other cells. Some cytokines increase the activity of white blood cells while others decrease it. Either inhibitory cytokines themselves or drugs that block the effects of stimulatory cytokines might be useful as immunosuppressants.

Impacted teeth

Q Do impacted wisdom teeth cause the other teeth to become more crowded in front?

A Generally wisdom teeth only become impacted if the mouth is already overcrowded. It has, however, been shown that impacted wisdom teeth do contribute to a small extent to the incisor crowding that affects many young adults.

Q My husband has an impacted upper canine tooth. His dentist says that this could be transplanted. Does this always work?

A Canine transplantation provides an instant method of moving a misplaced canine tooth that has failed to erupt into its correct position.

The tooth is taken out and then fixed into the jaw again. About 70 percent of such transplanted teeth are still in place after 10 years—the remaining 30 percent having been removed or fallen out as a result of some complication.

Q I am a professional boxer and have an impacted tooth. Will having it removed weaken my jaw?

A It is certainly possible that the jaw may be weakened for a few months after a lower wisdom tooth is removed, because this generally entails some removal of bone. After that time, however, the bone will have repaired itself and the jaw may actually be stronger than before, since before removal an impacted wisdom tooth represents an interruption in the continuity of the jaw and this forms a natural weak spot.

Q My son has an impacted wisdom tooth that never causes him any trouble. He is about to go to Africa for six months. Should he have it removed before he goes?

A There is always the risk of complications occurring with an impacted wisdom tooth; unless it is very deeply placed, it would be better to have it removed. He should discuss this with his dentist.

Impacted teeth are those that have failed to grow into the mouth correctly. You may not be aware that a tooth is impacted, and therefore a potential cause of trouble, until your dentist discovers it. This is one reason why regular dental checkups are so important.

Impacted teeth occur either because the path for their emergence is blocked or because they have formed in the wrong position in the mouth.

Causes

The eruption (emergence) of teeth into the mouth is not fully understood, but it is probably the result of rapid multiplication of the cells that form the tooth root (see Teeth and teething). The pressure from this thrusts the tooth through the overlying bone. In cases of impaction the problem is not usually one of failure within the developing tooth itself but either of its position or of its relation to the other teeth nearby.

When there is crowding—i.e., inadequate space in the mouth for all the teeth—the last teeth to erupt often have insufficient room, because the space available has all been taken by the teeth that have already emerged. Under these circumstances the later erupting teeth may grow through but be out of line. Alternatively, they may be unable to

Impacted wisdom teeth

The X-ray picture (right) shows a wisdom tooth that has become impacted, behind an impacted molar. This tooth (below, right) is also impacted and has insufficient space to come through. The only course of action for the dentist is to remove the tooth. Either a general or a local anesthetic will be given, depending on how difficult the tooth is to remove. Afterward the gum is stitched (below).

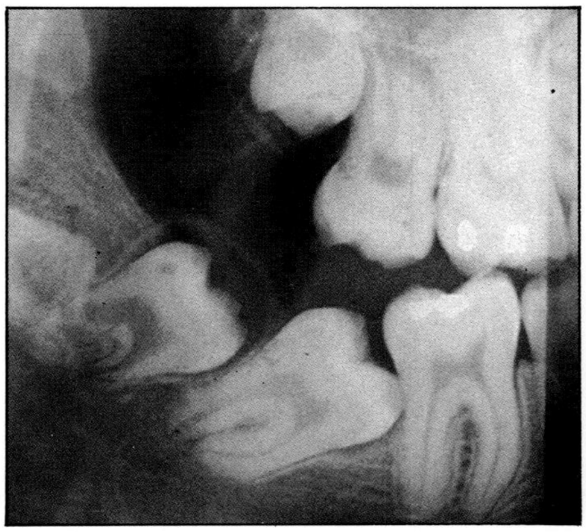

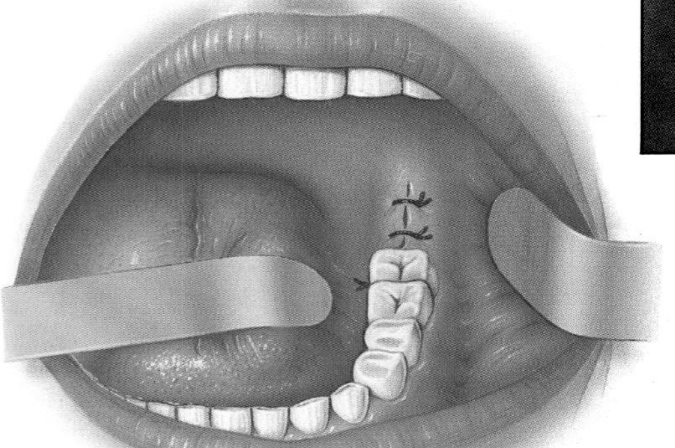

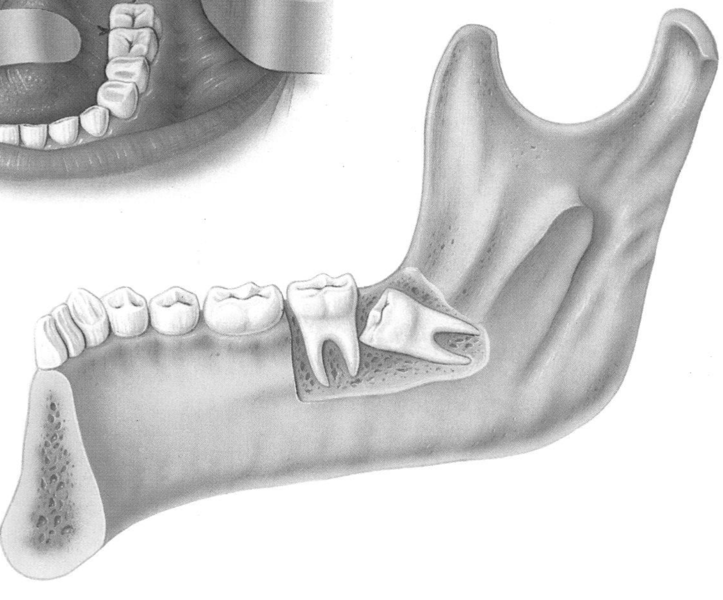

Mike Courteney

emerge fully. When a tooth fails to erupt, either fully or partially, it is described as being impacted.

The cause of the crowding that leads to most impactions is not really understood, but it may arise as the result of the individual inheriting large teeth from one parent and small jaws from the other. It has also been suggested that there may be an evolutionary process in progress, leading to a reduction in the size of the human jaw. Sometimes teeth are impacted as the result of their being formed in the wrong position. For example, upper canine teeth are sometimes too deeply placed, so that when they begin to erupt, they grow toward the roof of the mouth, instead of toward the alveolar bone (bordering the gums). It is then not usually possible for them to erupt properly.

Impactions are comparatively uncommon in the baby teeth (called the deciduous dentition), because they are small and crowding is usually less.

It is possible for any permanent tooth to become impacted, but impaction due to overcrowding most often affects wisdom teeth (third molars), canines, and premolars (situated in front of the molars). Impactions that are due to tooth development in incorrect positions affect upper canines more commonly than any other teeth, and the problem often runs in families.

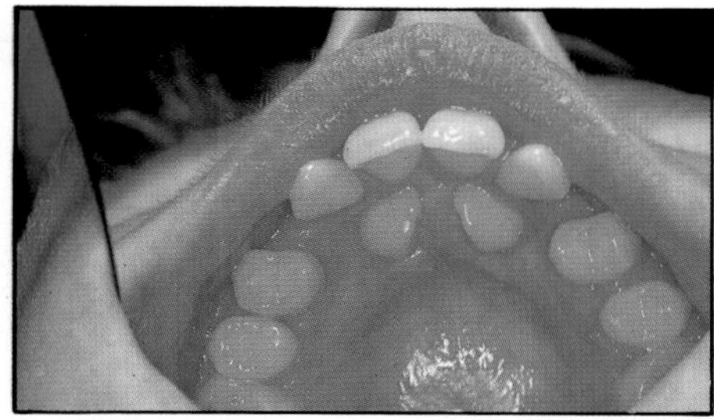

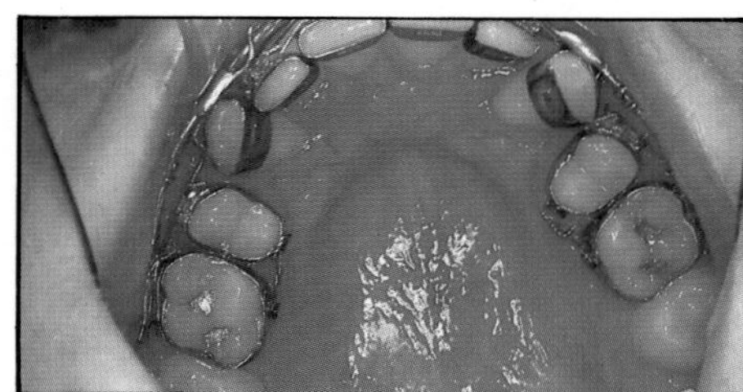

Zefa

Impacted canine teeth (top left) can be corrected by a fixed appliance (bottom left). Although this is cemented in place, the teeth can still be cleaned satisfactorily. The treatment takes about two years but produces good results (above).

Impacted canine teeth

The X ray (right) shows how canine teeth can grow in the wrong position in spite of having sufficient space. This is seen in the drawing (below); the teeth are growing toward the roof of the mouth. The dentist has the choice of extracting them or shifting their position. In the case of a child he or she might prefer the latter, using an appliance to bring them into their correct alignment in the mouth.

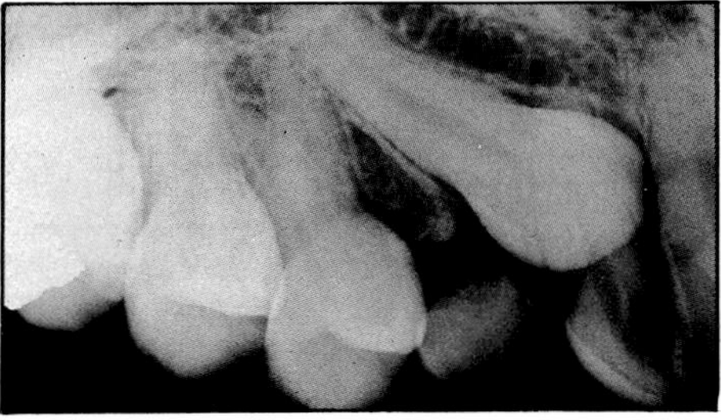

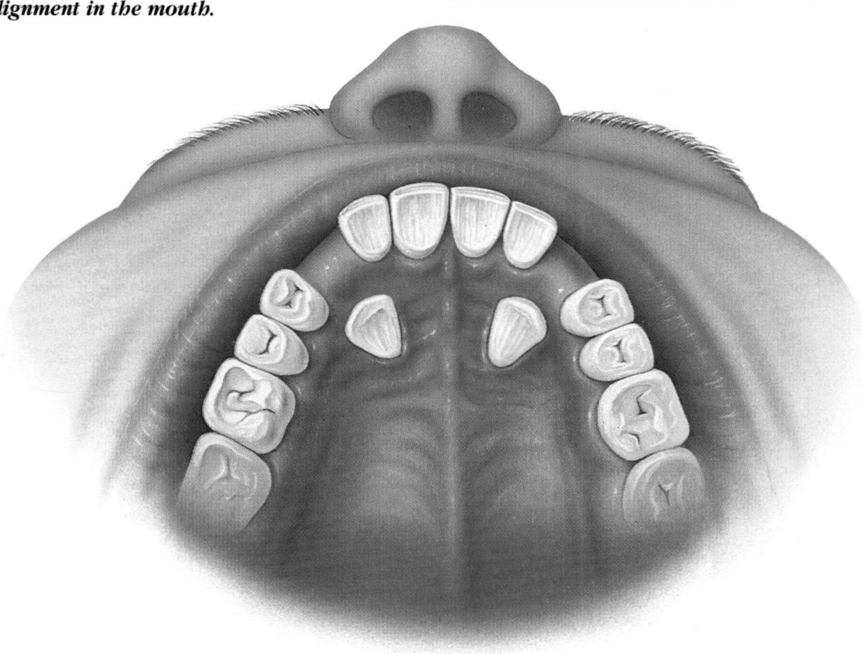

Mike Courteney

Symptoms

Many people have an impacted tooth or teeth without being aware of the condition because there are often no symptoms. The condition may only come to light as the result of a visit to the dentist. He or she may discover in the course of the dental examination that a certain tooth is missing, without ever having been extracted. If that tooth is impacted, it will be seen on an X ray of that particular area of the jaw (see X rays).

Some people may experience pain as the result of impactions of teeth. In most cases the pain occurs when an infection develops around an impacted tooth that has partially emerged into the mouth. This problem most often affects lower wisdom teeth. The sufferer is likely to experience tenderness and pain around the tooth concerned; pain may also be felt on biting. Sometimes a swelling may develop below the angle of the jaw, involving the side of the face, and the individual may be unable to open his or her mouth to the normal extent.

Usually teeth that are completely enclosed within the jaw cause no pain, and problems only arise if the tooth is partially through the gum, allowing access for infection (see Gums and gum diseases). A completely buried tooth is, by contrast, sealed off from sources of infection.

The only way in which your general health is likely to be affected by impactions is when an infection starts around an impacted tooth that has partially emerged. If this pain is sufficiently intense, you may feel ill and develop a slight fever (see Fevers).

Treatment

Impacted teeth that have become infected should be removed to prevent recurrent bouts of infection.

Another reason to remove impacted teeth is that it is generally inadvisable for an impacted tooth to be left in position indefinitely, because occasionally it may grow in such a way as to damage the roots of normal adjacent teeth. Another complication is a cyst (a type of swelling filled with fluid) that may develop around an impacted tooth (see Cyst).

There are, however, some cases where impacted teeth are so very deeply placed that their removal may endanger the other teeth, and these are generally left alone for this reason. In these cases your dentist will want an X ray to be taken occasionally to make sure that there has been no change in the position of the impacted tooth.

Cosmetic correction

One other reason for the treatment of impacted teeth is to avoid having a gap due to the tooth being in the wrong position. This problem often occurs in relation to upper canines. When an upper canine becomes impacted, the baby tooth may last for many years but will eventually be lost.

In these cases your dentist may consider it worthwhile to bring the impacted tooth into its correct position. This procedure can be done by cementing a hook onto the impacted tooth and pulling it into line by using an orthodontic appliance. (Orthodontics is the correction of irregularities in the position of teeth; see Orthodontics.) Alternatively the buried tooth can be surgically removed and then transplanted into its correct position.

Removal

Teeth that are impacted are often more difficult to remove than normally erupted teeth. In general the procedure takes the form of a minor surgical operation on the jaw. The gum is cut and peeled away from the underlying bone. A certain amount of bone is then removed to provide a pathway through which the impacted tooth can be taken out. The gum is then stitched back into position and left to heal again.

The removal of an impacted tooth can be performed either under a general anesthetic, which sends the patient to sleep, or under a local anesthetic, whereby the appropriate section of the jaw is made numb by an injection (see Anesthetics).

The choice of anesthetic is a matter for discussion between patient and dentist. Usually if the patient is very nervous, a general anesthetic would be used. In other cases a local anesthetic is preferable, because general anesthetics carry more risks than local anesthetics.

In cases where an infection is present around an impacted tooth, it must be eliminated prior to extraction to avoid spreading the infection. This can usually be achieved by a combination of antibiotics, the local application of antiseptics, and the use of a warm salt mouthwash.

The removal of impacted teeth under a general anesthetic is usually undertaken in the hospital because of its more extensive facilities for recovery from the anesthetic. The patient does not usually stay in the hospital overnight. When a general anesthetic is given, all of the impacted teeth are extracted during the same operation so that the whole procedure need not be repeated.

When impacted teeth are taken out using a local anesthetic, the extraction can often take place in a dentist's office. Usually only one side of the jaw is treated at any one time. When that side has healed, any impacted teeth on the other side are then removed.

Outlook

It is unlikely that the problem of impacted teeth can be avoided since the main cause, overcrowding or unnatural positioning, is largely genetically determined and present from birth.

In some cases, when teeth are extracted for orthodontic purposes to relieve crowding, this may provide space that can prevent wisdom teeth from becoming impacted, although this will depend upon the degree of crowding.

It is possible for impacted teeth to be removed in childhood, when it is often easier to do. This is not, however, frequently done since it would subject the child to a surgical operation.

As with other aspects of dentistry, regular checkups are invaluable in avoiding problems with impacted teeth (see Dental care). By this means future problems can be anticipated, and treatment can be carried out at the most suitable stage.

Also, in those cases where it is possible for impacted teeth to be brought in line, regular checkups provide the opportunity for treatment to be carried out at an age when it is most acceptable to the patient and before the impaction can cause serious trouble.

Modern dental techniques can help everyone to have a healthier set of teeth.

After a tooth extraction

- Avoid eating on the part concerned
- Maintain good mouth hygiene
- Use a mouthwash made from one teaspoon of salt added to a glass of warm water
- To stop any bleeding roll up a clean white handkerchief and bite on it for ten minutes
- Return to the dentist for removal of stitches after 3–5 days

Impetigo

Q Should children have their routine injections when they have impetigo?

A Doctors are very reluctant to give injections against diphtheria, tetanus, and whooping cough, as well as oral polio vaccine, when a child has any other infection at all, because the immune system, which fights disease, is already under stress.

Q My grandmother says that 50 years ago there seemed to be more impetigo around than there is now. Is this true?

A Yes, for several reasons. First, antibiotics are effective in curing the condition. Second, people are generally living in better housing, with less overcrowding, and they have a higher level of personal hygiene. Impetigo was also much more severe when there were more malnourished children.

Q All my brothers and sisters have had impetigo at one time or another. Can impetigo run in families?

A A tendency to impetigo is not inherited. However, if one family member has impetigo, the others are very susceptible to it, because it is highly infectious. Also a tendency to eczema is inherited and with this condition skin is more likely to be infected than normal skin, providing a perfect breeding ground for impetigo (see Eczema).

Q I recently had impetigo. Is it possible for the bacteria to stay in the house, for example, in the bedding, and cause an infection in the future?

A The impetigo bacteria will not survive in dry, well-aired, frequently washed bedding. They survive best in people and in moist materials, such as washcloths and towels, and thus these are common carriers of impetigo. For this reason the washcloths and towels of a person with impetigo should be kept separate from the rest of the family and boiled or washed with a disinfectant frequently to keep the infection from spreading (see Hygiene).

One of the most common skin infections that affects children, and occasionally adults, is impetigo. With prompt treatment it can easily be cured.

Impetigo is a highly contagious skin infection that may arise in both apparently healthy skin and in skin that has been damaged by eczema, insect bites, scabies, or cold sores.

Causes

Impetigo is caused by the staphylococcus bacteria that is found in the nose (see Bacteria). It may be transmitted by breathing or sneezing onto damaged skin, where it can spread rapidly, causing inflammation and weeping blisters. Unless hygienic precautions are taken and treatment is given, impetigo may spread quickly to other members of the household or school, either by direct contact or by contact with towels or washcloths used by the patient (see Infection and infectious diseases).

Symptoms

Impetigo first appears on the face, scalp, hands, or knees as little red spots. These soon become blisters that quickly break, exuding a pale yellow sticky liquid. They then dry to form large, irregularly shaped, brownish yellow crusts.

If only a small area of skin is affected, there are usually no other symptoms. However, if large areas are involved or if the surrounding skin is also infected with another type of bacteria, the patient will feel unwell with a temperature and swollen lymph nodes. Adults are usually less severely affected than children except in hot climates where the spread of infection may be extensive.

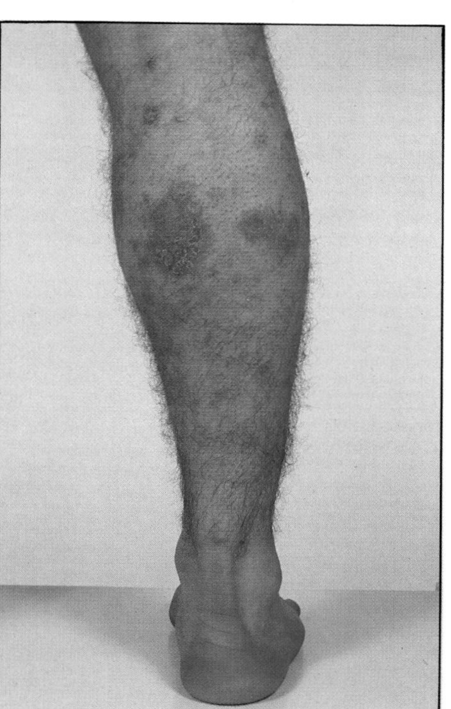

Dangers

Impetigo is a life-threatening illness for newborn babies, who have very little immunity, and so it is extremely important that no one with impetigo should come in contact with babies or their mothers.

Very rarely untreated impetigo may cause abscesses elsewhere in the body or nephritis (inflammation) of the kidneys.

Treatment

Treatment must begin immediately. If the area is small, then an antibiotic cream should be applied three or four times a day until the crusts have healed. Generally it is preferable to give antibiotics by mouth or occasionally by injection. Thick crusts may have to be soaked off with wet compresses.

Most importantly the spreading must be prevented, both to patients, who may reinfect themselves, and to others. Always keep patients' washcloths and towels separate and boil or wash with a disinfectant, together with clothing and bed linen, after use.

Children with impetigo should be told not to scratch the crusts, since scars may form. They should be kept out of school until the infection has cleared, usually after five days. If there is an underlying skin condition such as eczema, both this and impetigo should be treated together.

Impetigo initially looks like small red spots. These can turn to blisters (see eyebrow below). Once the blisters break and ooze pus, they dry and form oddly shaped crusts, such as the ones on this leg.

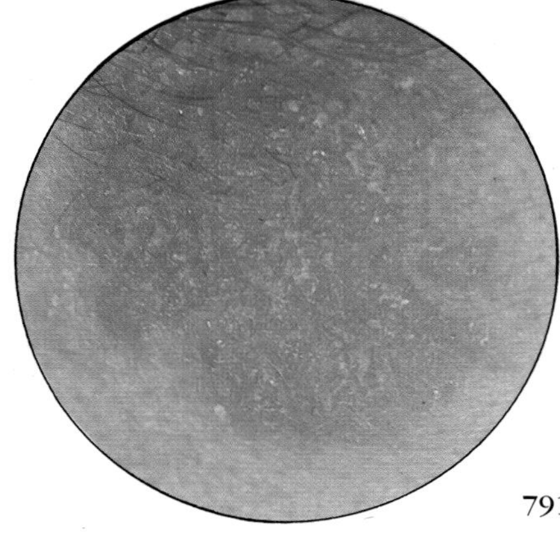

Impotence

Q I had been away on a business trip for a month and was very eager to make love to my wife when I returned, but when the time came I couldn't get an erection. I've never been unable to perform before. Am I going to be impotent for good?

A Almost certainly not. You would be amazed at how many men go to their doctors with the problem you describe.

Impotence is usually temporary, and probably caused by being too excited, rather than anything like incapability. The simple answer is to adopt a lighthearted attitude and just continue as usual. It's almost certain to be OK the next time or the time after. However, if the problem persists, see your doctor.

Q I don't have a particularly hairy chest and am worried that this means I am inclined to impotence. Could I be right?

A Absolutely not. You might be at a slightly greater risk of becoming impotent because you worry about it but not because of your lack of body hair.

Q Am I bound to become impotent in old age?

A No. Sexual desire does lessen with age, but you just have to come to terms with making love less often, less energetically, and in gaining a different sort of pleasure from it. Even so, a surprising number of men have been sexually active in their eighties. Even more are happily making love and fathering children in their seventies.

Q My first husband used to make love to me two or three times a night. My new husband can only do it once a night. Does this mean he is becoming impotent?

A No. Men vary enormously in this, not only between individuals but at different times during their lives. It would be unwise to suggest that your husband has a problem, as once you plant a seed of doubt, there is always a risk that it may become a reality through insecurity.

Impotence can be a worrying difficulty, but today a man can go to his doctor or to a sex therapist without embarrassment for effective treatment.

The physical aspect of sexual failure in men comes down to three things: non-production of sperm in the testicles; an inability to have or keep an erection; and an inability to ejaculate. Strictly speaking, only the second of these is impotence.

All men are likely to experience impotence at some stage during their lives. This is because sexual potency in the male involves a delicate balance of psychological and physiological factors—a balance that is very easily upset.

The female equivalent of impotence, frigidity, means that the woman cannot achieve orgasm (see Orgasm). Despite this, coitus is always possible, no matter how disinclined a woman may feel—unless, of course, she refuses or is suffering from severe vaginismus (when the vagina contracts to deny the penis entry). In men, however, disinclination is one of the many possible causes of erectile failure.

A small proportion of cases of impotence are due to organic disease, but even these cases usually have a psychological element as well.

Sexual arousal

The biological object of sexuality is procreation. This requires the penetration of the vagina by the penis so that fertilization (if contraception is not used) can take place. To do this the penis has to be stiff and erect. The stiffness is caused by blood flowing into three spongy cavities within the penis (see Penis).

Once a man has an erection, physical stimulation does the rest. Friction of the walls of the vagina on the head of the penis stimulates various muscles until, at orgasm, they contract, pumping semen out through the penis (see Erection and Ejaculation).

Psychological causes

As the primary stimuli of sexual arousal are sexual interest and inclination, and since these can be readily interfered with by any conflicting state of mind, there are many causes of erectile failure. One of the most prevalent of these is fear of failure, whether justified or not. Another common cause is lack of desire. Out of regard for the partner lack of desire may be concealed, but this in itself may make the problem worse. Lack of desire may be due to anything from boredom with the partner to active dislike; it may also be due to repeated past failure. Many men find this deeply humiliating and are determined to avoid it, even at the cost of a damaged relationship.

Psychological impotence is nearly always related to one particular partner. It usually starts fairly suddenly and tends to be intermittent. There is no problem in achieving a good erection during masturbation. Erection regularly occurs while sleeping—it is normal during the periods

The loving, relaxed encouragement of a partner is often the most effective means of regaining proper sexual functioning.

Peter Menzel/Science Photo Library

Overindulgence in alcohol is a cause of temporary impotence, often making a man willing but unable to perform. Fortunately drinking less usually solves the problem.

of rapid eye movement (REM) sleep—and is commonly present on waking. Psychological impotence is most likely to affect anxious, tense men with little idea of sexual technique, poor communication skills, and the inability to express affection. Such men often have strong sexual taboos and restricted ideas on how lovemaking should be conducted.

Physical causes

In men alcohol is the most common physical cause of impotence. Excessive alcohol can make them willing but unable to make love. There may be an erection but ejaculation takes a long time or does not happen.

Aging should be worried about least. At 60 a man is still able to perform sexually, although it usually takes him longer to reach orgasm.

Sexual powers are likely to be weakened by a bout of the flu. Severe diabetes may sometimes cause impotence, as may a few other degenerative diseases such as cancer of the colon or prostate.

Childhood events can make a man impotent later in life. Unhappy early relationships and sexual, physical, or emotional abuse can cause problems.

Other physical or organic causes of impotence include hormonal changes, local arterial disorders, multiple sclerosis, spinal cord disorders, diabetic nerve damage, and insufficient heart output.

Relative loss of the male sex hormones is an important cause of organic impotence. It is most commonly age-related, but it may also result from antihormonal medical treatment, such as that needed for treatment of prostate cancer, which, however, generally affects older men.

Sex hormone inadequacy causes loss of interest in sex, an absence of sexual fantasies and erotic dreams, and sometimes even loss of the male secondary sexual characteristics. Unlike psychological impotence, organic impotence usually comes on gradually. There is erectile failure during attempts at masturbation, and erection does not occur during sleep. The penis tends to be small and cold. Unless the underlying disorder is already known, full medical investigation is required without delay.

Treatment

Temporary psychological impotence can almost always be treated by a doctor at its first occurrence. He or she will try to identify the cause and offer reassurance. If this does not solve the problem, psychotherapy may be the answer.

Treatment of longer-term psychological impotence requires sexual education, sometimes sexual counseling, and occasionally the use of methods such as the temporary prohibition of sexual intercourse and the encouragement of touching and sensual massage (called the sensate focus technique).

Organic impotence may call for more extreme measures such as injections of a compound called papaverine, the use of vacuum condoms to suck the penis into a state of erection, or the use of a penile ring to exert a mild compression at the base and help to sustain erections. There is a range of implantable prosthetic devices available that can be inflated to produce a kind of pseudoerection. In a small number of cases in which the trouble is due to blockage of a major artery by thrombosis, vascular surgery can effect a cure (see Thrombosis).

If impotence is caused by a short-term illness or fatigue, the treatment is equally simple: an explanation followed by reassurance that normal sexual functioning will return. More than 90 percent of all cases of impotence are psychological and most respond well to treatment.

In vitro fertilization

Q Is a baby conceived by in vitro fertilization more likely to be abnormal than a baby conceived in the normal way?

A So far all the babies that have been born using this process have been healthy and normal. There has been no sign to date that in vitro fertilization is a danger.

Q We have been trying for three years to have a baby but without success. Should I ask my doctor about the possibility of in vitro fertilization?

A You and your husband should certainly go to your doctor, who will probably refer you to an infertility clinic. There are a number of causes of infertility, and the different treatments depend on the cause. If it is discovered that you have blocked or damaged fallopian tubes, then the greatest hope of success at the moment lies in microsurgery. This is carried out at special centers. Only if this fails should you consider the possibility of in vitro fertilization, and then very carefully, since the success rate at present is low.

Q Are test-tube babies very expensive to produce?

A Although there is no need for a great deal of expensive equipment, a high level of labor, skill, and experience is required—so such babies are very expensive in terms of human resources. Moreover the present low success rate adds to the expense of each successful birth.

Q Are there any dangers to a woman who has in vitro fertilization?

A There is little danger. The procedure for obtaining the ripened egg from the ovary is usually a straightforward one, which is carried out under general anesthetic. When the fertilized embryo is returned to the mother, via the vagina, no anesthetic is necessary. The problem that the woman may have to cope with is not physical danger but disappointment, should a longed-for pregnancy not result.

Of all the scientific breakthroughs of the century, the birth of the first baby conceived by in vitro fertilization (IVF) was perhaps the most remarkable. The technique offers hope to women who otherwise are unable to conceive.

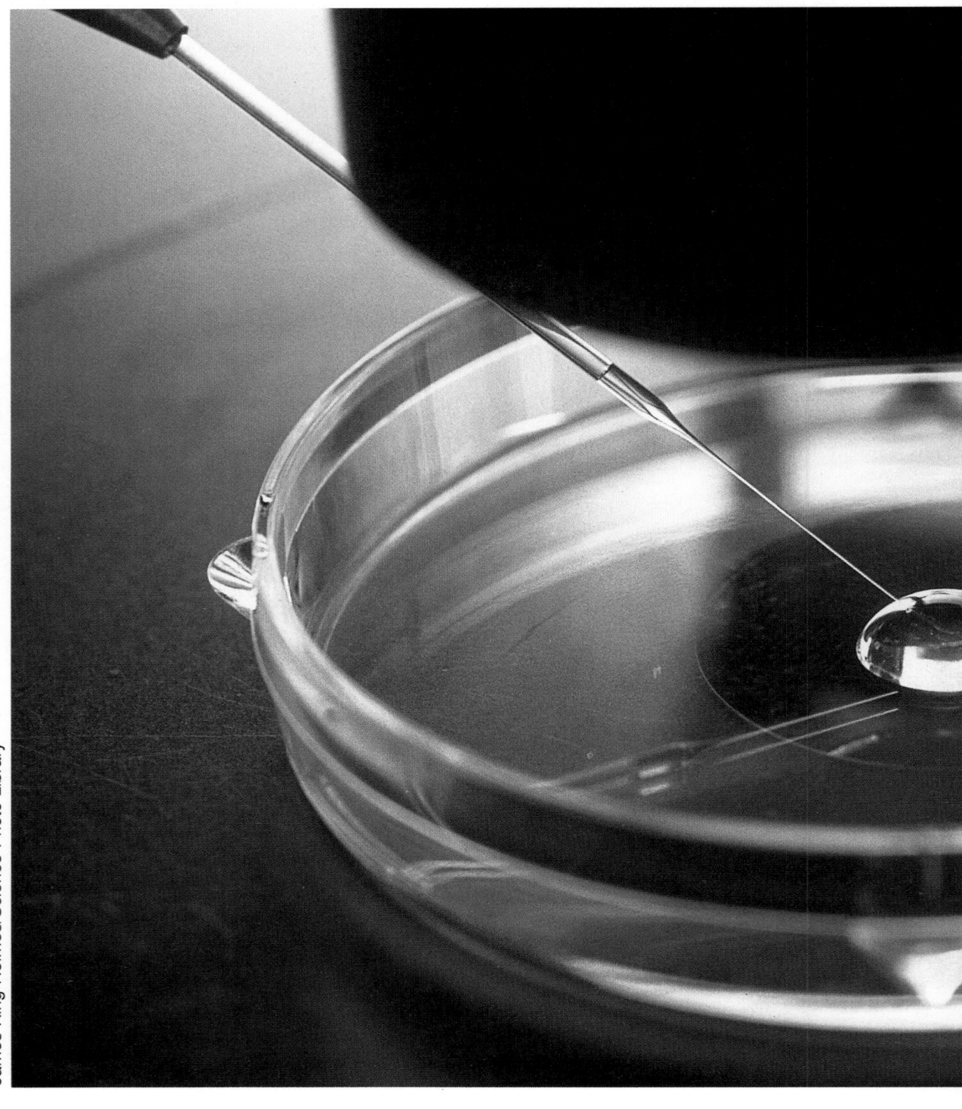

James King-Holmes/Science Photo Library

On July 25, 1978, at three minutes to midnight, a normal, healthy baby girl was delivered by cesarean section at Oldham General Hospital in Lancashire, UK. Louise Brown, weighing 5 lb 12 oz (2.6 kg), was the world's first test-tube baby. The birth was the culmination of 10 years of cooperation between gynecologist Patrick Steptoe and physiologist Robert Edwards. Their individual skills combined in a remarkable way to make this achievement possible.

To the parents Lesley and John Brown the birth seemed like a miracle. The couple had longed for a child for many years but had almost despaired of ever producing one. It had been discovered that Lesley's fallopian tubes were blocked and damaged, and surgery had been unable to repair them. Her inability to conceive, and her unfulfilled wish for a child, had depressed her deeply and put a severe strain on the marriage.

Causes of infertility

It is estimated that about one in eight couples has a problem with fertility. Exact figures are hard to establish because not everyone chooses to try to have children or seeks advice if there are

Computers can now be used to select fertile sperm. The sperm are viewed through a video microscope and monitored by a computer that identifies fertile sperm by their head movement, swimming speed, and tail thrashing. These sperm are sucked into microneedles and placed on a human egg in a glass dish.

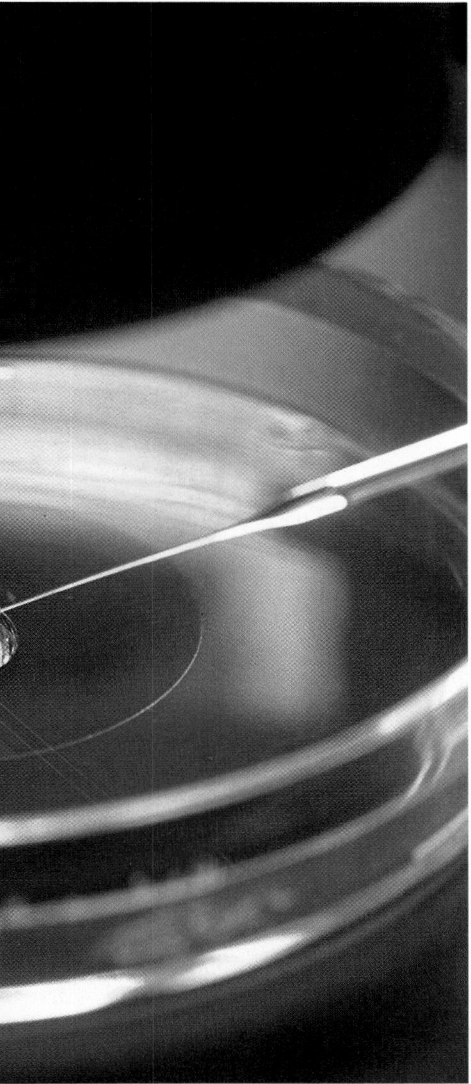

difficulties. In perhaps just under a third of reported cases, however, the problem lies with the woman's fallopian tubes, which are either blocked or damaged. Roughly the same proportion of women experience difficulties with ovulation, and in about another 30 percent of cases the problem lies with the man. In many couples more than one of these factors may be present.

Blocked and damaged tubes

In the normal course of events, the ripened egg passes into the fallopian tube, where it may be fertilized by a sperm (see Pregnancy). If the tubes are blocked, and the passage of the egg is prevented, chances of pregnancy in the normal way are ruled out. In the majority of cases some form of pelvic infection is responsible for blocked and damaged tubes, but there are also other causes. For example, tuberculosis infection, when it was prevalent (see Tuberculosis), caused this sort of problem, and infections in users of the intrauterine contraceptive device (IUD) have also been known to have this effect.

New developments in microsurgery (fine surgery carried out under a microscope; see Microsurgery) have greatly increased the success rate in dealing with tubal problems. At present it is only practiced at certain centers, to which women can ask to be referred. Only if such surgery proves unsuccessful should in vitro fertilization be considered as a last resort.

In vitro fertilization

In the case of Louise Brown and other test-tube babies, fertilization took place outside the mother's body. A test tube is not always used; it can be a glass dish—the Latin term *in vitro* means "in a glass."

One development that has made a vital contribution to this form of fertilization is laparoscopy (see Laparoscopy). The patient is given a general anesthetic, and the abdominal wall is pierced with a slim needle through which gas is passed to distend the abdominal cavity. A small incision is then made just below the navel, and the instrument known as the laparoscope is introduced. It works like a telescope, and provides clear views of the uterus, ovaries, and the fallopian tubes. Using a laparoscope the gynecologist can see exactly what he or she is doing and can carry out minor surgery if necessary (see Gynecology).

In the early 1960s Patrick Steptoe realized that the instrument could be used in conjunction with a hollow needle to remove eggs from the ovaries of a woman with blocked fallopian tubes. It was an article in a medical journal on laparoscopy by Patrick Steptoe that first attracted the attention of Robert Edwards and led to their famous partnership, resulting in the first in vitro baby.

Robert Edwards had been trying unsuccessfully for some time to fertilize a human egg in the laboratory. A decisive step forward was taken early in 1968 when a UK graduate student produced a new culture fluid that for the first time enabled a human egg to be fertilized by sperm outside the woman's body.

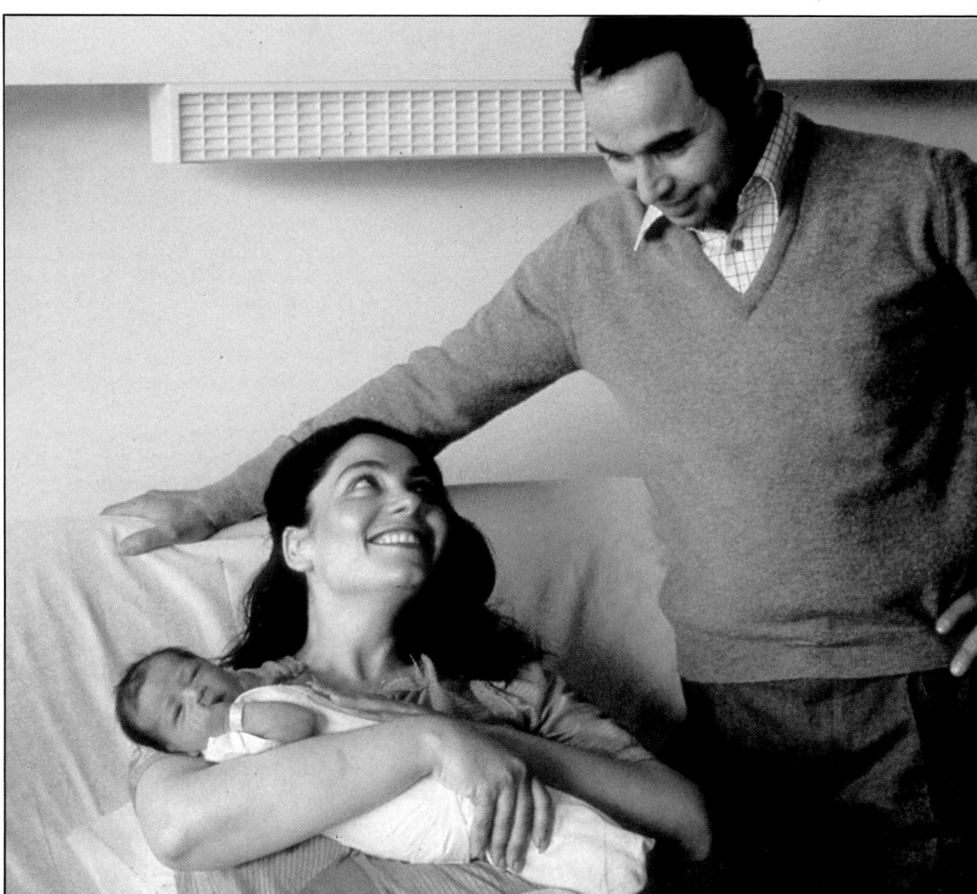

Rex Features

Researchers in several countries continued the pioneering work of the British team of Patrick Steptoe and Robert Edwards, and produced other test-tube babies, making parenthood a possibility for many who would otherwise be childless.

Hank Morgan/Science Photo Library

In today's in vitro fertilization procedure the woman is first given fertility drugs to stimulate the production of several eggs. These eggs are then collected and placed in a test tube together with sperm. The test tube is then put in an incubator, where fertilization may take place. If successful, several embryos—to give a better chance of success—are implanted in the uterus.

This done, there followed the excitement of watching the egg divide into two cells within a day, and into four cells within two to three days (see Conception). Eventually the team succeeded in developing an embryo to the blastocyst stage (the last stage of growth in the tube before implantation in the uterus). Now the main work lay in determining the right stage in the mother's cycle, and in the development of the embryo, for implanting it in the uterus, and discovering which hormones would assist implantation.

The method for implanting the embryo is painless and done without anesthetic. The embryo is placed in a cannula (a very fine tube) with an outlet at the side that is inserted through the vagina and cervix. Several days after insertion the woman is ready to return home, although if she becomes pregnant, she is of course carefully monitored.

Procedure

The original team of Steptoe and Edwards used the woman's natural cycle to obtain eggs from the ovaries, just before they were about to be shed. By monitoring the patient's urine, they were able to note the sudden rise in luteinizing hormone that precedes ovulation (see Menstruation). A naturally produced single egg was obtained through laparoscopy and placed in a solution. Today, however, fertility drugs are used to stimulate women's cycles, with the result that several eggs are produced at one time. The use of fertility drugs also means that procedures can be timed more conveniently for patients and doctors.

The egg is incubated for some hours in a special preparation and then the part-

In cases where a woman's fallopian tubes are blocked or damaged (1) and cannot be repaired by microsurgery, in vitro fertilization can offer her the chance of having a baby of her own.

The prospective mother is monitored around the clock so that the doctors can identify the hormone surge that precedes ovulation. The best time to remove the egg is at this preovulatory phase. The surgeon makes an incision in the abdominal wall and inserts a laparoscope to gain a view of the ovary. Through another incision he or she inserts the hollow needle of an aspirator and very gently sucks out the tiny egg (2). The egg is then transferred to a dish of nutrients kept at body temperature, and the father's (or, if necessary, donor's) sperm is introduced (3). Soon one of the sperm penetrates the egg. After about eight hours the egg and the sperm fuse into a single cell that divides and subdivides, doubling in size each time.

When it gets to the two-cell stage, or more rarely the four- or eight-cell stage (4, 5, and 6), the embryo is introduced through a cannula (a thin plastic tube) into the uterus via the cervix (7). This is a straightforward and painless procedure that is carried out without an anesthetic. Pregnancy can then develop normally as the egg becomes attached to, and then embedded in, the thickened lining of the uterus (8), and grows into a fetus (9). Naturally the health of both mother and fetus are carefully monitored until the time of birth.

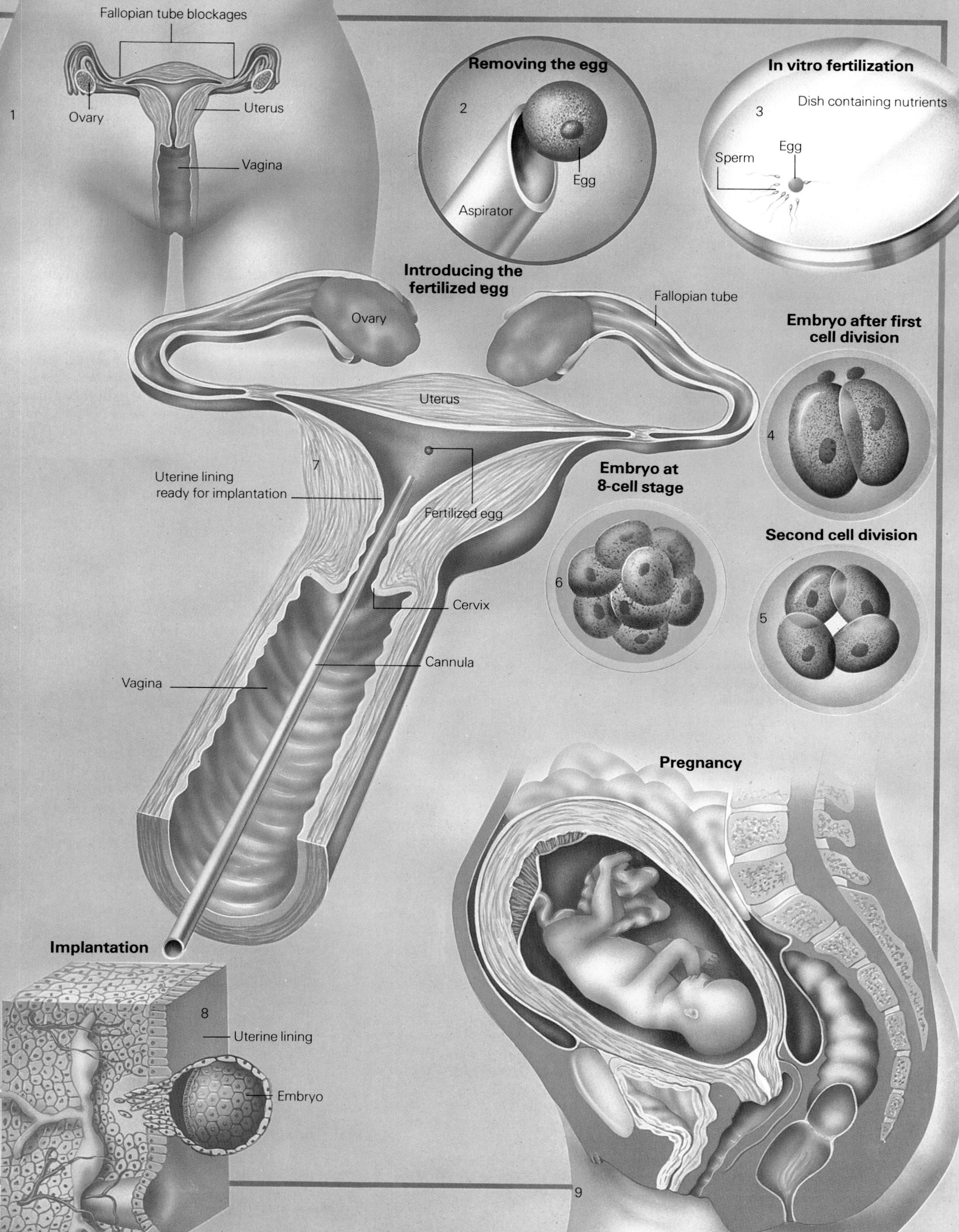
Fallopian tube blockages
1
Ovary
Uterus
Vagina
Removing the egg
2
Egg
Aspirator
In vitro fertilization
Dish containing nutrients
3
Sperm
Egg
Introducing the fertilized egg
Ovary
Fallopian tube
Embryo after first cell division
4
Uterus
7
Uterine lining ready for implantation
Fertilized egg
Embryo at 8-cell stage
6
Second cell division
5
Cervix
Cannula
Vagina
Pregnancy
Implantation
8
Uterine lining
Embryo
9

ner's sperm, which has been freshly collected, is added. If fertilization takes place it will be apparent after 18 hours. The fertilized egg is then transferred to another solution, where it will start to divide. In the early days of in vitro fertilization, research opinions varied as to whether it was best to transfer the embryo at the four-, eight-, or 16-cell stage. However, technological advances have been rapid, and now most embryos are transferred at the two-cell stage, with very few even reaching as many as eight cells.

Success rate

Most teams report a success rate of more than 90 percent for recovering a suitable egg cell from laparoscopy; fertilization is now also achieved in more than 90 percent of cases.

The real problem lies in implantation and achieving a successful pregnancy. Steptoe and Edwards claimed that nearly a quarter of the embryos they transferred into the uterus become implanted—similar to the natural rate of implantation. The majority of pregnancies achieved through in vitro fertilization do not, however, go to full term.

The future of IVF

With further refinements to the technique, it is likely that many more infertile women will be offered the chance of having a baby of their own. Obviously much more research is needed; one unexplained fact, for example, is that patients who receive their embryos at night seem to have a higher chance of becoming pregnant.

In vitro fertilization can also help couples with problems other than blocked fallopian tubes. As comparatively few sperm are needed to fertilize an egg with this method, a man with a low sperm count who would otherwise be infertile can father a child.

Should the procedure become routine, there is some hope that it could be used to help avoid the birth of some children with inherited disorders. The embryos of couples at risk would be examined and abnormal ones could be discarded.

In cases where the problem is damage to a woman's ovaries, preventing the release of eggs, a woman can now receive eggs from a donor, fertilized by her partner. The woman still carries the fetus to term and gives birth normally.

However, at present in vitro fertilization is scarcely out of the experimental stage. It is successful in only about 10 percent of attempts, and is generally regarded as a last resort in the treatment of infertility.

The current method for removing eggs from a woman's ovaries uses a transvaginal probe. An ultrasound monitor (right) is used to guide the probe through the cervix, uterus, and fallopian tubes to the ovaries, where it collects several eggs—the patient has taken fertility drugs to stimulate the production of more than one egg (see Ultrasound).

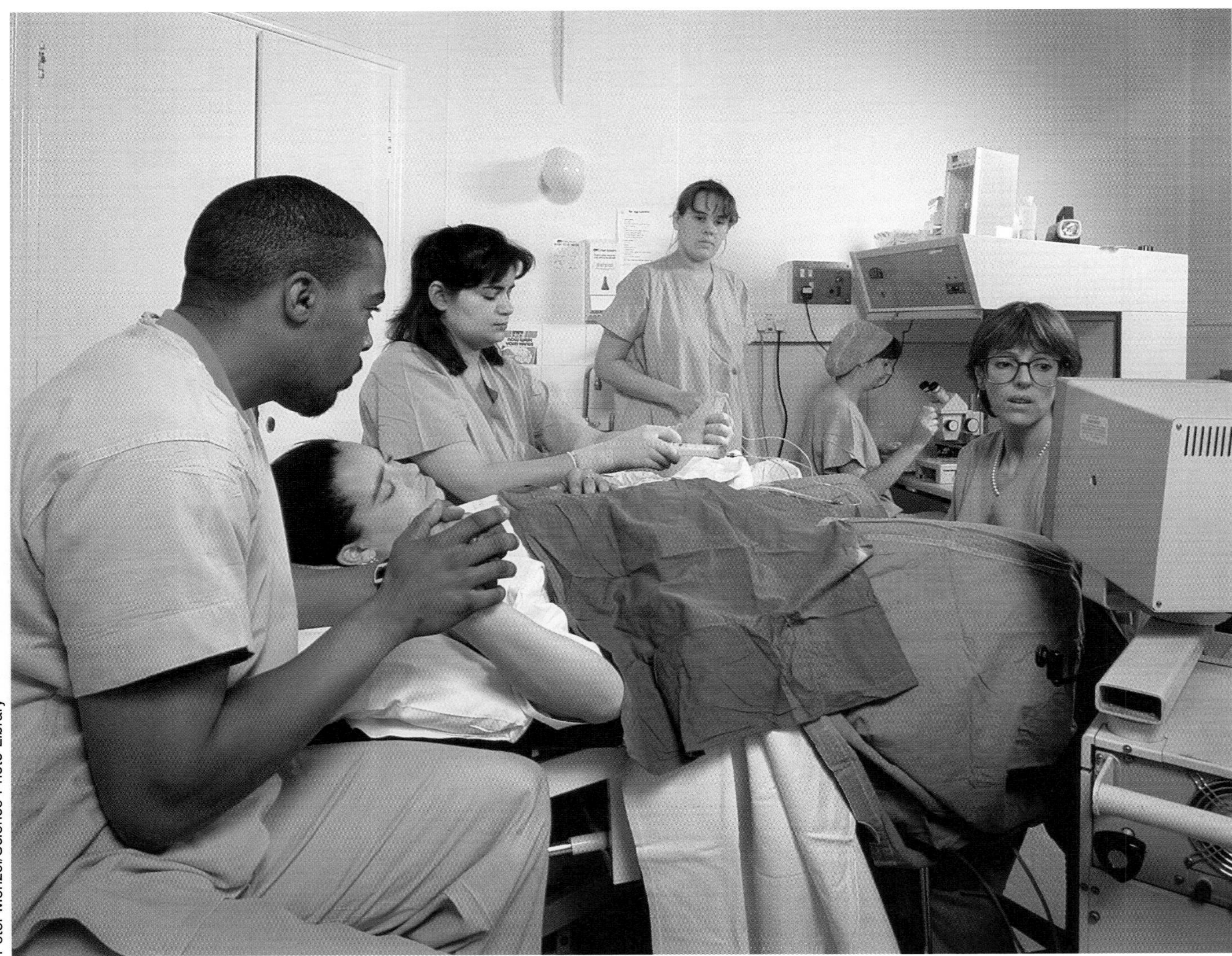

Peter Menzel/Science Photo Library

Inbreeding

Q My second cousin and I want to marry. Could our children be adversely affected because we are related?

A That depends on whether your second cousin is a blood relative or not. To be accurate, if you marry a blood relative, your chances of giving birth to an abnormal baby are slightly increased. However, a second cousin is likely to be far enough removed in the family tree to make this risk quite acceptable.

Q I have heard that in some countries first cousins can marry. Are there any genetic tests they can have before marriage to find out if there is a risk of abnormalities occurring in their children because they are closely related?

A Yes. It is now possible to spot the carriers of several inherited diseases. The family doctor can arrange for both partners to see a genetic counselor who will investigate their family medical history, carry out any necessary tests, and calculate the odds of the couple having an abnormal baby. However, in the United States marriages between first cousins are not allowed by law.

Q My British grandparents on my mother's side were first cousins. Could my children suffer from inbred defects?

A No. Any inherited abnormalities that you may be carrying are almost certainly going to be diluted if you marry someone who is not a blood relative. Only if you yourself were to marry a first cousin would there be any cause to worry.

Q I have fallen in love with one of my uncles, who is my mother's brother-in-law. We want to marry. Could any children we have be affected because we are related?

A No. He is not a blood relative. Your risk of bearing an abnormal child is no greater than if you married someone totally outside the family.

Genetic counseling has done much to help couples understand the risks of passing on inherited abnormalities to their children. Where partners are blood relatives, however, the risk may be increased and such couples should always take expert advice before having children.

Nancy Hamilton/Science Photo Library

An inherited genetic defect such as albinism, in which normal body pigment is absent, is more likely to be passed on if partners who are blood relatives have children.

Inbreeding is a commonly misunderstood term. People tend to think that it concerns certain physical traits that run in families—for example, a receding chin or a tendency to go bald early in life—that may be unattractive or undesirable.

These may be signs of inbreeding under certain circumstances, but what doctors and geneticists (experts on heredity) call inbreeding is something rather more serious. They mean disease or abnormality that is passed on to the next generation by blood relatives having children. Such relationships are described as consanguineous, and inbred disease can be caused by just one such union or a whole series of them.

As will be seen, the reason consanguineous relationships are associated with increased risk of inherited disease is just a matter of probability (see Genetics).

When inbreeding occurs

Inbred disease is actually quite a rare occurrence in these times of social mobility, when so many young people leave home to live and work in places far distant from where they were raised. The likelihood of marriages or relationships between relatives living in, for example, remote country villages is slight, but in the past it was a distinct possibility.

The other circumstance in which inbred disease can occur is at the opposite end of the social scale, in families where for reasons of power and politics people from various branches of the same family have to marry to make or cement alliances. Such families used to be mainly royal or aristocratic. It is possible, for example, to draw a family tree of all the present crowned and uncrowned royalty of Europe that traces them back to just two common ancestors in the seventeenth century, James I, King of England, and a German prince.

It is therefore no surprise that during the last century some European royalty did suffer from an inbred disease. This was hemophilia, in which the blood fails to clot in a normal fashion, and any slight scratch results in continuous bleeding (see Hemophilia).

How abnormalities occur

Everything we inherit from our parents comes to us on genes (the chemical codes that program the developing fetus). Geneticists know that genes work in a variety of ways, but the method of inheritance for diseases is usually one of the simpler forms, that is, by dominant or recessive genes. This means that a particular characteristic is seen in a baby as a result of the pairing of genes, one from each parent, which are either dominant or recessive. For example, if a gene for curly hair, which is dominant, pairs with a gene for straight hair, the child will have curly hair, but he or she will also carry the recessive straight-hair gene.

Luckily nature has arranged things so that most healthy characteristics are transmitted on dominant genes, which is why most mothers have normal, healthy babies. However, a few diseases can be inherited on dominant genes. Others are inherited on recessive genes.

If two people are related by blood the chances of them possessing a number of similar genes are higher than in two unrelated people; among these generally similar genes there may also be some abnormal genes. If they then pool their genes by having a baby, there is a greater-than-usual chance of the larger-than-usual number of abnormal genes actually pairing in ways that actually cause the person to develop symptoms and thus suffer from the disease itself.

Examples of diseases that are inherited on dominant genes are Huntington's chorea (a disease of the nervous system in which the nerves gradually degenerate; see Huntington's disease); achondroplasia (a type of dwarfism in which the head and trunk are normal in size but the limbs are abnormally short); and some types of muscular dystrophy (in which the muscles gradually become weak and ineffective; see Muscular Dystrophy).

For diseases to be inherited on recessive genes, both genes in the pair must be recessive. Diseases transmitted in this way include certain types of deafness and blindness; albinism (in which there is a complete absence of pigment, giving white hair, white skin, and pink eyes; see Melanin); cystic fibrosis (a disorder of the pancreas that drastically affects the lungs; see Cystic fibrosis); and galactosemia (in which a baby cannot derive any benefit from the sugar in breast milk).

Other types of disease are governed by more complex types of inheritance. Hemophilia, which is passed down by sex-linked inheritance, is transmitted on the X chromosome and behaves recessively in women because it is masked by the second, normal X chromosome. In men, however, the Y chromosome does not counteract the effect of the abnormal X chromosome, and the disease is expressed clinically. In theory, inbreeding between blood relations could increase the chance of offspring suffering from any of these inherited diseases.

Genetic counseling

If you suspect that you have an inherited abnormality that could be passed on to your children, you should discuss the subject with your family doctor who may refer you to a genetic counselor if he or she thinks there is reason for concern.

The counselor will draw up a detailed family tree for both partners, usually going back three generations. He or she will question you closely about your medical histories, and what you know of your families. If you are blood relatives, or if there have been consanguineous marriages further back in your family trees, the counselor will be particularly concerned.

If there is a problem, the counselor will be most careful not to interfere in your freedom of choice on whether or not to end a pregnancy, should it exist.

Knowledge of inherited disease is growing all the time and there are many instances when a genetic counselor can pronounce the risk minimal, even between blood relatives.

The hereditary risks of inbreeding

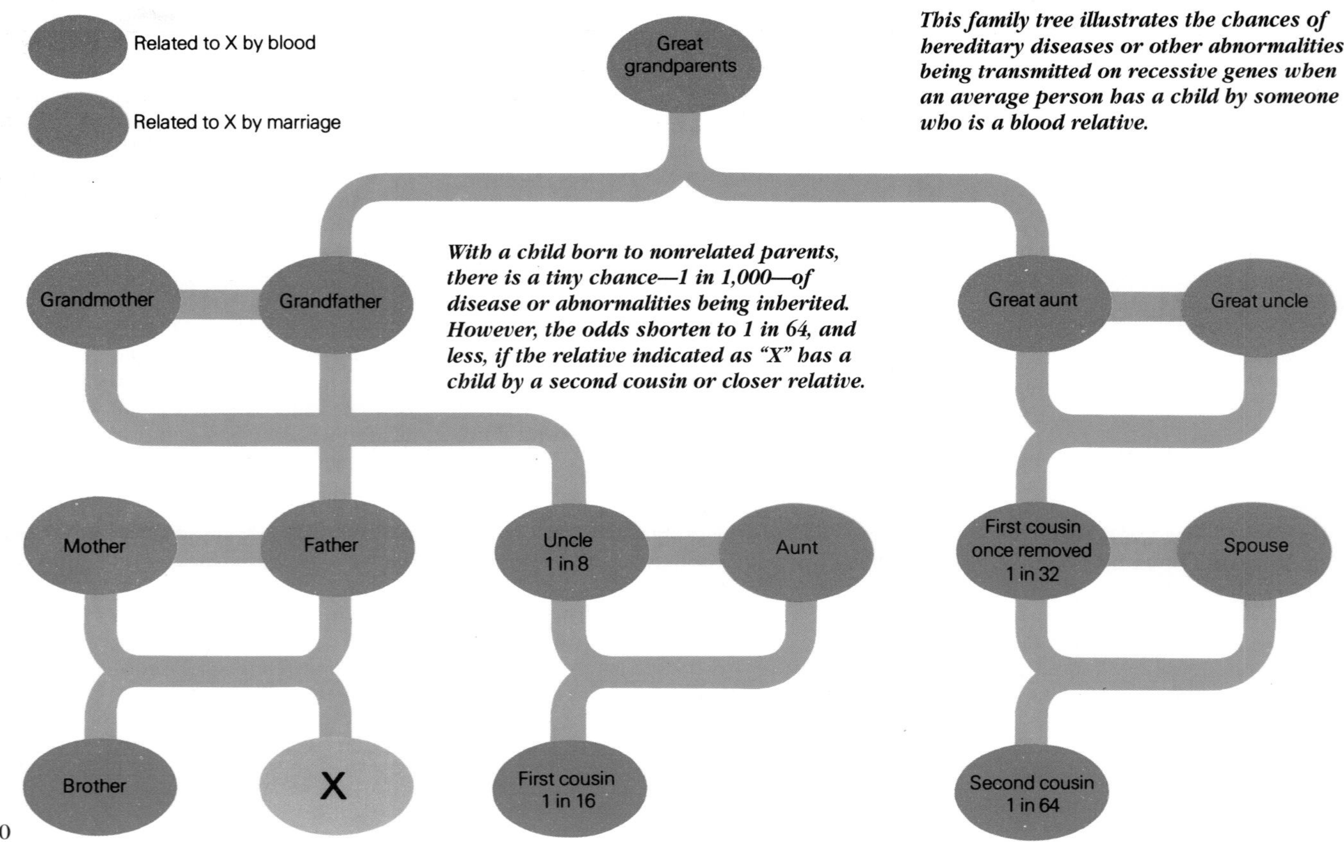

This family tree illustrates the chances of hereditary diseases or other abnormalities being transmitted on recessive genes when an average person has a child by someone who is a blood relative.

With a child born to nonrelated parents, there is a tiny chance—1 in 1,000—of disease or abnormalities being inherited. However, the odds shorten to 1 in 64, and less, if the relative indicated as "X" has a child by a second cousin or closer relative.

Incompatibility

Q My husband spends four nights a week out drinking with his friends. How can I persuade him that I need and enjoy his company?

A Have you tried telling him how much you miss him, and how lonely your evenings are without him? You might try suggesting that the two of you go out together one or two nights a week.

Q I want us to have a baby, but my wife doesn't agree. The arguments between us are tearing our marriage apart. Is there any way I can persuade her to change her mind?

A It is no use trying to force your wife to have a baby. Do you know and understand her reasons for not wanting one? Perhaps she doesn't feel that you both have enough financial security to support the considerable expense of bringing up a child. Perhaps she is not yet ready to give up her career—or she may be frightened of childbirth itself and need advice and reassurance from your family doctor. She may not even be sure of her own reasons.

If you feel that the two of you can't discuss the subject anymore without arguing, think about making an appointment to see a marriage guidance counselor. He or she could arrange to see each of you separately, and your wife may feel more able to talk about her feelings to a third person. The counselor may be able to interpret each of your feelings to the other and help prevent the disagreements that are threatening your relationship.

Q I got married three months ago after a whirlwind courtship, but now I feel that I don't know my husband at all. Are we incompatible?

A It is too soon to say. The image of marriage as shown in films, TV, or commercials hardly matches up to reality. You fell in love with a romantic ideal, but then, so did your husband. Try not to be too anxious, and give your marriage a chance to settle down. Maybe your husband feels the same way about you.

Some differences can add zest to human relationships, while others cause conflicts. But where incompatibilities are threatening a relationship, much can be done by the people involved—sometimes with the help of professional counselors—to resolve difficulties and restore harmony.

Adults sometimes do not realize that their children can suffer from incompatibility and are not automatically fond of each other just because their parents are.

The attraction of opposites can make for a very good relationship—in marriage, in friendship, or between members of a family. It is only when aspects of individual temperaments cause conflict that the problems of incompatibility arise.

Incompatibility in marriage

Many couples meet, fall in love, marry—and then have to get to know each other. If they are fortunate their first impressions hold true, and they get along together as people as well as lovers; but it can happen that, after a little while, they find that they are quite incompatible in many different ways.

Sometimes when the problem is too deep to be resolved, incompatibility can end in divorce. When differences are not too deep, marriage guidance counselors can help. Sometimes one partner is not even aware of what irritates the other, and this may emerge during counseling.

Sexual incompatibility

Sexual incompatibility, which can destroy a marriage, takes many forms. If one partner is more highly sexed than the other and enjoys sex more often, this can lead to resentment and frustration. Conflict is set up when one partner finds pleasure in forms of sex play that the other dislikes or when one partner wants children and the other does not.

If a couple love and respect each other enough, they should be able to talk over their particular problem and find a compromise. However, some husbands and wives are too reticent—or embarrassed—to do this, and because understanding between them is vital, they may need outside help. Marriage guidance counselors and sex therapists are trained to deal tactfully and gently with intimate problems.

Incompatibility over friends

It is not only incompatibility between the personality of the husband and the wife that can disrupt family life. Sometimes one or both partners cannot or will not accept the friends of the other. A familiar example is the husband's drinking

Bubbles/Jennie Woodcock

Incompatibility with in-laws may endanger a marriage. Doting grandparents who insist on overindulging their grandchildren may cause extreme irritation if they go against the parents' wishes.

friends, people he has known since before he got married and whom he is reluctant to give up. In the days before their marriage, his fiancée had probably joined in outings with his friends for the sake of being in his company, but if she wants to spend the evening in her new home or has a baby to care for, she resents her husband spending a lot of his leisure time with his friends. She also fails to understand what he sees in them, complaining that their conversation is limited, their jokes predictable, and their attitudes childish. She cannot see that the undemanding nature of their company helps her husband to relax.

This situation can, of course, be reversed. It may be the wife who has many interests, and friends who make it plain that they do not like her husband. The most practical solution when this conflict over friends arises may be for the couple concerned to develop a new interest that they can share together that will bring them mutual friends, and in time to give up some of the activities that have kept them apart. Any attempt to force a partner to give up, or to change, friends and interests almost always leads to resentment and usually to failure.

Incompatibility in the family

Incompatibility between relatives by marriage is complicated by the sense of family duty. This form of incompatibility often arises when a man or a woman has—unconsciously—chosen a marriage partner who is totally unlike their parent of the same sex. A woman may have married a hearty, sports-loving man who is the opposite of her father, a bookworm. In retaliation the father loses no chance to make his son-in-law look like an uneducated fool, while the latter runs down his father-in-law as someone who is less than manly. Time and knowledge of one another can ease the difficulties between the two men—if the wife/daughter never makes the mistake of playing one off against the other.

Parents and children-in-law

There are many reasons for incompatibility between parents and their children-in-law. The parents may genuinely believe that their children have made an unwise choice of partner. They could be right, but it is not necessarily wise for them to say what they think—and it will create a lot of friction. The child, on the other hand, may have chosen a spouse as much like the parents as possible—but it is not tactful if the child then criticizes its parents for failing to reach its perceived high standards.

The best way of dealing with incompatibility between parents and their children-in-law is for the whole family to talk over the difficulties calmly and to feel assured of their love and support—especially where matters such as the care and upbringing of any future offspring are concerned. In return for treating the parents-in-law courteously and tolerantly, the new spouse is entitled to courtesy in return. If such consideration is not received, then the new spouse is quite justified in wishing to spend less time with his or her in-laws.

Live-in in-laws

When a demanding in-law lives with the family and causes constant friction, it is wise for the couple to seek advice from their doctor, a social worker, or a marriage guidance counselor.

If no other solution can be found, it is better for an difficult elderly relative to go to live in a home for old people than for a marriage to be broken up, as harsh as that conclusion might seem to the relative involved.

Incompatible children

Just because they are siblings, children do not necessarily love each other. Within a family there may be one child who is the odd one out. He or she may be different in behavior, personality, or gifts, and if he or she also looks different from the rest of the family, the sense of being an outsider will be increased.

If the parents find the "different" child particularly difficult to understand and handle, a child guidance counselor may be able to help. Sometimes the child who does not seem to fit may grow into the young adult who gives his or her parents the most pleasure and companionship.

Outside the home

People with "difficult" personalities often suffer from incompatibility problems simply because they are so difficult to get to know, and they, in turn, find it hard to communicate and make friends. If a child is a loner, this will be obvious almost from infancy. The problems arise later, in school, work, or marriage, when communications break down and much unhappiness ensues. A parent who is aware of their own or their children's personalities can do much to avoid this—and professional counselors are available to help.

Incontinence

Q **My aged grandmother has always been fastidious, but when she had pneumonia she had incontinent diarrhea. She feels so guilty and is constantly crying. What should I do?**

A Old people with a serious illness can often get so weak that they are unable to control their sphincters. This is normal, and with understanding nursing and the use of incontinence pads, the problem is soon dealt with. Your grandmother has probably become depressed from worrying about it. Explain to her that she cannot help it. If her depression persists, she may need medical treatment.

Q **I caught my four-year-old actually playing with his feces, and I smacked his hand. Did I do the right thing?**

A Children do go through a phase when they are fascinated by their feces. Experts do not agree as to whether a child should be punished or not, but most would probably agree that you should show disapproval. However, this is a passing phase and drawing a lot of attention to it may prolong the problem.

Q **Can incontinence be a sign of rejection? My 12-year-old daughter has turned against me and is now soiling herself.**

A Such behavior at this age is uncommon and very serious. Smaller children do become incontinent of feces if severely emotionally disturbed but by 12 this is rare. She is more likely to be suffering from a physical condition —see a doctor immediately.

Q **Is bed-wetting the same as incontinence?**

A Bed-wetting is incontinence during sleep and is very different from incontinence when the person is awake and conscious. Most children stay dry at night by the age of five, and bed-wetting after this age can be a sign of emotional disturbance. However, bed-wetting in some cases can be caused by a urinary infection or bladder abnormality.

Incontinence is a problem that can be worrying and embarrassing both for sufferers and for those with whom they live. However, with proper treatment the condition can often be remedied.

Incontinence is the inability to control the excretion of urine and feces. It is a common problem that is associated with the very young and the very old.

People usually learn to control the muscular sphincters, the body's valves that retain urine and feces, from about age two. Bed-wetting may continue for longer, but most children stay clean and dry by the age of three or four.

In older people incontinence is usually caused by serious illness, weakness, or a physical problem. Mostly, it is occasional or partial and only rarely is there complete incontinence. In the elderly, however, incontinence can be a constant and disturbing problem. Aids can make the condition easier to handle.

Causes

Incontinence of feces is most commonly caused by spurious diarrhea (see Diarrhea). This is common in old age or during a weakening illness. Many older people have constipation, through poor bulk or fluid intake. They then take too many laxatives that make liquid feces push past the constipation and cause spurious diarrhea. This type of diarrhea can also be a side effect of antibiotics or iron therapy. Patients with severe neurological diseases such as a spinal injury that affects bowel control also develop incontinence, as do those with a serious abnormality of the rectum or anus, such as a tumor or anal prolapse (see Anus).

Fecal incontinence can be a sign of emotional problems in children; it is also common among the severely disabled and those with senile dementia (see Senility).

Incontinence of urine may also result from problems with one or more of the mechanisms that hold urine in the bladder (see Bladder and bladder control). Causes include the muscular sphincter at the base of the bladder; the muscular floor of the pelvis, which consists of the large levator ani muscles and the urogenital diaphragm; and the muscle wall of the bladder itself.

In women some degree of urinary incontinence is common, especially in those who have a weak pelvic floor as a result of childbirth. This is called prolapsed bladder (cystocele). The weakness of the muscle allows the front part of the bladder to bulge down into the vagina, making the sphincter less effective. This causes stress incontinence, where the urine leaks out whenever the patient coughs, strains as she lifts something heavy, runs, or laughs very hard. Women can also get urinary fistulas from trauma, radiation therapy, and automobile accidents.

A severe infection of the urinary tract will produce frequent urination, leaking, and dribbling with partial incontinence, especially in the elderly. The infection acts on the controlling muscles.

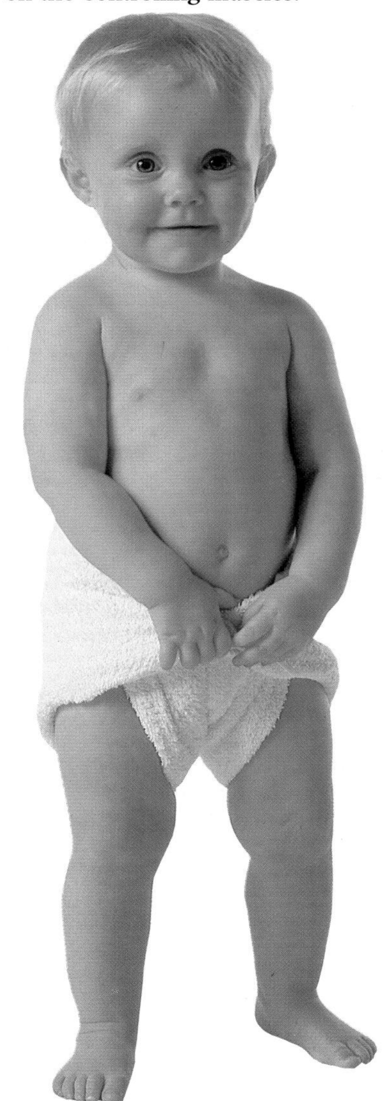

Jerry Harpur

Incontinence is normal in very young children who have insufficient muscular control of their bowel and bladder.

Male and female urinary systems

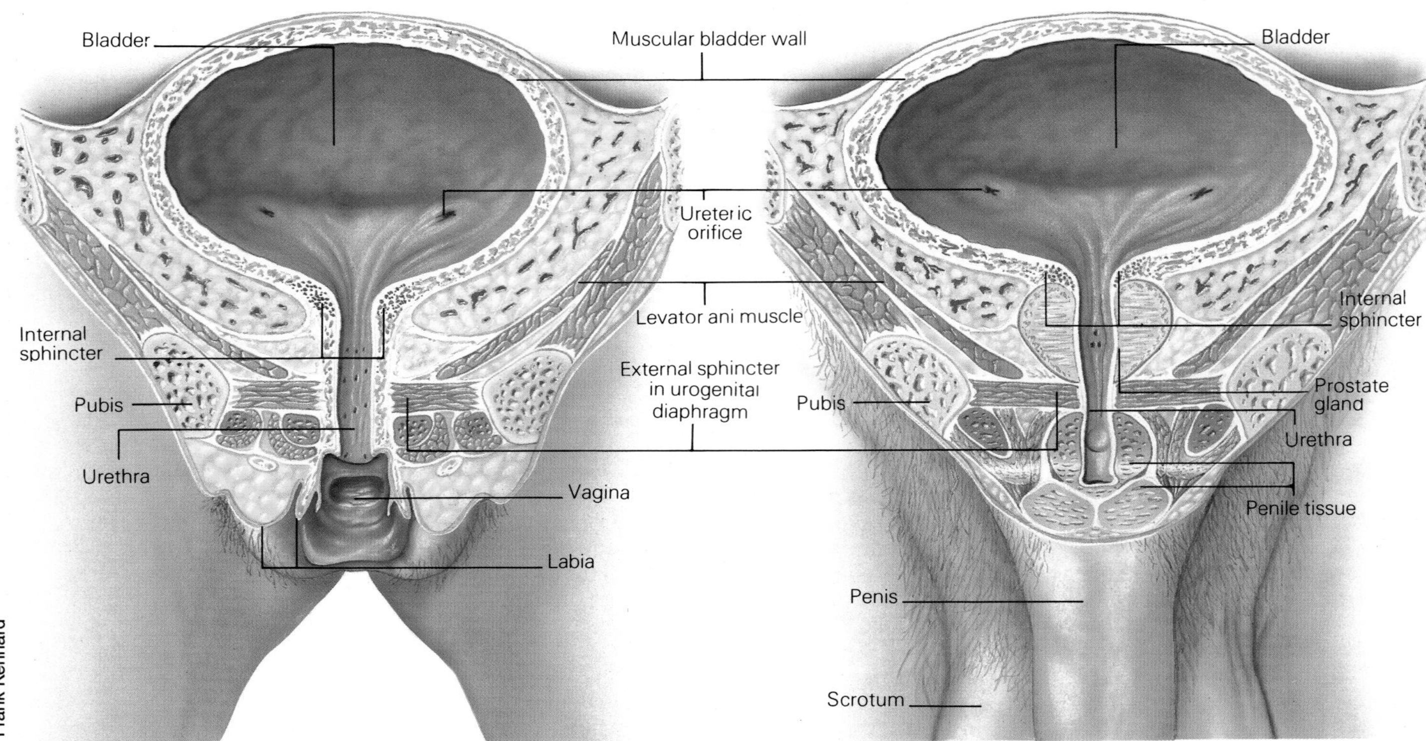

Frank Kennard

In men an obstruction of the prostate gland can lead to a retention of urine with a dribbling overflow. Alternatively an operation for an enlargement of the prostate makes some patients incontinent (see Prostate gland).

Incontinence in both sexes can occur where there is bladder cancer; a fistula (wound or ulcer; see Fistula); tuberculosis; or as a result of senility. Total lack of bladder control is much more rare and is usually caused by a neurological disease, such as multiple sclerosis.

In a few adult cases there may be severe behavioral problems. However, when incontinence occurs in children during the day it is nearly always a sign of psychological disturbance. Incontinence during sleep is called enuresis and is a slightly different problem as the incontinence is involuntary. Bed-wetting is a behavior-linked condition but it is not true incontinence.

Incontinence in itself is not dangerous, although the resulting odor, uncleanliness, and feeling of loss of control over bodily functions can be distressing to the patient and the person who cares for him or her. Incontinence is also a symptom of a number of diseases and as such warrants medical investigation.

Treatment

Fecal incontinence can almost always be cured, and it is only a permanent problem in a very small number of patients with neurological diseases. Regular use of enemas or suppositories will help empty the rectum. Alternately, surgery may be required to repair a prolapse of the anus or to remove growths causing incontinence. This is usually very successful.

Where the cause is impaction of feces due to constipation, then removal of the blocking feces, coupled with a very high fiber diet, is curative. Again, suppositories containing glycerol or laxative drugs may be recommended. Where patients have become incontinent following drug therapy from antibiotics or iron therapy, the condition will usually cure itself within a few days.

Children who defecate indiscriminately really need psychological help. They often have family problems or have become depressed, and they show their disturbance by soiling themselves.

If the problem is weak pelvic muscles, pelvic floor exercises may help restore function in the sphincter. However, reflex conditioning of the bowels is an exercise that is more easily learned by young people, rather than older people. Exercises to strengthen abdominal muscles include pushing up, bearing down, and contracting the appropriate muscles.

For short-term bouts of urinary incontinence, incontinence pads (with an internal pad to absorb the urine), changed immediately after the patient is incontinent, should be used. Incontinence pads can be used only in the short term because they may damage the skin.

Anticholinergic drugs may sometimes be used to relax the bladder muscle, particularly if irritable bladder is the cause. Occasionally an operation may be performed to tighten or lengthen the urethra.

In men the length of the penis is a valuable aid to collecting urine. A sheath or open-ended condom can be placed over the penis and linked directly to a specially adapted rubber tubing used to collect urine in a portable sterile bag. This can be used where there is urinary incontinence due to spinal injuries. Women may need to have a catheter (tube) inserted to collect urine in a bag. If all these methods fail, a urinary diversion operation may be carried out to bypass the bladder.

Aids for incontinence should never be purchased over-the-counter without medical advice, because if the wrong type is used it could lead to bladder and kidney infections.

Outlook

Punishing such a child will create a worse problem. The outlook for incontinent patients depends on the cause. Only the most severely mentally handicapped or neurological cases remain incontinent and the use of aids should make them more comfortable. In most other cases treatment will result in a cure.

Incubation

Q **Am I likely to be infectious during the incubation period of a viral infection?**

A Most viral infections are not contagious during the incubation period, but there are some exceptions, including the AIDS virus (see AIDS). With most infections once you begin to feel a bit ill, which is a symptom of many diseases, you will be infectious.

Q **My little boy was exposed to mumps three months ago. Is he still likely to get the disease now?**

A Mumps nearly always appears by the 21st day after exposure, so it is very unlikely that your son will get the disease now (see Mumps). However, it is possible that he had the disease without you being aware of it. This is called a subclinical infection, and it has two advantages. It means that the patient does not suffer from the effects of the disease and also that he or she becomes immune to it. Unfortunately, however, you cannot assume that your son is immune just because he has been exposed to the disease.

Q **Is it possible to have two diseases incubating at the same time, if you were exposed to one and then a few days later exposed to the other?**

A No. The first virus seems to stop the body from being invaded by a second virus (see Viruses). Many viruses instruct the cells in which they have become established to produce a substance called interferon, which prevents any further virus particles from invading the cells.

Q **Everyone in my office seems to have had the flu recently. When I had it last year I was very ill and would not like to repeat the experience this year. Can I take any special precautions if I think that I may be incubating the virus?**

A See your doctor, who may prescribe a medicine called amantadine that lessens the severity of influenza symptoms.

A person never displays symptoms of an infectious disease immediately after he or she has been exposed to it. Time is needed for the organism to establish itself and to multiply in the body.

When a person catches an illness, the bacteria or virus causing it invades the body and becomes established some time before the actual symptoms of the illness appear. The time that elapses between contact with the disease and the actual onset or start of symptoms is known as the incubation period (see Infection and infectious diseases).

Formally the incubation period is usually defined as the length of time between the entry of the infecting organism into the body and the appearance of the first sign or symptom of the resulting disease. Some definitions suggest that the start of the incubation period is the time at which the infection is established in the body.

Average incubation periods

Disease	Incubation period
AIDS	2–10 years
Chicken pox	14–21 days
Cholera	2–3 hours, may be days
Common cold	2–3 days
Gonorrhea	2–5 days
Influenza	3–4 days
Malaria	10–14 days
Measles	7–14 days
Mumps	12–31 days
Rubella	14–21 days
Scarlet fever	1–3 days
Whooping cough	7–10 days

Incubation of diseases

An incubation period may be as short as a few hours with diseases such as cholera; or it may be weeks or months, as with rabies. In the case of rabies the incubation period varies with the distance from the bite to the brain. If a person is bitten on the face, the disease might start as soon as 12 days after the bite. After a bite on the foot, the incubation period may be many months long (see Rabies). The reason for this is that the rabies viruses enter small nerves at the site of the bite and travel along inside these nerves until they reach the brain. The time they take to do so is determined by the distance they have to travel. For some diseases, such as tuberculosis, the organisms may lie dormant in the tissues for very long periods—sometimes even years. Such diseases do not have an incubation period in the normal sense of the word.

There has been much speculation about the incubation period of AIDS. Considerable information on this has

Chicken pox, a disease that most children get, has an incubation period of 14–21 days.

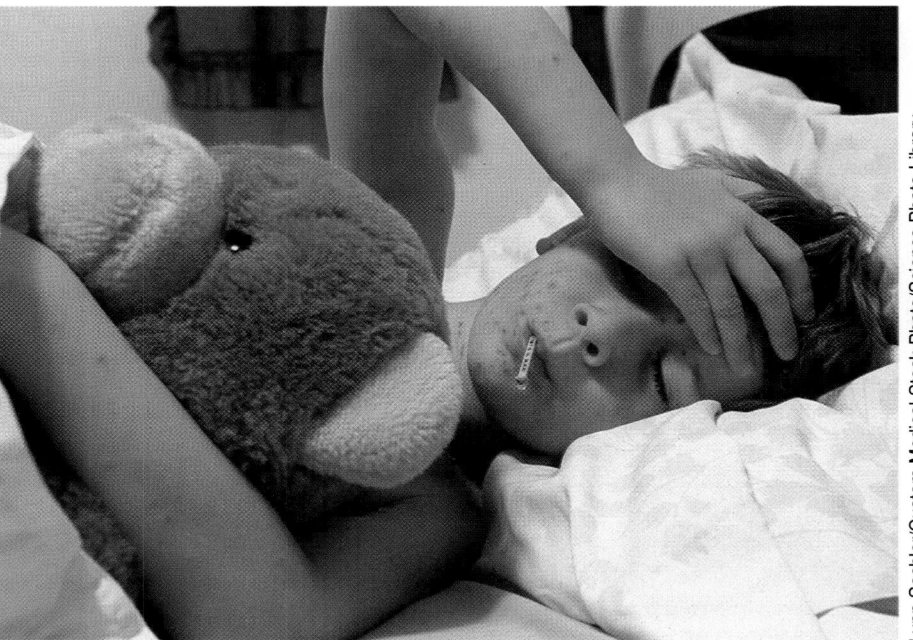

Lynn Sechler/Custom Medical Stock Photo/Science Photo Library

been derived from cases in which the infection was acquired from contaminated blood transfusions, thus establishing the time of onset. In about 50 percent of people who have become HIV-positive in this way, the incubation period was seven years or less. Children infected in this way before the age of five, however, commonly had incubation periods of less than two years. In infection by sexual transmission in adults, the incubation period averages nine to 10 years.

The virus that causes cold sores—herpes simplex—also remains in the tissues for some years and only emerges occasionally, usually when some other infection is present.

Portals of entry

Germs get access to the body in various ways, and the entry routes are called portals of entry. These include:

- the inhalation route, by way of the air passages and the lining of the nose, throat, bronchial tubes, or lungs
- any part of the digestive tract, after swallowing infected material
- through a break in the skin caused by cuts, scratches, bites, or abrasions
- through the mucous membrane lining of the eyelids and the membrane covering the whites of the eyes (the conjunctiva)
- through the mucous membrane coverings of part of the genital system, as in the case of sexually transmitted diseases
- through the mucous membrane lining of the anal canal or rectum
- through the urinary outlet tube (the urethra) to the bladder, especially in the case of females.

Most germs will cause infection only if they enter the body by their own particular route. Many germs can be safely swallowed because they are destroyed by the acid in the stomach; those that cause intestinal infections, such as typhoid or cholera, are resistant to the stomach acid. Some germs will cause infection only if introduced deeply into the tissues by way of a wound. The organism that causes tetanus, for example, will do so only if it is deposited in a deep wound. The same applies to the germ that causes gas gangrene (see Gangrene).

Incubation will not take place unless a sufficient number of germs pass in via the normal portal of entry. This necessary number, which is known as the infectious dose, varies considerably from one organism to another. In some cases it is possible for infection to occur after the entry of only a single germ. In others hundreds of thousands may be necessary before the immune defenses of the body are overcome. The dose is also affected by the general efficiency of the host's immune system, and this can vary with circumstances. It can, for example, be affected by malnutrition; a very low protein intake means that antibodies cannot be manufactured. In the case of immune deficiency diseases, such as AIDS, a much smaller number of germs than usual can cause infection.

Incubation of viral infections

Most common childhood illnesses, such as mumps and measles, are caused by viruses rather than bacteria. Viruses cannot exist outside the human body but depend on living cells to grow and multiply, whereas bacteria can be successfully grown in the bacteriology laboratory on culture plates that contain no living tissue.

Once a virus finds its way into the body, often through the lining of the nose or mouth, it invades the surrounding cells or is carried by the bloodstream to cells some distance away. Exceptions to this are the common cold and flu viruses, which establish themselves in the nose and throat.

Once the virus is inside a cell, it cannot easily be reached by the body's defense system. The virus uses the cell's own building system to make more virus particles. When these second generation viruses are released into the bloodstream the symptoms begin to appear and the person begins to feel ill.

Incubation of bacterial infections

In diseases that are due to bacterial infections, the bacteria must become established in the tissues, and the symptoms of the infection occur as soon as the organisms are present in large numbers. Bacterial infections become established extremely quickly, so incubation periods can be very much shorter than those of viral infections (see Bacteria).

Some bacterial infections have very short incubation periods—their effects are caused by highly poisonous substances called exotoxins that are present on contaminated food when it is eaten. This is the case with one form of food poisoning—staphylococcal food poisoning—that is caused by the contamination of food by infections, such as boils on the hands of catering staff. These toxins damage the intestinal lining and may be absorbed and cause more widespread damage in the body (see Food poisoning).

Other food poisoning bacteria, such as *Salmonella enteritidis*, need to reproduce themselves within the body until sufficient numbers are present to cause the disease (see Salmonella). The time this takes is the true incubation period. In the case of disease caused by preformed toxins, however, it is probably appropriate to speak of an incubation period.

Zefa

Schoolchildren often catch illnesses from others who are already infected.

Indigestion

Q **Whenever I get painful gas I take a little bicarbonate of soda in orange juice. Although it gives me more gas, it does relieve the pain. Why is this?**

A In some types of indigestion gas becomes trapped in the stomach, producing pressure and pain. Bicarbonate of soda causes more gas to be formed, and this is enough to release the trapped gas, making you feel more comfortable. The antacid effect of the bicarbonate of soda neutralizes stomach acid and also aids digestion.

Q **I often get indigestion following a big meal. How can I prevent it?**

A The most common cause of such indigestion is eating late in the evening, eating spicy or rich food, eating too much, and drinking alcohol as well. If you eat slowly and miss out one of the courses, you may reduce the indigestion. Whenever possible go for a walk after you have eaten, and allow time for your food to be digested before going to bed.

Q **I have never had indigestion until recently. Could I have an ulcer?**

A Your indigestion may be due to a change of lifestyle or foods. However, if the pain is severe, occurs in between meals, and is relieved by eating, it could be a sign of a duodenal ulcer—consult your doctor.

Q **Our entire family suffers from indigestion. Does it run in families, and will my children suffer from it too?**

A It is possible that indigestion runs in families, but it really depends on the exact nature of the symptoms and the situations in which they are experienced. Indigestion is so common that you could say that every family has sufferers because most people get indigestion at some time or other. However, children rarely suffer from indigestion because they tend to be sick, which solves the problem instantly!

Pain and discomfort after overeating or eating the wrong food is a common complaint but one that should never be ignored, since persistent and severe indigestion may have an underlying medical cause that requires treatment.

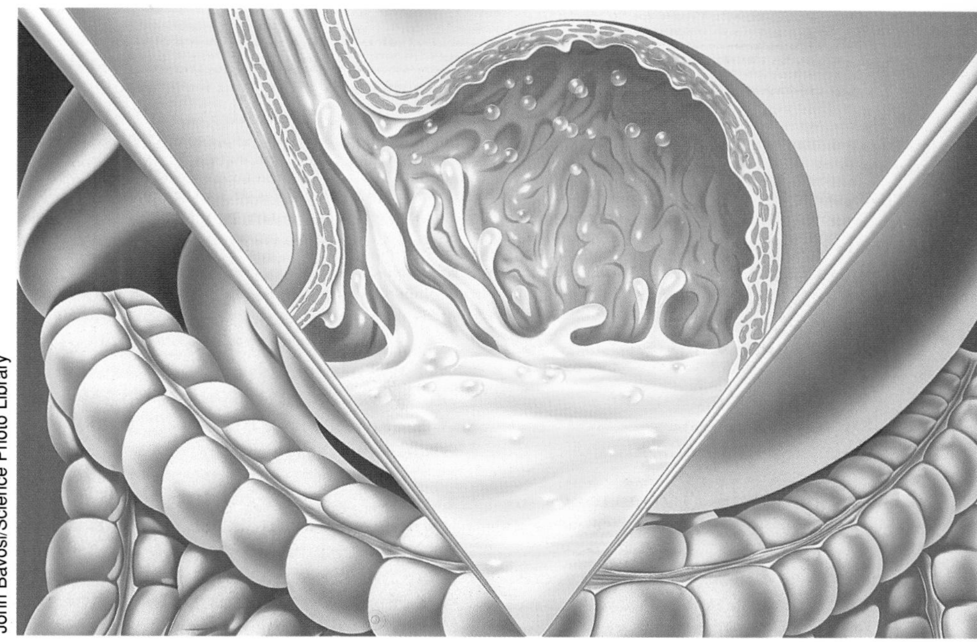

John Bavosi/Science Photo Library

Acidic juices flowing back up out of the stomach toward the throat cause the pain and burning sensation of heartburn.

Apart from the occasional rumble or belch, we do not usually notice the functioning of our digestive systems. For most people the term *indigestion* covers a wide variety of digestive complaints, but most commonly it means pain in the gut after eating, often accompanied by a bloated, sick feeling (see Heartburn).

Types of indigestion

Mild indigestion occurring after a heavy meal, particularly if rich or spicy food has been eaten, is extremely common. It is a complaint that mainly affects adults.

Chronic indigestion is more persistent and severe, and is often a symptom of a medical condition that can usually be treated. In some people the pattern of indigestion is indicative of a specific medical complaint, such as a peptic ulcer, a hiatal hernia (see Hernias), or a migraine (see Migraine).

Causes

Indigestion is either a symptom of illness or, much more commonly, the result of eating unsuitable food. It may also result from the way food is eaten.

Depending on the individual, certain foods can cause indigestion. Cucumber and pickled onions are common culprits, as are spicy foods, such as curry, and rich foods loaded with cream or butter. Unripe fruit, uncooked meat, and excesses of tea, alcohol, or tobacco can also cause types of indigestion. It is not that these substances cannot be digested, it is just that the stomach takes longer to deal with them and is slow to pass them on into the remainder of the intestine. The stomach contents and stomach acid lie in the stomach for a long time before being passed into the duodenum, and it is the acid that is poured out that causes heartburn and belching (see Digestion).

For some people indigestion is brought on simply by eating too quickly and failing to chew food thoroughly. Another cause may be poor dental hygiene, because bad or septic teeth may leak blood or pus around the gum margins, and this will taint food and produce chronic indigestion (see Gums and gum diseases).

There may also be psychological reasons behind bouts of indigestion. The nerve supply to the stomach is through the vagus nerve, which controls acid production and the rate at which food leaves the stomach. Both anxiety and depression affect this part of the nervous system. They can cause excess acid production and slow emptying of the stomach, both of which cause indigestion and can lead to the formation of ulcers.

Symptoms

There is no standard set of symptoms for this condition. The degree of indigestion produces an individual combination of symptoms, from mild pain and flatulence (gas) to severe discomfort and regurgitation of acidic food.

The symptoms also vary depending on the cause of the indigestion. There is usually pain, which is either colicky or constant, and may be situated in the pit of the stomach or the upper chest.

There may also be nausea, accompanied by a full and heavy sensation in the stomach; if the sufferer can vomit up the stomach contents, the indigestion is relieved immediately (see Vomiting).

Acid regurgitation from indigestion is another common symptom. Acid comes up into the mouth to produce hoarseness of the voice and a pain in the chest, better known as heartburn.

Sometimes a person with indigestion will experience a symptom known as waterbrash—where saliva flows like water—accompanied by excess belching, flatulence, or hiccups.

In chronic indigestion the tongue is dry and is coated with a brown furlike substance, and the breath is stale.

Dangers

Isolated bouts of indigestion following heavy meals or drinking sprees are not dangerous. However, where the indigestion is chronic, or when the pain does not pass or becomes extremely severe, it is important to see a doctor since some serious conditions produce pain and symptoms that often mimic the symptoms of indigestion.

Inflammation of the gallbladder, for instance, produces gas, sickness, and central abdominal pain. Occasionally some cases of appendicitis can produce the same symptoms (see Appendicitis).

A heart attack or a blood clot on the lung may also appear at first to be a bout of acute indigestion, but the pain remains fixed or worsens and is not relieved by taking an antacid.

Where chronic indigestion is caused by an undetected peptic ulcer, the ulcer may perforate or bleed. Persistent indigestion may also be the first indication of stomach cancer. Failure to diagnose any of these conditions is dangerous and in some cases could even be fatal (see Ulcers).

Treatment and outlook

In the case of chronic indigestion where a medical condition, such as a hiatal hernia, stomach cancer, or a peptic ulcer, is suspected, the sufferer will usually need to have a medical investigation, such as an X ray or an endoscopy, to establish the precise cause (see Endoscopy).

If the cause of the indigestion is a hurried way of life, stress (see Stress), or a poor diet (see Diet), this must be corrected. In the case of isolated bouts of indigestion, it can be treated with antacids.

The outlook for people with a medical cause for their indigestion varies depending on the particular cause. Many people who are suffering from a hiatal hernia experience severe heartburn. In most cases their condition can be controlled by taking small meals; avoiding certain foods, especially fatty foods; avoiding aspirin and other nonsteroidal anti-inflammatory drugs that irritate the stomach lining; and by taking antacids regularly. If these measures fail, a surgical operation may be needed.

People with peptic ulcers can normally be cured by either medical or surgical means. However, if the ulcer was originally caused by stress, another ulcer may form if the person does not alter their way of life.

For the great majority of indigestion sufferers, an occasional dose of antacid is all that is needed. This will relieve the indigestion symptoms quickly and effectively and allow them to eat freely. Others with more severe indigestion symptoms need to modify their lifestyles, in particular their eating habits.

Jerry Harper

A dose of antacid offers quick relief from the occasional bout of indigestion.

Avoiding indigestion

- Eat regularly and slowly, chewing food thoroughly so that it is swallowed easily
- Do not eat when wet or cold, because the digestive mechanism will be slowed down
- Avoid heavy drinking or smoking
- Get plenty of exercise
- Eat plenty of fiber to avoid getting constipation
- Visit your dentist for regular checkups
- If anxious or depressed seek help from your doctor

Home treatment for indigestion

- Take a dose of antacid. Bicarbonate of soda or magnesium trisilicate are both good but neither should be a substitute for better eating habits
- Take sips of water and sit in the cool air. Sit up rather than lie down; it may help to walk around
- If the indigestion persists or is more severe than usual, you should get medical advice
- If you have never had indigestion before, be sure to tell your doctor to aid him or her in making a diagnosis

The natural way to aid digestion is to get plenty of exercise.

Induction of labor

Q **The birth of my first child was induced because the baby was long overdue. Could this happen again?**

A Postmaturity is less likely in a second child; second labors are also nearly always quicker and easier. However, there are so many reasons for induction that a different complication could arise. All you can do is wait and see.

Q **Is it true that mothers having their first child are always induced?**

A From an obstetric point of view, the first baby is often the most difficult, and it is true that some such mothers run over the normal 40-week limit for pregnancy. An induction is only performed when there is a risk of harm to the mother or baby—there has never been any medical recommendation to induce all first pregnancies. However, it is more likely with older first-time mothers.

Q **A friend of mine had a difficult time with her third child and had to be induced. She has suffered from depression ever since and feels that it was her fault. How can I reassure her?**

A All induction does is to start off the natural process of birth. Although your friend feels guilty that she had to be helped, surely this is much better than risking harm to her baby or her. Tell her that there was no reasonable alternative to accepting a little assistance, and refer her to a psychiatrist. In the meantime help her get over her depression, perhaps by taking care of the children for a morning.

Q **I have heard that induction can be difficult and you have to be monitored. Why don't doctors just do a caesarean?**

A Natural birth is more beneficial for the baby. The obstetrician will prefer, therefore, an induced natural delivery to a caesarean section, which is only performed when there is no other alternative. Monitoring is just a way of keeping watch on the baby.

The birth of a baby is a natural process, but sometimes help is needed to get labor started. The procedure is called an induction and is performed to insure the safety of both the mother and the baby.

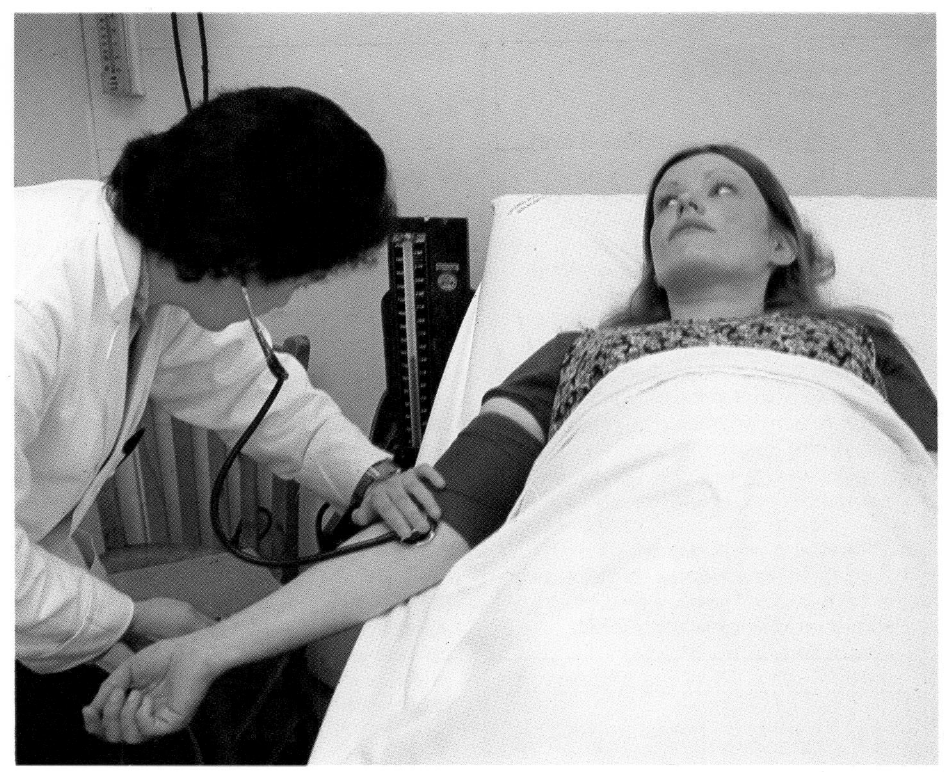

Camilla Jessel

During the course of labor a very careful check is kept on the expectant mother's blood pressure.

Induction is an artificial process of starting labor. It is carried out by doctors if the health of the mother or her unborn child is considered to be in danger. However, an induction is only performed when it is considered medically unavoidable. The procedure is less common now in developed countries. This is because it is now easier to measure the health of the fetus by means of laboratory tests (see, for example, Amniocentesis and Ultrasound) which give more accurate results. Some women manage to have several children without needing an induction, but a woman who does need an induction should not worry. On the contrary, without this technique and caesarean sections, many more women and their babies would die during childbirth (see Pregnancy).

In a normal pregnancy it is thought that hormone signals from the developing baby (the fetus) start up labor, and this occurs at about the 40th week. The neck of the uterus ripens (softens), the membranes covering the baby break, or rupture, and labor begins the process of birth. However, sometimes it is necessary to bring the birth forward for definite medical reasons. The two most common situations where an induction is needed are when the pregnant woman develops high blood pressure or if the fetus is postmature (that is, overready).

High blood pressure

In this condition, known as preeclamptic toxemia (PET) of pregnancy, the presence of the fetus induces high blood pressure in the mother (see Preeclampsia). If untreated the pressure will continue to rise and the mother's kidneys will be affected. In serious cases she can have epileptic-type seizures and die. The mortality risk for the baby is also high and it is for this reason that the prenatal checks are so important. Three common symptoms are: rising blood pressure, protein in the urine, and swelling of the feet or hands (see Edema).

Q After I had my baby the nurse told me that I had had a dry labor. Would this have been caused by having the birth induced?

A No. *Dry labor* is a term used when there is very little amniotic fluid (water) in the uterus. This is more likely to occur when the baby is late and induction is needed.

Q My sister was induced and within 20 minutes she was having a caesarean section. Why was this?

A One of the rare complications of pregnancy must have arisen. Either the umbilical cord must have prolapsed and rushed out with the amniotic fluid, or for some reason the fetus must have been in distress. In such cases a caesarean section is urgently needed and is the only way to save the life of the baby.

Q When my baby was due to be born, the nurse gave me a bath and an enema and then did what she called a sweep. I went into labor almost immediately. What did she do?

A A bath and enema are well-established methods of getting started. A sweep involves examining the neck of the uterus and sweeping the index finger gently around inside the bulging uterus. This stimulates the cervix, and within a short time the membranes rupture naturally and labor is well under way. It does not work when the cervix is not ripe (soft), so its use has declined, since there is a slight risk of infection being introduced.

Q I know several people who think too many inductions are done to suit the staff of the hospital. Are we right?

A When it is possible to plan an induction 24 hours beforehand, it seems reasonable to aim the delivery time for a period when there is maximum staff cover and hence maximum safety. An induction should never be done just to suit the convenience of the staff.

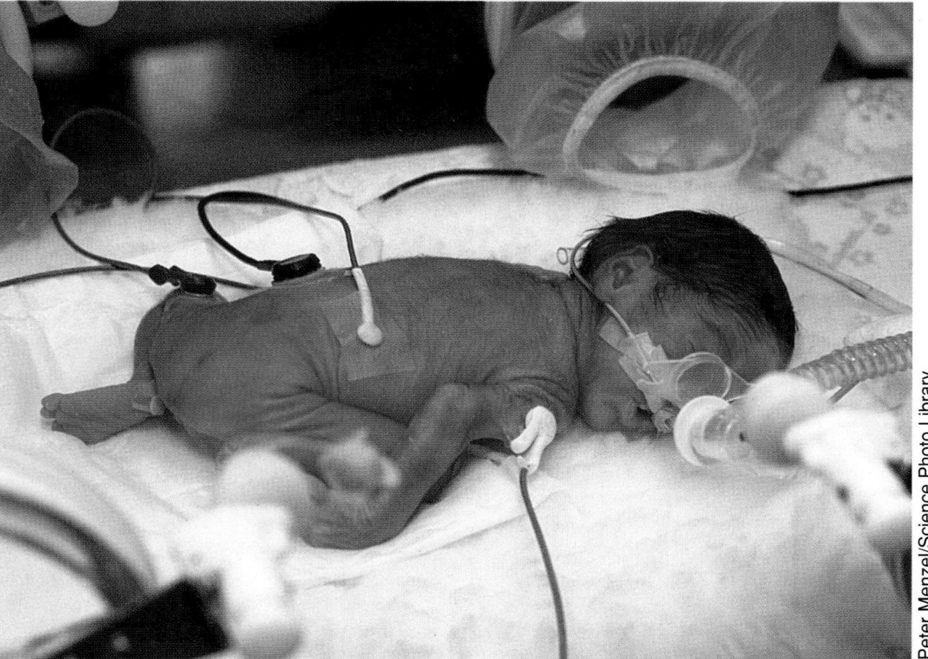

Peter Menzel/Science Photo Library

Sometimes babies must be induced prematurely and they may then need to be cared for in an incubator in a premature baby unit.

Thankfully this condition only develops late in pregnancy, but if it does occur, rest in bed and drug treatment are essential to control the blood pressure, followed by induction of labor. During labor an anesthetic is sometimes given; this not only numbs pain but also keeps blood pressure down (see Anesthetics). Provided that the pressure continues to be kept down, the subsequent delivery of the baby should be completely normal.

Postmaturity

This is a common situation where the fetus remains in the uterus after the normal 40-week period. It is slow to send out signals to start labor and at the same time the placenta is becoming old. The essential function of the placenta is to supply nutrients and oxygen to the fetus, without which it would die. For this reason, when a baby is overdue, tests of placental function are performed to check that the placenta is still working properly. These are done on specimens of the mother's blood and urine.

If it is found that the placenta is failing and the baby is no longer growing, the doctor will recommend induction of labor. In the rare case where a previous pregnancy has resulted in a fetal death, induction would be performed earlier. Otherwise the doctor may recommend waiting until 42 weeks.

Other reasons

Other situations where inductions may be necessary include: the serious illness of the mother; conditions such as diabetes, heart disease, or active tuberculosis; cases where the placenta has failed and the fetus has died and must be delivered quickly to avoid risk of infection; and cases of Rhesus blood disease (where the mother develops antibodies that destroy the blood of the baby; see Rhesus factor). In the relatively rare condition where the placenta lies over the cervix and blocks the birth canal, or when examination reveals that the head of the baby is larger than the outlet of the pelvis, a caesarean section will definitely be required.

When induction is possible

Provided that the baby is born in a hospital that is equipped with a modern obstetric unit and facilities for the care of premature babies, an induction can be performed at any time after the 28th week of pregnancy (see Obstetrics). However, there are serious hazards to the baby if it is born so early (see Fetus).

If the reason for induction is the mother's high blood pressure, it will be carried out between the 36th and 40th week of pregnancy, depending on circumstances.

When the problem is postmaturity, provided the baby is growing and the placenta is working properly, most doctors now prefer to wait until the full 40 weeks have definitely passed.

Making the decision

In every case the doctor has to weigh the risks involved and decide on induction only when it is thought to be necessary. In many cases the mother herself may be given a choice, but the final decision is based on the patient's previous obstetric history, the risks to the mother and baby, and the facilities available where the child is to be born. Unless the case is an emergency, the decision is made 24 hours beforehand. The patient knows and is ready and so is spared any last minute dash to the hospital.

Induction is never recommended as a matter of convenience for the staff or doctors of the hospital, although the time of day that an induction is performed may be taken into consideration. Mothers cannot request a special birthday date.

Methods of induction

The doctor or nurse explains to the patient the method that has been chosen for her; she is bathed and in some hospitals pubic hair is shaved if a caesarean section is at all likely.

To establish how ready the uterus is for labor and how easy induction would be, the doctor performs a vaginal examination. If the cervix is unripe, drugs called prostaglandins will be rubbed on the cervix or given orally (see Prostaglandins). An enema is always given before any delivery (see Enema).

Before any attempt to induce labor is started, the doctor will insure that the patient knows exactly what is going on and why. He or she is also likely to tell the patient that the length of time the process will take cannot be guaranteed. For example, if the induction is started in the morning, there is no guarantee that the baby will be delivered that day. It might be necessary to repeat the process the following day or even on the next two days before labor starts. Throughout the entire induction process, the condition of the baby will be carefully and frequently monitored.

In the past the most common method of inducing labor was rupturing the membranes: deliberately cutting the amniotic and chorionic membranes that enclose the bag of water in which the fetus lies. This was done with scissors, which were passed through the widened cervix and used to make a hole in the membranes so that the water gushed out. This was a highly effective way of getting labor under way but had the disadvantage that as soon as the membranes were cut, the interior of the uterus was in contact with the outside world and could no longer be considered sterile. The risks to the mother and fetus were minor so long as labor followed quickly, but if labor was delayed for more than about 24 hours, there was a risk of a uterus or fetal infection developing. If this happened, it was usually necessary to perform a caesarean section (see Caesarean birth).

In the 1970s this method was improved by combining membrane cutting with the administration of the drug oxytocin—a hormonal drug that causes the muscular wall of the uterus to tighten so as to force out the baby.

For a time this was considered to be the best way of inducing labor. The method was successful in about 80 percent of cases. But in the 1980s a major advance occurred when it was found that prostaglandin drugs placed in the vagina could produce a sequence of events almost identical to natural labor. With this method labor can be induced successfully in 95 percent of women. Equally importantly, the method causes fewer complications, both in the mother and the baby, than any previous procedure. It is now considered to be the method of choice. Using this method the membranes can usually remain intact until the baby is close to delivery.

Prostaglandins

Prostaglandins are a range of natural body products with many important functions. Various members of the group are capable of inducing labor and can be given by mouth or by injection. These routes, however, tend to be unreliable and the vaginal route is now preferred.

The drug most commonly used to induce labor when the baby is alive is prostaglandin E2. This is available commercially under the name dinoprostone and is formulated as a pill, pessary, or gel. Many obstetricians prefer the gel and find it more reliable than the pill or pessary. There are other and more powerful prostaglandins than E2, but these are restricted to use in bringing about the expulsion of a dead fetus.

To start the induction prostaglandin gel is placed high in the vagina, using the single-dose delivery syringe in which it is provided. A notable advantage of the prostaglandin method is that the mother is free to move around during the early stages of induction and the early part of labor. With the alternative method—the use of oxytocin—the mother must be connected to an infusion pump, which

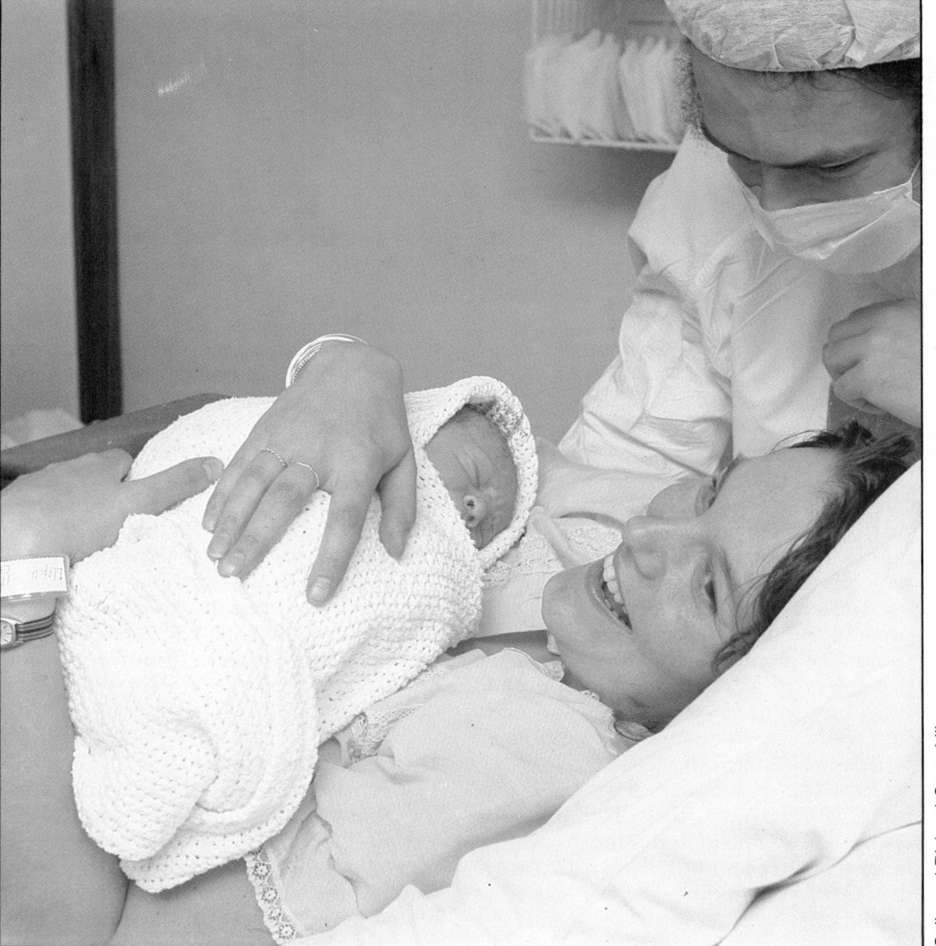

Sally and Richard Greenhill

The moment that makes it all worthwhile: a new mother holds her baby in her arms for the very first time.

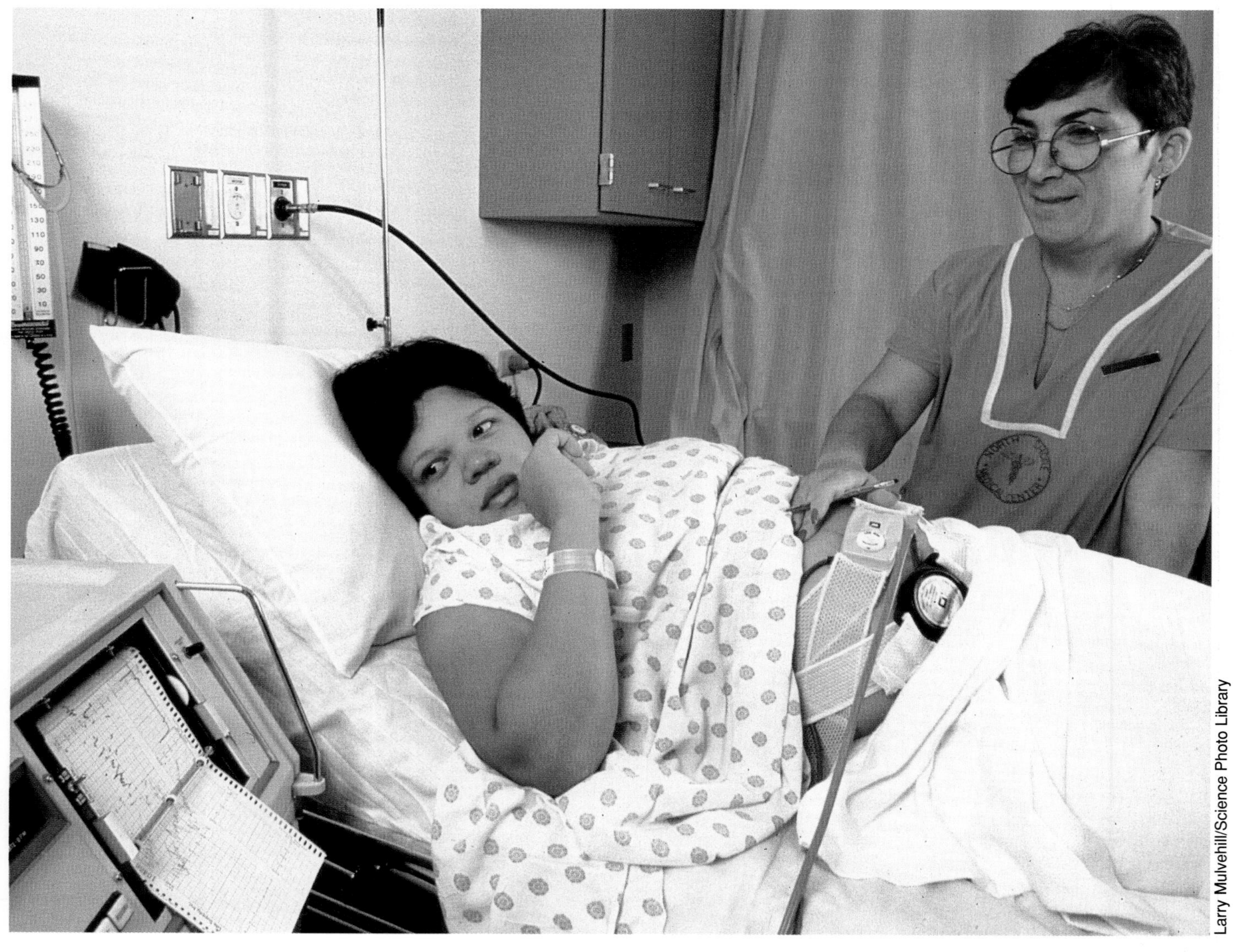
Larry Mulvehill/Science Photo Library

A fetal monitor attached to the mother plots the baby's heartbeat in the uterus during the induction process.

severely limits mobility (see Intravenous infusion).

Once labor has been started by the prostaglandin method, it is best not to cut the membranes but to let nature take its course. Sometimes oxytocin is still used after labor has been started with prostaglandins, but in this case it is usual to cut the membranes so as to avoid the possible risk of forcing amniotic fluid into the uterine blood vessels and causing a dangerous amniotic embolism, which could harm the fetus.

Once the membranes have been ruptured, it is essential to deliver the baby within 24 hours since the uterus will no longer be sterile, but it is usually only a matter of ten minutes to half an hour before contractions start.

If necessary the patient may be connected to all kinds of sophisticated machines that monitor, or keep an eye on, the baby's heartbeat, the contractions, and so on. This essential information about the condition of the baby and the progress of labor insures that the maximum precautions are taken to insure a safe delivery of a healthy baby. Often an anesthetist is on hand to revive the baby.

Of course progress depends on each individual case, but most women will go on to have normal deliveries. Some women will need help from forceps and only a very small proportion will need a delivery by caesarean section.

Dangers and outlook

The greatest risk is of inducing a premature baby. If the mother's dates were wrong she could believe she is 40 weeks pregnant while only being in the 36th week. If the baby were to be induced, it would be premature and need the facilities of a premature baby unit.

Reasons for inducing labor

- Pregnancy-induced high blood pressure (preeclampsia)
- Bleeding (antepartum hemorrhage)
- Unduly prolonged pregnancy
- Growth retardation in the fetus
- Changing fetal position (unstable lie)
- Rhesus problems (hemolytic disease)
- Diabetes in the mother
- Severe fetal abnormality
- Death of the fetus
- Voluntary pregnancy termination (abortion) during the 2nd semester

Infection and infectious diseases

Q Is there any difference between an infectious and a contagious disease?

A Strictly speaking, a contagious disease is one that is caught by touching an infectious person. However, people use the word *contagious* just to mean infectious.

Q My neighbor told me that you can catch some forms of cancer. Is she right?

A No. It is true that viruses may be involved in producing the irregular division of cells that is the basic abnormality in cancer. A disease called Burkitt's lymphoma, which is a cancer affecting African children, is caused by the Epstein-Barr virus. It is also suggested that viruses may be involved in producing cancer of the cervix. However, you cannot actually catch cancer from another person.

Q My husband has just had a very bad case of mumps. Are childhood diseases more severe when you are an adult?

A Although this does not apply to all the normal childhood illnesses, as a general rule, yes. It is particularly true of mumps, which can cause severe inflammation of the testes in men. Chicken pox in adults can cause a very severe pneumonia that is often fatal.

Q Is it possible to have a disease without knowing it?

A Yes. This is called a subclinical infection. Some people may be exposed to an infection and gain immunity to it without developing the full-blown symptoms of the disease. This seems to occur in young children with mumps, and in quite a high proportion of the population with rubella (German measles).

Q Can people catch diseases from animals?

A Yes. Birds, dogs, and insects carry infections that can be transmitted to humans. However, only those who work with animals are very likely to be affected.

Infectious diseases were once the most common cause of death. Improved sanitation, housing, hygiene, immunization, and antibiotics and other drugs have greatly reduced deaths from infection.

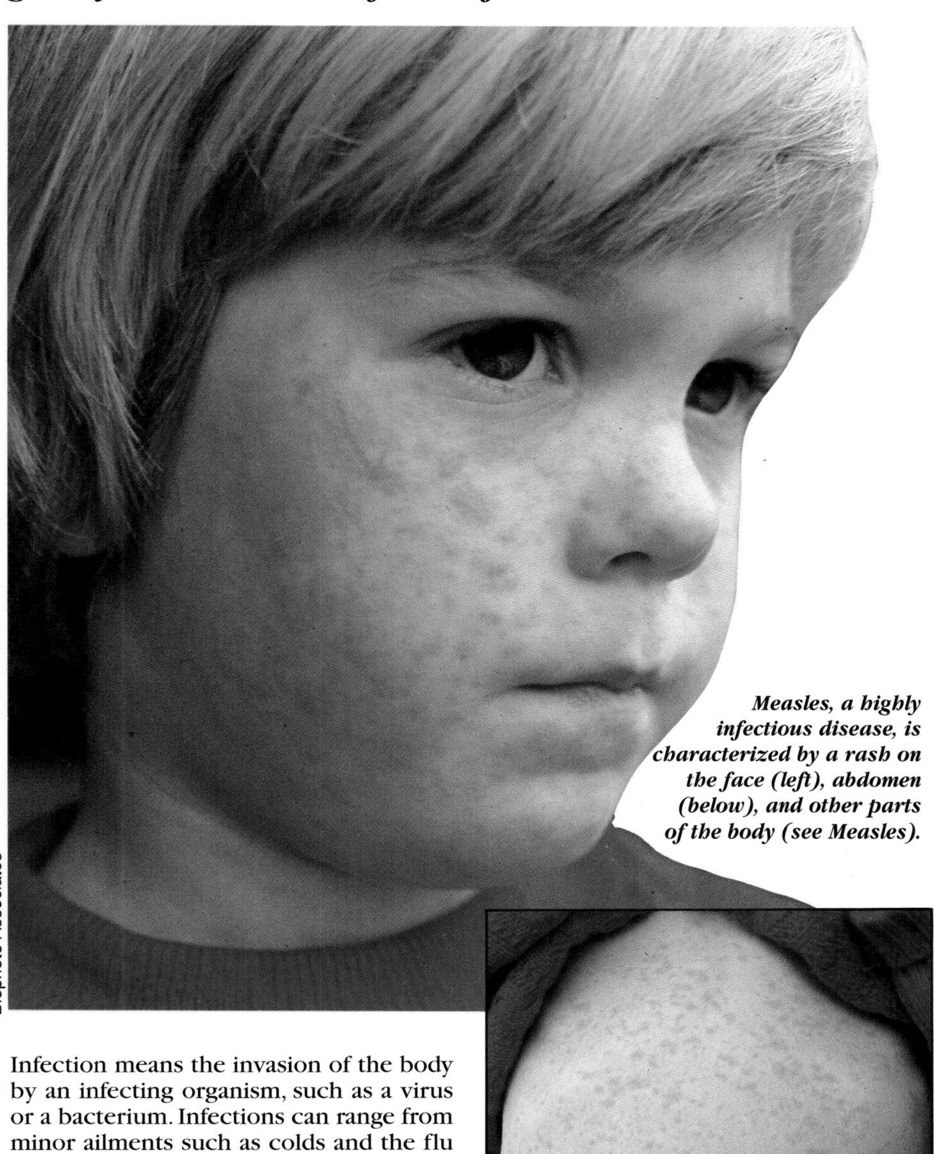

Biophoto Associates

Measles, a highly infectious disease, is characterized by a rash on the face (left), abdomen (below), and other parts of the body (see Measles).

Infection means the invasion of the body by an infecting organism, such as a virus or a bacterium. Infections can range from minor ailments such as colds and the flu to invariably fatal illnesses such as rabies. Infections may be localized, affecting only a small area of the body (an abscess, for example) or a single system (the way that pneumonia affects the lungs), or they may be generalized, affecting a greater part of the body, as in septicemia (see Blood poisoning).

Causes

Infections are caused by tiny organisms that are too small to be seen with the naked eye; they are therefore called microorganisms. Two different types of microorganism—the virus and the bacterium—cause the vast majority of infections.

Viruses are not really complete organisms on their own. In fact, they are unable to maintain a separate existence outside the cells of another living entity (see Viruses). Many viruses infect human beings, and there are also viruses that infect other animals, plants, and even infect bacteria.

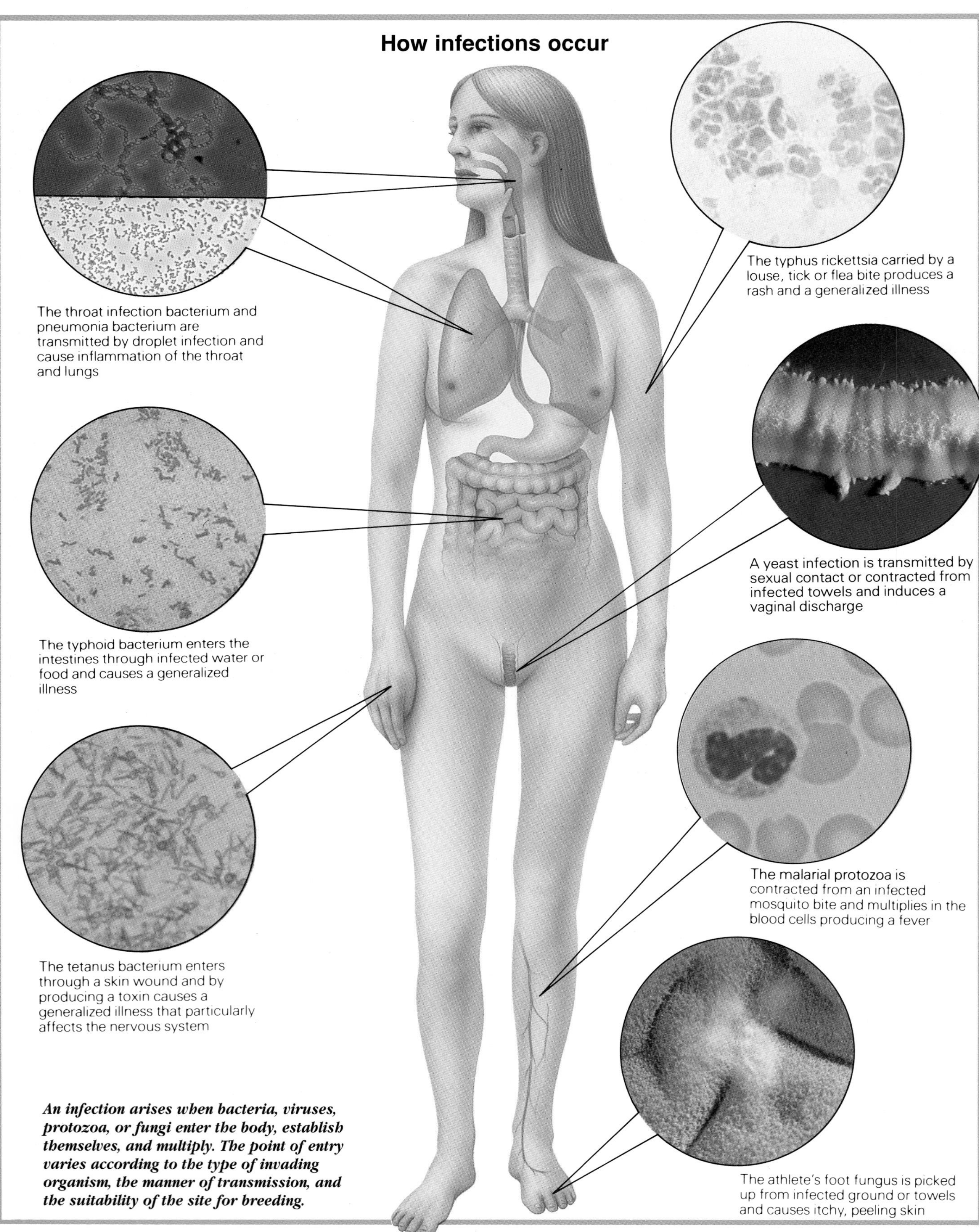

An infection arises when bacteria, viruses, protozoa, or fungi enter the body, establish themselves, and multiply. The point of entry varies according to the type of invading organism, the manner of transmission, and the suitability of the site for breeding.

A virus consists of an outer shell of protein that contains a core of genetic material (DNA or RNA). When this genetic material infects a cell, it instructs the cell to make other viruses and in this way it can reproduce itself.

In contrast bacteria are single-celled organisms that can exist quite happily away from other living things (see Bacteria). Many bacteria live in the soil and do not cause any infections. In humans some bacteria enter cells during the course of infections, while others remain outside. Many bacteria are normal inhabitants of the colon (large intestine), where they do no harm and may even be helpful, preventing the growth of other more dangerous bacteria. These are called commensal (literally, "eating with") bacteria.

A third type of infective microorganism is the protozoan, which is a larger single-celled organism. Malaria is caused by a protozoan called plasmodium (see Malaria).

A further class of infecting organisms are the fungi. Fungal diseases include thrush (candidiasis; see Thrush); athlete's foot (tinea pedis; see Athlete's foot); various other similar skin fungal infections (epidermophytoses), such as ringworm (tinea corporis; see Ringworm), jock itch (tinea cruris), and kerion or scalp tinea (tinea capitis); and the lung infection histoplasmosis.

In general internal fungal infections are uncommon except in people with severe immunodeficiency disorders (see AIDS). In these conditions, which include AIDS, congenital immune deficiencies, and the results of immunosuppressive treatment for organ grafting (see Grafting), internal fungal infections frequently occur.

How infections begin

Once a microorganism has entered the body, it proceeds to reproduce itself using the plentifully available supply of nutrient substances as its food source. Viruses go one stage further by using the chemical building apparatus of the cells to build new viruses. In contrast the bacteria reproduce simply by means of each individual bacterium splitting into two.

Microorganisms cause disease in a number of different ways. A disease occurs when the microorganism interferes sufficiently with normal body processes. Potentially dangerous organisms may be present in considerable numbers without causing enough change in the body to produce symptoms. In some of these cases the people infected in this way are carriers of disease.

One of the most important properties of disease-causing microorganisms is invasiveness, or the ability to make their way across tissue planes into new areas. They are able to do this because they produce chemical activators called enzymes (see Enzymes). One of these enzymes, called hyaluronidase, breaks down hyaluronic acid, the substance that glues together the cells of connective tissue. Organisms that synthesize this enzyme can spread rapidly through body tissues. Other bacterial enzymes can break down the protein collagen, which is an important structural protein in the body. This also allows rapid spread of bacteria. Some bacteria produce enzymes that dissolve blood clots by breaking down the fibrin of which clots are made. Others produce enzymes that are capable of destroying red blood cells and various tissue cells (see Blood).

The principal way in which microorganisms cause disease is by producing remarkably poisonous substances known as toxins. Bacterial toxins are among the most poisonous substances known and can produce serious illness and death when present even in minute quantities. It has, for instance, been estimated that one gram of botulinum toxin could kill well over 200 million people—every single person in the United States.

In some cases these toxins are called exotoxins because they are actually released by germs and may be carried by the bloodstream to remote parts of the body. This is the case with the organisms that cause diphtheria. These germs remain in the throat but produce exotoxins that can severely damage the nervous system, the heart, and various other organs (see Diphtheria). Most toxin-producing organisms, however, secrete endotoxins, poisons that operate only at the site of the colonies of the germs and are released on the death of the microorganism, when its cell membrane ruptures.

Bacterial toxins act in various ways, all of them damaging. They can interfere with many vital processes within cells and lead to cell death; interfere with the body's synthesis of proteins; block transmission of nerve impulses and hence cause paralysis; damage the lining of blood vessels so that they become leaky and may lose so much fluid that the heart cannot maintain the circulation (shock); interfere with the action of vital body enzymes; cause red

Viruses reproduce by instructing the cell's DNA to make new viruses that are directly or indirectly transferred to other cells.

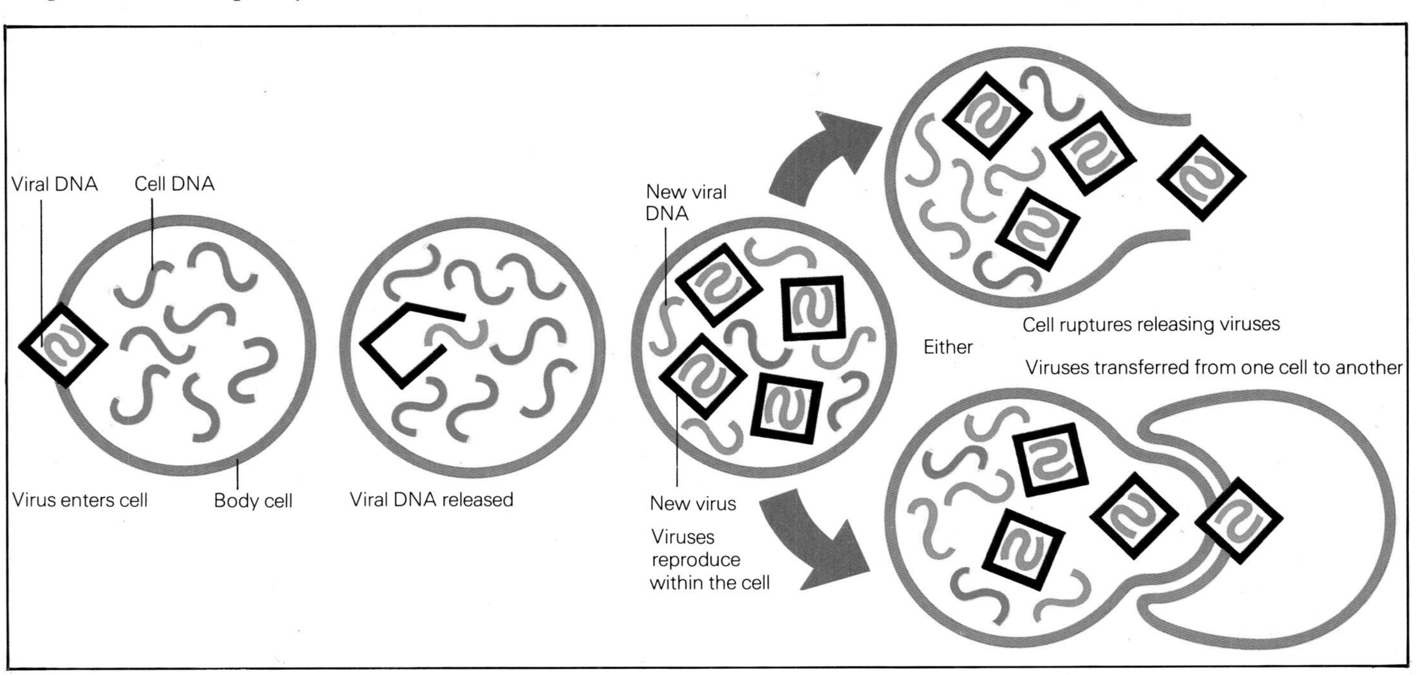

Q I seem to catch one infection after another. Could there be something wrong with the way my body copes with infection?

A People vary in their ability to fight off infections, but it is equally true that having had one infection, your resistance is lowered and therefore you are more likely to catch another. Viral infections often leave the way open for further infection by a bacterium. This is why some people with diseases like chronic bronchitis take antibiotics at the first sign of any cold. Although the antibiotics will not help to treat the cold, they may stop it spreading to the chest in the form of a bacterial infection. So even if you do seem to have nasty runs of infections, you are probably quite normal in the way you respond to them.

Q Could I catch AIDS from someone at work or socially?

A The virus that causes AIDS is not infectious in that it cannot be caught as a result of someone coughing or sneezing, or by using the same cup or toilet. Shaking hands or hugging has also never been found to be a source of infection. Do not, however, share items like razors or toothbrushes that could carry blood, and if you are looking after an infected person, cover cuts on your own skin with a waterproof dressing and avoid contact with blood or any other body fluid from the patient.

Q Like everyone else I can't stand having colds or the flu. Why can't scientists develop a vaccine against them?

A The common cold is caused by many different viruses, so even if a vaccine were to be successful against one sort of virus it would not protect against all the others. Influenza has the capacity to change the way it appears to the body's immune system, so if you have the flu one year it does not necessarily mean that you will be immune to the disease the next (see Influenza). The makers of the flu vaccine have to try to predict which strain is likely to be about in any one year and to produce a vaccine against that one.

blood cells to rupture; and produce severe inflammation of various tissues, especially the lining of the intestine.

Bacterial toxins that damage the intestine are called enterotoxins. It is such toxins that cause cholera and typhoid (see Cholera).

The damaging effects of viruses are different from those of bacteria. Viruses do not produce toxins, but they are still readily able to kill cells. They can do this by multiplying so vigorously within cells that the sheer bulk of viral material bursts the cells; by coding for proteins known as fusion proteins that cause cells to join together to form highly abnormal giant cells; and by forming new markers on the surface of body cells that label these cells as foreign and cause the normal processes of the immune system to attack and destroy them.

How the body defends itself

The body deals with infection by a remarkable and complex defense system called the immune system (see Immune System).

Before an organism reaches the cells of the body, it must break through the skin, which acts as a primary barrier against infection. However, many infections enter the body through the respiratory tract or the alimentary (digestive) tract and thus avoid having to cross the skin. Once inside the body the organism may be consumed by a phagocytic cell (a cell that swallows up and destroys viruses and bacteria). These are the white cells of the blood (although there are similar cells in other tissues). In some cases both the organism and the phagocyte will die, and this leads to the production of pus, which is no more than a collection of dead organisms and phagocytes (see Pus). The activity and effectiveness of phagocytes depends on the health of the immune system.

Rex Features

In crowds (above) try to avoid coughing or sneezing if you have a cold. Fungal infections of the skin, such as ringworm (below), cause redness and itching. Internal fungal infections are uncommon.

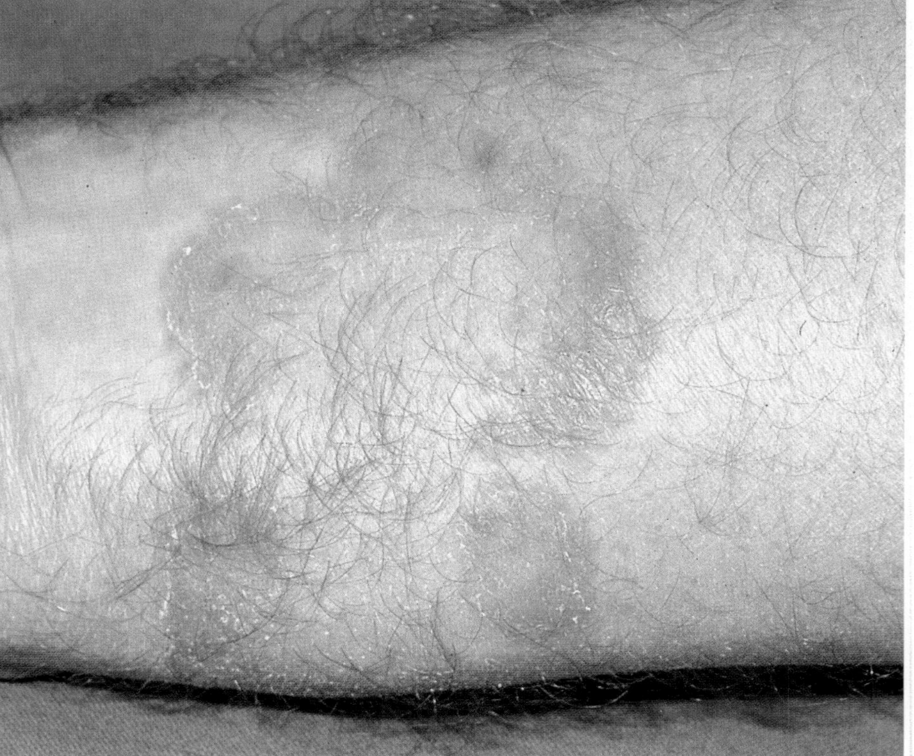

Dr P. Marazzi/Science Photo Library

Infectious diseases and their treatment

Disease	Caused by	Method of transfer	Immunization available	Symptoms	Medical treatment
AIDS	Virus	Contact with infected blood	No	Resistance to infection reduced	Antiviral drugs, HIV protease inhibitors
Chicken pox	Virus	Person to person	Yes	Rash	None
Common cold	Virus (many types)	Person to person	No	Runny nose	None
Diphtheria	Bacterium	Person to person	Yes	Obstructed throat, localized paralysis	Antibiotics
Gonorrhea	Bacterium	Sexually transmitted	No	Genital discharge	Antibiotics
Hepatitis	Virus (at least three types)	May be via skin, via infected food, or by sexual transmission	Available for Type A and Type B	Jaundice	Chronic Hepatitis B can be treated with Interferon
Influenza	Virus (many types give flulike illness)	Person to person	Yes, but not 100 percent effective	Cold, sore throat, muscle aches	Amantadine
Legionnaire's disease	Bacterium	Air-conditioning or water systems	No	Pneumonia, general ill health	Antibiotics
Malaria	Protozoa (three types)	Mosquito bite	No	Fever	Antimalarial drugs (also given to prevent infection)
Measles	Virus	Person to person	Yes	Runny nose and eyes, rash, ill health	None
Meningitis	Virus (many types) or meningococcus (bacterium)	Person to person	For meningitis caused by hemophilus	Neck pain, pain on looking at light, drowsiness	Nursing care for viral, antibiotics for bacterial
Mumps	Virus	Person to person	No	Swelling of salivary glands	None
Pneumonia	Bronchopneumonia (usually bacterial, may be virus)	Person to person	No	Cough	Antibiotics
	Lobar pneumonia (bacterial)	Person to person	Yes, for patients at risk	Cough and chest pain	Antibiotics
Ringworm	Fungus	Person to person (contact required)	No	Skin rash	Antifungal drugs applied to skin
Scarlet fever	Bacterium	Person to person	No	Skin rash and shedding of skin	Antibiotics (penicillin)
Syphilis	Bacterium	Sexual contact	No	Many symptoms, often years later	Penicillin
Tetanus	Bacterium (disease caused by poison)	Soil infection of wounds	Yes	Lockjaw and other spasms	Antitoxin; support on respirator if necessary
Tuberculosis	Bacterium	Person to person, by infected phlegm	Yes, but effectiveness varies	Affects lungs, causing cough with blood	Special antibiotics
Typhoid	Bacterium	Infected food or water	Yes	Fever and headache, later diarrhea	Antibiotics
Typhus	Rickettsia (different types)	By lice, ticks, or fleas	No	Fever, rash	Antibiotics and tetracycline
Yeast infection	Fungus	Sexually transmitted or on infected towels	No	Irritating white genital discharge	Antifungal drugs

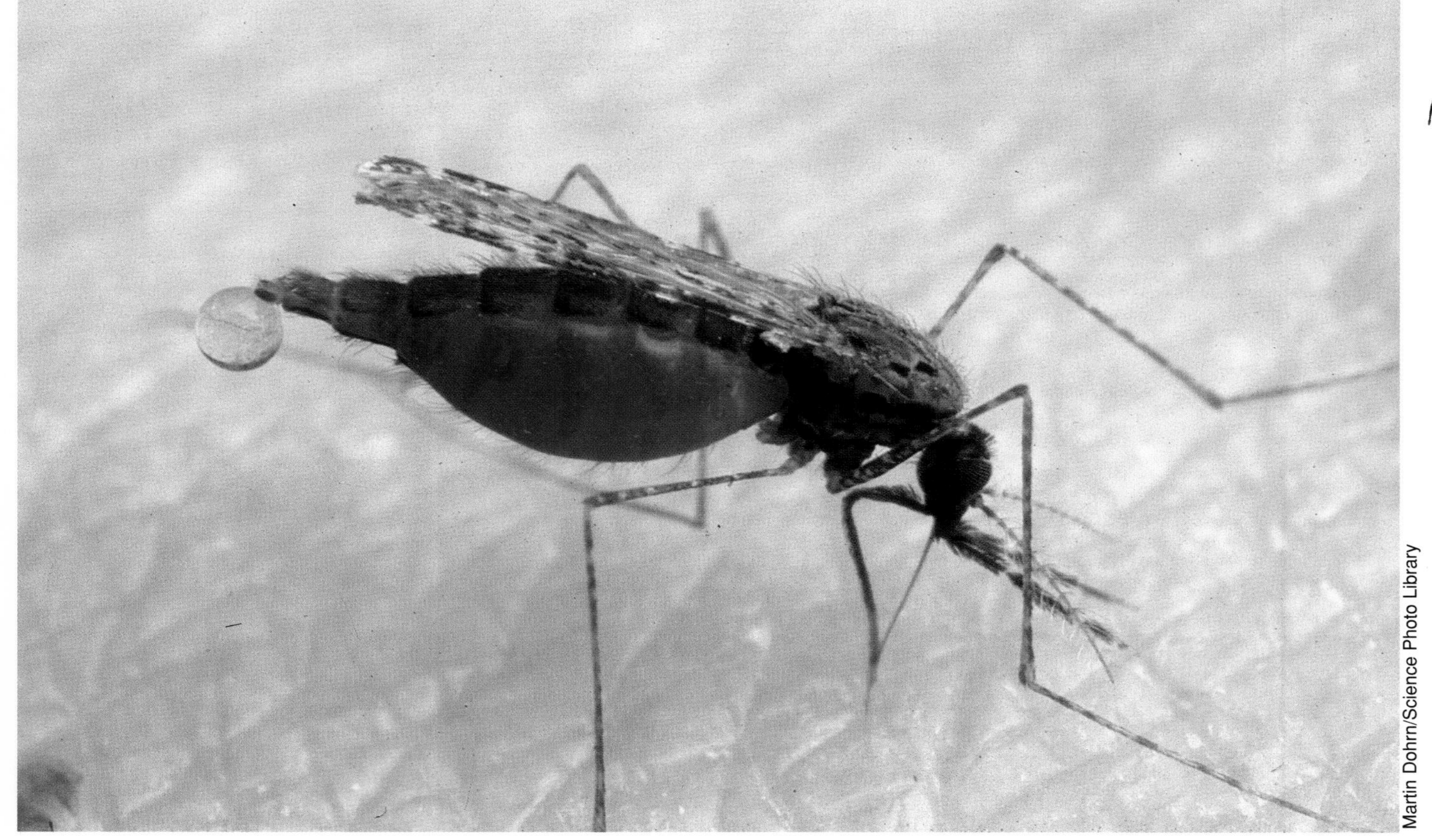

Martin Dohrn/Science Photo Library

The immune system has two major ways to combat invasion by foreign organisms. One is the production of antibodies; these are protein molecules that travel in the bloodstream and tissues and bind to the surface of specific microorganisms. This makes it easier for the phagocytic cells to attack. Antibodies may also stop organisms from being effective; for example, they may stop viruses entering cells. Finally, antibodies may trigger a system that leads to the breakdown of invading bacterial cells.

The other arm of the system is called cell-mediated immunity. The cells of this system, which are called lymphocytes because they come from the lymphatic system, may be specially primed to kill particular organisms (see Lymphocytes). They may also produce substances that help phagocytes attack infecting organisms. However, the immune system will not work if AIDS is present (see AIDS).

The development of vaccines to protect against infection has been one of medicine's major contributions to health. All vaccines rely on one basic idea: to find a substance that will cause the immune system to react to a specific disease without producing the disease itself. Most vaccines rely on the production of dead bacteria or viruses that have the same cell wall structure as the live organism and so cause antibody production (see Vaccinations).

Diseases and their symptoms

Most viruses enter the body and then spread throughout the body via the bloodstream. They enter other cells and produce more viruses. The symptoms of the disease usually start as this second wave is released from the cells.

Many organisms tend to infect only one organ. For instance, the hepatitis virus lodges in the liver (see Hepatitis, and Liver and liver diseases); the bacterium pneumococcus causes pneumonia in the lungs (see Pneumonia, and Lung and lung diseases); and the meningococcus, which causes meningitis, results in an inflammation of the membranes lining the brain (see Meningitis, and Brain damage and disease). Why organisms show this preference is unknown.

Other organisms, like the staphylococcus, may produce disease in any system. Once this organism has entered the bloodstream it gets carried around the body and settles in organs far away from the point where it originally entered. Once settled, the staphylococcus can multiply and produce an abscess (a cavity containing pus and surrounded by inflamed tissue; see Abscess).

Finally abscesses may produce toxic substances that poison particular areas of the body. Tetanus produces such a toxin that only affects the nervous system, and the cholera organism produces severe diarrhea as a result of toxins (see Tetanus).

Insects can be carriers of infectious diseases. Mosquitoes transmit malaria by piercing human skin with the proboscis, allowing the protozoan that causes the disease to enter the bloodstream.

However, in many cases a large part of the problem that a disease may cause results from the effect of interaction between the infecting organism and the body's defense mechanism. For example, in pneumonia, the production of large amounts of phlegm is really a result of the immune response, and this phlegm is often the leading symptom of the disease. Similarly the lung destruction that may follow from tuberculosis is primarily caused by the immune response rather than the disease itself (see Tuberculosis).

Treatment

Antibiotics have made a great difference in the treatment of infection. These drugs are toxic to bacteria but not to human cells. Many act by interfering with the bacterial cell wall, which has a different sort of structure to human cell walls (see Antibiotics). Unfortunately antibiotics are ineffective against viral infections, protozoa, and worms, so other drugs must be used in such cases (see Worms).

Infectious mononucleosis

Q My sister has infectious mononucleosis. She is uncomfortable and is most unhappy. Why is this?

A One of the side effects of mononucleosis is malaise and depression. This arises because many patients feel low and lack energy and drive, often for several weeks. It is important that you explain this to her and help her through her moods, while at the same time being sympathetic. Within a few weeks she will return to normal.

Q Is infectious mononucleosis harmful in pregnancy?

A Pregnant women virtually never get mononucleosis, because pregnancy enhances their immunity. However, virus infections in pregnancy are very dangerous, so a pregnant woman who suspects she has the disease should see her doctor immediately to check that no harm has been done to the fetus. This can be done through an amniocentesis test on the fetal fluid (see Amniocentesis).

Q Why should infectious mononucleosis make some people very ill and others hardly at all?

A There is no explanation for this. The response to a virus depends on the susceptibility of the patient. Some people have a built in immunity, others only a partial immunity; others have none at all, and for them the illness can drag on for many months.

Q Is there anything you can do to avoid catching infectious mononucleosis?

A No. There are no really effective preventive measures because the virus is carried long after the illness is over, and some people seem to carry the virus without any symptoms at all. The virus is only transmitted by close personal contact, so staying away from people who have the disease will help. It is just one of those illnesses young people may or may not get.

Infectious mononucleosis is a viral infection that mainly affects young people. Most cases are mild, but sometimes there are serious complications. However, in almost all cases, complete recovery is usual.

Infectious mononucleosis is sometimes known as glandular fever, but this term is inaccurate because the lymph nodes that are swollen in this disease are not glands (see Lymphatic system). It is caused by the Epstein-Barr virus, one of the herpes group of viruses (see Herpes).

The virus causes some of the white blood cells, called lymphocytes, to multiply and enlarge, and the increased activity of the immune or lymphatic system causes the lymph nodes to swell and become tender (see Immune system).

The virus lives in the mouths and noses of people who have the disease, and can remain there for several months after the illness is over. Although it has been referred to as the kissing disease, it is passed between people in close contact, including in exhaled breath (see Viruses).

Symptoms

After a symptomless incubation period of between four and seven weeks, the patient begins to feel listless and fatigued. Headache and chills are followed by a high fever, sore throat, and swollen lymph nodes in the neck and sometimes in the armpits and groin. The spleen may also become swollen, and weight loss occurs.

Two sorts of rashes may appear, and it is these which help the doctor make the diagnosis. In about 15 percent of cases a redness appears under the skin of the trunk and inner surface of the arms and legs. Patients have a temporary rash to the antibiotic ampicillin, so if the doctor misdiagnoses the condition and prescribes ampicillin, the tell-tale rash will occur.

In mild cases the illness may be missed or mistaken for another illness. In severe cases the symptoms are more obvious and there may be dangerous complications. The liver may become inflamed, producing jaundice (see Jaundice). The spleen may become so enlarged while it makes white blood cells to fight the infection that it becomes painful and tender. If pressed too hard or bumped in error, such a spleen may rupture (see Spleen). This would mean an immediate blood transfusion and the surgical removal of the organ.

The virus may also affect the nervous system, producing a form of meningitis (see Meningitis); the lungs, causing pneumonia; and the heart, causing inflammation of the pericardium (the fibrous sheath surrounding and enclosing the heart).

Treatment

There is no cure for infectious mononucleosis, only treatment for the separate symptoms. In mild cases the patient should gargle frequently for the sore throat and take painkillers for headache. Bed rest is advised, particularly in the early stages.

In severe cases bed rest is essential. The patient should have fluids and a light diet, and take some aspirin or acetaminophen for the fever and sore throat (too much of these medicines, however, can damage the liver). A hot water bottle will help relieve the swollen glands. Rarely, infectious mononucleosis is accompanied by thrombocytopenia (an abnormal decrease in blood platelets, the cells that clot blood), and hospitalization and steroids must be given (see Steroids).

Outlook

Most cases of infectious mononucleosis disappear in one to three weeks, but sometimes the patient feels ill, weak, depressed, and tired for weeks or even months. This can be the most distressing aspect of the disease. However, those affected in this way can be reassured that they will make a full recovery sooner or later.

A tiny proportion of patients suffer a relapse that causes a renewal of such symptoms as fever and swollen glands.

People who have infectious mononucleosis should avoid mouth-to-mouth kissing.

Zefa

CLARKSTON

WITHDRAWN